MORE PRAISE FOR *Rosalie Edge, Hawk of Mercy*

"In the years leading up to World War II, Rosalie Edge's stinging critique of the conservation establishment rocked it to its very core. Furmansky does a wonderful job of capturing the triumphs and defeats of this indomitable spirit whose ideas and actions anticipated the modern environmental movement."—Mark V. Barrow Jr., author of *A Passion for Birds: American Ornithology after Audubon*

"With Dyana Furmansky's authoritative biography, conservationist Rosalie Edge deservedly joins John Muir and Rachel Carson as a historic figure in the environmental movement. Furmansky's story of Edge's preservationist quests details her battles with special interests—from gun manufacturers to logging companies—that had powerfully infiltrated leading conservation organizations, as her crusades to save the nation's natural wonders took her to Washington D.C. During the Great Depression Edge mapped cunning strategies to prevail, and did so, whether over fellow conservationists, federal bureaucrats, government agencies, Congress, and FDR's White House. Born of privilege, Edge, a New York suffragist with a flair for publicity, transformed herself into a militant organizer and lobbyist, at home on Capitol Hill or in the ancient forests of the Olympic Peninsula. *Rosalie Edge, Hawk of Mercy* will captivate and surprise you." —Lynn Sweet, Washington Bureau Chief, *Chicago Sun-Times*

"A product of extensive research, *Rosalie Edge, Hawk of Mercy* chronicles the many accomplishments of a remarkable person while it reveals the often dramatic story of her life and sheds light on her times. What more can be asked of a biography? Furmansky reveals the early history of land preservation in America to be a story of intrigue, betrayal, anger, and, occasionally, victory. At the center stands a hero, Rosalie Edge—tragic, imperious, and obsessed."—Doug Carlson, author of *Roger Tory Peterson: A Biography*

"In *Hawk of Mercy*, Rosalie Edge soars again. The unscrupulous—as well as the scrupulous—are laid bare for all the world to see in Dyana Furmansky's biography, just as Rosalie Edge exposed them in her own day. Passionate, provocative, and precise, the book provides important new insights into the life and times of one of conservation's most original thinkers. A must-read for those who want to know more about this remarkably successful woman."—Keith L. Bildstein, Sarkis Acopian Director of Conservation Science, Hawk Mountain Sanctuary

"Finally, a full and appreciative biography of one of the most significant environmentalists of the twentieth century. Rosalie Edge was unique, a rare species, and nobody else could have achieved what she did. At a time between the world wars when conservation had become too cautious and conservative, too organized, Edge revived the movement by returning to its roots, to the former role of fearless amateur radicals like her. In the independent founding spirit of John Muir, she called out nature's enemies wherever she found them, from industrial polluters to the halls of Congress to the august chambers of the National Audubon Society. Dyana Furmansky, with the authority of her deep research, tells the story in full detail, and thereby places Rosalie Edge where she belongs in the pantheon of great American environmentalists."—Stephen Fox, author of *John Muir and His Legacy: The American Conservation Movement*

"It is high time that the full story be told of Rosalie Barrow Edge, an indomitable and early preservationist of birds—especially of hawks and eagles. Furmansky details Edge's battles with the Audubon Society as well as with despoilers of national parks in such a way that Rosalie Edge's role in the history of environmentalism will be restored to its rightful place."—Polly Welts Kaufman, author of *National Parks and the Woman's Voice: A History*

"*Rosalie Edge, Hawk of Mercy* does an excellent job of bringing Rosalie Edge to life and defending the importance of her contributions to conservation, especially during those doldrums decades from the 1920s to 1962. It fits well with biographies of other women conservationists—especially Rachel Carson and Lady Bird Johnson."—Vera Norwood, author of *Made from This Earth: American Women and Nature*

Rosalie Edge, Hawk of Mercy

Rosalie Edge, Hawk of Mercy

The Activist Who Saved Nature *from the* Conservationists

DYANA Z. FURMANSKY

With a foreword by Bill McKibben &

an afterword by Roland C. Clement

The University of Georgia Press ¤ Athens and London

© 2009 by the University of Georgia Press
Athens, Georgia 30602
www.ugapress.org

Set in Minion Pro by Graphic Composition, Inc.
Printed and bound by Maple-Vail

The paper in this book meets the guidelines for
permanence and durability of the Committee on Production
Guidelines for Book Longevity of the Council on
Library Resources.

Printed in the United States of America

13   12   11   10   09   C   5   4   3   2   1

Library of Congress Cataloging-in-Publication Data

Furmansky, Dyana Z.
Rosalie Edge, hawk of mercy : the activist who saved nature
from the conservationists / Dyana Z. Furmansky with a foreword
by Bill McKibben and an afterword by Roland C. Clement.
        p.   cm.
Includes bibliographical references and index.
ISBN-13: 978-0-8203-3341-0 (hardcover : alk. paper)
ISBN-10: 0-8203-3341-7 (hardcover : alk. paper)
1. Edge, Rosalie.
2. Conservationists—United States—Biography.
3. Suffragists—United States—Biography. I. Title.
QH31.E17F87 2009
333.95'16092—dc22
[B]   2009008551

British Library Cataloging-in-Publication Data available

FOR HILARY AND ARIEL, AND FINALLY FOR BERT

What has come of it all—of all that I had hoped for?
And now when the shades of evening are beginning to close in
upon my life, what have I left that is fresher, dearer to me,
than the memories of that brief storm that came and went
so swiftly one morning in the spring?

IVAN TURGENEV, *Torrents of Spring*

Contents

Foreword

There's so much history that it has to get written in shorthand—we take up the civil rights movement and invariably end up talking about Martin Luther King Jr. There's nothing wrong with that, except that it leads us to believe he sprang full-blown on the scene, instead of emerging, invariably, from a tradition.

This wonderfully informative biography helps us understand that tradition in the conservation movement, by focusing on the quite marvelous Rosalie Edge. If, in the civil rights tradition, organizers like A. Philip Randolph and Bayard Rustin paved the way for the explosion of the sixties, in the conservation movement Edge is one of the people who made Rachel Carson and David Brower possible. We've tended to focus on the years either side of World War II as sleepy ones in the American environmental movement—the excitement of John Muir and Teddy Roosevelt gone, the country's attention focused on expansion and then on the Depression and then on war and then once more on prosperity. But Edge and others—Robert Marshall, Aldo Leopold—were building the framework for much that would come.

Was there ever anyone better named? Edge had the same patrician access that defined conservation for most of the twentieth century, but thank heaven she didn't play by the same rules. She wrote new ones, most importantly with her willingness to forego politeness and accommodation when necessary. She spoke and wrote with vehemence and urgency, and hence was a thorn in the side to the more staid environmentalists of her day. These kinds of battles are still under way, of course, and she is an inspiration to those of us who must sometimes fight almost as hard to move the establishment "green groups" that dominate Washington discourse as we do the Congress or the White House.

Her life story suggests some of the necessary resources for this kind of work (though no one can ever really know the sources of the fearlessness that allows one to stand out from the crowd). Above all, I think, she was grounded in place: there was a center to her universe, Hawk Mountain, that let her understand her place in the great world. She paid back that gift, of course, protecting the mountain for the hundreds of thousands who love its unmatched spectacle.

It does not surprise me that it took a woman to shame many of the more conservative environmentalists of her day. She came of age in the suffrage movement and hence was used to the idea that she'd need to roar a little to make her voice heard. She reminds me not only of Carson, who stared down the chemical industry and its congressional lackeys, but of other grand women of the present: writers and activists like Terry Tempest Williams or Janisse Ray or Lois Gibbs or Vandana Shiva or Arundhati Roy. For those of us in the trenches, slogging it out each day in the high-stakes fights of our time on questions such as climate change, this is an invaluable piece of history, one that gives guidance and courage in equal measure.

Bill McKibben

Acknowledgments

I could not have dreamed of writing this book had I not been given two things: first, a powerful suggestion, and second, a suitcase packed with old letters. The suggestion came from the late T. H. Watkins, my friend, co-author, and editor at *American Heritage* and *Wilderness*. Watkins discovered Rosalie Edge's Emergency Conservation Committee (ECC) papers in the Conservation Collection of the Denver Public Library while working on his biography of Secretary of the Interior Harold L. Ickes. Since I lived near Denver, I checked what the library had on Edge, and as Tom predicted, I became hooked.

That suitcase—with about three hundred of Rosalie Edge's handwritten personal letters, original memorabilia, and family documents dating to the 1850s—was presented to me by the activist's seventy-seven-year-old son, Peter Edge, about a year after I began my research. I went to Winnetka, Illinois, several times to interview the generous and gracious Peter before he died in 2002. At the end of one of my visits, he handed over the suitcase with the stipulation that I use its contents to recover a forgotten bit of history and tell the best story I could about his mother's life. I have been blessed and burdened with Peter Edge's faith in me to do so ever since. I am further indebted to Deborah Edge, who adhered to her father's wish that I be permitted complete freedom to write this book as I felt it needed to be written.

While the character of *Hawk of Mercy* derives from the wealth of primary material I was privileged to have available, I want to acknowledge five published histories that helped me put Edge within the context of the conservation movement: Steven Fox's *John Muir and His Legacy: The American Conservation Movement*; Carsten Lien's *Olympic Battleground: The Power*

Politics of Timber Preservation; Irving Brant's *Adventures in Conservation with Franklin D. Roosevelt*; T. H. Watkins's *Righteous Pilgrim: The Life and Times of Harold L. Ickes, 1874–1952*; and Frank Graham Jr.'s *Audubon Ark: A History of the National Audubon Society*. I am also grateful to Clark N. Bainbridge's 2002 PhD dissertation, "The Origins of Rosalie Edge's Emergency Conservation Committee, 1930–1962: A Historical Analysis." Clark knowledgeably discussed Rosalie Edge with me and as one of my manuscript readers suggested corrections. Any errors or omissions that remain are my own. Clark's admiration for Edge strengthened my belief that she was the sort of hero others would want to know.

A dozen agents and publishers rejected this notion, but the book proposal did grab the plucky and persistent acquisition editors at the University of Georgia Press. I am grateful to Barbara Ras for her spontaneous enthusiasm and to Christa Frangiamore for her periodic calls gently rousing me from stagnation. Andrew Berzanskis's bracing note still hangs above my desk; next came the stalwart and resourceful Judy Purdy, who grasped all that I was trying to accomplish and guided manuscript revisions through to the end. Developmental editor John Tallmadge provided essential validation of the story's worth and gave me elegant solutions to address the narrative's shortcomings. Barb Wojhoski proved the value of having a fine copyeditor.

At the Conservation Collection of the Denver Public Library's Western History/Genealogy Department, Bruce Hanson, Joan Harms, Abby Haverstock, Janice Prater, and Ellen Zazzarino were of enormous assistance. The library's helpful staff and unique resources further convinced me that along with national parks, free public libraries are the greatest contribution the United States has made to the world.

I am thankful to archival collections large and small, public and private. Hawk Mountain Sanctuary's staff and volunteers tolerated my erratic visits for a decade or more and gave me permission to go where no one had gone before: into the dark, dank, mouse-infested basement of the Visitor Center, where Rosalie Edge's yellowed correspondence pertaining to Hawk Mountain's establishment moldered in rusty file cabinets.

At Hawk Mountain, Nancy Keeler, Keith Bildstein, and Mary Linkevich remained as enthusiastic about the project as they were patient, and proffered a thousand kindnesses. Hawk Mountain volunteer Karen Wolzanski and interns Emily Brodsky and Nicole Barko ably assisted me in the Julian Hill Memorial Archive–Hawk Mountain Sanctuary Archives, the bright, clean space that was later funded so that Edge's papers could be preserved and cataloged.

Muhlenberg College's Maurice Broun Library–Acopian Center for Ornithology in Allentown, Pennsylvania, was also indispensable in my research. At this tiny repository, Daniel Klem Jr. gave me access to Rachel Carson's correspondence with Hawk Mountain Sanctuary and promptly responded to my requests.

Rosalie Edge's conservation associates, family, and friends in the United States, England, and Italy eagerly shared their personal recollections with me; the names of everyone I interviewed are listed in the bibliography. I am also grateful for the guidance and enduring interest of my own family members and friends, who had never heard of my subject until I started talking about it. I thank Michael Edesess for going through those times with me when sorting out our story dominated my ability to tell Rosalie Edge's; I thank my sisters Nina Brodsky and Rita Zaslowsky, my uncle Daniel Zaslowsky, and almost-family members Ira Sohn, Rose Rappaport, Wayne Silverman, Laura Silverman, and the Furmanskys Leif, Nik, and Eliza for other times when Edge's story dominated the ones they wanted to tell.

A few favors done on behalf of this book deserve special mention. Jennifer Gantwerker spent one summer vacation voluntarily photocopying about six inches' worth of public records at the courthouse in White Plains, New York. Linda and Jules Kroll graciously gave me a tour of their house at Parsonage Point in Rye. Deborah Mefferd, Richard Smith, and Pamela Smith not only read portions of my manuscript at various stages but also personally introduced me to the American expatriate experience in Hong Kong. In Denver Michael Gilbert read my complete manuscript carefully. So too did Jessica Bondy, who made up stories with me when we were children.

Other readers provided invaluable comments that I believe improved the end product. Of note are my sister Nina, my friend Bonnie Kossoff, and Hawk Mountain ornithologist Keith Bildstein. Joyce Fine, Audrey Friedman Marcus, and Rebecca Reynolds critiqued my output at our monthly meetings and formed a dedicated community of writers on which I have come to rely.

I owe much to Charleen Edge, Charles Nightingale, Martha Hill Schafer, Tim Ernst, Barbara Badger, Steve Cardin, Rabbi Sara Gilbert, Rabbi Howard Hoffman, Peggy Eggers, Peter Eggers, Bert Newman, Pat Newman, Martin Fleischman, Colleen McGrath, Elizabeth McCarty, Don Cook, Patty Cook, and Todd Tantillo for their abiding interest and confidence-replenishing friendship over this long haul.

This book was raised alongside my daughters, Hilary and Ariel, who grew into the indomitable and loving young women I am proud to call my friends. I don't think it ever occurred to me on those starry nights when I read *Huckleberry Finn* to them as little girls that they would light out for so many new territories.

In my own way I try to follow in their footsteps. The adventures ahead I share with my husband Bert, a man of panache and sensitivity. I thank him with all my heart for being so very present: as my sounding board, tireless booster, bike companion, and dance partner.

I thank my parents, Joel and Shirley Zaslowsky, of blessed memory who gave me so much though they died too young. Their early passing daily reminds me to thank God for enabling me to reach this season of life.

THE AUTHOR AND THE PUBLISHER gratefully acknowledge the following for permission to excerpt material:

All writings of Rosalie Edge, published and unpublished, used by permission of Peter Edge and Deborah Edge.

Adventures in Conservation with Franklin D. Roosevelt, by Irving Brant. Used by permission of Robin Lodewick and Ruth Brant Davis.

Hawks Aloft! The Story of Hawk Mountain, by Maurice Broun. Used by permission of Julian Hill Memorial Archive–Hawk Mountain Sanctuary Archives.

"Keeper of the Kittatinny," by Kenneth Kranick. Used by permission of Kenneth Kranick.

Letter from Gifford Pinchot to Rosalie Edge, 1939. Used by permission of Peter Pinchot.

Letters and diaries of Maurice Broun at the Maurice Broun Library, Acopian Center for Ornithology, Muhlenberg College, Allentown, Pennsylvania. Used by permission of Daniel Klem Jr.

"Mrs. Rosalie Edge, Free to Choose a Career, Prefers Conservation Work, and She Encourages Other Women to Serve Usefully," by Marjorie Shuler, 1938. Courtesy of the *Christian Science Monitor*.

"My Life," by Richard H. Pough. Used by permission of Julian Hill Memorial Archive–Hawk Mountain Sanctuary Archives.

Olympic Battleground: The Power Politics of Timber Preservation, by Carsten Lien. Used by permission of Carsten Lien.

"The Origins of Rosalie Edge's Emergency Conservation Committee, 1930–1962: A Historical Analysis." Used by permission of Clark N. Bainbridge.

The Pennsylvania Game Commission, 1895–1995: 100 Years of Wildlife Conservation, by Joseph Kosack. Used by permission of the Pennsylvania Game Commission.

Roger Tory Peterson's profile of Ludlow Griscom, published in *The Auk*, 1965. Used by permission of the American Ornithologists' Union.

Saving American Birds: T. Gilbert Pearson and the Founding of the Audubon Movement, by Oliver H. Orr. Reprinted with permission of the University Press of Florida.

Silent Spring, by Rachel Carson. Used by permission of Frances Collin, trustee.

George Miksch Sutton's article on Hawk Mountain, published in *The Wilson Bulletin*, 1928. Used by permission of the Wilson Ornithological Society.

"To Peter and Other Storm Petrels," originally published as "Sonnet to a Navigator" in the *Bulletin of Massachusetts Audubon*, 1944. Reprinted with permission from Mass Audubon.

Voices and Votes: A Literary Anthology of the Women's Suffrage Campaign, edited by Glenda Norquay. Used by permission of Glenda Norquay.

Rosalie Edge, Hawk of Mercy

Introduction

The widow of Charles Noel Edge was sitting in the swank lobby of the Robert Driscoll Hotel in Corpus Christi, Texas, when she was spotted by staff members of the National Audubon Society.[1] The sighting on November 12, 1962, caused a muffled stir, as if a rare bird had been identified. Mrs. Edge—Rosalie, as her few intimates called her—was the legend of the conservation movement. At eighty-five she still ran the two organizations she had started in the 1930s: Hawk Mountain Sanctuary in Kempton, Pennsylvania, the world's first preserve for birds of prey, and the Manhattan-based Emergency Conservation Committee. The ECC was the most militant nature advocacy organization of its time and, some said, one of the most effective ever.

Edge, who lived in New York, had flown to Texas to attend the Audubon Society's fifty-eighth annual meeting. Renowned bird artist and guidebook author Roger Tory Peterson was among those surprised to see her.[2] He had met her when he was a teenager birding in Central Park in the 1920s, and in 1934 Rosalie Edge was among the first to receive an autographed copy of his groundbreaking *Field Guide to the Birds of North America*. At her invitation, Peterson joined the Hawk Mountain Sanctuary board of directors and served for almost twenty years. Though Madame Chairman often reprimanded him for arriving late at her meetings, he retained a soft spot in his heart for her based on the early faith she showed in him.

Others who noticed Edge in the Robert Driscoll lobby that day were conservation eminences Richard Pough, cofounder of the Nature Conservancy, and senior Audubon biologist Roland C. Clement, who was quietly working on the side to start a new organization that would be called the Environmental Defense Fund.

In their youth, Peterson, Pough, and Clement had all admired Edge immensely.[3] While acknowledging her powerful influence on them in particular and the conservation movement in general, they were also wary of her. Her tiny Emergency Conservation Committee succeeded by not caring whom it might offend.

New Yorker writer Robert Taylor Lewis described her deportment as a cross between that of Queen Mary and a nervous pointer, and her use of the word *committee* was something akin to the royal *we*. It was not a committee that a person could join. The ECC's fluid and phantom collaborators, whom she selected, briefly swelled to about twelve after she formed it, but for most of the ECC's thirty-three years, the committee was Rosalie Edge. As the formal and ferocious embodiment of the committee, Edge lobbied congressmen, hounded federal bureaucrats, and aroused public indignation. She edited or wrote, published, and distributed more than 140 pamphlets and circulars on a wide range of topics that reached one million readers across the country. She asked only for modest contributions to cover the cost of production and mailing. ECC pamphlets became essential reading for anyone who wanted to know what was really happening in the nature-saving movement.[4]

For too long the answer had been: nothing. Edge declared that her ECC pamphlets told truths to the public that nobody else dared tell, and they told these truths with a passion sorely lacking among the professional conservationists. With sensationalist titles and shrill pronouncements, the pamphlets, letters, and broadsides recounted what certain major organizations and federal agencies were not doing to protect wildlife and lands and what the people must do. Her conservation achievements, according to the profile of her in the *New Yorker*, were "widespread and monumental." One project merged so seamlessly into another that it was difficult to find the right word for her set of talents. She complained of how professional conservationists pigeonholed themselves and drew unnatural boundaries around their particular specialties. Rosalie Edge wished to defy categorization.[5]

Vice President Al Gore's inconvenient truth about global warming uncannily echoes the "unpleasant facts" Edge began to expose in 1929 concerning the human-caused degradation of the natural world. In the unpublished memoir she began to write in 1950, she attributed the great public "awakening" in large part to her alarming reports of ignorant human complicity in rampant species and habitat destruction. "Thousands of people who had within them a yearning toward nature, a deep-seated need to preserve its beauty, had been in very truth asleep. I know, for I was one of them," Edge wrote. Singer Melissa Etheridge's song "Awakening," composed to accompany Gore's 2007 Oscar-winning documentary, could well have been Edge's theme song too.[6]

Rosalie Edge was not a naturalist prophet and wilderness sojourner like John Muir. Nor was she a college-educated biologist and best-selling author like Rachel Carson. Edge's credentials were different. She grew up in privileged New York society, in a family related to Charles Dickens and James McNeill Whistler. She married a brilliant and ambitious Englishman and lived abroad with him for several years. She became a suffragist and eventually a bird-watcher. As a wife and mother, she confronted family crises she dared not speak of. With only this background, Rosalie Edge made herself a citizen-scientist and militant political agitator the likes of which the conservation movement had never seen.

Hyperbole and myth tried to explain who she was. The *Christian Science Monitor* observed, "She is that peculiarly powerful being, an individual who has private means, who accepts no salary, no expenses, no gifts, and whose independent social position helps her to speak fearlessly and to act uncompromisingly"; the *Brooklyn Daily Eagle* called Rosalie Edge "the Paul Bunyan of Conservation," and the *Altoona Tribune* anointed her the "Glorious Joan of Arc of conservation." *Time* settled cautiously on "peppery." A comparison she preferred was one made of her to Boadicea, the warrior queen of the ancient Brits who confronted Roman invaders in her chariot with wheel spokes forged from spears.[7]

The characterizations of Rosalie Edge that are most memorable originated with Willard Van Name, another of her contemporaries who admired her from a distance to avoid being trampled by her, again. It was Van Name who, in 1948, said she was "the only honest, unselfish, indomitable hellcat in the history of conservation."[8] One wonders what Rosalie Edge might have been called had she been a man. As a woman and an older one at that, she was depicted as an eccentric, even a grotesque. Today we would use another word to describe her: environmentalist. In the sheer breadth of her conservation activism, Rosalie Edge was, arguably, the nation's first.

IN ADDITION TO publishing pamphlets that reeducated an entire generation of conservationists, Edge created the first sanctuary for birds of prey
with private funding; for three decades she opposed the indiscriminate
use of pesticides and toxins from strychnine and thallium to DDT.[9] In 1935,
Edge decamped from New York's Upper East Side to fight for skyscraping
trees in Washington State and California, with Olympic National Park and
Sequoia–Kings Canyon National Park resulting from her efforts. Edge succeeded in persuading Congress to restore other big trees to Yosemite National Park, from which they had been illegally traded, and kept Yellowstone
Falls in Yellowstone National Park from being diverted. No one person had
ever taken on so many conservation causes at once.

With no job of her own at stake, Edge shielded men whose career insecu-
rities prohibited them from expressing their own qualms about conservation's somnolence. Their stifled concerns about excessive use of toxins to
control predators and insect pests were among the most strident complaints
she aired over thirty years.

"I am the means through which scientists express themselves," Edge aris-
tocratically declared during a 1942 Senate hearing.[10] Before Rachel Carson,
Rosalie Edge was the nation's premier example of how one person could
wed science to public advocacy for the preservation and restoration of the
wide natural world. Edge's decades of accomplishments, however, were
eclipsed by the publication of Carson's *Silent Spring*, conventionally cited as
the beginning of the environmental movement.

Conservationists had been steadily losing ground for twenty years or more
when Rosalie Edge arrived on the scene in 1929. Outraged by their indolence
and hypocrisy, she revived the movement, firing it with the rabble-rousing
spirit of the suffragist she had once been. Through Edge, two of the most
important progressive movements of the twentieth century—women's suffrage and environmentalism—would be incidentally linked. Her greater
claim to fame is as the person who forged the bridge stretching from the
sainted John Muir's quest for national parks to the highly esteemed Rachel
Carson's revelations about pesticides.

Although Edge had no credentials and no clear constituency when she
began her protests, by the end of her life her style of political activism defined a movement reborn, one she had made more dynamic and universal
than it had ever been. For Edge, conservation advocacy was the duty of
every individual.

OUR HEROINE WAS BORN and raised in the world of wealth and manners depicted in Edith Wharton's memoirs and novels of New York's Gilded Age. As a wife and mother, Edge fell into the pampered idleness customary of even the brightest women of her class. Nannies cared for her son and daughter, and Cook prepared the family dinner. It was not until 1929, when Edge was fifty-two, that she bolted from her refined prison and ended up at a dull meeting of the nation's most respected ornithologists. Few women were present, and at first Edge's white gloves and ladylike demeanor signaled passivity to the gentlemen in attendance.

But the men learned they were mistaken. "Let any of them think that the sword has been left at home and they are due for a great surprise," the *Christian Science Monitor* warned. "Her sword is a folding one. It can fit into an evening bag, or even into a delicate glove. And it accompanies its owner wherever she goes."[11]

Twenty-five years after this *Monitor* profile appeared, Rosalie Edge's name still elicited bitterness and resentment in certain organizations. The National Audubon Society was chief among them. So it was with understandable trepidation that Carl Bucheister, Audubon's current president, received the news that the society's old foe had registered for his annual meeting in 1962. One of Bucheister's aides asked her why she had come. Edge replied that she wanted to see what was going on. When the aide later reported her evasive answer, he allegedly pretended to faint from fear of what Edge might do. Bucheister put these unpleasant facts before his staff: "Rosalie Edge hates us and we hate her, but she is the officer of two national conservation organizations."[12]

Seated in the lobby that day, the old woman did not look menacing. She was smartly dressed as usual, though wisps of white and wiry hair strayed from the bun gathered at the back of her neck.[13] Stooped shoulders canted her forward. Edge facetiously attributed her bowed frame to years spent hunched over her typewriter crafting denunciations of milquetoast conservationists and springing muskrat and mink from the steel-jawed traps that the Audubon Society had profitably used in the 1920s and 1930s. Edge's pale, piercing gaze was clouded with age, making her appear less raptorial.

Perhaps the passing years had eroded her ire. Or perhaps not. Bucheister needed to know her intentions to avoid another nasty confrontation, this time before a gathering of twelve hundred National Audubon Society members who had assembled for the society's largest annual meeting in its history.[14] The Audubon president deliberated carefully.

WHAT FOLLOWS is the neglected story of the events that led up to Carl Bucheister's anxious minutes. They are events that would define the modern environmental movement. Rosalie Edge's enemies and even her friends wondered what on earth drove her out of her cushioned comfort to become the nation's most militant conservation activist. Her unpublished memoirs offer a few hints. More insights are gleaned from the cache of about three hundred family letters and documents made available to the author. These writings recount a woman's history that is cultural and environmental in equal parts and that intersect with momentous events between the 1860s and the 1960s. By weaving Edge's private words into her forgotten public legacy, our story approaches the heart of one woman's fury and becomes a perverse kind of romance.

Part One

CHAPTER ONE

Noblest Girl

When Rosalie Edge spoke of her late start in conservation work, she mentioned Central Park, which she could see from her apartment on Fifth Avenue.[1] In the 1850s landscape architects Fredrick Law Olmsted and Calvert Vaux had designed the beloved New York greensward to transform eight hundred acres of naked granite and marsh into pastoral woods, meadows, and ponds. For the last thirty years of Edge's life, the tall Beaux Arts windows of her building refracted Central Park's green relevance into her gracious rooms.

Rosalie Edge—baptized Mabel Rosalie Barrow—had been brought up on Central Park's engineered version of nature. By the time of her birth on November 3, 1877, millions of trees and shrubs, vines and flowers of more than one thousand botanical species had been planted in the red soil ferried over from New Jersey. Dirt by the ton had been transported to the chosen site, for "a crowbar thrust anywhere into the ground would meet rock," Edge wrote.[2] Her mother, Harriet Bowen Barrow, remembered the endless carts of earth drawn by draft horses lumbering up from the river dock to the future park.

What Edge saw of Central Park's virtuous beauty from her apartment could be deceptive. After heavy downpours, the New Jersey soil so laboriously excavated, transported, and deposited on Manhattan washed down the steep bank and entry drive on Central Park's perimeter. The Fifth Avenue sidewalk across from Edge's building would be caked in mud. She was piqued every time she saw men shovel the eroded soil into a truck, drive to the East River, and dump their wet load in.[3]

CENTRAL PARK'S INFLUENCE on Edge's life, however, can be traced further into the territory of her memory, bounded on its far side by her childhood in the elegant carriage days of the early 1880s. This was long before she was drawn to wildness of either the manufactured variety or the natural type. The spectacle of New York's ruling class on parade made a deeper impression. Central Park was the place she visited with her family when she was a pampered child called Mabel clothed in ermine and velvet, and the birds she loved were the stuffed ruby-throated hummingbirds that circled her white silk bonnet.[4] The park was then "innocent of hard pavement. A good macadam was overlaid with earth—'dirt' as you say—and riders inter-mingled often with carriages on the drives—the little coupes, or heavy ba-rouches drawn by big horses with silver-plated chains on their bridles, mak-ing music almost like bells. New York then was a proud city with a proud aristocracy."[5]

Her British father, John Wylie Barrow, was a wealthy accountant, re-spected Orientalist, skilled horseman, and most wondrous of all, first cousin to Charles Dickens. With Mabel's penetrating blue eyes and mass of wavy dark hair, she was said to bear a "wonderful likeness" to her father, who, judging from the oil portrait of him painted in 1864, resembled Dickens.[6]

According to Barrow family ritual, John Wylie, astride his favorite horse, Ottawa, arrived at the park ahead of the carriage that brought Harriet and the children. The groom followed a few paces behind Barrow leading Har-riet's spirited white mare, Coquette. Mabel remembered how her mother, dressed in a slim black riding outfit, stepped down from the carriage and dramatically paused. Barrow did not permit her to mount her horse until, "imperious as a prince," he ran his handkerchief over the mare's neck and flanks to make sure she was clean and dry. Barrow scolded the groom if Coquette failed his inspection. Attentive little Mabel took mental note of her father's confident exercise of authority.[7]

On one afternoon in April, the Barrows arrived at Central Park to see a procession heading to a statue of William Shakespeare in commemoration of the Bard's birthday.[8] Leading the way was Edwin Booth, renowned Shake-spearean actor and despairing brother of the assassin John Wilkes. As the Barrow party neared the Shakespeare devotees, Harriet's horse reared and pranced "like a ballerina" as though performing her old act in the circus that had previously owned her.[9]

The walkers scattered, and Edwin Booth turned to regard Harriet Barrow and her white mare. "His face lighted with genuine enjoyment, and he was applauding and saying 'Brava! Brava!'" Harriet, however, was embarrassed by the scene she and Coquette had created. "John," she murmured nervously, turning toward her husband. Barrow beamed at his wife, who looked as confident on her mount as if she "were dancing the lancers in a ballroom." He sidled close but did not catch Coquette's bridle or try to stop the performance. As he leaned toward Harriet, Mabel could hear her father say, "It's beautiful. Enjoy it, dear heart."[10]

LIKE OTHER MEMBERS of the city's social elite, the Barrows came to the park to see and be seen. John Wylie and Harrie, as Barrow nicknamed his wife, were "well-known to many people who never had the pleasure of meeting them," or so it seemed in the golden light of reflected childhood. Harriet's eyes were "china blue," and John Wylie was as handsome as his wife was lovely, according to Mabel. When dressed to go out in the evening in his velvet doublet, brocade knee breeches, with the ostrich feather bowing from his hat band, her father was "far superior to the fathers of the other little girls" she knew.[11]

Their affection for each other was mutual and conspicuous. John Barrow called Mabel his "Noble Girl," even his "Noblest Girl," lest there be any doubt about her supreme place in his heart. She was the youngest of the five surviving Barrow children, and John Wylie's pet names for her contrasted with his collective references to her much older sisters, Margaret Dubois and Anna Evertson, and to her brother Archibald Campbell. In one letter to Mabel, they were described as her "subordinates."[12]

"I cannot allow anyone to be disrespectful to the Noble Girl in her own house," Barrow wrote to Mabel in 1882 while he was away. She was four years old, and it seems she had complained to her father about sibling disobedience to her wishes that needed to be addressed when he returned. During another absence, Barrow wrote: "I hope your two maids continue to merit your approbation by their humility and obedience." Mabel was probably too young to read the letter herself; one of these obedient maids may have read it to her.[13]

Since she loved animals, Barrow dutifully reported any he saw in his travels; alligators, cockroaches, cats, and dogs merited mention. He bought her canaries and parakeets to keep in the conservatory at home, where he raised orchids. Mabel once directed her nurse to inform her father that the silent canary had started to chirp again. Barrow wrote back that he was relieved the bird had "come to his senses again, and shown his appreciation for his fine new cage and elegant surroundings by singing in the proper manner."[14] But there is no evidence she preferred birds over other creatures, such as her cat, Orange.

Mabel and her father observed their own Central Park ritual. When the rest of the family did not accompany them, he took her on pony rides and bought her ice cream. While away, he once wrote of how much he missed seeing her in the park "running about in the grass and directing and taking charge of things generally."[15] It was an appropriate training ground for Mabel, at the tender age of five or so, to exercise her freedom of expression under her father's powerful auspices.

Although Mabel's early tendency to take charge charmed John Wylie, her sisters and her brother Archibald did not find it adorable. There was much quarreling and divisiveness among them. For confirmation of her superiority, the child Mabel kept her father's letters of devotion. The habit of preserving what mattered most to her had begun.

ON THE FAMILY's Central Park outings, Mabel rode in the carriage with her three subordinate siblings. She had no memory of her elder brother, William Woodward, accompanying them. Mabel had no memory of William at all. He was already a student at Columbia College when she was two and left home soon afterward. When William married a woman his parents disliked, mention of the young man's name was forbidden in his mother's presence.

Three other Barrow daughters had died before Mabel was born, which explains the age gap between her and her older brothers and sisters. John Wylie and Harriet donated a marble altar to St. Bartholomew's Cathedral in their infants' memory; somber Harriet wore a locket with a portrait of one of them painted on it and a tendril of the baby's hair coiled within. Perhaps John Wylie overcame his own grief by devoting himself to Mabel, who robustly survived. He was forty-nine years old when this last daughter was born. Financially secure enough to semiretire, Barrow had both the time and the means to lavish his attentions on his youngest.

William, Margaret, Anna, and Archibald Barrow had been given middle names plucked from the family's distant past. Mabel's middle name, Rosalie, was of more recent origin and was tied to yet another tragic loss. Harriet Barrow's sister Mary Putnam had given birth to four babies, all of whom died before they were eight months old. A Putnam daughter had been baptized Rosalie. Mary was widowed shortly after the last child died.[16] With no children of her own to raise, Aunt Mary busied herself with resurrecting her family's genealogical past rather than tending to the future.

Aunt Mary's genealogy efforts supported her sister Harriet Barrow's pride in their family's descent from illustrious Kiliaen Van Rensselaer, "the first Patroon of Rensselaerwyck in New Netherland" and a "merchant-prince of the Seventeenth Century, buying and selling precious stones and other wares, and a banker." In 1630 Kiliaen acquired his "great fief in the New World through his Lord-Directorship of the West India Company."[17]

Almost three hundred years later, Harriet instructed her children Margaret, Anna, Archie, and Mabel to "remember [they] were all baptized in the Killaen [sic] Van Rensselaer bowl." It may have helped for the society-conscious Harriet to stress this fact to offset her husband's blood relation to the celebrated Charles Dickens. Harriet's ancestor was not as well known as Dickens, but at least he had been known for much longer. In the New York circles in which the Barrows traveled, old Dutch kin held their value better than more recent English ones.[18]

Years later Rosalie Edge, who remained almost as conscious of her upper-class origins as her mother might have wished, conceded as much: "Recent biographies have all stressed his [Dickens] lowly origin and the mean beginning to his life," she wrote. "We have been reticent about proclaiming him our first cousin, removed by but one generation."[19]

John Wylie shared his sister-in-law's passion for genealogical digging and delved well beyond his relation to Dickens. After tracing the Bowen-Woodward-Barrow lines, he discovered that he was related to his wife, who was his "fourth cousin, once removed" by way of Gaulterius Du Bois, another seventeenth-century Dutch progenitor. Du Bois came to New York to serve as a minister in the Dutch church. In America, Du Bois's son John married a woman named Jean McNeill. By tracing the McNeill-Du Bois offspring forward to his own day, John Wylie Barrow was pleased to confirm that he was not only blessed by close kinship to Charles Dickens. He was, as he had suspected back in England, also "a near relative" of the contentious American painter James McNeill Whistler.[20] It is said that Barrow introduced himself to Whistler's mother, Anna, soon after he arrived in America, and according to Barrow family lore it was Anna Whistler who introduced this ambitious young Englishman to his future wife, Harriet Bowen Woodward.[21]

BACK IN ENGLAND twenty years before John Wylie was born, his father, Thomas Culliford Barrow, had been responsible for initiating a far more significant courtship, at least as far as British literature would be concerned. Thomas Barrow introduced his pretty and petite sister Elizabeth to his friend and coworker in the Navy payroll office, John Dickens. Thomas's father, Charles Barrow, ran the office. It was a prestigious appointment and one in keeping with the Barrow family's bourgeois standing in wool manufacturing, musical instruments, and newspapers. John Dickens was of a much lower class than the Barrows and made considerable progress up the social ladder when he married Elizabeth Barrow in 1809. The Dickenses' son Charles was born in 1812. Decades later Charles Dickens's Barrow cousins of New York City still insisted that it was "generally considered that the great novelist's gifts were inherited" from Elizabeth Barrow's side of the family.[22]

Charles Barrow, however, was convicted of embezzlement from the Navy office not long after Elizabeth married John Dickens. Barrow testified in his own defense that he had only pocketed the money to support "the very heavy expenses of a family of ten children, increased by illness."[23] The court was unsympathetic, and Barrow fled the country to avoid imprisonment. His crime and abandonment heaped shame and financial ruin on his family.

John Dickens lost his Navy office job and had trouble finding employment that paid enough to support the extravagant spending habits he had acquired in his marriage to Elizabeth. He borrowed heavily from his brother-in-law, Thomas Barrow, and other Barrow family members and incessantly squabbled with them and his wife over money. When he did not pay his wine bill, John Dickens was sent to prison, which heaped more shame on the socially tarnished family.[24] The misfortunes of the Dickens household provided an endless source of dramas for young Charles.

Through it all, Uncle Thomas Barrow remained on excellent terms with his talented nephew. Uncle Thomas, his wife, who was also named Harriet, and their son, John Wylie, lived above the bookstore on Gerrard Street that Dickens frequented, and Uncle Thomas was one of those who encouraged Charles to be both a serious writer and a reader. In subtle tribute to his uncle's influence, the lawyer Jaggers in Dickens's semiautobiographical *Great Expectations* lives on Gerrard Street, and his rooms are exhaustively detailed in the novel.[25]

Dickens might have witnessed a grisly scene in Uncle Thomas's flat after Barrow broke his leg. The leg became infected and had to be amputated. "Where's my leg?" Uncle Thomas is said to have asked when he recovered from his unanesthetized swoon of agony. "Under the table," was the reply, according to Dickens, and the novelist's depictions of amputees and wooden legs may have been colored by what happened at his uncle's Gerrard Street flat. After Uncle Thomas recuperated, Dickens reminded him of how he had diligently behaved as his "little companion and nurse, through a weary illness."[26]

AS CHARLES DICKENS's popularity soared, little John Wylie Barrow, sixteen years younger than his cousin, was displaying another kind of family genius for language. By the time he was eight, he could read Dickens's serialized novels on his own, and at that age bought a copy of Homer from the Gerrard Street bookstore. John Wylie taught himself to read the Bible in Greek and won prizes at school for his translation ability.

At fourteen John Wylie was "obliged to go into an office" to support his family, presumably because his father, as an amputee, could no longer work. But the urge to study prodded the youth; he quit work and went to college in London and then in Heidelberg to learn Arabic and Hindustani. At twenty-three John Wylie abandoned "an early dream of entering the East India service" and pursued the study of Chinese, Latin, Italian, French, Russian, and German at the university. But again "a want of means and determination not to be dependent upon others" derailed his quest for formal education, and he never returned to it.

His knowledge of ancient Greek, "Hebrew, 'Chaldee' and the Talmud" was nonetheless extensive enough to win him an appointment as a secretary with the British legation to the Vatican. Though "warmly attached to the Church of England," John Wylie was granted access to the Vatican's closely guarded copy of the Codex Sinaiticus, one of Christianity's oldest texts.[27]

German Lutheran scholar Constantine Tischendorf had discovered 129 leaves of the codex in a trash bin at St. Catherine's Greek Orthodox monastery in the Sinai Peninsula in 1844. Tischendorf wanted to present the original Greek manuscript dating from the third century to his Eastern Orthodox patron Czar Alexander II and accompany it with a Russian translation. He engaged Barrow to do the work, which was completed in time to celebrate the one-thousand-year anniversary of Christianity's arrival in Russia. Barrow received one of the five authorized copies of the codex from Tischendorf in return for his services, and Czar Alexander presented the young man with two egg-sized amethysts bearing the Romanoff seal.[28]

In 1853 Barrow's fluency in German and Italian won him employment with the Austrian and Italian delegations to New York's Exhibition of the Industry of All Nations. Barrow selected costly examples of Austrian and

Italian crystal, silver, porcelain, and linens to display in the glass-domed Crystal Palace built in Bryant Park specifically for the exhibition. His representation apparently pleased yet another sovereign; Austro-Hungarian emperor Franz Joseph gave the Bible scholar a book containing the Lord's Prayer in 608 languages.[29]

By the time the exhibition closed, Barrow had decided that he wanted to stay in America permanently, and he joined the import firm of J. R. Jaffray & Company in New York. The knowledge of exquisite wares that he had gained would help the importer satisfy rich New Yorkers' desires for the best that European artisans had to offer. At thirty Barrow eased out of importing and into accounting and quickly demonstrated his mastery of the language of numbers.

With promising business prospects and American citizenship within reach, John Wylie proposed to nineteen-year-old Harriet Bowen Woodward, whose father, William, was a prosperous New York City businessman.[30] The couple was married on April 27, 1858, at St. Thomas Church in New Windsor, near the farm the Woodwards owned on the Hudson River. Twenty guests attended the wedding, including Charlotte Thompson, an "old colored servant of 1801" who marked an X beside her name as one of the witnesses.

With each of Barrow's professional advancements, his growing family moved to finer residences. Mabel was born at their Stuyvesant Square house, but then like other fashionable New Yorkers, the Barrows moved uptown to a mansion at 3 West Forty-sixth.

As respected translator of early Bible texts and classics, tasteful importer of housewares, and finally as partner in a public accounting and actuarial firm, Barrow prospered in every direction he turned. His natural mathematical abilities were enhanced by his use of a machine known in England as an "arithmometer" but apparently unknown to businesses in America.[31]

In 1883, when Mabel was five years old, a British accountant named Edwin Guthrie came to New York to pursue a bankruptcy case and hired John Wylie Barrow, "an estimable American gentleman of culture and refinement, held in the highest esteem by all," to help him. The partnership went so well that Guthrie persuaded Barrow to leave Jaffray and join him and a third British accountant, Charles Wade, to form Barrow, Wade & Guthrie. It was "the first step in the beginning of the great profession of public accounting in the United States of America."[32]

Barrow, Wade & Guthrie's prosperity gave John Wylie time to again pursue his love for studying classic texts in their original language. His fortune enabled him to buy rare books and manuscripts, some dating to the mid-1400s. Mabel played nearby when her father retired to his library, where he pored over his beloved Horace and Virgil, perhaps stopping to read her some favorite passage.

Barrow kept dictionaries of a dozen languages within easy reach in his library. Renaissance-era books on music, botany and gardening, philology, and astronomy filled the shelves. His library also housed leather-bound mathematical and engineering tables from the early 1600s; first editions of Goethe and Schiller, Turgenev, Balzac and Racine, Dante and Boccaccio; the nine-volume engraved folio of John and Josiah Boydell's Shakespeare; and the fifty-three autographed volumes of Cousin Charles's *Complete Works*. The early nineteenth-century *History of British Birds* with diminutive engravings by Thomas Bewick, and an 1864 copy of the epochal *Man and Nature*, by George Perkins Marsh, would have held little interest for Mabel; they would not become relevant until she reached middle age.

More fascinating to the child Mabel was the microscope her father kept in his library. With him standing beside her or lifting her to peer through the eyepiece at one of nature's invisible wonders, she became his equal in access and in awe. At such times John Wylie was not only a prince who publicly redressed his groom. He was a humbler man who openly marveled at biological intricacy made visible by the magnifications of science.

Writing from the vantage point of an old woman, Rosalie Edge could still picture the microscope on the table and the "serried ranks" of Whistler's Thames River etchings on the library walls.[33] A verse Barrow kept on his desk summed up the intellectual oxygen that restored him as his little darling bore adulatory witness.

> The pleasant books, that silently among
> Our household treasures take familiar places,
> And are to us as if a living tongue
> Spake from the printed leaves or pictured faces.[34]

Mabel's earliest childhood was steeped in literature more than in studies of nature, and it was through great books that the world was first revealed to her. Cousin Charles's novels ranked supreme in this regard. Although Dickens died ten years before she was born, and the Barrows were reluctant to acknowledge him as their near relative in polite society, the author dominated the family's household culture.

Dickensian characters were spoken of as though they were personal friends and the novels' plots could be treated as genuine. In an 1884 letter Barrow wrote to his wife from Florida, he described "a thick mist all over the river," noting, "[S]uch parts as I could see reminded me forcefully of Dickens' [*sic*] description of Eden in 'Martin Chuzzlewit.'"[35]

Barrow had acquired a large photograph of Cousin Charles, which Dickens autographed while John Wylie, Harriet, and their oldest children were living in England at the end of the Civil War. Apparently Margaret sat on Dickens's lap as he wrote his name, a warm salutation, the day, and the year 1865. She squirmed and bumped his hand, smearing any immortal words he might have written, along with his famous signature; the year remained clear. From that day on chubby, asthmatic Margaret was designated the clumsy one in the family. Back in New York the photograph of Dickens was always hung in a place of honor so that guests could admire the photo and then puzzle over its inky smear. The story of Margaret's ignominy would be trotted out, to everyone's amusement but Margaret's.

Immersed in a cult of Dickens and of great literature, Mabel Barrow developed an intuitive sense of how a good story could be made a better one. She usually preferred the literary truth to the literal one that mere facts might support, and her interpretations of past events had a novelistic flair. And so, many years later Rosalie Edge wrote a fictionalized account of Margaret's lifelong aversion to the Dickens photograph. According to this telling, Margaret inherited the photograph, and when it was given to her, she smashed its frame and glass with an andiron, shattering the cherished cousin's image as Anna, Archibald, and Mabel looked on, "shocked to a paralysis of silence and inaction."[36]

But a curious disclaimer appears at the top of the manuscript: "This is confidential. Essentially, but not accurately true," Rosalie Edge confessed. "Margaret did not smash the picture, but she said that she had always wanted to, and she refused to have it."[37] The story was not a factual telling but one from which a greater truth emerged. Rosalie's "essentially, but not accurately true" disclaimer would frequently apply to the style of her later conservation pamphlets as well.

Indeed, her conviction that one should "never let the truth spoil a good story" was so fixed in her character it may well have been genetic. She would often be accused of wandering from proven facts. Her novelistic preference for the greater truth would serve conservation well. In time new facts arose and proved her right.

ON APRIL 25, 1885, fifty-seven-year-old John Wylie died at home after a brief illness, according to the *New York Times*. The obituary also stated, "[Barrow] bore an untarnished record, and his untimely death removes from our midst one of our most valued citizens." The American Orientalist Society acclaimed him "altogether a very symmetrical and great character."[38] Barrow was buried at the cemetery in Newburgh, a town about sixty miles up the Hudson River from New York City near Keewaydin, his in-laws' farm.

If Barrow indeed died at home after a brief illness, it seems odd that he was taken to Newburgh for burial. Years later Rosalie Edge wrote a fictionalized explanation of her father's death. According to this version, John Wylie and Harriet were riding together near Keewaydin when Ottawa slipped and John Wylie was crushed beneath him. "Papa was killed instantly," Rosalie wrote. This too seems an essentially but not accurately true version of her father's death since it conflicts with his obituary.[39] Perhaps Barrow did not die instantly as Rosalie's story claimed, but something else surely did: the family's sense of financial security.

The oral history on the subject that was passed down as gospel was that John Wylie's hand was crushed in a riding accident near Keewaydin and became infected. The injury and his distance from New York City prevented him from signing an agreement with Barrow, Wade & Guthrie that would have assured Harriet's portion of the accounting firm's future profits in the event of his death.

The Barrow women lived from then on in dread of destitution.[40] (Most galling was that Barrow, Wade & Guthrie thrived for years after Barrow's death, swallowing one accounting firm after another until it ultimately disappeared into the Big Four accounting company that is today KPMG.)[41] Around 1888 Mrs. Barrow was forced to sell the Forty-sixth Street mansion and bought a handsome brownstone off Park Avenue at 113 East Seventy-second. The brownstone, though substantial and impressive, had no orchid conservatory for Mabel's canaries and parakeets nor a stable for horses. Short of cash and having no place to keep her husband's magnificent library in their new home, Mrs. Barrow sold most of his 1,835 books at auction.

These traumatic circumstances following Barrow's demise posed a dilemma that it seems Mabel, her mother, and her sisters dared not confront.

John Wylie Barrow—the perfect, princely husband and father, the father in velvet doublet far superior to the fathers of other little girls—had made no prior arrangements to preserve his family's welfare. Rather than focus on that unpleasant fact and perhaps turn against him, Rosalie took comfort in literary license. The explanation that "Pappa died instantly" seemed to cover what was perhaps her princely father's arrogant oversight.

PSYCHOLOGICALLY SPEAKING, the Barrows had skidded to the precipice of what novelist Edith Wharton referred to later as New York's social aristocracy: those committed to "the concerted living up to long-established standards of honour and conduct, of education and manners."[42] The Barrows fervently clung to these standards even though during the Gilded Age, the concerted living-up part required a great deal more money than they had.

Fortunately they were invited to partake in the spillage of great wealth. Cornelius and Alice Vanderbilt II, whom they knew from St. Bartholomew's, charitably offered them seats in their box at the opera, and other friends also provided favors.[43] Margaret and Anna, who were in their twenties when John Wylie died, volunteered their services in socially appropriate ways in return for the crumbs of patronage they received. For a short time Anna also worked for the banker J. P. Morgan. The great financier, she declared, taught her how to balance her checkbook.

At about twenty Archibald was hired to be the personal assistant to Louise Whitfield, a Barrow family friend who had married industrialist Andrew Carnegie in 1887. Archie worked for Louise Carnegie until her death in 1946, accompanying her between the Carnegies' sixty-four-room red-brick Georgian mansion in New York City and their Skibo Castle retreat near Dornoch in the Scottish Highlands. After Andrew Carnegie died in 1919, Archie Barrow assisted Mrs. Carnegie in giving away the family fortune.[44]

Margaret and Anna continued to live at home. Neither seems to have been considered pretty even by family members.[45] With their family's diminished wealth, the hope of either of them finding a suitable mate faded further. Although they were both intensely erudite young women, college was also out of the question. Margaret read and translated Latin and Greek, and Anna studied accounting and astronomy, but careers were no more appropriate for these cosseted young women than college. Dependent spinsterhood under their mother's roof was the most acceptable option if they wished to remain in the class to which they were born. And yet, given the fine home and few servants Harriet managed to keep despite the economic cataclysm, the Barrows seem not to have been as impoverished as they pled.

EIGHT-YEAR-OLD MABEL's childhood became lonely and cold in a household where her sisters were too grown up to play with her and her reserved mother was too distracted by grief to nurture her daughter. Visits with Harriet Barrow were conducted with great formality. Each night before Mabel went to bed, her nurse dressed her in fine clothes to present her to her mother. Mrs. Barrow was "always sad." Though Harriet had known "so well the joy of perfect human love herself" in her marriage to John Wylie, she seemed to have little of it to show her fatherless girl, and it was Mabel's nurse who tucked her in for the night.[46]

Gone was the child's golden aura of paternal favoritism. Although Margaret could be attentive, she did not lavish the sort of affection on her little sister that their father had. The Noblest Girl who had been placed above reproach no longer had permission to be in charge of everything.

For the next twelve dreary years, Mabel did not seem to venture out very much. She stayed home and kept mostly to herself. Her maternal grandmother, Frances Evertson Woodward, paid Mabel's tuition at Miss Doremus's, the exclusive girls' school from which Margaret and Anna graduated. Mabel excelled: one grade report commended her for having "done almost faultless work in most English studies" and noted she had "not been absent or late."[47] Grandmother Frances also paid for her youngest granddaughter's piano and voice lessons. Although Margaret and Anna had apparently abandoned any hope of careers or husbands, Mabel studied music so assiduously that she considered teaching music and performing as a way to earn money when she was grown. When she was about twenty, the choral director of Grace Church asked her to help him coach the boys' choir, probably without pay.[48]

A recent widow herself, Grandmother Frances brightened Mabel's spirits when Mabel visited her at Keewaydin. The old woman refused to wear black as was expected of her, and after sixty years of marriage she was happy to do as she pleased. She drove herself around in her small carriage and complained of the vulgar class of people moving into her town of Vail's Gate. Frances could identify the newcomers by the large and noisy carriages they drove down the narrow country lanes. When one of the offensive contraptions passed, she politely inclined her head in greeting toward its occupants before turning to Mabel to whisper, "In trade . . ." Grandmother Frances showed the lonely girl how to enjoy being outdoors and walked with Mabel in the woods bordering her gardens to "visit" her favorite trees.[49]

In 1899 Frances Woodward died at the age of eighty-eight. The inheritance Harriet Barrow received from her mother seems to have eased her financial worries.[50] Mabel, who was twenty-two when her grandmother died, missed her terribly. Frances's habit of visiting favorite trees had not yet become her own.

AT TWENTY-TWO Mabel Rosalie Barrow was a well-read and opinionated young woman. Raised as the only child among erudite adults, she seems to have been particularly precocious.

Though she was no arresting beauty, Mabel was at least more attractive than either of her older sisters. Her features were plainer than her mother's delicately delineated Liberty-dollar profile, she wrote in gentle self-deprecation. Mabel's nose was sharp, and her chin receded. Overlapping teeth made her self-conscious, and she pursed her lips to hide her smile, which frequently gave her a look of aristocratic disdain.[51]

But Mabel was, at five feet five, slender, and the arresting contrast of her pale eyes and dark crown of hair attracted some male attention. At least, she was courted "by a moderate few," while her sisters were not.[52] Mabel Barrow's few suitors were far too humble, from her mother's point of view, and Mabel accepted this judgment.

Her best girlhood friend was Louise Schanck, a classmate from Miss Doremus's who was not much sought after either. Another of Mabel's closest friends was Louise Johnson—or Beautiful Louise, as Mabel called her. Beautiful Louise played piano and lived with her mother at the home of wealthy cousins who knew the Barrows. Her father, William Johnson, remained in Ithaca; it seems William Johnson's lackluster social standing was interfering with his beautiful daughter's strongest marriage prospects. For Beautiful Louise to come out in Manhattan might repair the situation.

At fifteen Louise Johnson met Charles Marston, a wealthy industrialist from the British Midlands nine years older than she. Marston owned the Sunbeam Company, which his father had founded in the mid nineteenth century to make pots and pans, two-wheeled bicycles, and eventually small automobiles.[53] He frequently traveled to the United States on business. Marston discovered that he liked American girls because they were friendlier than English girls. Beautiful Louise was particularly appealing. She had

read "most of the regular run of the average books, and, on the whole, reminds me of the average English schoolgirl, except she is an improvement,"
he wrote.[54] Because of the difference in their ages, he waited four years to
marry her.

On January 30, 1895, eighteen-year-old Mabel was one of Beautiful Louise's "seven pretty bridesmaids in pink" at the All Souls Episcopal Church
in New York City.[55] The Johnson-Marston match was a toned-down version
of the American-Anglo marriages much in vogue. There were at least nine
such high-profile unions that year alone, the most glittering and infamous
of them being between Consuelo Vanderbilt and the man she reportedly
detested, the 9th Duke of Marlboro, impoverished heir of Blenheim Palace. Consuelo was in love with another man, which did not stop her brash
mother, Alva Vanderbilt, from promising $2.5 million to the duke if he mar-
ried her daughter and made her a duchess. The marriage of Louise Johnson,
who was not an heiress, to wealthy Charles Marston, who was not a member
of the nobility, would have received little attention, probably a notice in the
newspaper.

MABEL WENT TO ENGLAND to visit the happy Marstons at Afcot, the
couple's rambling brick mansion in Tettenhall Wood outside Birmingham.
The estate's gently sloping lawns and gardens opened to misty views of the
Malvern and Clee Hills. After 1902 her visits to Afcot preceded or followed
those she made to Skibo Castle in Scotland, where she visited her brother
Archie and his wife, Elizabeth.[56] Skibo's lands rambled over more than one
hundred square miles of moor and meadow, golf course and glade, encom-
passing a dramatic view of the North Sea. Seven-hundred-year-old beech
and yew trees lined the driveway leading to the castle entrance.[57] Mabel
learned to swim in Skibo's indoor "Saltwater Swimming Bath" heated to
seventy degrees, considered quite warm, at least for Scotland. She loved to
wander freely over the bright green grounds, admiring the trees and all the
scenery as she might have on the walks she had taken with her grandmother
at Keewaydin.

A full array of intensively planned activities awaited Skibo's official guests,
beginning at seven each morning, when a piper woke them by playing traditional Scottish melodies as he circled the castle. Archibald Barrow was
indispensable in helping Mrs. Carnegie fulfill the myriad duties that made
running Skibo much like serving as mayor of a village filled with the rich
and famous. When Woodrow Wilson visited, he wrote to his wife that the

castle's "perfect stream of visitors . . . would utterly wear poor Mrs. Carnegie out." She relied heavily on the "assistance of her personal secretary," none other than Mabel's brother Archibald.[58]

Despite Skibo's glittering roster of the world's richest and most famous people, Mabel Barrow was a guest of lower stature owing to her brother's position. But at the Marstons' estate in Wolverhampton, where Louise and Charles entertained in great style, she was the equal of the other guests. "These were the days when entertaining on a large scale was possible and lavish," even among the rich whose net worth fell considerably below that of the stratospheric Carnegies.[59]

Afcot's visitors may not have been as luminous as those Mabel encountered at Skibo Castle, but she found its young, international mix of Louise's American family and friends and Charles Marston's British family more pleasurable.

Until Louise Marston moved to the town, Americans had been considered exotics by Wolverhampton gentry. The Midlands natives were friendly as long as the Yankees displayed an "enthusiasm and genuine reverence for things English." With her manners burnished in the high societies of both Manhattan and Skibo, and with Charles Dickens as her first cousin once removed, Mabel Barrow might scarcely have seemed out of place. She loved to pass as English, and did so easily with her patrician New York pronunciation that easily blended into the proper British she had picked up from her father and English nannies.[60]

Among Afcot's frequent visitors was a mob of Charles Marston's cousins on his mother's side; Ellen Edge Marston's brother Hall Travers Edge lived in neighboring Edgbaston and had fathered seventeen children by two wives. The Edge family traced its respectable lineage to 1340.[61] Edge linens and stationery bore the family's crest, consisting of a silver eagle with its wings extended on a field of red and black. On Edge sterling was engraved the family's centuries-old emblem, a mythical creature whose upper half was that of a boxing lion and its lower one a seal with flukes resting on a wave.

The Edge family was not only large in number. Some of its individuals were gigantic. One of Charles Marston's favorite cousins was six-feet-eight Charles Noel Edge, a handsome civil engineer who had graduated from Cambridge.[62] Mabel, fifteen inches shorter and four years older than Charles Edge, did not seem to mind the difference in either their height or their ages. They became a couple during the "tennis parties, tournaments, [and] river picnics on the winding Avon a long cycle ride away." In the evenings there was music and dancing at the manor, and she and the other girls "indulged in friendships and flirtations."[63]

Mabel Barrow was an avid participant in all the games in the parlor or outdoors; Charles Edge took her hunting, and she taught him to swim. Her formidable intellect and sense of spontaneous adventure offset Charles's sheer physical dominance. What perhaps impressed Charles more than anything about Mabel was her "beautiful mind."[64]

Just as Harriet Bowen Woodward had been smitten by a brilliant and ambitious Englishman fifty years earlier, so too was Mabel Rosalie Barrow. She was hopelessly in love, this time with a man who would meet her mother's exacting social requirements. Doubtless John Wylie Barrow would also have approved of this magnificent specimen of his native countrymen.

IN JUNE 1908, twenty-six-year-old Charles Edge went to New York City to consult on the Queensboro Bridge, which was then under construction. Charles, as a civil engineer, was an expert in bridge design. The completion of this elegant, cantilevered span linking the Long Island suburbs to Manhattan had been stalled after a section collapsed in a wind storm, and a firm he worked for was hired to assure the bridge's safety. His business trip to New York gave him a chance to call on Mabel. In a quadrant of the Cloisters overlooking the Hudson, he asked her to marry him, and Mabel said yes.[65]

There was one hitch. Charlie would leave New York in a few days for the Orient to work for Metropolitan Vickers, a British industrial firm. The company was sending him to China to acquire railroad construction contracts for them. His employment agreement with the firm stipulated that unless he was already married when he started the job he would not be allowed to marry for a year.

Charlie offered to wed Mabel the week before he sailed so that she could join him immediately. This idea must have horrified Mrs. Barrow, who refused to approve such a hasty marriage, perhaps fearing what people would think if her daughter married and immediately disappeared for a year or more. Chaste spinsterhood for thirty-one-year-old Mabel may have seemed far more respectable than an impromptu ceremony to a man the family did not know.

Harriet decreed that if her daughter wished to marry Charles Noel Edge she would wait out the year in New York and then go to Asia, since Charles was not free to return until the end of his second year with the company. It is not hard to imagine why a grief-stricken seventy-two-year-old widowed mother who had buried three children and disowned a fourth did not share Mabel's jubilation at becoming a bride so far from friends and family. Harriet may have come to expect that her three daughters would live with her until she died, to compensate for the ones who had departed far too soon.

Mrs. Barrow struck a compromise with her daughter and prospective son-in-law. She agreed to give the match her blessing and help Mabel prepare for her marriage in a year's time. Margaret would accompany Mabel to Yokohama, where Charles would meet them and they would marry. In exchange for her approval of their delayed marriage, Harriet insisted the couple keep their marriage plans a secret for at least six months.

Charles departed New York with this understanding, and the secret engagement was sealed. A few months later, however, Mrs. Barrow changed her mind and decided she, and not Margaret, would accompany Mabel to Yokohama. Charlie was inexplicably adamant in his protest. "I should be terribly distressed if you insisted on coming so far," he shot back in a letter to Mrs. Barrow. His vehemence may have surprised his future wife and mother-in-law: "You must remember that last June you consented to our marriage in one year's time and that we both placed absolute reliance in your helping us in every way in your power. Supposing either Mabel or I had not felt that confidence, have you ever realized that we should have been married there and then?"[66]

He threatened to break his two-year contract with Metro and return to New York without a job to marry Mabel in the sort of wedding Mrs. Barrow wanted her daughter to have. Such a move would severely prejudice his future employment opportunities, he warned.

It is hard to understand why Charlie so strenuously opposed Mrs. Barrow's attending her own daughter's wedding—unless his intentions toward Mabel were not yet fixed in his own mind. Curiously, although there are several letters Charlie wrote to Mrs. Barrow among Rosalie Edge's private papers, there are none written to Mabel in that year they were apart.

Mrs. Barrow relented. Margaret would be the one to go with Mabel to Yokohama as the family's emissary at the wedding as originally planned. Once the decision was made, Mabel displayed a bit of her own grit. It was "a waste of good time and good tears to weep for me," she announced to her mother. "I always said I would see the world before I died, and by marrying Charlie I seem in a fair way to do it." Mabel had perhaps agreed to marry Charlie on his terms not only because she loved him, but also because as Mrs. Charles Noel Edge she would have the means to travel, a yearning she had acquired even before her trips to England and Scotland. At thirty-two Mabel would be an unusually old bride, and perhaps she considered Charlie's proposal her last chance to make all her dreams come true.[67]

WITH HER ENGAGEMENT veiled in secrecy during the summer of 1908, Mabel received an unusual assignment from Harriet Barrow's good friend Alice Vanderbilt. Alice asked Mabel to serve as a spokeswoman for her youngest daughter, twenty-two-year-old Gladys, after she had wed Count László Széchenyi of Hungary the previous January. The Vanderbilts perhaps wished to neutralize the sort of toxic publicity that had saturated Consuelo Vanderbilt's disastrous marriage thirteen years before.

New York tabloids insisted on knowing how this Vanderbilt heiress would fare with her noble husband in her adopted country. The Széchenyis' ancestral castle near Tatra-Lonnicz in the Carpathian Mountains was not as grand or as modern as The Breakers in Newport, Rhode Island, one of the palatial residences in which Gladys Vanderbilt had been raised. Reporters also demanded to know how an American and a commoner would be accepted in Count Széchenyi's circle. "The fact that she is a Vanderbilt would, of course, establish a place for her," Count Anton Sigay explained reassuringly.[68]

Nevertheless, the honeymooning Széchenyis were pursued relentlessly by the press as they proceeded in style toward Hungary. A spokesperson for the Vanderbilts—presumably Mabel Barrow—placed the following clarification in the *Times* under the soothing subtitle "The Countess Delighted": "Although it had been borne abroad in some manner or other that the reception of the new Countess László Széchenyi, formerly Miss Gladys Vanderbilt, on the ancestral estates of her husband was a trifle rough and simple, bespeaking too much of poverty-stricken slav peasantry to suit her taste, nothing could be further from the facts."[69]

The Vanderbilts asked if Mabel might continue emphasizing this editorial slant from Budapest while the countess settled in.[70] Mabel quickly assented. Keen to travel, the literarily adept Miss Barrow was the ideal person to spin a happy story and deflect attention away from Gladys, who was understandably fragile in her new role. Mabel could have empathized with her Vanderbilt acquaintance somewhat; both had accepted proposals of marriage from foreigners and were moving to backward countries amid doubts about the wisdom of their choices.

Whenever Mabel returned from the Széchenyi castle to the posh Hotel Gellert in Budapest, where the Vanderbilts put her up, she made herself conspicuously available to a snooping reporter or perhaps filed her own rhapsodic account of the countess's well-being. The exuberant prose in one *New York Times* article that ran in August 1908 presages the style of our future pamphleteer.

> The Count and Countess are very happy, and always in each other's company, making excursions about the country like a pair of young lovers, which they are. A few days ago they went to the famous ice cavern at Dobsina, where skating can be had in midsummer. Both the Count and Countess skated, while Mrs. Cornelius Vanderbilt, who was with them on the occasion, contented herself with looking on. Gladys was perfectly enchanted with the experience, and told the general manager, who had personally received the distinguished guests, that if the Dobsina ice cavern were located in America it would be visited every year not by 5,000 to 8,000 persons, as in Hungary, but by five to six millions.

The mention of the ice cave's beauty seems odd in such an article and may have reflected Mabel's nascent interest in Dobšiná's natural wonders. It also seems doubtful that Countess Széchenyi skated, since she was seven months pregnant at the time. Mabel Barrow, however, loved to ice skate and may have done so that day. That fact would not have been of any interest to the *Times'* readers. She perhaps improved the story by putting the countess in her skates. As small as the cause of preserving Countess Széchenyi's privacy might seem, it was the first cause that Mabel would energetically champion.

Perhaps Mabel's reports bought the Széchenyis some months of peace. There was no more speculation about the count and countess's happiness together until their daughter was born nine months to the day after they were married.

Coincidentally, Mabel was asked to come to the aid of another of the world's richest women that summer. Her brother Archibald, who was Mrs. Carnegie's personal assistant, had injured his back on a dive into the Skibo swimming pool, as the Carnegies' social season was going full tilt.[71] She helped Mrs. Carnegie organize events and kept up with the correspondence as Archie would have.

After Mabel completed her assignments at Skibo and in Budapest, she went to Afcot. Her fiancé was, of course, in China, but Mabel had another reason to visit the Marstons. Louise and Charles had asked her to be the godmother of Melissa, their second daughter, and Mabel had not yet seen the six-month-old baby. Mabel kept her promise to her mother and breathed not a word of her engagement to one of her best friends. It must have been a difficult secret to keep under the circumstances, particularly since Charlie's brother Cyril, who lived nearby, was aware of it. He told Mabel that he approved of his family's upcoming "acquisition" and hinted at the engagement to his parents, "the Dad and the Mater."[72]

Although Mabel purposely kept Louise in the dark, she felt that her dear friend was being willfully clueless. Through Cyril, Charles made sure Mabel received flowers every day at Afcot, but Louise never commented on their arrival. She complained of exhaustion and stumbled when she walked. At the time of Mabel's visit, it seemed Beautiful Louise was simply recovering from childbirth slowly; it would be another year before she was diagnosed with multiple sclerosis.

Sadly, Louise's early symptoms of the disease coincided with the happiest time Mabel had known since her father died. It was Louise's turn to feel slighted when she finally learned of the secret engagement from one of the Edge cousins months later. "I had imagined if you and Charlie had wanted us to know you would have written and told us," she wrote from her sickbed, then graciously added that she thought the match "lovely indeed."[73]

In New York Mabel's good news raced around the Barrow circle of intimates. Dozens of congratulatory notes expressed surprise and puzzlement over Mabel's choice of a British husband and a Chinese home. It left one of Mrs. Barrow's friends "gasping for breath." Countess Széchenyi wrote to wish Mabel as happy a marriage as her own was proving to be and promised to send her a wristwatch as a wedding gift.[74]

Grace Church's rector was also stunned when he learned of Mabel's engagement. Mabel and he were walking in Central Park and talking about the differences between Norway maples and Carolina poplars when she blurted the news. In retrospect it is striking that she made her important announcement while engrossed in nature study. Mabel was in her latency, that long period between human nature's stimulus and the human response to it.

Meanwhile on East Seventy-second Street, the Barrow women read ravenously and talked endlessly of the Orient. Mabel read everything she could about the political situation in China and was thrilled by the book *Indiscreet Letters from Peking*, which dramatically recounted the Boxer Rebellion of 1900. She was undeterred by the rebel banners that flew over Peking a short time before proclaiming, in four Chinese "dread characters," "Death and destruction to the foreigner and all his works."

Presumably she also read the encyclopedic *Things Chinese*, published in 1904, which warned her to expect the unexpected in the land of "Topsy-turvydom."

> The Chinese are not only at our antipodes with regard to position on the globe, but they are our opposites in almost every action and thought. He laughs when he tells you his father or mother, brother or sister, is dead; a bride that did not wail as if for the dead would be a fraud. He asks you if you have eaten your rice, instead of saying, "How do you do?" and locates his intellect in his stomach. For "goodbye" he says "walk slowly." Instead of telling you to take heart and be brave when any danger threatens he tells you to lessen your heart; he makes the most earnest enquiries, not only as to your health, but asks your age, and compliments you if you are old; he wishes to know what your salary or income is, what your rent is, and numberless other polite questions which we think impertinent. On the other hand, let no enquiry cross your lips as to the welfare of his wife; nor had you better ask after his daughters—his sons he will be glad to parade before you; but do not compliment him on the chubby cheeks and healthy looks of his baby boy, as any accident or disease happening to the youngster will be laid to your account. While you have doffed your hat while entering his house, he has put his on before receiving you. He shakes his own hands instead of clasping yours; he places you on his left as the seat of honor; and if he hands you anything he does so with two hands. He, perhaps, shows you with pride the set of coffin boards which his dutiful son has presented him.[75]

Mabel also plunged into her wardrobe preparations. There were fittings at Senora Tucci's and the acquisition of porcelain, sterling tableware, and monogrammed linens to jot down in a small brown leather notebook.[76] By the time she and Margaret were ready to sail for Yokohama, her trousseau filled twelve trunks piled in a spare bedroom.

In the first week of May 1909, Mabel and Margaret left New York and traveled north. The quickest route to the Orient was by way of Canada, then across the Pacific Ocean aboard the Canadian Railway's sleek ivory-hulled steamer, the *Empress of Japan*. Their stateroom was crammed with bouquets from Charlie and eight pounds of chocolates. In a letter to Mrs. Barrow, Charlie took a conciliatory tone: "I am sure too that I regret as much as Mabel that it was impossible for us to be married in New York," he wrote. "She would have dearly loved to have had you with her and to be married in Grace Church."[77]

The *Empress of Japan* headed north, angling toward the Aleutian Islands to make up for its delayed start. The islands were veiled in icy fog. "If you looked us up on a map you might easily think we had gotten by mistake on a polar expedition," Mabel wrote to her mother. "We are so cold we are just cross." She "longed to be grilled," and ship stewards promised she would be when the ship neared Japan.[78]

Mabel's letters to her mother reveal for the first time how opinionated she could be. She dismissed another fiancée bound for Yokohama as "a most noisy little person" who permitted men to say anything they pleased to her; a passenger from Iowa behaved so badly Mabel was ashamed to let it be known that she too was an American. The ship librarian recommended Dickens's novels to bored passengers, however, and so won her respect.[79]

One night Mabel's hot-water bottle burst. She was scalded, and her berth was drenched. She screamed for help, and a Chinese steward materialized within moments. "You should have seen with what calmness and quiet and dispatch he put everything right," Mabel reported to her mother. To mop up the wet floor, he removed his shoes, then "coiled his queue around his neck, knotted it neatly on one side and set to work."[80]

Hours before daylight on May 27, 1909, Mabel woke—if she had slept at all—to prepare for her reunion with Charlie. Her sister Margaret gave her mother the detailed account of her sister's toilette, explaining that since she had no groom to meet she could stay in bed and simply watch. As Mabel and Margaret stood on the ship's deck at ten in the morning, Mount Fuji's white symmetry billowed up before them, a solitary cone shimmering in the blue sky. A steward informed them that such a clear view of the great mountain god was an auspicious omen for those disembarking in Japan the first time.[81]

Minutes later the sisters spotted the man-mountain Charles Noel Edge, balancing precariously in a small tender, his arms heaped with yet more bouquets. Mabel had previously ordered Margaret to "disappear" when Charlie boarded, but she seemed to have forgotten her instructions and gripped her sister's arm tightly to keep her from leaving. Margaret stood by superfluously. She recalled feeling "so lonely in the reunited lovers' company that I lifted up my voice and was prepared to howl for the benefit of the passengers to my eternal disgrace." Charlie, according to Margaret, "was so excited and flustered that he could not think what to do next." He behaved so manically that she wondered if the Japanese thought he was an "escaped lunatic." A friend who had come aboard with Charlie noticed

Margaret Barrow's discomfort and gallantly escorted her off the ship to the waiting carriages.[82]

After a year spent apart, Mabel and Charlie were too overcome to eat any of the elaborate lunch prepared in their honor at the home of Reverend W. P. G. Field and his wife, on the bluff overlooking Yokohama where foreigners lived. They spent the day admiring their wedding gifts and mooning over each other, Margaret wrote to Mrs. Barrow. The wedding gifts, she assured her mother, were too numerous and wonderful to describe, although the diamond pieces Charlie gave Mabel were noted, as was a check for one hundred dollars from Alice Vanderbilt to the young couple. The next morning Mrs. Field's *awah* (maid) hooked the bride into her ivory lace gown. Mabel donned the diamonds Charlie had given her and went downstairs to meet her groom, who was pacing in his frock coat, striped pants, and lavender tie.[83]

During the ceremony in the church's steamy garden, the acting United States consul general to Japan gave the bride away. Margaret confessed to her mother that she wept as a small choral group sang "The Voice That Breathed O'er Eden" and "O Perfect Love." At the reception Margaret surprised everyone by producing a wedding cake she had smuggled from New York and placed it beside a vase of calla lilies.[84]

As the newlyweds got into their carriage, Margaret and Mrs. Field blanketed them with confetti, contrary to Mabel's expressed wishes to avoid tacky displays. "I was so overjoyed, because she thought that being married here she could control matters and not have any frivolities," Margaret wrote triumphantly.[85]

The "two inane children" packed five trunks for their two-week honeymoon; Charlie insisted on seeing all her finest raiments as soon as possible. Mrs. Field tied an old shoe to the back of their carriage, a final act of disobedience that Mabel protested as she drove away with her husband.[86]

CHAPTER TWO

Wife of Charles Noel Edge

For their honeymoon, Charles Edge had reserved a suite at the elegant Fujiya Hotel, nestled in the wooded mountains on Mount Fuji's perimeter. The Fujiya, with its natural hot springs and odd blend of Victorian and traditional Japanese architecture, was the first hotel in Japan built for Western tourists, in 1878. Of greater contrast than the architecture were the women of the East and the West: dainty and delicate Japanese maidens prettily shuffled about in their sandals, as they waited on "sour-visaged European females," dismissively noted one Englishman who had stayed at the hotel. This group was composed of "veritable ogresses, bespectacled, loose-bloused, curled, broad-waisted women of the type whose sole mission . . . is to vulgarize the world."[1] The ogresses were often recent brides. In the long letter that the new Mrs. Charles Noel Edge wrote to her mother from the Fujiya, she gives a unique counterpoint to the Englishman's harsh judgment.

1st June 1909
Fujiya Hotel
Minyanoshita

Dearest Mother—

   This is Tuesday, and I have been a British matron since Friday—and yet have not written to you! We are both very well—happy? And we are in the loveliest spot in the world and do the most delightful things. I send you a postcard of the

hotel—it is said to be the finest in the East—delicious chow, which being
interpreted means food and excellent service. We have delightful rooms
and for days at a time do not need to penetrate to other parts for we usually
dine upstairs. Our first day I am afraid you would have said "poor children"
for Charlie was quite ill, it seems since he came to Japan and looked a very
ghost. My nose bled violently before my wedding and continued for two days
and when it came to Saturday evening dinner being all served I was flat on
the floor and Charlie looking so frightened that my desire to laugh revived
me. We took counsel after that and spent Sunday quietly on the hills—quite
a procession—two coolies carrying tea, books, rugs, knitting, Marquis
chocolates—we climbed a mountain—little heat and spent the entire day
in the open air and since that, there have been no nosebleeds and Charlie
is getting very bonny and his cough sounds less graveyard-like. There is
an ideal swimming bath, water clear as crystal always, running in and out
from a hot spring carved out of this side of the greenest hills and we swim
there at any and all times of the day—always before breakfast, having first
had coffee. Yesterday we had a long ride—horses very bad, trappings truly
remarkable—but a lovely ride in the mountains and a delicious swim after-
wards. What I have seen of Japan is too beautiful—it is like Scotland—the
same bare hills but in all the sheltered places this most delicious almost tropical green—perfect all except the people—the men servants I don't mind but
how I loathe the impertinent giggling women. Oh! You should see Charlie's
Chinese "boy" Wang! He calls me "Missy" which does not seem quite proper.
The hotel is crowded with brides and grooms there is scarcely anything else
here, and we all eye one another with frank interest. I am beginning to speak
pigeon [sic] English quite fluently. Margaret promised to write you full par-
ticulars of our lovely and complete wedding—our bridesmaids, our breakfast, the beautiful decorations—everything complete. I don't wonder Charlie
was ill, no little thing forgotten—and I can assure you the champagne was
good—Best of all I loved my bouquet, though Charlie was horrified—it
was to have been all white but turned up orchids every known shade—one
would never have had the imagination to order it but it was beautiful. We
had our pictures taken in the garden as we came out from the church so you
will see a little what it was like. You should see Mabel's diamonds and new
silver—oh! If you could see my coffee set: The Mater and Dad are sending
a diamond brooch but I will not get it until I get to Shanghai. Thank you so
much for the cameo and the Horace. I loved them and was much touched.

I can't write more. C. is buried to his neck in work and if I can get off a few letters for him we may get out to enjoy a little of this loveliest day.
Much much love to Anna, Affectly, Mabel[2]

Despite Mabel's unfavorable opinion of the Japanese people, the tranquility of Japan's landscape may have touched something deeper in her. Around the Fujiya Hotel, wild forests and thoughtfully tended gardens were saturated in soothing gradients of the color green bathed in spectral green light. Vistas were softened by the several species of condensate suspended in the air—columns of steam from natural geothermal pools, low-bellied clouds, and ribbons of fog wrapping around the mountains.

In the Land of the Gods, ancestral spirits inhabited trees, rocks, and water. Nature was sacred. Countless deities on land and sea had to be appeased to avoid devastating earthquakes and typhoons. But as Japan rushed headlong toward modernity in the 1900s, there was the possibility that the Japanese people would lose their sense of profound connection to the natural world. Kenji Miyazawa, a scientist who would become one of Japan's greatest poets of the twentieth century, began composing Thoreau-like verse that implored his industrializing brethren to live in balance with all the earth's elements and creatures.

The Edges could not have avoided seeing Shinto shrines in forest openings or rising out of Japan's coastal waters. These were constant and countless reminders of the traditional ethic that Miyazawa feared might get lost. Entry to the shrines was through a simple torii gate of stone or wood and shaped like a character of Japanese calligraphy: two upright pillars topped by two overhanging spans, the upper one slightly arched. Torii, Mabel might have learned, was the Japanese word for "bird perch," and birds were considered the messengers sent from spirits of the nether world.

Japan's moist air was pungent with cedar and hinoki cypress, a smaller version of the tree that had once dominated the country's forests. Old-growth hinoki had attained two hundred feet in height and thickened to immense girth. For centuries remnants of these majestic trees stood as structural timbers in the great Buddhist temples built at Nikko and Nara. It would be almost thirty years before Mabel would see the like of such ancient trees standing in a living forest.

Understandably, the Fujiya's ambient sexuality was far more pertinent and interesting: she noted the women's shoes placed beside the men's shoes outside each bedroom door and described bridegrooms "mostly wrapped in gloom and the brides defiant." A married woman of but a few days, she was all-knowing and longed to give the couples in pettish moods "little words of advice to help them over their rough places!"[3]

But "the Chief end in life," she wrote perhaps only half-sarcastically, was her jewelry. She and Charlie spent hours admiring the diamond, pearl, cameo, and amethyst treasures he had given her. Together they chose the right brooch, bracelet, and pendant to be worn with each dress.[4]

Charlie appraised his wife's appearance. She was "very vain but surpassingly beautiful," he wrote to Mrs. Barrow. "She is simply made for pretty clothes and she adores them!" Charlie promised Mabel he would buy her emeralds and pearls when they went to Siam, all of which Mabel dutifully reported to Anna, who no doubt would convey the husband-affirming information to their mother. Charlie, acquiescing to his wife's style of ancestor worship, complimented the pendant she wore with her father's silhouette. "How great a thing it would have been to me to have known him," he wrote to Mrs. Barrow.[5]

When they returned from their honeymoon, Margaret was moved by the sight of her sister: "the most radiant thing I ever beheld, absolutely transfigured she was so happy." Margaret had remained with the Fields and attended to such postwedding matters as packing up the remainder of the cake and mailing the fifty-three engraved wedding announcements she had brought: "Mrs. John Wylie Barrow has the honor of announcing the marriage of her daughter Mabel Rosalie to Mr. Charles Noel Edge on Friday, the twenty-eighth of May at Christ Church, Yokohama, Japan." The day Margaret left, Mabel "wept inconsolably" in a rare display of feeling. Again Margaret was moved by her sister's newly soft demeanor: "It was a pleasure and a comfort to see her, and she was very gentle and sweet to me, perfectly wrapped up in her husband, and he in her, really the most happy looking and acting couple, except that poor Charlie looked wretchedly ill, which he certainly was with a touch of malaria."[6]

Mrs. Barrow could not have ignored the "touch of malaria" Margaret slipped into her report of Mabel's transfiguration, adding it to Mabel's casual acknowledgment that Charlie had been sick during their honeymoon. He had been gravely ill from the moment the sisters landed at Yokohama, and his feverish activity on the deck of the *Empress of Japan* was truly that. During much of their honeymoon, he lay wasting in the marriage bed from what Mabel suspected was either malaria or dysentery, or both. Charlie told all to Mrs. Barrow in his letter thanking her for the sixteenth-century volume of logarithms from John Wylie's library. He confessed, "[I have] gone and disgraced myself entirely—felt very sick right there in the middle of our honeymoon."[7]

Indeed it took "Rosalie's whole will and energy" to keep him alive during the arduous two-day trip by steamer from Yokohama and then on the sweltering train to Shanghai, where they would be based.[8] Charles's confession of his illness was one bit of surprising news. That he called his wife Rosalie was the other; from that moment Rosalie was the name she preferred. Her new identity dated to the first days of her marriage, to the time when she began her new life by saving her husband's.

FROM THE DECK of the *Yamaguchi Maru*, Rosalie Edge, the only woman aboard, was dismayed by her first sight of the Chinese mainland. "Seen from this side it seems desirable chiefly as the place where I will get the Dad's pendant and the Countess's [Széchenyi] watch," she wrote diffidently.[9] Charlie's valet, Wang, met them in Shanghai and was horrified by his master's deterioration, particularly in contrast to his new mistress's robust health.

A rickshaw brought Rosalie and ailing Charlie to the first home they would share, the elegant Palace Hotel in the International Settlement, the part of Shanghai where foreigners were permitted to live. The luxurious rooms delighted Rosalie; they each had their own bathroom, which meant that she could brush her teeth whenever Charlie had enough strength to shave.[10]

But his health was a source of great worry, for since their honeymoon he had gotten so much worse that there were times she feared he would die. Rosalie confided to Margaret that she tended him around the clock: "It has been a serious thing—how serious I am (Fortunately) only just beginning to realize but it was almost (certainly) dysentery—a thing which, whatever it may be at home, is spoken of here with bated breath and is considered well nigh hopeless."[11]

His giant frame had shrunk to "a cadaverous skeleton" with "bony wrists, hollow cheeks and great eyes—a horrid looking object." Rosalie spoon-fed him boiled milk and bananas and left his side only to scrub books, clothing, and cookware with ammonia, for dark mold threatened to colonize every surface. Her hands turned red and raw from the work.[12]

Though she would have liked to go outdoors when Charlie slept comfortably, she would not have enjoyed refreshing air. Shanghai's summer heat and rain provided little relief from their own hot, muggy rooms. "I do not like a climate that includes a rainy season," she declared. Her writing paper was so damp the ink sometimes ran. She did not open her trunks for fear mold would invade the pretty clothes.[13]

Sometimes Charlie felt strong enough to sit up in bed and do paperwork. On such occasions Rosalie complained, "[He sat] propped up, studying, lost in figures, perfectly unconscious that he numbers such a thing as a wife among his possessions, but if I move it's, 'O Dearie, aren't you going to sit in here?'" Rosalie wryly observed, "Charlie does not need too much fussing—like you and Margaret he needs nothing as long as one does not occupy oneself with anything or anyone else."[14]

He found the secretarial skills she had used during her brief stint as Louise Carnegie's assistant quite useful. Rosalie had a gift for organization. She cataloged his two hundred engineering drawings, recopied his notes in her fine hand, and composed business letters, marveling at the peculiar technical knowledge she was picking up as she became acquainted with her husband's work. Charlie the designer of bridges worked on one project that stipulated the span must bear the weight of three elephants. What, Rosalie wondered, did one elephant weigh?[15]

On some days Charlie felt strong enough to schedule meetings in their suite and asked Rosalie to serve as hostess. When the other men were there, Charlie summoned her with "'Dearie, can Mr. P. have tea?' Or, 'Dearie, haven't we a currant cake?'" She concluded that he really only wanted to show off how becoming she was with the silver belt he had given her on her slender waist.[16]

They acclimated to their strange new relationship in this strange land. "I say 'my husband' in true English style, and 'Master' to the [servant] boys and 'Mr. Edge' to promiscuous inferiors—but I have never known C's courage to rise to either 'my wife' or 'Mrs. Edge,'" she wrote.[17] Wang, who had previously taken care of all his master's needs, seemed to object to her intrusion. She had to break the Chinese servant's habit of walking into their bedroom every morning to wake Charlie as he had done before the marriage. Half asleep Rosalie ordered Wang out, but the servant refused to leave. In his feeble condition, Charlie interceded. "If Missy no like Wang, Wang goes," he told his valet firmly. "And Wang is a canny man," Rosalie victoriously reported to Mrs. Barrow. After a few more weeks she was referring to him as "Our Wang" in her letters, and he congenially waited on them both. Charlie disapproved though when she asked the valet to button her dress for her.[18]

In July the rain stopped and Rosalie was able to escape the oppressive heat of their rooms by going to the hotel's rooftop rose garden, "a delicious place at the truly remarkable height of six stories." She dropped exhaustedly into a fat chair and inhaled the garden's fragrance.[19]

She also began to venture out into the International Settlement but was bored by it because its neighborhoods looked so much like places she had seen in Europe. Depending on the particular nationality dominating each section of the settlement, it looked exactly like parts of London or Paris or Berlin. In 1909 Shanghai's four hundred thousand Chinese dwelled close by but a world away from the five thousand foreigners.[20]

On her excursions beyond the International Settlement, Rosalie made her way through the sea of rickshaws. She passed wizened Chinese men holding fans to shade their eyes, poses that struck her as stray bits of Gilbert and Sullivan. The Chinese portions of Shanghai contained much that was too vulgar for a well-bred young woman from New York to see. Westerners had never seen "such loathsome beggars," and few cities smelled as "vile" as Shanghai.[21] A slave trade thrived, royal eunuchs fluttered past in gorgeous silk robes, and privileged women shuffled by on bound feet no bigger than their fists. Starving parents thrust dead or dying children in the faces of foreigners, and along some streets the sickly sweet odor of opium hung in the air.[22]

Rosalie did not describe any of these street scenes in her letters home but wrote confidently that after a few weeks in Shanghai she had gotten used to all its strangeness. Shanghai seemed to her, as to other Westerners, "a capacious prison." "There are *no roads* so that it is not possible to roam the country," she wrote to her mother, signifying that this freedom was something she missed. From the little she had seen of China, she concluded it had no natural beauty, and the fact that she noted this suggests that she sought it out. The elaborate needlework on both men's and women's clothing, however, won her wholehearted approval. "Don't talk to me about the Chinese being civilized though undoubtedly they know how to embroider," she would write to Mrs. Barrow.[23]

If Rosalie had seen the city's bird market, she did not mention it, although it made a memorable impression on other foreigners. Grimy coolies kept their pet birds in varnished bamboo cages nearby, and at the end of each day hundreds of men gathered at Soochow Creek with their exquisite cages to listen to the sunset serenade of their captive larks.[24]

In his compendium *Things Chinese*, J. Dyer Ball elaborates:

No Chinese gentleman, at least in the South of China, takes a dog out to
walk with him; but on a fine day numbers may be seen each with a lark in
a cage on the outskirts of town, or sauntering leisurely along the streets, or
standing in some square, or squatting on their haunches on some green spot,
while their favorite bird enjoys himself, occasionally even with a little ramble
on the grass. His master cum dignitate gravely taking his pleasure in watching his pet, or even unbending so far as to occupy himself with the pursuit of
grasshoppers amongst the turf, though more frequently such a hunt is left to
the boys or to the wretched grasshopper hunters, who, armed with a bunch
of twigs and tiny baskets to hold their victims, from dewy morn till darkest
twilight, wander up and down the hills, beating every tuft of grass for the
active, springing, startled insects, which, when caught, they sell for a cash or
two apiece, to the bird shops and bird fanciers; their ultimate fate of course,
to be gobbled up by pet birds.[25]

Larks could cost twenty-five dollars a piece, but all birds were deities and
royals, and the sound for the Mandarin words for "noble rank" also referred
to "birds," according to Ball. Golden eagles were kept for hunting. Rosalie might also have observed fishermen with cormorants tethered to their
flimsy rafts. The birds dove into murky rivers to scoop out fish, ten or twelve
filling their gullets at a time, with fish tails flopping from their distended
bills. The cormorants were forced to disgorge the booty onto the raft, after
which the fishermen rewarded their birds with a bit of the catch.[26]

Rosalie Edge, however, never remarked on Chinese bird keeping in her
letters home or years later. Despite her childhood fondness for kept canaries, China's pervasive culture of captive birds seemed to have eluded her.

FOR THE FIRST three months of their marriage, Charlie was too ill to do
much work. With the stiff competition among hundreds of foreign investors for China's railroad contracts, he could little afford to be sick. Some
days he rose from his sickbed to call on prospective clients, only to stumble
from one relapse to another. The pattern terrified Rosalie. She made an ally
of one of Charlie's associates who lived at the hotel and had almost died of
dysentery. The man promised to order Charlie back to bed if he saw him
out. His opportunity to scold Charlie came the next day. When her husband
returned to their suite a chastened man, Rosalie launched yet another "discourse upon the duty of caring for himself in order to discharge his duty to

his firm and care for the wife of his bosom." He was so contrite she thought she had changed him.[27]

But Charlie's impatience is also understandable, given the frenzied international competition for China's railroad business once the decaying Qing royal house began to promote industrial development. Traditional Chinese had long loathed the clanking and sulfurous belching of the iron behemoths and the landscape-scarring rails that destroyed the earth's natural harmony. China's "stupendous prejudices" against modernity meant that not more than a mile of railroad track had been laid for every million in population; by 1909 Europe had one mile of track for every 2,400 of its citizens.[28] Thus in 1909 there was no shortage of foreign investors trying to reap profits from China's belated rush to modernize. Though Charles Edge played an infinitesimally small role in the Western nations' determination to slice China like a melon—to use the parlance of the day—the only way he earned his living was in making sure that Metro got a piece.

Rosalie had not changed her husband at all. Though ailing, he stayed in the competition. Not more than a week after Rosalie's secret ally had ordered Charlie back to his room, a business tip in Nanking somehow came his way, and he was ready to leave before dawn the next day. "The excitement, the smell of a tussle with a few Chinese officials braces him up," was his wife's rationalization as she joined in his enthusiasm for finding hot prospects.[29]

Nanking was the "oldest and most Chinese of Chinese cities," Rosalie wrote to her mother. Outside the few diplomatic residences, it provided none of the comforts of home foreigners insisted on having in Shanghai's International Settlement. Charlie warned that their hotel would be filthy and dangerous. He told her to clean and pack the pistol he had given her. She replied that the thought of having to defend herself with it was too terrifying for her to carry it. Charlie looked "wondrous solemn" at her. "Remember I would not give it to you if I were not sure you were very brave. Remember the first thing to learn about a pistol is never use it." She found her husband's contradictory response puzzling, she wrote to her mother. It left her, she remarked, "in some doubt as to what my responsibilities in the matter are!" She put the pistol in with her belongings and the chest containing Charlie's restricted diet of dried milk and bananas, and cocoa for herself.[30]

Nanking was as horrid as Charlie had promised. The temperature of 105 degrees made it far too hot for Rosalie to visit the Ming tombs as she had hoped. The streets were too disgusting for her to want to go out at all. While

Charlie was away during the day, Rosalie occupied herself by sponge bathing herself from the single basin of water brought to their room each morning. She carefully wrung each drop of the precious water back into the basin to be reused. Clouds of mosquitoes swarmed in their room, and the view from their window at night was "all very sordid." The streets were packed with beggars, who slept wherever they could find enough space.[31]

They had one "tantalizing taste of bliss" in Nanking, however, when the British consul invited them to a banquet. His lush compound was shielded by high walls from the pervasive human misery. They dined while servants fanned them with punkahs. Afterward the Edges rode in the consul's carriage back to their squalid hotel "through all the weirdness of the Chinese city by night."[32]

By September Charlie was well enough for a new pattern to take shape. It was one of frenetic travel, usually by steamship, for which Rosalie would reluctantly put down the *Ladies' Home Journal* her mother had sent her, repack, and go. The Edges lived, according to Rosalie, "in a chronic state of going on the next boat." They caught steamers to Hong Kong, Canton, Amoy, Singapore, Bangkok, Kuala Lumpur, and Yokohama. The pace was a punishing one for both Rosalie and Charlie, who occasionally relapsed, but Rosalie was relieved to leave China with its retreating view of the "horrid yellow" Yangtze River effluent spewing into the blue Eastern Sea.[33]

The circumstances encountered en route to any of their destinations were perhaps not what she had pictured when she declared her devotion to seeing the world. She was not going, after all, to Scotland or the Continent aboard a luxury ship. In Oriental waters the Edges were subjected to equatorial heat, typhoons, flies that blackened the ceiling in cramped berths below deck, shipboard cholera quarantines, bad food and water or sometimes none at all.

The Japanese seemed to be in charge everywhere, and their engineers were second to none. Charlie marveled at how he had to do his best work to match theirs if he wanted to win any business. As far as Rosalie was concerned, however, the Japanese people she encountered made "bad servants, their utter conceit depriving them of any wish to please."[34]

On one Japanese steamer, the Edges' cabin was too hot for them to sleep, and Charlie hauled their bedding onto the top deck. A steward tried to stop him. "He looked like a toy monkey prancing with rage in front of Charlie, who with the mattresses on his shoulder was rather too formidable to be interfered with," Rosalie wrote.[35] Charlie prevailed, and that night they slept under the stars.

They found relief from the heat and welcome modernity in the city of Dairen. The Russian-built terminus for the Trans-Siberian Railway would become one of their favorite destinations. The city's former name of Dalny, Russian for "far away," referred to its distance from St. Petersburg. With Russia's defeat by the Japanese in 1905, Dalny became Dairen (now Dalien in China). New shops were so well stocked with Pears soap, ribbon, chocolate, pâté de foie gras, and Lucca olive oil that Rosalie thought she might have drifted back to New York.

She sent the hotel menu to her mother so that with roast chicken, grilled beefsteak, capon, pâté, artichokes, and exotic boiled green corn, Mrs. Barrow could see that at least here her daughter was suffering no privations. Rosalie and Charlie, who never ate raw fruit and vegetables in China for fear of getting sick, devoured fresh peaches and plums. The late summer air was "delicious to a degree."[36]

At sunset each afternoon they hired a Chinese junk and paid a rough-looking boatman twenty-five cents to take them about a mile from shore to swim in the bay. They stripped down to underclothes—Rosalie dropped the raincoat and frock she wore unbuttoned over her tights—and dove into the water. She admired how Charlie's swim costume revealed his manly grace. "A husband is a great institution—without which one would never dare to board a junk and dive in the middle of Dalny Harbor," she wrote appreciatively.[37]

Their daily swim "was a joy that was forever new." The Edge marriage was at last unfolding as they had dreamed: as a union between two intrepid souls in love, wandering the wide world. They looked for other swimming opportunities, and in Amoy found a secluded beach cove where they could sleep. They carried bedding from their hotel coolie-style on long poles balanced unevenly across their shoulders. One night the bright stars kept Rosalie awake. She woke Charlie to ask him to explain shooting stars to her. They talked of constellations until the dark faded to dawn.[38]

AS CHINA's political unrest spread, the security of foreigners was of grave concern. Before each of Charlie's trips, he weighed whether Rosalie would be safer if she accompanied him or stayed in Shanghai; whichever way they decided, they next had to decide who should keep their only pistol. At this point in the discussion, Rosalie would insist that if she needed a pistol to protect herself when she was alone, then she would rather be with Charlie. At least by accompanying him she could monitor his extravagance, for he had none of the qualms about spending that she had acquired since her father's death. Rosalie succeeded in convincing her husband to drink ginger beer rather than claret, but the economies she imposed were no match for his insistence on their staying in the best hotels a city offered.

On their first visit to Hong Kong in September 1909, they booked a suite at the elegant Peak Hotel that cost an exorbitant fifteen dollars a night. The Peak presented Rule Britannia in all its imperial glory. The hotel was accessible to Western guests only by one of the steepest tramways in the world; Chinese coolies pulled baggage and provisions up the seemingly vertical slab of jungle on sedan chairs.[39]

The views from the Peak's rooms afforded "views of unrivalled loveliness," noted one guest in 1907. There were "views of the greatest conglomeration of shipping on earth; of mountains and islands and sea; of handsome residences clinging to the steep face of the hill; views of precipices and ravines; of groves of dense vegetation; and the busy, throbbing town far below, with its stately buildings, and its crowded native tenements; no panorama like this can be found anywhere."[40]

"We are in the most beautiful spot I almost ever was—H. K. is too wonderful," Rosalie wrote, happier than she had been for months. The air was cool in the morning and evening, and for the first time they slept without mosquito netting around the bed. One moonlit night Rosalie and Charlie strolled around the summit park, stopping to admire shimmering vistas of sea and sky. Precipitous mountains jutted up in almost every direction, and the intoxicating scent of wild ginger clung to the darkness. It was, Rosalie declared, "the most marvelous walk I ever had in my life—the beauty of Hong Kong is past any words to describe."[41]

But typhoons came frequently that season. Storm signals were posted in Victoria Harbor daily to let ship captains know when to sail and when not to. The dismal forecasts gave Charlie and Rosalie an excuse to extend their Hong Kong stay. "The vessels make dashes from port to port like blind man's bluff," Rosalie explained to her mother on September 19.[42]

A stiff wind had picked up. Rosalie and Charlie ended their daily outing earlier than usual and returned to their room. Suddenly a "large game bird" flew in through the open window and tarried on the inside sill. Charlie looked up from his reading and observed that it was a pheasant. "After contemplating us some time, [it] came into the room, but seemed most ill at ease when it got there, though it made no attempt to go," wrote Rosalie, puzzled by the bird's presence.[43]

She called the servant to chase it out. He shooed the bird away and closed the windows, but a few minutes later a strong gust blew them open again and a different bird stepped into the room, "a wee one this time." Again Rosalie summoned the servant to drive the bird out, but before he could secure the windows the wee one fluttered back in. After the birds returned for the third time, Rosalie ordered the boy to bolt the windows tightly so that they could not come back.[44]

"I was completely bewildered but the boy explained 'Typhoon!'" The next sentence she wrote in the letter to her mother contained a prophecy, so potent it is hard to believe that she never referred to it again, particularly after she founded her Pennsylvania bird sanctuary: *The birds were taking refuge wherever they could.*" But it seems she never made the connection.[45]

The light in the room was dim as she and Charlie sat very still, listening to the gale. The next morning they left during a lull to make a dash for Shanghai. Once they were under way, a new storm formed on the ocean, and their steamer was forced to take shelter on the lee side of a small island and wait. The situation was "quite sufficiently exciting," she wrote to her mother. The captain zigzagged to avoid other typhoons that formed along their intended route, and a passage that should have taken two days stretched to five.[46]

A few weeks later they returned to blissful Dairen. One morning Charlie finished dictating his correspondence to Rosalie and proposed they take the rest of the day off to go "snipe hunting." Charlie was a gifted athlete but did not like to walk as much as she did, unless he was hunting. "Shooting [was] a great way out of the difficulty" she learned and declared the sport to be "heaps of fun."[47]

Off they went, stopping to hire a coolie to carry the picnic basket and supplies. They took the train as far as it went and then headed into the countryside on foot. "The weather was glorious beyond words and how I did enjoy the tramp and such excitement getting the birds," Rosalie wrote Margaret. At some point a bog slowed their progress, and with each step Rosalie's feet sank into a glutinous mixture of mud and water: quicksand. She took a few more laborious steps, and the ground sucked her in to her knees. In a panic to extricate herself, she sank deeper. Rosalie called to Charlie, who was ahead, and he turned to make his way back to her. By the time he reached her, she had sunk even more.[48]

Charlie dropped everything and spread his weight carefully over the surface, reaching for her hands to pull her out. Rosalie, dragged from the mud hole to what seemed a safe place, sat panting. Her clothes were so caked with slime that she could barely stand. She was peeling off as much clothing as she could when Charlie suddenly "went under." He struggled to extricate himself. "I gave him a hand but he was pretty far away from me for a good grip and the ground was none too safe," Rosalie wrote. "But somehow, by the grace of Heaven, he got out." Using the mud-caked clothes she had discarded, Charlie buoyed himself up and inched toward his wife.[49]

They spent at least an hour lightly and quickly stepping back to firm ground. Several times they sank in above their knees, and Rosalie was certain it was the end of them. Charlie dragged her across the mud for the final distance because she had no strength left to move. Safe at last, they collapsed, frightened and breathless, and wept in each other's muddy embrace. Her relief instantly mixed with rage when she realized that their coolie had idly watched everything that had occurred from a solid distance: "He had taken the precaution of skirting well around it evidently knowing it well but with their absolute indifference to life (their own as well as anyone else's) he did not trouble to tell us nor had we been up to our necks do I think he would have gone to the village for help."[50]

After they had recovered, they ended the day by killing five birds, which their cook prepared for dinner. Both realized neither would have made it without the other. Suspecting the episode was too harrowing for her mother to read, Rosalie confided it to Margaret. Her tale ended on a high note: "Still it was a good morning and great good sport and I did enjoy it." Once she was clean and full of the bounty they had shot, Rosalie could acknowledge that she loved the hardships associated with confronting nature, whether on rough seas or on land.[51]

Yet despite her professed enjoyment of such typically masculine challenges, Mrs. Charles Noel Edge missed close female companionship. Too few of the expatriate wives were to her liking, and she implored unmarried Louise Schanck to visit. Charlie objected. He was, Rosalie wrote to her sister, "just as jealous as can be."[52]

He might have been drunk when he scribbled a protest in the margin of her letter. He wished Margaret was coming instead: "I want to take my eldest sister away by myself, put my arm around her, and talk to her in brotherly fashion, telling all the secrets of my life, and receiving hers in return," he wrote. Charlie's inexplicable hostility toward Louise made Rosalie wonder how her husband would behave in New York surrounded by her family and friends.[53]

After Louise arrived in November, she sent Mrs. Barrow a glowing report of the Edges' life in Shanghai. "[The couple look] so radiantly happy that it is all one can see—they quite fill the atmosphere with it!" Louise wrote. She was so frankly appreciative of everything: the luxurious suite, the bountiful bouquets Charlie sent each day, the two servants in obedient attendance upon them. Mabel—as Louise still referred to her childhood friend—had trained them to hook up their dresses "with the ease of a French maid." Rosalie wore her wedding dress and the diamond pendant Charlie had given her to dinner one night.[54]

> I just can not keep my eyes from her she looks so stunning and so well— even after Charlie's illness. I am trying to train myself into being a sweet-tempered old maid—but I really am green with envy of her and I have never gotten my natural color back since the other night when I saw the rest of her wedding presents. She had, I thought, enough at home for anybody but to add to that her diamond bracelet and the Edges' pendant and the rest of her silver, well, I tell you—the married state for me.[55]

The women preened and gossiped until they were "both as hoarse as crows." Lou reported that their friend Daisy had been offended by the richness of Rosalie's trousseau when she saw it in New York, proclaiming it unnecessary to "get so much for the Chinese." Rosalie was indignant.[56]

> O Lord! I have all my dresses with me and all I can say is this—that I could scarcely have done without one of them, and looked as I wanted to . . . especially as most of the people are charming, one would be glad to know them in any part of the world—sprightly, gay, and themselves beautifully dressed. Daisy, I suppose, has no idea of the ports, where one leads only the gayest European life and might be thousands of miles from anything Chinese.[57]

After months of tending to Charlie and being dictated to by his travel schedule that never factored in the time it took Rosalie to look her best, Lou's companionship was liberating. "I don't have to be so discreet when Charlie isn't with me," Rosalie wrote. "In fact Lou and I gallivant about in our best clothes with the deliberate purpose of shooting arrows into the hearts of our already numerous men friends!"[58]

They decided to go to Peking. Though Charlie hated sightseeing, he gallantly agreed to escort them as their protector. They stopped in Tientsin on the way and visited a wealthy American businessman whom Charlie knew. The unidentified man's wife and daughter had returned to America, and Rosalie was quite happy to find herself and Lou the only women at the table of gentlemen—"six as delightful specimens as one would care to see." She would always prefer being in groups where men far outnumbered women. Rosalie's flirtatiousness in such company depended less on her comeliness than on her extroverted intelligence. Their host had invited a bachelor named Mr. Blunt to the dinner. Rosalie was disappointed when no romance ignited between the man and Lou, for with his surname she thought it would have been clever of Lou to marry him: "While I have an Edge she should become Blunt!"[59]

At a dinner in Peking, Rosalie and Lou spoke in their British accents, which were so convincing that the British diplomat who sat between them elaborated on the failings of American women—"'the lightness of their minds, the superficiality of their knowledge,' and ended by pontificating he could imagine 'no worse fate for a man than to marry an American.'" Rosalie dared not glance at Lou for fear they would burst out laughing.[60]

When they went sightseeing in Peking the next day, thousands of rickshaws were stopped to make way for the funeral procession of China's Empress Cixi, "The Holy Mother, Compassionate and Fortunate, Upright Protector, Reposeful and Firm, Glorious and Happy, Grave and Sincere, Long-Lived and Reverent, August and Gracious, Noble and Brilliant." Although China's last empress had died the previous year, her remains had been preserved until her lavish tomb seventy-five miles from Peking was completed. Hundreds of colorfully glazed life-sized terra-cotta statues of soldiers and horses and altars with offerings filled the streets.[61]

The Chinese multitudes that Rosalie and Lou had expected to see lining the cortege's route did not show up, however. "The common people were not allowed to look at anything so sacred," she explained in a letter to her mother. The empress's procession was an impoverished affair consisting of a yellow catafalque attended by "dirty coolies trigged out like ragamuffins."[62]

Early the next morning, Charlie, Rosalie, and Lou left Peking for the Great Wall. There the three walked hand in hand into Mongolia. "I decline to describe either it or my own sensations, but I shall never forget standing on top and looking down on China on one side and Mongolia on the other side, the great panorama spread out with the moving line of pack mules and camels fading toward the horizon, on the trail that leads across the desert to Europe—this wall rising to the crest of every mountain on every side."[63]

Despite Rosalie's joy at Lou's coming, she and Charlie argued during her visit. One night Rosalie slammed her bathroom door in Charlie's face so hard that it could not be opened. Charlie had to climb in through the window to rescue her and lead her out the way he had come in.[64]

AFTER LOU LEFT, Rosalie complained more frequently about her life in China. Violent confrontations between Dr. Sun Yat Sen's Revolutionary Alliance and imperial troops had increased. Though foreigners were not directly targeted, the Revolutionary Alliance, like the Boxer rebels ten years earlier, demanded immediate nationalization of all foreign-owned railroads and industries. The mounting apprehension about the country's political and economic future exacerbated the difficulties of travel and her isolation.

In January 1910, Charlie had so few engineering prospects to pursue that he had time to go ice-skating with Rosalie. She had perhaps not put skates on since she had spoken on behalf of Countess Széchenyi in Hungary eighteen months earlier, and she welcomed the exertion in the cold. "At any rate it means exercise, which is so hard to get here as walking is almost always impossible," she wrote.[65]

A directive from Metro finally arrived, telling Charlie to return to England as soon as possible for reassignment. Rosalie was elated. Charlie decided they should take the Trans-Siberian Railroad from Harbin to Moscow because it was the most direct route, and because as one who engineered railroads he could not miss the experience of traveling on the world's longest line.

They had to sail north one last time, however, then head to Harbin. Since it was winter, the S.S. *Kaiping* rammed ice night and day until it reached open water. The "beastly boat" crashed and bucked so noisily and jarringly that sleep was impossible. "It was bright moonlight and I sat up in my bunk and looked out—just a waste of what might well have been polar ice, a desolate sight which brought all we have lately read of Peary and Cook and Shackleton vividly to mind," she wrote. Charlie was too seasick to eat, as were most of the passengers, but hale Rosalie kept her food and appetite. Rather than try to sleep, she spent one night playing bridge with a hardy Austrian count and countess who had "known everyone—Kitchener, Curzon, Mark Twain, Bismarck, and now Mrs. Charles Edge!"[66]

Next came the ordeal of the eleven-day Trans-Siberian train ride that skirted the empty Gobi Desert and crossed the Russian steppe. At each station they got off the train to inhale the icy Siberian air. "Most of Siberia and all of Russia is a white snowy flat, unrelieved by anything," she wrote. As they traveled west, coffee rather than tea was served on board, the people they passed looked less and less Chinese, and the landscape bespoke fences and hedgerows, draft horses, and lawns. She welcomed these familiar features as evidence of "the first civilization of many months."[67]

But Moscow seemed so antiquated and backward to Rosalie that she decided civilization had again retreated. Charlie, however, still found ways to spend too much money at an antique store. He bought a silver icon and a painting, both from the fifteenth century. When Rosalie pointed out that his purchases left them with no money to buy food until they reached England, he reluctantly returned the painting. Rosalie assured her mother that Charlie's spending habits were really quite compatible with the Barrows'. Like the rest of them, she noted, "he was not quite sure where the necessities of life are to come from but he is quite ready to consider the luxuries." That night the Edges dressed in their finest and "went down to a sumptuous dinner in a sort of fairyland of a room with a Russian orchestra playing."[68]

IN ENGLAND two months later Mrs. Charles Noel Edge pronounced herself "altogether satisfied with life" as she and her husband toured the countryside and visited friends and plentiful Edge relatives. At Afcot they were shocked by Louise's condition. "More sunshine" was the remedy Rosalie prescribed and urged Charles Marston to take his wife to Brighton.[69]

In May Rosalie witnessed her second royal funeral procession in six months. The British wore uniformly dark clothing in mourning for King Edward V, and buildings were draped in black crepe. She approved of these stately rites to publicly mark a monarch's passing and compared them favorably to what she had witnessed in China as she had watched Empress Cixi's ragamuffin cortege pass.

Amid reports to Mrs. Barrow of the historical processions she had witnessed, Rosalie planted one vital bit of personal information: she was pregnant. With this in mind, her long journey by icebreaker and Trans-Siberian Railway seem even more arduous. "I must really tell you the awful thing I contemplate landing you in for," her letter began. "Nothing less than staying with you until I have a baby! . . . Don't ask me when it is going to be! I haven't the remotest idea—but I am hoping you may be able to cast some light on the matter."[70]

Rosalie guessed she was due in October or November and asked if she could stay with her mother and sisters at 113 East Seventy-second Street until after the baby was born. She would be wholly dependent on her family since Charlie would have to return to China long before the baby was due.

> I have made no preparations at all, of course, for the Wee Girl's trousseau either. You must positively direct me there. It is the "Wee Girl!" I would not dare to suggest to Charlie even the possibility of its being anything else. He is an engineer, and accustomed to having his designs delivered exactly according to specifications! He had never thought, spoken nor considered the matter as relating to anything but the "Wee Girl" or "My Daughter." I would not face Charlie with an offspring of the male gender. If it is a girl you may borrow her when you choose—kiss her, feed her potatoes, and treat her as you think best.[71]

Rosalie warned that her maternal instincts might be deficient. If the child turned out to be difficult she would engage "a thoroughly good nurse and leave her with the highest bidder, for I paddle after Charlie the moment I get up."[72]

CHAPTER THREE

First Awakening

In the spring Rosalie and Charles were living in Malaysia when she wrote to her mother that her strength was finally returning, although her "nerves were still not much to boast about." She hoped they might "get steadier."[1]

These days she did not paddle after Charlie as he frantically sought railroad business in Asian countries other than China, which in 1911 was rapidly sliding toward anarchy. Rosalie usually stayed behind in paradisal seclusion at either the famous Raffles Hotel or another British outpost of luxury. She preferred to adhere to her own compass, which pointed to long walks every morning before the heat of the day bore down, and to reading or singing on the veranda when it grew too hot for her to venture beyond it.

It bothered her that the British—including her husband—refused to wear clothing adapted to Malaysian heat. They dressed in wool suits, silk dresses, and ankle-length motoring coats as if they were still in England. She told her mother she had tried to convince Charlie to be sensible. "But faith! . . . Charlie's whites and beautiful pongees are not good form if you please, and poor dear must wear cloth suits. Did you ever hear of such idiocy?"[2]

While Charlie insisted on dressing like the rest of his countrymen, she floated about in light sarongs, having learned that if she dressed according to the dictates of heat and humidity and slowed her pace, the climate was bearable, if not pleasurable.

Charlie endured eye strain and incapacitating headaches brought on by heat stroke. But about herself Rosalie wrote, "I am very brown and handsome and feel another being."[3]

Mrs. Barrow might have been particularly relieved to hear of her daughter's well-being after all Rosalie had been through. The baby had lived five days. Rosalie left no personal record of how traumatic this birth and swift death were for her, but Charlie acknowledged his wife's emotional state. "The sad news of our dear son," he recalled, reached him in China weeks later. "Rosalie feels his loss so deeply that I am still very anxious about her," he wrote to his mother-in-law, in the only personal mention of the Edges' deceased son that survives.[4]

Charlie had bought Rosalie a pearl pin before the baby was born, which he wanted her to wear always in the boy's memory. "I shall do anything in my person to help her from the minute she is with me again," he wrote. The baby, Hall Travers Edge, named for Charlie's father, was laid to rest in the Barrow family plot in the Newburgh cemetery near Rosalie's father, John Wylie Barrow.[5]

The Edges' five-month separation during the last part of her pregnancy and its aftermath had proved difficult for them both. "I have felt most horribly lost without her and the feeling gets no better," Charlie's letter to Harriet Barrow confided in October.[6]

He had spent ten days in a Peking hospital after he got into a brawl with a man who had offended him. "I wh——pped someone," he illegibly wrote, as if to obscure the incident. He feared his employer might impose its own penalty on him. Charlie's letter was touching and tough in its empathy for his wife mingled with his disarmingly candid acknowledgment of an explosive temper.[7]

In November 1910, after her ship weathered a "perfectly good typhoon," Rosalie and Charlie were reunited in Yokohama. Six months later she was resting her nerves in Kuala Lumpur and sending her mother optimistic reports on her health and cultural reflections far more vivid than those she had provided from China.[8]

Rosalie loved Singapore's mix of people, declaring its racial mélange much more appealing than "mere China or Japan." She enjoyed the "real black savages with painted faces" and satiny skin, and black women so "tastefully, gracefully and withal chastely dressed in one or at most two veils that one cannot but think of Salome a prude with seven." She was "much amused" by the sight of a "black, woolly-headed savage, with only a very scanty loin-cloth and gold necklace [who] put up a capacious European umbrella when it began to rain and walk[ed] away with much dignity."[9]

Almost imperceptibly, doubts about her husband's purpose in Asia seemed to be forming in the back of her mind. She regretted how civilization—via the railroad—rolled so resolutely through primitive cultures, making them seem comic in their transition. The entrepreneurial Japanese were every-where; she wished they would stay on their own island. She immediately amended this sharp opinion by adding that it was the British who ought to stay on their own island, since they and their culture ruled a quarter of the world's population. And it seemed that she was no longer pleased to be mistaken for an Englishwoman after visiting the Edges in England. America was the country where both her beloved father and little son were buried, and where her elderly mother was growing weaker. She feared she might not see Mrs. Barrow again.

In her reassuring letters to her mother, Rosalie did, however, let slip that she was "mostly alone." Charlie worked night and day and on Sundays, as though he were "reconstructing the entire system of the Federated Malay States Railway." She grumbled that her husband suffered from "Abnormal Distortion of the Conscience" in his incessant work habits.[10] At least Char-lie's absences gave her time to practice her singing without interruption, and she was so pleased with the quality of her voice that she wrote she "might have been something" had she continued her lessons. She hastened to amend this claim as well, noting that if she had become a professional singer she "never would have married Charlie or have had these wonderful experiences in the East."[11]

As the nearby jungle became her steady companion, observations about its beauty also crept into her letters. Recalling Tennyson, Rosalie loved the "limpid silver path" the moon made as it rose and the way the dense green canopy refracted equatorial light. Wildness made Singapore and Malaysia "the crown" of their travels in the Orient, she declared.[12]

She loved the blooming poincianas and chameleons that "walk gayly [sic] over the walls to Charlie's utter horror."[13] A bat that swooped through their villa one night revolted Charlie but did not faze her, and she toler-ated a large rat that cohabitated with them. In Johore she went walking in the jungle and strained to spot a tiger, and heard, but perhaps did not see, loud monkeys and jewel-toned birds. "The tigers are there," she reported confidently. "There is not a man in Johore who will patrol the Railway alone at night—and it has to be done in parties of three together, with guns."[14]

She watched a crocodile slide over Federated Malay States Railway tracks one day—a creature thirty feet long, she improbably guessed—and next saw it hanging on the wall of an Englishman's billiard room. Of its fate she offered no judgment one way or the other. Elsewhere, she noted, "the wild elephants delight in rubbing their backs against the telegraph poles and although they stud them thick with spikes, the lines are more often than not out of commission."[15]

THE EDGES CELEBRATED their second anniversary in Bangkok. Charlie gave Rosalie a pair of Zeiss binoculars as a gift, presumably along with the emeralds he had once promised, although these she did not note in her letter to Mrs. Barrow. On her visit to the Royal Monastery at the Grand Palace, Rosalie turned her double scopes upward to observe the Emerald Buddha, the most venerated object in Siam. The Buddha was a gorgeous flash of carved jade enshrined high above the temple floor in an aerie of gilded wood and many-colored mirrors and was difficult to see without magnification.[16]

The sight of the three sacred white elephants on the palace grounds aroused new sympathies. "I should say their captivity was very cruel," she wrote to her mother, in the first recorded statement of her indignation over the treatment of animals. "They have a house to themselves and attendants and they enjoy titles of nobility—but they stand chained on a small platform so that they cannot walk a step or lie down!"[17]

The Malay idyll ended when Metro ordered Charlie back to Shanghai. The Edges reluctantly returned but were not there long when new instructions came. The Chinese Revolution had begun, apparently by accident. An explosion at a house occupied by rebel bomb makers in Hankow was misinterpreted and triggered major uprisings that the emperor's armies could not quell. On this misfire of October 9, 1911, the Manchus' 250 years of governance of the largest nation on earth ended, and so did Charlie's Asia assignment.

Rosalie glided over the revolution's start when she next wrote her mother, lightheartedly telling her that regardless of what the world might think of the China situation, the "big news" as far as she was concerned was that she would be home again by spring. "I want to get rid of all my trunks and pretend for the time-being that I am really settled down. I want to swim and have some music (all I can get—I'm so hungry for it) and do choir work and brace up Lou Schanck and have tea with you and eat clams and ice cream. I often wonder if I will really do it! For you know I hate to leave Charlie."[18]

Despite the rapid departure they anticipated, the Edges stayed in Shanghai for another two months. Charlie's Abnormal Distortion of Conscience kept him working at a new enterprise in the field of unbridled capitalism. He decided to become a stockbroker. Ironically he was finding his best business opportunities amid China's upheaval and had begun to attract clients for his new profession among the expatriates who had not yet left.

Although Charles Edge had been less successful than he might have wished in acquiring railroad building contracts, he had meanwhile been investing his own money in the stock exchanges of London and New York. Handsome stock returns explain the Daimler Silent Knight that he ordered for himself before leaving China, so that it would be ready to pick up when they reached England.[19] He was confident he could do as well with others' money as he had with his own, as well as earn fees on his investment services.

Rosalie assured her mother that although the events in China sounded terrifying, foreigners in Shanghai were in no danger. In private she and Charlie were less certain in this regard, for he refused to let her stay behind when he traveled. "Oh! Such a hullabaloo!" she complained after Charlie forced her to go with him to Tientsin and Peking to call on investment clients. He hustled her off before she could say, "Knife!"[20]

Peking, unlike Shanghai, lay under the heavy pall of revolution. One day Rosalie managed to slip away from Charles's watchful eye and headed to the Forbidden City, curious to see if it had changed since she had last seen it. The human flood still surged through the massive gates, but the people seemed gray and restive. "I doubt that I would have cared to have walked far alone, as I used to do, but it may have been my imagination," she wrote. Surveying the somber masses, she did not have much hope for China's political prospects.[21]

She bought a memento of Imperial China, brought to its knees before her eyes. It was an intricately embroidered Mandarin robe. The luxurious silks with their fine needlework depictions of birds and flowers were what she loved most about China, and the exquisite remnant of the great, topsy-turvy civilization, she wrote, "quite satisfies the longing of my soul."[22]

CHARLIE CHOSE TO base his brokerage business in England. They rented a cottage in Malvern not far from the Marston and the Edge estates. Rosalie occupied herself with being a dutiful wife to an ambitious young stock operator and paid the obligatory visits to "the Mater and Pater." She liked the quiet village life, but Charlie was quickly bored by it. He missed having people around who were of his intellectual caliber, a lack addressed by visits to Cambridge, where he could socialize with "delightful *worldly* people." Rosalie wrote wistfully that they stayed in separate rooms when they went to the university, giving her husband "a salutary change" from her company.[23]

They moved to London. Rosalie was sad to give up her small country cottage with its garden for the cramped city flat, but she gamely made yet another life for herself. She shopped at Liberty of London and contemplated how the bolt of velveteen in a "wonderful queer blue" would look made up as a winter evening dress to wear to the theater and symphony.[24] But her enthusiasm for this prosaic turn her life had taken seemed hollow. The choice of winter evening dress did not satisfy the longing in her soul quite the way her old Mandarin robe did.

Under November's leaden skies, she accompanied Charlie to London's annual motor show and gazed blankly at the automobiles he coveted. While the show was tedious for her, the fatigue she complained of had a different source. At thirty-five years old, she was six months pregnant. This time when she broke the news to her mother, Rosalie made no flippant remarks about "a wee girl" in her womb but rather referred to her baby as a gender-neutral "Edgeling." She insisted again on giving birth in New York and "wanted most especially" to have Charlie there.[25]

In December 1912 he reluctantly granted her most heartfelt wish: that they move to New York for good. As happy as she was with this decision, the prospect of another hard trip in winter while she was in late pregnancy was almost too much for her to face. She was due at the end of March, and they would not reach New York until February. She nearly changed her mind about going but feared that Charlie might change his mind about emigrating if she delayed. "You will see that when Charlie proposed to take me to America *to live* it was not for me to make terms," she wrote.[26] He already had $100,000 of clients' funds under his investment management and seemed confident he could make his fortune as a stockbroker as easily in New York as he could in London.

Despite the death of their first baby, Rosalie still expressed ambivalence about motherhood. "We'll joggle it up well and kiss it profusely," she assured

Mrs. Barrow. She predicted there would be many days when she would leave the Edgeling with Grandmother Harriet and her sisters to feed it "with potato and beefsteak gravy while [she] gad[ded], say, to a bridge-party."[27]

ABOARD THE *MAURITANIA* in February 1913, Charlie exercised his Abnormal Distortion of Conscience by cultivating investment clients. Rosalie, who was about eight months pregnant and had been ordered by her doctor to rest, avoided public exposure. It may have been her delicate condition that encouraged another passenger named Sybil Haig Thomas, the Lady Rhondda, to befriend her. Sybil's husband, Lord Rhondda, or David Alfred Thomas, was a client of Charlie's.[28] Lord Rhondda was a liberal MP from Wales, where he owned coal mines.

Both Lord and Lady Rhondda were enormously sympathetic to the Cause, as the women's suffrage movement in Great Britain and the United States was known. The Cause was a euphemism that might have made the women's movement more palatable to the uninitiated, since the word *suffrage* sounded too much like *suffering* and could reinforce a negative feeling about giving ladies the right to vote. The Latin word *suffragium* means "a decision," and voting is a most powerful form of deciding.[29]

Rosalie apparently had been oblivious to the social forces colliding in the streets of London and throughout Great Britain. She had come from China, where the 1911 revolution had left her largely unruffled even as she witnessed its chilling hold on the Forbidden City and acquired the embroidered silk robe that represented the old order. Though China's convulsions had ended her husband's civil-engineering career and forced him to find another profession on a different continent, she could reason that what happened in China did not concern her.

What was happening in England, however, ought to have had a very great effect on her, as on every woman. In China the masses' struggle for a voice in governance was not her struggle; the struggle for this voice in England and the United States was. During that weeklong crossing to America, Lady Rhondda enlightened her insular and pregnant young friend. The voyage between Liverpool and New York was long enough for her to provide a thorough and personal account of social events rocking the nations on both sides of the Atlantic.

Sybil and David Thomas's thirty-year-old daughter, Margaret Haig Thomas Mackworth, was making headlines in Britain even as her parents were befriending Rosalie and Charles Edge. Margaret was a prominent street fighter for women's right to vote and employed some of the tactics favored by its most radical element. England's shrieking sisterhood hawked the offensive newspaper *Votes for Women* on street corners, jumped on the running board of Prime Minister Herbert Asquith's car to scream their demands in his face, and barged into men's clubs to speak, despite a pelting with herrings and tomatoes.[30]

Gutsy Margaret Thomas had married Hugh Mackworth, a neighboring coal baron much older than she, but soon found her marriage stultifying. She preferred the way her father treated her even when she was a child, because he "talked business" to her, and when she was old enough Lord Rhondda invited her to help him run the Rhondda coal company. She probably would have accompanied her father on the business trip he made to America in the winter of 1913 if not for the recent scuffle that had landed her in jail. She had been convicted of blowing up a letterbox and was confined to a cell reeking of vomit and urine. Margaret was released after going on a hunger strike with other women offenders.[31]

Sybil Thomas's fascinating accounts of her daughter's defiance made Rosalie more captive to her parlor chaise, imprisoned as she already was by advanced pregnancy. We can imagine that Sybil Thomas discoursed long and with impressive feeling about her daughter's convictions as well as her escapades. Margaret Mackworth would later write her own history of them, explaining that a casual conversation with another young woman had impelled her to act.

> In one unconscious phrase, she summed up all that was by then trying to become articulate in my revolt against the life the average well-to-do woman was expected to lead. She was setting off to play bridge. It was a lovely afternoon in late April and the country was looking perfect. It seemed great waste to spend the day indoors unless one need. "Why," said I, "do you play bridge in the afternoon?" A shadow crossed her face and a queer, discontented inflection came into her voice. "One must do something," she said. "I'd sooner wear out than rust out." And playing bridge was "wearing out." . . . that is a definition which I shall never forget.[32]

This innocent declaration "had come like a draught of fresh air into our padded, stifled lives," Margaret wrote, and militant suffrage quickly became "the very salt of life" for her.[33]

She joined a women's rights march through Hyde Park, more than likely the one held on June 21, 1908, when half a million women assembled in the largest public demonstration in England up to that time.[34] The march, held just one month before Margaret's wedding day, posed one of those quaint clashes between entrenched custom and revolutionary change. Her mother insisted on marching with her for not one but two reasons: although she strongly believed women ought to be given the right to vote, she believed just as strongly that a young unmarried woman should not go out in public without a chaperone. Margaret was thrilled by the sight of thousands of screaming viragos on the march; Sybil was not. Her mother "came of a generation which took the gutter and casual street insults hard," Margaret wrote forgivingly.[35]

In England the women's rights movement had crept along for more than a century. Mary Wollstonecraft's *Vindication of the Rights of Women*, published in 1792 and inspired by French revolutionary rhetoric, was perhaps its first memorable utterance. Now and then other declarations for women's right to vote appeared; in 1846 the Quaker abolitionist Anne Knight published "A Plea for Women," and in 1848 Benjamin Disraeli spoke passionately in the House of Commons for a woman's right to vote.

In 1869 John Stuart Mill, with the help of his wife, Harriet, produced a significant treatise, "The Subjection of Women." The Mills opined that "legal subordination of one sex to another is wrong in itself, and is one of the chief hindrances to human improvement." They declared that it "was an altogether unnecessary solitude" for men to impose prohibitions on women; "what women by nature cannot do is quite superfluous to forbid them from doing."[36]

In England not much else happened because of the deeply entrenched fear among women of appearing "unmaidenly" if they demanded the right to vote.[37] Their concern for appearances suddenly abated in 1912 with the formation of the Women's Social and Political Union. The WSPU was formed by Christabel and Emmeline Pankhurst, another mother-daughter suffrage team that had lost all patience with Great Britain's demure womanhood. At her speech in Albert Hall, Mrs. Pankhurst prodded women to use violent means if necessary with her proclamation, "I incite this meeting to rebellion."[38]

Margaret Mackworth was among the thousands who enlisted in this volatile army of socially privileged women, donning their uniform of purple, green, and white. WSPU adherents from England's most illustrious families heaved rocks at dignitaries and bit and kicked police who tackled them in the mud. The Cause martyred one woman, who flung herself under a racehorse owned by King George V. The shrieking sisterhood torched churches, schools, and country estates. They slashed art in the National Gallery, broke store windows, and, as Margaret Haig Thomas Mackworth had done, blew up letterboxes. Many women who went to prison and held hunger strikes were physically restrained as they were painfully force-fed through a tube inserted in the nose.

The women who were willing to go to such extremes to advance the Cause were derisively known as "suffragettes," a term first used by the *Daily Mail* in 1906.[39] Public brawling distinguished the suffragettes from the milder "suffragists," who continued in a ladylike manner to circulate yet more petitions.

For Rosalie, Lady Rhondda's shipboard indoctrination would be momentous. "It was the first awakening of my mind," she would recall more than thirty years later.[40] It may have struck Rosalie that at precisely the time she was immersed in her secret engagement plans, the newly married Mrs. Mackworth was busily busting up domestic tranquility. And while pregnant Mrs. Charles Noel Edge was writing to her mother about gadding off to bridge games after her baby was born, Margaret Mackworth had sworn off both bridge and babies.

Rosalie had thought herself so very bold for venturing off to see the world. Suddenly she was confronted by Margaret Mackworth, who went to prison in order to change it.

WHEN THE EDGES landed in New York, Rosalie's best intentions to get involved in women's suffrage were overtaken by more urgent matters. She had only weeks to find a place for them to live and establish a household before she went into labor. Her preoccupations were legitimate procrastinations, particularly given the death of her first child, which made this time all the more anxious. On March 25, scarcely a month after the *Mauritania* docked in New York, the Edges' son, Peter, was born.

As if Mr. and Mrs. Charles Edge wanted to make their own fresh start in America, their baby's name had no precedent in either side's extensively delineated genealogy. Her mother was too ill to care for the baby as Rosalie had hoped, but she could afford to hire the requisite live-in nurse and cook. Harriet Barrow died eight months after Peter was born. And although Mrs. Charles Noel Edge did manage to gad off to a bridge game now and then, she had many other things to consume her attention. The Edge family of three and their two servants moved into Mrs. Barrow's brownstone at

113 East Seventy-second Street. Margaret and Anna Barrow may have stayed on for a while since the house could easily accommodate all, but their inheritances enabled them to finally live on their own.

Charlie had been hired by a Manhattan brokerage house and prospered. On July 7, 1914, he penned a celebratory note to Rosalie, who had gone to the Hamptons with baby Peter to escape the city's brutal heat: "Dearest, I bought your birthday gift today. I hope you like it. I wanted to write just a line as this is the first day we ever made $10,000—to be accurate $11,300. Looking forward to seeing you on Thursday."[41] Charles rode the stock market's dramatic surges up and down, partaking of the 82 percent return the market earned in 1915, the best year in its history.

Rosalie modernized and refurbished the East Seventy-second Street house. Their luxurious home was an eclectic mix of East and West, combining her early Dutch and English inheritances with the Edges' acquisitions in China and Japan. Charlie's precious Russian Orthodox icon, her embroidered Mandarin coat, Japanese watercolors, and antique Chinese porcelains were scattered among the Whistler etchings, Boydell's Shakespeare engravings, and Reynolds's mezzotints.[42] As a New York matron, she went about building the sort of life that Margaret Mackworth had found so personally unfulfilling.

When Peter was seventeen months old, Rosalie, at thirty-six, was again pregnant, and again her decision to become involved in the suffrage movement had to be delayed. This time the trials of pregnancy and labor ought to have been easier for her to face, since little Peter was healthy and for the first time she was settled in her own home long before her due date.

Yet in the days before she gave birth on May 14, 1915, Rosalie was seized by a terror she had not known with her previous two pregnancies. The terror was so potent that she vividly recalled its unusual effect decades later in one of her unpublished memoirs: "At that trying moment, confident that death was at hand, I had grabbed my cheque-book, and dispatched donations to every organization which interested me," she wrote.[43]

She never specified the source of her panic, but she did identify two organizations that benefited from her spontaneous generosity. One, understandably, was the Equal Franchise Society, a prominent suffrage organization in New York. The other was the National Association of Audubon Societies.[44] This was an odd choice, since she had never before evinced an interest in the welfare of wild birds.

There is a more important question to ponder here: what might have convinced Rosalie Edge that her death was at hand in the days before her labor commenced? The news of that week offers a most persuasive explanation. On the afternoon of May 7, a German submarine torpedoed a British luxury passenger vessel called the *Lusitania* in international waters off the Irish coast, killing twelve hundred of the two thousand people aboard. The ship had embarked from New York the week before, and more than one hundred of the victims were Americans. Although the United States declared its neutrality and would not enter World War I until 1917, such premeditated aggression against innocents was thunderously proclaimed in the nation's eventual battle cry, "Remember the *Lusitania!*"

The imperial German government had sent an ominous warning before the ship was torpedoed. On April 22 the *New York Times* published a notice reminding travelers that a state of war existed between Germany and England. The notice, printed in a box funereally bordered in black, asserted that ships with noncombatants sailing in the war zone, which included "the waters adjacent to the British Isles," did so at "their own risk."[45]

Apart from sharing in the nation's mood of disbelief and horror over such premeditated aggression, Rosalie had other reasons for feeling close to the sea tragedy. The *Lusitania* was sister ship to the *Mauritania*, the craft on which she had sailed from England while pregnant and received her suffrage indoctrination from Lady Rhondda. Little more than two years had passed, so perhaps her crossing was a fresh memory.

But there was something else still: there were reports that two of the *Lusitania* survivors pulled from the sea were Lord Rhondda and his daughter, the suffragette Margaret Mackworth, who had accompanied him on this particular business trip. This time, Lord Rhondda's wife was not along. Despite the United States' proclaimed neutrality, Germany correctly surmised that the *Lusitania* was transporting war munitions to England, and at least one British war agent, purportedly Lord Rhondda.

Margaret Mackworth's frightening firsthand accounts of the sinking were among the first survivor stories transmitted to newspapers in both England and the United States. "We were not, as I thought, sixty feet above the sea," the suffragette later wrote. "We were already under the sea. I saw the water green just about up to my knees. . . . The ship sank and I was sucked right down with her."[46] She did not know how to swim and was knocked unconscious but was buoyed up from the depths by her lifejacket.

Margaret was found floating, sitting upright in a wicker chair from the wreckage that had bobbed beneath her. A sailor on the rescuing ship took her for dead and laid her on deck with the corpses. Naked beneath a blanket, Margaret awoke on the rescue ship's deck that night. Lord Rhondda also survived, and the two found each other before midnight.[47]

As the newspapers filled with harrowing stories such as these and stunned New Yorkers spoke of nothing else, the Edges' third child, a daughter, entered the world alive and well. They named the baby Margaret Dubois in honor of Rosalie's childless oldest sister, but Margaret Mackworth's miraculous rescue seems to have influenced the choice too. "Margaret" conjured the memory of the week Rosalie spent captivated by Lady Rhondda aboard the *Mauritania* and was linked to the news of how Margaret Mackworth had been plucked from the sea—from the same waters Rosalie had sailed over with this other Margaret's mother.

Bestowing the name Margaret on her newborn daughter was perhaps less consciously tied to the growing certainty that America would enter Europe's bloody war. In those last days before she brought forth life, Rosalie may have reflected too much on untold death and destruction. Fear gripped her, but all she could do to forestall these inevitabilities was make donations. The one to the Equal Franchise Society was two years overdue.

"Waking from a twilight sleep some hours later, delightedly happy, but personally impoverished, the consequences of my rash action rushed upon me," was what she ultimately wrote of the emotional trauma she had suffered before Margaret Edge's birth. When her daughter was a few weeks old, Rosalie Edge wrote that she turned the baby over to the second nurse she had engaged and went out to enlist in the fight for women's voting rights.[48]

DO PEOPLE SAVE what they value? Mabel Rosalie had done so beginning in her childhood, long before she took it upon herself to save the nation's wild birds and biggest trees. Her habit of preservation began with written artifacts of her personal history: the letters her father wrote to her and the dozens of letters she wrote to her mother from Asia. The letters remained neatly folded and bundled in their original envelopes bearing foreign stamps with postmarks visible, a trail left in paper and fading ink.

A second set of writings Rosalie preserved among her private papers were her unpublished autobiographical short stories, poems, and the 230-page memoir she worked on toward the end of her life.

The third bundle of words that she saved is the bulkiest. It consists of papers and pamphlets she wrote as a suffragist. It also contains the white sash trimmed in marigold that she wore across her chest when she marched through the streets of New York shoulder to shoulder with hundreds of women. The sash proclaims "Votes for Women," suffrage's slogan on both sides of the Atlantic. Rosalie would keep this sash as one of her cherished textiles, another bolt of the social fabric of her life that had satisfied her soul as the embroidered Mandarin coat had.[49]

The "Votes for Women" slogan was something America's suffrage movement shared with the British version, but differences were significant. American women were more "suffragist" than "suffragette" in their methods. They did not make much use of prison hunger strikes or the torching of public property. Unlike the British form, America's suffrage movement could date its genesis precisely, to July 19, 1848, when Elizabeth Cady Stanton and Lucretia Mott held a hastily organized public meeting in Seneca Falls, New York, to protest and discuss the inferior social status of women.

The idea for such a conference, however, had originated in London in 1840, at the World's Anti-Slavery Convention. Stanton and Mott had been among the women in the American delegation who were not allowed to take their seats at the men-only event. Women's participation in the antislavery proceedings would be "subversive to the principles and traditions of the country, and contrary to the word of God," a leading British representative told the American delegates.[50]

The female delegates had crossed the ocean for nothing. William Lloyd Garrison angrily refused to take his seat or enter into the antislavery debates, declaring that he preferred to join the ladies behind the thick curtain that separated them from the proceedings. Stanton and Mott waited eight years to address the indignity of their exclusion.

The Seneca Falls meeting drew three hundred people, most of them women, and included the great orator and former slave Frederick Douglass. The assembly listened to Stanton deliver her ten-point "Declaration of Sentiments and Resolutions," modeled after the Declaration of Independence, and voted to pass it. Point 9, asserting "the duty of the women of this country to secure to themselves the sacred right to the elective franchise," was its most controversial resolution, and was approved only after Douglass's impassioned plea.[51]

The Civil War derailed the drive for women's suffrage, and in 1869 a new obstacle was placed in its path. The Fifteenth Amendment to the Constitution, which granted blacks the right to vote, specified "men"; previously the Constitution had made no mention of gender. Unless women resided in certain territories of the West, the U.S. Constitution now expressly forbade them to vote. That same year the Wyoming Territory extended voting rights to its female residents, and the Colorado Territory did so in 1893; Utah and Idaho followed suit in 1896. Women's suffrage spread across the country one new state at a time but was blocked as it headed east. New York, the most populous state, was also the most contentious, and whenever the campaign to extend voting rights to women reached its boundary, the movement stopped.

WHEN ROSALIE presented herself to the Empire State Campaign Committee after her daughter, Margaret, was born, Carrie Chapman Catt, a brilliant campaigner for women's rights from Iowa, had recently taken charge of it. Catt had succeeded Susan B. Anthony as head of the National American Woman Suffrage Foundation but had been retired from it for ten years when she was pressed back into service. Catt's calm, methodical political prowess was needed in intransigent, cacophonous New York. Catt, twice widowed, agreed to head the New York movement in partnership with her best friend and housemate, New York suffragist Mary Garrett Hay.

By this time the American suffrage tide was so strong that it seems Rosalie Edge could not have avoided being swept up by it even without her previous association with Lady Rhondda and Margaret Mackworth. The campaign engulfed her, as it did thousands of women. With few discretionary funds of their own to donate to the Cause, New York women held bake sales and bazaars, rummage sales and card parties. In 1914 New York City hosted "Sacrifice Day," during which ladies donated their bracelets, watches, and wedding rings, dropping them into pots placed around the city.[52]

But Catt had come back to the suffrage movement too late to win in the November 1915 election, which posed the question of women's voting rights on the ballot. The measure failed by a small margin, defeated in part by the dissenting voices rising from a plethora of suffrage organizations. In New York City the demand for voting rights was lost in the broader demands of "heterodoxy," which championed free sex, birth control, and careers for women and exhorted married women to keep their maiden names.

Pursuit of such socially unacceptable goals strengthened the National Association Opposed to Woman Suffrage. Among those who spoke against giving the right to vote to women was Archibald Barrow's employer, Louise Carnegie, who, alarmed by the heterodoxists, asserted that giving women the right to vote would destroy families.[53]

Nevertheless, Carrie Chapman Catt saw that victory was within reach even in New York if the suffrage movement did not splinter into heterodox and other factions. Her winning plan, as her secret strategy became known, called for close collaboration of the nation's disparate women's groups for just one purpose: constitutional change. When confronted by the need to address other social issues, Catt retorted, "We do not care a gingersnap about anything but that Federal Amendment."[54]

To assure that New York's suffrage efforts coordinated with those of the rest of the country, Catt agreed to head both the state and the national organizations. The reconceptualized New York State Woman Suffrage Party (NYSWSP) was formed to work in lockstep with the National American Woman Suffrage Association, based in Washington, D.C.

The Equal Franchise Society was one of the organizations absorbed into Catt's NYSWSP. Rosalie not only marched in its parades but also was one of NYSWSP's twelve thousand women mobilized to serve as "the front door lobby." The women knocked on every door in their assigned precinct and delivered the suffrage message to whoever opened it. As an itinerant orator, Rosalie gave "blistering" stump speeches.[55]

For her dedication and obvious ability, Rosalie was elected corresponding secretary and treasurer of the NYSWSP and had opportunities to work directly with both Catt and Mary Garrett Hay.[56] Her swift ascent in the NYSWSP may also have been assisted by Margaret Norrie, who had lived in China with her husband, Gordon, while the Edges were there. Margaret Norrie was one of the few women Rosalie had befriended while abroad. Norrie and her unmarried sister, Ruth Morgan, were wealthy in their own right and generously donated their efforts and money to advance suffrage. In Hyde Park, New York, the sisters' estates neighbored that of Franklin and Eleanor Roosevelt.[57]

From her position on the NYSWSP board, Rosalie Edge was able to closely observe a well-run campaign. It was the best advocacy education she could have received, for she previously had known "nothing of organization, publicity, policy or politics." These skills were "taught [her] under the leadership and through the friendship of such women as Carrie Chapman Catt, Mary Garrett Hay, Ruth Morgan and others, to whom women of [her] time, and of all time to come, must ever be grateful."[58]

Service to the NYSWSP gave Rosalie Edge, first cousin to Charles Dickens, the opportunity to hone her inborn sense of how stories could advance social justice. She exercised her literary acuity by composing impassioned pamphlets for the NYSWSP press and publicity council. Under publicity director Vira Boardman Whitehouse, Rosalie produced a stream of suffrage propaganda at NYSWSP's Fifth Avenue headquarters. The material is strident and packed with arguments that are essentially if not absolutely true, two trademarks of the conservation pamphlets she would begin to edit or write fifteen years later.

The pamphlets mixed practical suggestions and lofty ideals. The plea for a woman's right to vote might be accompanied by advice on how to make a meal of leftover spinach, stale bread, and meat scraps. It is unlikely this was one of Rosalie's own recipes, since she did not prepare the Edges' meals and Charlie's income and tastes demanded richer fare.

Another of her pamphlets was *Better Babies*:

Five times as many babies die in crowded tenement districts as in well-to-do quarters of a city. Lack of air and sunshine, poor food, bad sanitation, over-work of mothers, both before and after marriage, above all ignorance on the part of the mother are responsible for most of these deaths. . . . The lowest death rate of babies in the world is New Zealand. Why? Because the government realizes the value of babies and does everything in its power to educate the mothers and protect the baby. WOMEN HAVE HAD THE VOTE IN NEW ZEALAND FOR 20 YEARS.[59]

WHY NOT? shouted yet another pamphlet:

In the United States all men are allowed to vote. WHY NOT women? Women own property and are taxed the same as men are. WHY NOT let them have representation? Women make the home. They care more about it than men do because it is their business. WHY NOT let them have something to say about laws which protect the home? Women take care of children. They are held responsible for their welfare. WHY NOT let them have something to say about the laws which govern the food, clothing, schools and playgrounds for children? These things are largely questions of voting. Over two million children are at work in mills, shops and factories. WHY NOT let women vote about this?[60]

"Woman Suffrage, a War Measure" was the text she trumpeted in one of her stump speeches: "And make our glorious country a Democracy—'for the right of those who submit to authority to have a voice in their own government.' We shall, ourselves, observe with proud punctilio, the principles we profess to be fighting for. Show that you are a true American. Work for the N.Y. Suffrage Amendment November 6th 1917. Vote for the N.Y. Suffrage Amendment November 6th 1917."[61]

Catt commended the organization writers' persuasiveness. "For the first time," the suffrage leader noted, "there was a strongly organized press department with an auxiliary body, the famous 'publicity council,' the two together devising and spreading broadcast suffrage publicity in 26 languages in which newspapers were published in New York State."[62]

Despite the inspiration of Margaret Mackworth, who broke laws and went to jail for the Cause, Rosalie never subscribed to these examples of militancy. In the United States, Alice Paul's breakaway National Woman's Party, with its picket lines and effigy burnings of Woodrow Wilson, was associated with these tactics. Catt's determined sisterhood eschewed them. The NYSWSP's social radicalism was characterized by the forceful repetition of its simple demand as often as possible and to as many people as possible, until the idea was beaten into the collective conscience. It was a highminded form of nagging. For Charles Dickens's New York first cousin once removed, word deluges were the best weapons at her disposal.

On November 6, 1917, New York State granted its women citizens the right to vote, becoming the first state in the East to do so. Victory in the bottleneck state assured not only that the New York constitution was amended on June 16, 1919, but that the U.S. Constitution would be changed as well after required ratification by other states. "The right of citizens of the United States to vote shall not be denied or abridged by the United States or by any State on account of sex," declared the new law of the land, which took effect in 1920.

Meanwhile, Margaret Mackworth, who had been elevated to Lady Rhondda after her mother died, was stirring up new trouble in England. Her father, Lord Rhondda, had been made a viscount before he died in 1918 and had willed that his daughter and only heir should inherit both his viscountancy and his seat in the House of Lords as a son would have.

Margaret Mackworth gained the title of Viscountess Rhondda, but she had to fight to sit in her father's seat. Bernard Shaw proclaimed the new Viscountess "a terror of the House of Lords" and "a peeress in her own right," as she battled for entry to the chamber. If Viscountess Rhondda sat in the House of Lords, Shaw warned, "there would be such a show-up of the general business ignorance and imbecility of the male sex as never was before."[63]

Viscountess Rhondda lost her bid; what is more notable is that Great Britain's women did not achieve full voting rights until ten years after American women did.

WITH VICTORY ACHIEVED, the NYSWSP changed its name to the New York State League of Women Voters, mirroring the national suffrage organization's name change to the League of Women Voters. Rosalie Edge joined both leagues, though it seemed her ardor for the women's movement had dissipated by the time the Nineteenth Amendment passed.[64]

To reward her for her service to the NYSWSP, Rosalie's friends Ruth Morgan and Margaret Norrie nominated her for a coveted membership in the Colony Club, New York's most exclusive private organization for women. The sisters were among the club's founders in 1903, and Ruth was Colony president when the call for younger members went out, and Rosalie was invited to join. A hopeful applicant might be well past fifty by the time her candidacy would be voted on, but under Ruth's tenure both Rosalie Edge and Eleanor Roosevelt—who was seven years younger than she—went to the head of the waiting list.[65]

A club where only women came together to relax and socialize was a bold idea when first proposed in 1900 and generally considered a bad one as well. Former president Grover Cleveland protested, insisting that women already had a place to relax, and it was called their home. Nevertheless, the Colony's forty founders raised $400,000 to build the sort of home they had in mind and hired architect Stanford White to design the building at 120–124 Madison Avenue. White asked the actress Elsie de Wolfe, one of the Colony's founders, to furnish the interior according to her refreshingly bright, spare tastes, which were a revolutionary departure from darkly draped Victorian modes.

Colonists—as these women referred to one another—could bring their lap dogs with them and keep them in the club's kennel. Styles of relaxation often took energetic forms, as in the organized horse buggy races up Third Avenue and swims in the marble pool, which resembled a Roman bath. There was a ballroom where the women could dance and an indoor track where they could run.

The Colony Club had outgrown the building White had designed for it before Rosalie Edge became a member. A large lot was purchased at Sixty-second Street and Park Avenue, and a new, Georgian-styled clubhouse opened in 1915. Edge cherished her Colony Club membership. She went almost daily to play bridge, swim, and lunch with her suffrage comrades. Her children were not neglected, as each had a nurse. She raised her children as her mother had raised her, with formal visitations when they were small. Rosalie Edge, like Harriet Barrow, may not have been affectionate toward her children, but she was dutiful.

Practically the only times the Edges were together as a family were at Parsonage Point, a rugged four-acre parcel in Rye that jutted into Long Island Sound. Charlie had bought the land around 1915 with his Wall Street killings. Even before a house was built on the land, the property was a refuge away from the demands of suffrage and the stock market, and from the steaming city heat that Rosalie refused to tolerate after the brutal summers in Asia. The Edges adopted a rambunctious "red chow doggie" named Ching, or R.C.D., as Rosalie nicknamed him, and she was his favorite.[66]

During the war the cost and scarcity of building materials delayed the construction of a house. Instead the Edges lived in tents the first few summers. It was Charles's vision that first "beheld the garden" they planted together. "No suggestion of its later beauty appeared in the rough weeds of those few acres," Rosalie wrote admiringly. Charlie, who had once been a designer of bridges that could support the weight of three elephants or the iron horse, also entertained a vision of a bridge that reached from Parsonage Point's shore to a bleak islet where Rosalie liked to sit at low tide.[67]

> The ring of fine rocks and the ever-changing beauty of the sea beyond had filled the Big Man with a desire to beautify that little piece of sterile land. His part was the making of drains, the building of walls, the erection of a bridge. Such a serious bridge it was. It spanned with heroic determination the narrow blue channel to our outer rocks and lay like a chastisement on the gaiety of the garden pattern. Its every line insisted that life was real and earnest. Its masonry piers frowned 'mid the warm rocks. Alas! Its philosophy of life was too well justified and it shared the end of many another philosopher. One night the great northeaster came. The pines waved their branches in the figures of a wild dance, the birches bent their lissome length. The bridge met the assault undaunted and wrestled until dawn. We found it slain. The steel beams were torn away and lay twisted and misshapen on the shore. The pride of masonry was laid low.[68]

On the mainland Rosalie was in charge of "planting, unplanting and replanting" and trained "heedless and untidy vines to lead ordered lives." It was up to her to praise "the sturdy and [bid] them shelter the weak. So, as in human relations, the Man was interested in material things, the Woman in the care of life."[69]

Peter and Margaret toddled after her. Rosalie gave them pansies to plant, flowers "so peculiarly responsive to the efforts of baby gardeners." Neither child looked like a baby for long. Each growth spurt made it apparent they had inherited their father's height; Rosalie called them her "Baby Giants."[70]

It was as she puttered in the soil with the children that she began to notice birds. Despite her fraught contribution to the National Association of Audubon Societies after the *Lusitania* went down, it seems she was not fully conscious of her liking for birds until the summer of 1919. By that summer her preference had clearly shifted from women's issues to birds. She woke early to watch the birds, perhaps with the binoculars Charlie had given her to view the Emerald Buddha in Bangkok.

Each morning she quietly pulled her cot onto the landing between her tent and Charlie's so that she could watch a family of what she would learn were kingfishers nesting in an earthen slot near the beach. Quail, as she would also discover, darted through a nearby patch of wild buckwheat, and a pair of what she called sparrow hawks nested in a tall tree. These hawks—or kestrels, as she later found they were more correctly called—were "a delightful couple, they were very much in love."[71]

Nothing in Rosalie's prior history explains this sudden interest in birds. She had made a few fleeting references to them in early letters, but they were not fond ones. There were the caged canaries and parakeets her father bought her when she was about five; the day in 1909 when birds repeatedly flew into the Edges' Hong Kong hotel room and she ordered the servant to bolt the windows to keep them out; and the times she went hunting with Charlie and proclaimed shooting to be great fun.

In Rosalie's detailed letters home, she never mentioned China's famous bird markets nor noted any offense she had taken at the ubiquitous old men walking with their bird cages filled with melodious captives. She could never satisfactorily explain, perhaps even to herself, the source from which her bird love sprang. One day she came into the city from Rye too late to deliver her committee's report at a meeting of the New York League of Women Voters. Vira Boardman Whitehouse, her old boss at the publicity council, noted her tardy entry and looked at her "with cold reproach." Rosalie wrote, "Convicted of negligence, I blurted out, 'A great blue heron was sitting in our maple tree.'" Vira Boardman Whitehouse was not amused. "I learned to keep separate the different departments of my life," Rosalie commented.[72]

She confined her bird love to Parsonage Point on Long Island Sound. When Charlie was not repairing the serious bridge he had built to her wild islet off the rocky point, she persuaded him to construct bird feeders and sheltered baths on the main property. Charlie's bluebird boxes attracted bluebirds, and a different kind of box he made according to her instructions and lodged in a dead tree lured a second pair of kestrels.

Loons, mergansers, and thrashers reliably visited. In August Rosalie saw one hundred terns, and "great black-back and laughing gulls mixed with the herring gulls on the rocks." She adored her own soft work of planting "bird allurements" that she ordered from the gardening magazines, garlanding shrubs and trees with suet and scattering birdseed on the grass. She wreathed the grounds with gardens, and Charlie built a Japanese-style meditation shrine in one of them. For Rosalie attracting birds to Parsonage Point was what she and Charlie did together even though he lacked enthusiasm for her purpose. Charlie still preferred birds he could hunt, and she no longer joined him in his pleasure.[73]

Charlie also liked to plan what to build, and toward the end of the Great War when construction material became more available, he began working on Parsonage Point's main residence. A long driveway led to a parcel where the land abruptly ended at the savage line of the sea. The family tents came down as walls went up. Rooms rambled outward from Charlie's paneled study at the center, in roughly a nautilus pattern. He named the house Treasure Island, and it billowed into nine rooms leading off a palatial entry, with the pounding surf of the sound visible—sometimes threateningly so—on three sides.[74]

From the house his bridge and her islet could be observed in unspoken competition between man and nature. Between man and woman the competition was verbal as he fretted about his bridge and she told him he never should have built it. Charlie monitored how the steel-enforced structure withstood the harsh elements blowing off the Atlantic. This too was part of nature, though that of a civil engineer. Rosalie rooted for wind and sea and the rugged islet, apparently content that it was unreachable at high tide until the next time Charlie succeeded in spanning the narrow channel.

Despite the bridge's frequent need of repair, Treasure Island was as much a sturdy monument to Charlie's stock-market prosperity as to his expertise as a civil engineer. In time the grounds included a swimming pool, a garage big enough for the Silver Knight and the other cars he collected, and a cottage for his chauffeur, Oscar Brice.[75] As impressive as the evolving estate was, Treasure Island received few visitors.

Louise Carnegie and other suffrage opponents had predicted that the American family would disintegrate if women got the right to vote; for whatever reason, the disintegration of the marriage of Mr. and Mrs. Charles Noel Edge dated to about the time women achieved this right. Rosalie recalled one of the typically oblique exchanges with Charlie:

"What kind of day did you have dear?" Charlie asked.

"Thirty-two finches, twelve titmice, a pair of blue jays, six ordinary or house wrens and a robin," Rosalie replied, in the way a man who put his faith in numbers might appreciate. But it did not matter, for he was gone.[76]

IN THE SPRING of 1921 the argument broke out, perhaps in their bedroom or in the paneled study. Rosalie recalled years later that it felt as if the ground had shifted beneath the house, so forceful and destabilizing was Charlie's loss of temper this time. He was a tower of rage, and his booming voice woke Peter, who was barely nine. She was also shouting, but her anger was high-pitched and piercing, with a ripping quality to it rather than a thundering one. Something or someone, perhaps Rosalie, crashed into a wall and there was a cry of pain. She ran out of the room. Clutching her arm, she entered the boy's bedroom, then the girl's.[77]

Rosalie told the children to get up because she was taking them back to the city immediately. They dressed, and she hurried them across the cold, dark lawn to the garage, to the relentless rhythm of waves crashing on rock. They climbed into a car with Rosalie behind the steering wheel, but her arm hurt too much for her to shift into gear. She got out and went to wake the chauffeur, Brice, who drove them to New York before the sun came up. For weeks afterward Rosalie's arm was cradled in a sling and perhaps set in a cast.

Mr. and Mrs. Charles Noel Edge never lived together again. Until Peter and Margaret were old enough to take the train from the city to Rye by themselves, Brice shuttled them and their nannies between their mother's brownstone on East Seventy-second Street and their father's mansion at Parsonage Point. It was not until about twenty years later that Rosalie captured those predawn hours in a memoir, referring to them as "my earthquake."[78]

She also wrote a poem called "Storm," undoubtedly composed under the later influence of the Columbia University creative-writing classes she would take.

Your love—it swept with stinging lash
Of rain torrential, with the crash,
Of thunder, with fierce lightning flash
Of bolt that severed with one gash
The all-pervading mists; again
The temple-veil was rent with twain;
Your love, it was storm-driven rain,
Reverberating with the pain
Of revelation. . . . Since . . . long night,
Forever blinded with the sight
Of space uprolled to timeless height
Made plain in one zigzag of light.[79]

There are more words that perhaps explain why the storm came up that night. These were penciled by Charlie on a sheet of Hammermill Bond typing paper.

Dearest Heart,
    I love you with all my heart and soul and my life is truly in your hands.
A great sorrow may come upon us—oh God forbid it! I am trying today
to do my duty and when you get this shall have asked you to share my fear
and trouble. My own fear is nothing but my fear for you is very great. If you
love me I need your faith and all your love now oh so very very [sic] much.
If you want to, may I come and cry in your arms and will you comfort me?
I love you now so much, my heart is in my throat as I can hardly see to write.
These things may not be—but the very thought has shown me how altogether dear to me you are and that your love for me means more than life.
I want to kiss your hair and eyes and lips. Oh dearest say your prayers with
me tonight.
Charlie.[80]

Was Rosalie the "Dearest Heart" for whom Charles's passionate letter was intended, whose hair and eyes and lips he yearned to kiss? The neatly folded paper on which these words are written is preserved among dozens of her personal letters, with those she wrote to her mother from Asia and those her father wrote to her. But circumstances indicate this letter of devotion was not meant for her eyes.

We might surmise that Charlie's confession of love for another woman was discovered by his wife. Perhaps she confronted him with it. We might further imagine that he lunged at her to retrieve the damning evidence but failed, leaving it forever in her possession. This letter among Mrs. Charles Noel Edge's precious cache is like a prime suspect attempting to melt into a crowd. Even after so many years have passed, it guiltily stands out from the rest.

Part Two

CHAPTER FOUR

Amateur and Dilettante

For the next few weeks following her flight from Parsonage Point, Rosalie lived "mechanically," alternating between "dumb and stunned" existence to searing pain that ripped through her again, leaving her nerves dreadfully alert.[1] The lingering ache in her arm left her with a physical sensation reminding her of Charlie's betrayal. She was forty-four years old.

So soon after Rosalie helped women achieve the greatest power they had ever known, her identity as a woman, as a wife, had been crippled. She resolved that "the Baby Giants must never know" the circumstances that had ended their family. "The Big Man, the treasured garden, the air, the sky, the gulls flying high, the bluebirds newly arrived, the bulbs just out, the spring about to bloom in fullness—were gone. My earthquake took all these, but the Baby Giants were with me and I must see that their joy of life was not destroyed."[2]

When Rosalie was growing up, "adultery" was whispered only when the Ten Commandments were recited, cracked the bold Alva Vanderbilt, Consuelo's mother. While dictating the terms of daughter Consuelo's marriage to the Duke of Marlboro in 1895, Alva had caused a second public sensation by becoming the first society lady to accuse her husband of infidelity and sue for divorce. Once free of William Vanderbilt, Alva quickly married his best friend, Oliver P. Belmont.

"All around me were women leading these half lives, practically deserted by their husbands who not only neglected them but insulted them by their open and flagrant infidelities," Alva Vanderbilt wrote.[3] But for women not as inured to social or financial ruin as a Vanderbilt might have been, divorce was still beyond consideration. New York's finest ladies still left the room when the subject came up, and the state's draconian laws in contested cases spelled catastrophe for both husband and wife.

To protect their status and preserve their economic well-being, the Edges settled for half-lives rather than for divorce. Keeping their altered living situation as private as possible, they secured a judicial separation on February 14, 1924. Legal separation kept the details of their breakup confidential and ended cohabitation without terminating Charlie's financial obligations to his estranged wife.[4] Only to the outside world did the Edges still look married.

Charlie's monthly allowance to Rosalie was generous and dependable. Gifts and furnishings passed back and forth between them, and written communications were cordial at first. Either Charlie's Abnormal Distortion of Conscience was working again, or he feared what she might do to hurt him professionally. His earliest letters after their separation pandered and placated: "I am afraid you are overestimating the value of the little fur jacket—I bought it as a beautiful intriguing garment—but I did not buy it as ermine. . . . Your husband Charlie." In another he wrote: "My Dear I realize your need of a garden. If this summer you will find a place you like I will try to buy it for you and in a little while you shall have a garden again. Your Husband Charles." And in still another he wrote: "I have deposited $1,000 in your account. . . . This account is for you and not the children." "Thank you so very much for the Japanese embroidery. . . . I remember so well buying it in Hong Kong." "I enclose check for $1,000. It seems that you might like to buy some new clothes." "Please, everything in the house is absolutely yours, to do with as you will. It would hurt me very much that you should part with any of them, or think that at any future time I might claim them."[5]

Charlie told her he had drawn up a new will and "left to [her] and the children rather more than three quarters of everything," so that in the event of his death her circumstances would improve. This message ended with what is perhaps unintended irony, given the length of the separation, "Wishing you a very happy summer I remain your husband Charles N. Edge."[6]

Yet her smoldering indignation gave him no room to do otherwise.

Dear Charlie,

I am very unhappy over an attempt to change the arrangement to which you agreed before Christmas. I do not believe this to be your idea. The letter telling me and lilies from you chanced to be brought to me at the same time. I knew only the lilies came from you. They are still fresh and white and pure—and so are the thoughts of you which they released in me.

Your wife R. E.[7]

Knowing how much Rosalie hated spending summers in New York, Charlie encouraged her to travel with the children. She took Peter and Margaret to Europe, and they toured castles and cathedrals and museums at a relentless pace. She bought lace from Ireland, muted wools from Scotland, sumptuous velvet from France, and silk from Italy and spent hours with dressmakers. Indolently she resumed piano lessons and was admitted to the summer program at the prestigious Fontainebleau Music School in France. Once again she toyed with the idea of teaching.[8]

In England Rosalie and the children stayed at Wolverhampton with Sir Charles Marston and her thirteen-year-old goddaughter, Melissa. Beautiful Louise died slowly and in 1921 had succumbed in a nursing home in her birthplace of Ithaca, New York. The timing of her childhood friend's death coincided with Rosalie's own loss and bound her in grief to the Marstons in a way she had not experienced for a long while.[9]

All these things Rosalie did to save her life; what she did not do was watch birds. After her father died, she had similarly deprived herself of the outdoor pleasures she had enjoyed with him, perhaps because of the grief these once-shared activities renewed in her if she went about them alone. Bird-watching belonged to the world she and Charlie had created at Parsonage Point. In the city birds were invisible to her.

But on November 19, 1922, one breached the emotional wall she had erected, and she scrawled this notation after one of her walks: "Hermit Thrush Hunter College." Another year went by before she made a written note of a "yellow throat" she had seen in Central Park; in 1924 a wren caught her eye in her yard.[10]

At sunset one day in May 1925, Rosalie sat by an open window in the East Seventy-second Street house, pining for her gardens blooming profusely at Parsonage Point. "From high above came the note of birds," she wrote years later. She remembered from her days in Rye that it was the call of nighthawks. "Their sharp 'speek, speek' was so insistent," she recalled. "I looked up and wondered what bird could love to hover over a city when all the reach of green was within the compass of its wings."[11]

Suddenly curious, Rosalie walked out of her brownstone and into the cool lavender dusk. One of the birds she had heard swooped low. Since her earthquake she had not noticed birds, perhaps assuming it would hurt too much to be reminded of the life that was no more.

The thing that had caused her to love birds, she wrote decades later, was buried so deep she would have had to go to a psychologist to discover what it was. Looking back on her life near the end of it, Edge wondered if the joy of birds came "as a solace in sorrow and loneliness," or if it gave "peace to some soul wracked with pain."[12] She did not acknowledge that she had personally known such sorrow or possessed a wracked soul. But suddenly it seemed to hurt more when she did not see birds. With the nighthawks' gentle allurement, Rosalie Edge's pain-wracked soul finally began to heal.

ROSALIE SAW BIRDS everywhere. To learn the names of new varieties she spotted each day, she pored over mystifying bird guides at night, at first assuming the arrangements on the pages were artistic imaginings, drawn only "to balance the picture, to fill space" as on a Mandarin robe or a Japanese watercolor. On one outing a flock of little birds floated out of a tree toward her, looking exactly the way yellow warblers were clustered on a page of her guidebook. The vision of yellow birds and their crisply articulated song belonged to her. "The lust of possession seized me and forth I fared to win for myself feathered prizes," she wrote. It struck her that she was alive to hear them sing. Her bird love was buried deep indeed.[13]

One morning she decided to go to Central Park to see if there might be any birds there. "I thought that this was my own, original exclusive idea," Rosalie later wrote. "I laugh to remember it."[14] Central Park was the place she had loved to go with her father when she was a little girl, but in the years since then she had been unaware of the renown it had attained for its remarkable variety of bird life. Park architects Fredrick Law Olmsted and Calvert Vaux had meant nature to flourish in their botanical creation; as a draw for birds, however, it exceeded expectations. At Parsonage Point, Rosalie Edge had deliberately selected plants to attract different species of birds, but somehow the extravagant application of the same principle in Central Park had eluded her. The park's thirty-eight-acre Ramble was a microcosm of an Adirondacks woodland, and it in particular was filled with migrant songbirds in early May. More than two hundred species of birds visited Central Park during the course of the year, and for many it was their permanent home.

As a new Central Park bird-watcher, Rosalie thought it would be fun to bring her chow and children along, just as she had done at Parsonage Point. Peter and Margaret noisily accompanied her as she held on to the straining R.C.D. with one hand and tried to focus her binoculars with the other. "The eager questions of the Baby Giants do not help—'Where Muz, where? What bird is it, Muz?'—and a shriek of joy if it is recognized," she wrote. "It was a bird with steady nerves, indeed, that waits to hear my replies."[15]

The park's veteran bird-watchers eyed her critically. Once she hesitantly approached a group of them gathered around a tree, "their gaze fixed on an atom of nature." Someone whispered, "black-throated blue." Rosalie wheeled her binoculars around to track the bird but saw only a small green speck with not a trace of blue. "Green," she murmured. "No, not the black-throated green, the black-throated blue," came the hissed correction. Dejected, Rosalie turned away from the speck on the branch and resignedly wrote down what the other person had said.[16]

At forty-eight she feared she was too old to learn to see what the younger bird-watchers saw. Her eyes were for "sewing buttons, reading receipt books and for watching Baby Giants." Her self-esteem was still at low ebb, yet with each bird she correctly identified it rose, and Central Park birders warmed to her company. "The persistence of Dog and Giants and Mad Seeker-for-bird-truth may have touched their kindly hearts," she wrote. "Baby Giants and Chow Doggies waste not time nor vitality doubting themselves," she observed and resolved that neither would she.[17]

"TO MUZ FROM PETER" reads the inscription in the leather-bound date book that twelve-year-old Peter gave his mother for Christmas in 1925.[18] In it she began to keep track of the birds more earnestly. That winter she went to Montauk; Cape May, New Jersey; and the Palisades to see them. She traveled to Rye a few times as well, with bird-watching at least part of her purpose for making the trip. Her bird notations were still so infrequent, however, that after two years the date book's pages were mostly blank.

Peter came to love bird-watching as much as his mother did, although Margaret was bored by it. Her mother and brother's conversations about birds excluded her, and it seemed that the bird bond made Peter the preferred child.[19] Like their father, both Margaret and Peter grew extremely tall, yet excessive height in a teenaged boy was not the stigma that it was for a teenaged girl. Rosalie did little to ease her six-foot-tall daughter's awkwardness and adolescent ostracism; referring to Margaret as a "giant," whether a baby one or otherwise, might have made matters worse. In time Margaret came to prefer spending more time with her father and less with her mother.

Meanwhile, Rosalie's bird bond with Peter was so strong that she frequently phoned Lincoln School with instructions to her son about which birds he should look for on his walk home through Central Park. After the school refused to deliver any more bird alerts, she sent Peter a telegram about a rare sighting. At Lincoln School, "a telegram rather awed them," Rosalie wrote. But "when Peter came home that evening he had both the prothonotary and the yellow-throated (warbler) on his life list."[20]

Improved binoculars and more-comprehensible bird guides were making Rosalie Edge's entry into the avocation easier. A knowledgeable teacher was also essential, and she found her first mentor in Ludlow Griscom, one of the nation's best birders. Griscom, the gruff, thirty-five-year-old Harvard-educated bird curator at the American Museum of Natural History, possessed legendary bird-identification skills. It was widely rumored that he had accurately identified an upland plover making an unprecedented pass over New York City one foggy night by only its brief call. Like Griscom's other acolytes, Rosalie checked the notes he left in a hollow tree on the "Point" in the Ramble each morning.[21]

She often arrived early enough to talk to the great man himself and tagged along on his rounds. Griscom's idiosyncratic patter delighted a young birder named Roger Tory Peterson, whom Rosalie had met in the park. "Let's stop here and flap our ears," Griscom would say. "Now someone find a bird with some zip in it. . . . Please lower your voice to a howl!"[22] Griscom showed Rosalie her first Philadelphia vireo and once hurried her off to make a quick sighting of a bobolink that he warned "would not tarry."[23] It was years before she saw another bobolink in the park.

If Griscom was said to be the god of the Central Park birders, his 1923 *Birds of the New York City Region* was their bible. Its emphasis on visual and auditory identification was a major departure from the conventional way of identifying a bird, which was to kill it and stuff it. New York ornithologists and bird collectors typically headed for Cortlandt Park, where, for the sake of science, they were "perfectly free to shoot as many warblers in the morning as [they] could skin in the afternoon." Griscom wrote that "when visiting a friend in New Haven, in whose shade trees a pair of warbling vireos were nesting, by first ringing the doorbell, hat in hand, and courteously requesting permission, it was entirely possible to blaze away and shoot the warbling vireo out of the treetop onto the lawn."[24]

Elliott Coues, a leading nineteenth-century ornithologist, had defined the serious bird student as one who "goes out to study birds alive and destroys some of them simply because that is the only way of learning their structure and technical characters."[25] In the laboratory permeated by fumes of arsenic or formaldehyde, wild specimens were measured, eviscerated, and stuffed for future reference.

Coues had been a Union army medic stationed on the lightly embattled western frontier during the Civil War and had the leisure and the army-issued weapon necessary to advance his bird knowledge. His *Key to North American Birds* was the landmark study resulting from his tour of duty. Coues's 1874 work, *Field Ornithology: Comprising a Manual of Instruction for Procuring, Preparing and Preserving Birds*, spelled out collecting techniques in detail: "The double-barreled shot gun is your main reliance. Under some circumstances you may trap or snare birds, catch them with bird-lime, or use other devices; but such cases are exceptions to the rule that you will shoot birds, and for this purpose no weapon compares with the one just mentioned."[26]

The manual gave advice not only on shooting but also on poisoning, cleaning, skinning, stuffing, and wiring specimens to prevent decomposition. Reliance on its instructions enabled the first members of the American Ornithologists' Union, which Coues cofounded in 1883, to classify the nation's birds. The AOU's membership was composed not only of Coues-trained ornithologists who collected specimens to study but also those who concentrated on "economic ornithology." AOU member Theodore S. Palmer defined this specialty as "the study of birds from the standpoint of dollars and cents."[27] Palmer's buttoned-up accounting method necessitated making judgments about which birds benefited people and which did not. This specialty was so important that the Division of Economic Ornithology and Mammalogy was established within the Department of Agriculture.

When the economic ornithology division's name was changed to the Bureau of Biological Survey in 1896, Palmer served as assistant director under C. Hart Merriam, its founding chief. So many employees of the Biological

Survey were also members of the AOU that the two most prominent bird organizations in the country spoke with one voice and, whether for their own
pleasure or for professional purposes, collected birds as Coues prescribed.

The Biological Survey's collection was vast; assiduously labeled cabinets
and drawers at the Smithsonian Museum housed its inventory of well over
100,000 field specimens. Other museums provided additional storage for
them. Frank Chapman, who besides Griscom had also curated birds at the
American Museum of Natural History, offered this description of his job:

> If he is true to his name, a curator's first duties are the care of the collections
> under his charge. Each specimen must be identified, labeled, catalogued,
> and given its proper serial number before being stored in a manner that
> it will thereafter always be immediately available for examination. . . . The
> mounted birds are placed in the cases of the exhibition halls. The usually far
> larger number of unmounted skins (resembling in appearance a dead bird)
> designed for study, are placed in containers which will protect them from
> insects and dust as well as from the bleaching effects of exposure to light that
> so detracts from the scientific value of exhibited specimens.[28]

The number of specimens of both game birds and nongame birds shelved
in museum cabinets was small, however, compared to the millions destroyed in the pursuit of pleasure or profit: the desire to bag trophy animals,
supply restaurants with delectable menu items, or accessorize fashion was
annihilating many bird populations. AOU members determined that while
their reasons for collection in the name of science were defensible, all others
demanded control. The organization drafted a law each state could adopt to
regulate the killing of birds within its borders.

As well-intentioned as it was, the model law failed due to both a lack of
state enforcement and the bickering among the types of bird-takers. Nevertheless, the desire or economic necessity to kill birds continued to unite the
various bird factions to some degree.

LUDLOW GRISCOM'S REIGN over Central Park birding ended when he returned to Boston in 1927, but his novel methods of identification had gener-
ated a new faction among the Central Park bird-watchers. It was comprised
of people like Rosalie Edge, who watched living birds for the sheer pleasure
of it. With magnification powers of seven or eight times normal vision in
hand, those with no formal ornithological education or field training could
distinguish one bird from another. These callow interlopers' reliance on

binoculars annoyed the traditional collectors.[29] "Ornithology as a science is threatened," decried California zoologist Joseph Grinnell. "It should not be allowed to lapse wholly into the status of a recreation or a hobby, to be indulged in only a superficial way by amateurs and dilettantes."[30]

An innovation as simple as two scopes mounted side by side for viewing—double barrels loaded with prisms and mirrors rather than buckshot—encouraged amateurs and dilettantes. Rosalie Edge and others of this ilk in Central Park swapped bird observations with one another. As Griscom had taught them, no pigment was unworthy of comment; no outline of beak or arch of wing was too insignificant to mention to a fellow bird-watcher, and the collegially pooled observations filtered in to steadily improving bird guides. Griscom's Central Park adherents, the great majority of whom were young men, "were contributing to the very law and gospel of bird study," wrote Rosalie, who would also add to this fount of knowledge.[31]

As she contributed, she also acquired a visceral hatred for traditional ornithologists. Simply hearing of them brought to mind the odor of death that pervaded "the trays that hold hundreds of thousands of skins of once lovely, lively birds." For ornithologists "birds were their job, not their hobby," she dismissively wrote.[32]

CHAPTER FIVE

Like a Man

In August 1929 a stack of mail was waiting for fifty-two-year-old
Rosalie Edge at her hotel in Paris, where she and the children
were ending their customary summer tour of the Continent.
A bigger envelope bore a return address she did not recognize.
Inside was a densely printed sixteen-page pamphlet titled in a
bold font *A Crisis in Conservation*. Its three authors were identified as employees of the American Museum of Natural History,
but Rosalie did not recognize their names: Dr. Waldron DeWitt
Miller, who was also vice president of the New Jersey Audubon
Society; Dr. Willard Gibbs Van Name, an invertebrate zoologist; and Davis Quinn, who appeared to be a young protégé of
Van Name's but otherwise of vague professional affiliation. Edge
assumed that someone from her Central Park community—she
guessed the lepidopterist—had given one of these strangers her
mailing address.

"If bird students and nature lovers are led by self-congratulatory
reports of bird protection organizations . . . they are due to get a
rude awakening," the *Crisis in Conservation* pamphlet stated:

> Let us face facts now rather than annihilation of many of our
> native birds later. . . . Our success is far from complete; in many
> cases there has been no success at all and no sincere effort is
> being made to achieve any. The results that we are paying for
> we do not get, and the outlook for longterm survival of many of
> our most beautiful and most conspicuous and most interesting

native birds has become a poor one. The earnestness, activity and efficiency
which characterized our bird protection efforts and our organizations for
that purpose during the early years of the present century has [sic] not been
maintained.[1]

According to the three authors, the whooping crane, the trumpeter swan,
the ivory-billed woodpecker, the California condor, the white pelican, and
the bald eagle were poised on the brink of extinction. The unidentified bird
protection organizations were condemned for their repeated failure to oppose Alaska's bounty on bald eagles, which the authors claimed was a desecration of the national emblem.

> The number of eagle bounties paid in Alaska had risen to 41,812 (with an
> estimated total destruction of at least 70,000). . . . Did they promise any
> active campaign to put an end to the slaughter? Far from it. They are largely
> anti-eagle propaganda. Their general purport and intent is such as to give
> any uninformed reader seeking information the idea that the eagle is pretty
> destructive of game and fish and that it is not in danger of extinction, . . .
> and who do[es] not want to be bothered with any such troublesome matter
> anyway.[2]

The pamphlet authors further asserted the unmentionable protection organizations had plenty of money to save the birds at risk, but ammunition
makers and hunters had gained so much influence over them that they saw
"birds merely as fodder for shotguns."[3]

Though *Crisis* was coy about which bird protection organizations it referred to, there was no doubt about the name of one. The authors had cited
deficiencies in *Bird-Lore* at one point in the diatribe. This was the official
publication of the twenty-four-year-old National Association of Audubon
Societies, a loose confederation of private bird protection clubs with affili-
ates in most states. Rosalie read the *Crisis* pamphlet and quickly realized the
NAAS was its target. It dawned on her that the NAAS had scarcely entered her
mind after she dashed off that check for a life membership in the organization in those horrific days before Margaret was born. Fourteen years had
passed since then.[4]

Remarkably, the NAAS, the nation's oldest and most prestigious bird-
protection organization, had played no part in Rosalie's bird education. She
barely glanced at *Bird-Lore* when it arrived and had not attended any of the
Audubon programs or meetings in New York. Exhausted from a long day

of sightseeing and dress fittings, she now considered the *Crisis* pamphlet's charges. It was a moment of epiphany for her, worthy of being canonized in conservation history:

> Before me now is a vision of my bedroom in the hotel, hung and upholstered in brocade, as the French do in their kindly effort to persuade one that a bedroom is also a drawing-room. I paced up and down, heedless that my family was waiting to go to dinner. For what to me were dinner and the boulevards of Paris when my mind was filled with the tragedy of beautiful birds, disappearing through the neglect and indifference of those who had at their disposal wealth beyond avarice with which these creatures might be saved?[5]

Rosalie was so disturbed by what she had read that she forgot to change into evening clothes for supper. Famished Peter and Margaret waited impatiently, and when the three finally went down to dine Rosalie could speak of nothing but the pamphlet's charges. The Edges sailed home a few days later. After her leadership in conservation was well established, Rosalie described how she sat on a deck chaise studying *Crisis*.

The image she painted of herself in anguished contemplation was reminiscent of the transatlantic turmoil unleashed in her by the long suffrage talks with Lady Rhondda more than sixteen years earlier. Given Rosalie's novelistic regard for the past, she might have embellished this self-portrait with literary devices she had gleaned from her reading. Henry James found his heroine Isabel Archer sitting before a fire, energetically reviewing her life until she burned with new insight; so too had Ivan Turgenev caught the conflicted Dmitry Sanin in the simmering act of revelation.

However long Rosalie Edge sat pondering in a "visible tension of thought" she did not know.[6] What Edge must have known was that this conservation awakening, unlike her suffrage awakening during a previous oceanic journey home, would not lead her to a social ferment roiling America. This time there was no social ferment. There were only three disgruntled members of the NAAS.

THE NAAS WAS not much more than a pamphlet itself at its beginning, in 1887. Rosalie would not have known of these societies then; she was a fatherless girl of ten, still groping her way out of the fairy-tale childhood that had shattered two years earlier when her father died.

But the first pamphlet of the NAAS, like the appeal Rosalie received in Paris, was an impassioned appeal to protect wild birds, written by Yale paleontologist George Bird Grinnell. Grinnell grew up in rural New York near the estate of bird artist John James Audubon and attended a school run by Audubon's widow, Lucy, in the old Audubon home. Though the great artist was notoriously wasteful of bird life, killing one hundred birds a day if he could, his magnificent paintings depended on collection. In rooms crammed with the painter's art and taxidermy, Grinnell learned to read, write, and love birds. After such exposure he became the editor of conscience for the hunting magazine *Forest and Stream*.

Though Grinnell did not oppose hunting, he condemned unregulated market hunting that kept restaurants and meat vendors supplied with fresh game. Women were another target of his censure, owing to the feathers and wild-bird parts that decorated dresses and hats like the one with stuffed hummingbirds that little Mabel Rosalie Barrow had worn.

In the 1880s the American Ornithologists' Union estimated that about 5 million birds of fifty species were killed annually in the production of women's hats and clothing. Whenever women were present, "church gatherings and other social events often resembled aviaries." Ladies' hats resembled miniature museum dioramas filled with taxidermied warblers, cardinals, baby owls, and bluebirds.[7]

Among the easiest birds to catch were herons and egrets, and fashion's insatiable demand for their feathers was gutting coastal rookeries. The gory shores were out of public view and far from the elegant streets of New York. Dead herons putrefied on the ground, their bald, bloodied backs offering vivid evidence of plumes ripped out while the birds were still alive. Beside the corpses orphaned young birds screamed to be fed.[8]

The AOU's inability to persuade states to pass bird protection laws led Grinnell to take a new approach based on Great Britain's privately funded Royal Society for the Protection of Birds, which supported public education and legislative advocacy. In an 1886 issue of *Forest and Stream*, Grinnell broached an American version of the idea: "We propose the formation of an Association for the protection of wild birds and their eggs, which shall be called the Audubon Society. Its membership is to be free to everyone who is willing to lend a helping hand in forwarding the objects for which it is formed. These objects will be to prevent, as far as possible, (1) the killing of any wild birds not used for food; (2) the destruction of nests or eggs of any wild bird; (3) the wearing of feathers as ornaments or trimming for dress."[9]

Forty thousand people signed pledges not to harm birds. Oliver Wendell Holmes gave his promise, as did Henry Ward Beecher and John Greenleaf

Whittier. Grinnell published his first educational pamphlet, which he named for the great bird painter, and included an essay called "Woman's Heartlessness," by poet Celia Thaxter. The essay recounted how Thaxter tried to persuade a well-dressed woman to stop wearing the plumes of wild birds. The fashionable woman was not convinced and "went her way, a charnel house of beaks and claws and bones and feathers and glass eyes upon her fatuous head."[10]

But Grinnell had neither funds nor staff to continue publishing his Audubon pamphlets and abandoned the effort in 1888. He had far better luck forming the Boone and Crockett Club in 1887, which promoted the conservation of mammals among big-game hunters. The storied marksman Theodore Roosevelt served as founding president of the "club of American hunting riflemen," and Roosevelt's electric personality no doubt boosted its appeal.[11]

The Audubon Society's swift demise came as a bitter shock to Grinnell. "Fashion decrees feathers; and feathers it is," he wrote. The "moral idea" he predicted would quickly lead to repudiation of fashions that threatened marine and wading birds with extinction had not been persuasive enough; eight years later the demand for egret plumes and body parts was as high as ever.[12]

Frank Chapman, the natural history museum's bird curator, opposed the day's fashion along with Grinnell. As Chapman walked through New York, he saw far too many owls and woodpeckers perched where Nature had not intended them. Chapman, who had renounced personal collecting and market hunting, could personally attest to the power of transformation; as a youth he had shot two passenger pigeons, "unaware of their value," and eaten them for dinner.[13] After trading in his shotgun for binoculars, Chapman initiated an enduring compensatory tradition—the annual Christmas bird count.

Grinnell's moral idea did not die. Beginning with Massachusetts in 1896, it materialized in one state after another, spreading to Pennsylvania, New York, Connecticut, and New Jersey. By 1903 Audubon Societies had sprouted in thirty-four states. These independent organizations published pamphlets about the birds headed for extinction and advocated for their protection in their state legislatures using the AOU's model law. To make it easier for these distinct Audubon Societies to share news with one another, Frank Chapman and his wife, Fannie, started the magazine *Bird-Lore*. The publication was well received and became a "a sisyphean task" the Chapmans ran from home.[14]

Bird-Lore attracted so many subscribers that the loose union of state Audubon Societies gained enough clout to negotiate with the powerful New York City milliners. Author Mabel Osgood Wright, who was also president of the Connecticut Audubon Society, forged an agreement with hatmakers not to use wild species, in exchange for Audubon Societies' consent not to oppose the continued use of domestically raised feathers and fowl parts. Grinnell's moral idea gradually caught on. The fashionably feathered woman, targeted as Bird Enemy Number One, would become a fashion pariah.[15]

William Dutcher, a wealthy executive with the Prudential Life Insurance Company and another reformed hunter and bird collector, shared Grinnell's and the Chapmans' sentiments. Soon Theodore Palmer of the Bureau of Biological Survey joined the vocal brigade. Chapman, Dutcher, and Palmer, all AOU members, campaigned particularly hard to get the model law passed in coastal states, where they also proposed guarded bird reserves be established. Chapman knew of four acres of mangrove swamp in Florida with unspoiled rookeries and believed President Theodore Roosevelt, his former hunting buddy, would be sympathetic to his cause. At Chapman's urging, Roosevelt established the first federal bird refuge on Pelican Island by executive order.

Agreements with milliners and the establishment of the Pelican Island refuge confirmed William Dutcher's intuition that state Audubon Societies might achieve much if they unified and operated on a national level—perhaps even an international one, since birds traversed the globe.

Albert Willcox, another rich insurance executive who loved wildlife, moved the protective organization that Dutcher envisioned closer to realization. Elderly and ailing, Willcox promised to leave at least $100,000 to the thirty-seven independent Audubon Societies if they merged into a single dues-paying organization dedicated to the protection of the nation's wildlife. Willcox's terms also stated that prominent men and women must hold leadership positions in the new organization, and that it must hire a "paid secretary, or financial agent" to solicit additional memberships and contributions.[16]

With Willcox's financial backing secured in January 1905, Dutcher, Chapman, and Palmer, along with key state Audubon Society leaders, met at the American Museum of Natural History to establish the NAAS for the

Protection of Wild Birds and Animals. Dutcher was named president. As Willcox had stipulated, the new society's governance was composed of peerless individuals, the most energetic and knowledgeable bird experts of the day, among them, *Forest and Stream* editor George Bird Grinnell; American Museum of Natural History bird curator Frank Chapman; Bureau of Biological Survey assistant chief Theodore Palmer; and Connecticut bird author Mabel Osgood Wright, all of whom also belonged to the AOU.

The new NAAS assured Willcox that it would tend to the welfare of beneficial wild animals as well as that of game and nongame birds.[17] As a final step, Willcox interviewed the financial agent whom Chapman and Dutcher wished the association to employ: a thirty-two-year-old ornithologist from North Carolina named Thomas Gilbert Pearson. Chapman had hired Pearson during his former hunting days to locate birds he wanted to collect. Willcox, in failing health, interviewed Pearson and was impressed by how deeply the young man felt about the nation's "two great evils": the destruction of birds and game animals, and "the abuses heaped upon the Negroes of the Southern states." Pearson, a Southerner known for his shrewd diplomacy, acknowledged later that he "did not talk much about the second point, but had something to say about bird and game protection." In addition to Pearson's vast knowledge of bird science, he was a standout candidate for the job of NAAS financial agent because of the unusual success he had enjoyed in raising money for bird protection in his home state of North Carolina.[18]

While still in school, Gilbert Pearson had summed up the NAAS founders' common cause in a speech: "O fashion, O women of America, how many crimes are committed in your name!"[19] At its root NAAS was far more closely linked to the need to curtail women's vanity than men's. The association—or the society, as it would ultimately be referred to—built its protection mission largely on its agreements with the milliners and the informed fickleness of women. Once women were educated, they stopped making fashion statements that encouraged species extinction.

To be fair, American women's styles had not resulted in any species' utter eradication, as men's excessive hunting had in several instances. Those who loved birds most continued to kill them the most; seeking their deaths was a form of respect if the creatures provided food, advanced science, or graced hobbyists' homes. Some birds were loved to death, while others, such as birds of prey, were hated to death. The constituencies of the bird lovers and haters came together in the NAAS's mission.

Despite the NAAS's protective mission, the culture of bird killing was embedded in its marrow, whether for the illustrative purposes of the nation's greatest bird artist, or for collection by the most expert naturalists and ornithologists, or for the pastime of America's best sportsmen. The three organizations that embodied these interests—the AOU, the American Museum of Natural History, and the Bureau of Biological Survey—flowed seamlessly into the NAAS. Their powerful union must have pleased Willcox. When he died in 1906, he left the Audubon Association triple the amount he had promised.

T. GILBERT PEARSON's bird love had presented itself in the usual way, with much youthful shooting and preserving of the wild specimens he killed in the woods and fields surrounding his family home. The Pearsons were hardworking farmers who scratched their living out of the earth near Archer, Florida. Thirteen-year-old Gilbert proudly killed his first bird and took his prize to bed with him. This grackle "proved to be covered with parasites which promptly swarmed over the bed filling me with discomfort and my mother with dismay," he later recalled.[20]

At eighteen Pearson joined the AOU, and by nineteen he was recognized as an ornithological prodigy. He was most content when he was outdoors alone. He collected eggs from bird nests and traded eggs for a copy of Elliott Coues's *Key to North American Birds*. "To build an egg collection Pearson needed calipers for measuring eggs, drills for making holes in them, and blowpipes for expelling the contents. Hooks and scissors were used for extracting embryos; the insides of the shells were washed with syringes. When the shells had dried, holes were patched with tissue paper, which could be bought already gummed. Cracks were mended with cement."[21]

To attend Guilford College, Pearson traded his collection of one thousand eggs from more than two hundred species to the school's museum in exchange for tuition. After earning a second bachelor's degree from the University of North Carolina in 1899, he not only taught about birds but also lobbied the state legislature for their preservation. In the rural South, where concern for wildlife was not expected to be as progressive as it was in the Northeast, Pearson demonstrated an uncanny knack for raising both funds and awareness. In his first year as head of the North Carolina Audubon Society, the country fellow attracted twelve hundred new members and raised an astounding seven thousand dollars.

The success of North Carolina's Audubon Society was, according to Dutcher, "an object lesson of the greatest force to other societies who complain[ed] about the difficulty in securing funds for their work."[22] Indeed, after Pearson was hired as NAAS financial agent, he was surprised to learn how naive the gentlemen from the rich and sophisticated Northeast were when it came to asking for money.

Pearson was clean-cut and courtly, his hair precision-parted in the middle, pasted down, and slicked back on either side. He orated masterfully, combining the sincerity of a southern preacher with the enthusiasm of a chamber of commerce booster. He respected the opinions of both poor farmers and rich hunters; to secure passage of the AOU model law in North Carolina, for example, he agreed that shooting of all hawks and owls should continue. When Pearson accepted the NAAS position, he had certain reservations about its bird protection philosophy, which by its species-inclusiveness "indicated the presence of extremists in the field."[23]

For the next five years, William Dutcher and Gilbert Pearson worked together to build a national bird-protection organization that would own guarded sanctuaries, produce educational materials for school children, develop enough state and federal political clout to influence legislation for bird protection, and nurture close working ties with game agencies. Pearson, the consummate fund-raiser, quickly attracted the kind of financial support this far-reaching agenda required. "One of the most pleasant sounds I ever hear is the clink of a life membership fee as it drops into the money box," he once remarked.[24]

Yet while Pearson handily adapted his methods to suit the well-heeled NAAS members, he was not comfortable among them. With his wife and children remaining in North Carolina during his first year in New York, Pearson was perhaps lonesome. After leaving the Audubon office each day, he went back to his hotel room and worked into the night. His dedication to his NAAS work and to the men who had hired him spilled into his private life. Though he did not socialize much with his wealthy employers, he named his two sons William and Theodore, in gratitude to Audubon Society founders Dutcher and Palmer.[25]

Despite Dutcher's and Pearson's professional closeness, ideological fractures between them began to show. As early as 1906, Dutcher was concerned when Pearson did not oppose the use of automatic and "pump" guns or protest their high kill ratio. Pearson explained that it did not matter what sort of gun a hunter used as long as state game laws were in place.[26] Meanwhile, Dutcher was becoming increasingly vocal in his opposition to hunting and collecting, and hunters and professional ornithologists within NAAS began to regard him as too radical. At one meeting with Connecticut hunters, Pearson acknowledged this concern, which he had initially shared, and reported that his audience "frankly stated that heretofore they regarded the Audubon Society as a company of long-haired fanatics."[27]

Although Pearson himself no longer hunted or collected, he never lost his respect or friendship for those who did, and he feared that the existence of a small antihunting faction within the Audubon Society would erode the key financial support he had built. Militant sentimentalists, as Pearson and others referred to hunting opponents, could never be counted on as an important source of money for wildlife protection; physical possession of birds in one form or another was the prerequisite for buy in.

In 1910 a stroke left Dutcher unable to speak or write, and he remained paralyzed until his death ten years later. As Pearson assumed Dutcher's organizational responsibilities but not his philosophy, the gifted southern oologist's troubles began.

IN MAY 1911, William Dutcher was too incapacitated to curb Pearson's zeal for a new funding arrangement. Harry Leonard, vice president of the Winchester Repeating Arms Company, stopped by Pearson's Audubon office to discuss organizing a new game-protection association that Winchester would handsomely fund. Since Winchester's profits were derived from the sale of guns and ammunition, the company's interest in perpetuating certain wildlife populations was obvious; "as the game declines, our business grows less," was how Leonard put it to Pearson.[28]

Pearson quickly embraced Leonard's idea and carried it further by noting that since other gun makers would also benefit, the major ones should be asked for their financial support as well. All participants could then split the $125,000 that Pearson estimated would be needed to run the new organization during its first five years. Leonard liked the idea and by the end of the day had gotten enough endorsements to create a new group with Pearson as its head. "As we told you, we have looked the situation over thoroughly and decided for ourselves at least, that you were the one who could best handle an organization of this kind and make it productive of results," Leonard wrote.[29]

Pearson agreed to take the job and remain head of the Audubon Society as well if the gun makers would donate the $125,000 directly to NAAS. Under such an arrangement, it seemed fair to Pearson that the Audubon Society should double his pay so that he could receive an "adequate salary, this to be not less than $6,000 a year" using a portion of the gun makers' $125,000 contribution each year to fund the difference.[30] Leonard promised that if Pearson decided not to take on the additional responsibilities, the gun makers would still contribute $25,000 a year to the society.

Pearson may have felt further justification for accepting the gun makers' offer by recalling Willcox's requirement that the NAAS protect game mammals as well as song and insectivorous birds, and that it seek additional donors for its mission. To Pearson, a man living apart from his family and suffering from the pangs of financial inadequacy compared to those around him, the gun makers' offer was too tempting to reject. The additional income would at last enable him to bring his family to live with him in New York.

But Pearson's annual salary of $3,000 was already a substantial one compared to the nation's top professional conservationists. Gifford Pinchot, the chief of the United States Forest Service, drew $3,500 a year; Bureau of Biological Survey chief C. Hart Merriam made $2,750; and individual national forest supervisors were paid $2,500. As financially savvy as Pearson was, he "appears not to have anticipated hostile reactions to the proposal."[31]

Or perhaps he intuitively understood the sentiments of the NAAS board and expected little opposition to Leonard's proposal. On this point he would have been right, for there was not any—at first. All but two NAAS board members voted in favor of the alliance with Leonard's gun group. One of the dissenters presented the situation in a different light. "Just think what a row these subscribers would kick up," he said.[32]

George Bird Grinnell had been the other member to oppose the proposal but changed his mind and persuaded the remaining "no" voter to vote "yes." At that June meeting, the NAAS board of directors, along with Gilbert Pearson, who also voted, approved the gun makers' offer. The board decided not to announce the new partnership until the absent board members had a chance to sign a written statement showing unanimous support.

But that night someone leaked the Audubon Society vote to two outsiders, Andrew D. Meloy, president of the New York Fish, Game and Forest League, and G. O. Shields, an outdoor magazine publisher and president of a game-law enforcement organization. Meloy and Shields called a *New York Times* reporter with their scoop. The story, claiming that the gun makers' money was a payoff to buy the NAAS's silence in upcoming hearings about hunting regulations, ran the next morning. A similarly damning variation of the story appeared in the *New York Herald*.

"Winchester Arms Co. has for some time been endeavoring to get control

of the National Association of Audubon Societies," charged the antihunting zealot William Temple Hornaday in the *Herald*'s version.[33] Hornaday,
founding director of the New York Zoological Park in the Bronx, claimed
the gun makers had offered him ten thousand dollars to drop his opposition
to automatic guns. But Hornaday refused to cooperate. In his opposition to
Pearson's ambivalence on this issue, he blew the whistle shrilly.

William Temple Hornaday, like Frank Chapman, Gilbert Pearson, and
many other men in the wildlife conservation movement, had undergone
a dramatic transformation from game hog to game guardian. Unlike his
peers, however, Hornaday could not stand those who continued to behave
as he once had. By his own admission he had been among the most blood-
thirsty of trophy hunters, praising that glorious day in Southeast Asia when
he shot seven orangutans and would happily have given up a box at the
opera for the pure pleasure of dismembering them.[34]

Hornaday's voraciousness provided the Smithsonian Institution with
many of the birds and animals displayed in its realistic dioramas. In the
1880s while shooting bison in eastern Montana on a Smithsonian assignment, Hornaday and his party killed twenty-five animals when the museum needed only six. It had been a small herd to begin with, and the last
that roamed free in that region. From that day the need to protect wildlife
weighed on Hornaday's conscience.

By the turn of the twentieth century, when free-ranging bison had
dwindled to one thousand including twenty-two animals in Yellowstone
National Park, Hornaday atoned by forming the American Bison Society
to regenerate wild herds by mating captive pairs at the Bronx Zoo. The
twenty-two thousand bison that were born in Hornaday's captive breeding
program were reintroduced into their once vast habitat. Then, having accomplished its mission, the Bison Society disbanded in 1933.

Hornaday also participated in other landmark species rescues. He saved
fur-bearing seals in the Pribilof Islands and worked in close partnership
with T. Gilbert Pearson to halt the use of wild plumage by milliners. Despite this alliance, however, Hornaday nursed suspicions about where NAAS
loyalties lay, and Pearson's acceptance of the $125,000 contribution from
hunting interests confirmed they lay with his former friends.

Hornaday's published allegations were only the first wave of criticism
hurled at the Audubon Society. His opinions were predictably intemperate
and therefore easy to dismiss. The sharp censure of Chief Forester Gifford
Pinchot, a conservationist second only to Theodore Roosevelt, however,

was more problematic for the NAAS board. Pinchot was so disturbed by the society's deal with gun makers that he threatened to resign his NAAS advisory position unless the board rescinded its approval.

"It is not the active dictation of the contributor that is to be feared, but the quiet shaping of actions and policies which follows from the fears that the contribution may perhaps be discontinued," Pinchot wrote.[35] After a letter that Catherine Dutcher sent to Pearson on behalf of her incapacitated husband, William, was made public, the exposé became a highly personal one.

My Dear Mr. Pearson:

Mr. Dutcher wishes me to write to you regarding your acceptance of this $125,000 gift from the manufacturers of guns and ammunition. I can not, of course, say what he wishes me to say, but I do know that if he could speak he would plainly give you to understand how he does not at all approve of what you have done and so taken advantage of his helplessness. I am greatly disappointed in your friendship for Mr. Dutcher and now look upon you as one of his greatest enemies, inasmuch as you have taken the opportunity of doing him the greatest injury.[36]

Then G. O. Shields stirred things up further in another letter to the *Times*:

If the gun and ammunition people are so anxious to preserve wildlife, why not cut down on the output of cartridges? Why not advance the price on those they do sell, and on their guns, to such an extent as to put them out of reach of the hordes of men and boys who have no regard for decency, or the rights of other human beings, and who slaughter everything that flies when they go out with guns? Why turn out all these deadly guns and all this vast quantity of deadly ammunition for the destruction of birds and then subscribe to a bird protection fund? It looks fishy.[37]

The *Philadelphia Inquirer* was more sanguine and suggested, "The members of the Audubon Society should restrain their indignation, hold their peace, and proceed to make good use of the money which is tendered them."[38]

The public firestorm did not die, however, and persuaded Pearson and the Audubon Society board to reject Harry Leonard's offer. Their refusal of so much money only added to NAAS notoriety. "The idea that any board of directors should fail to accept a gift of $125,000 was such an unusual news item," Pearson wrote.[39] Commendations of the NAAS's principled act poured in.

Chief Forester Pinchot accepted Pearson back into his good graces; Mrs. Dutcher invited the Audubon executive to dinner to patch things up. Even the vituperative Hornaday seemed to have forgiven Pearson, praising him in his 1913 book, *Our Vanishing Wildlife*. Pearson's credibility seemed restored, and his leadership in wildlife protection led to the first international treaty for the protection of migratory birds, laws banning spring hunting, and the sale of wild game to commercial markets. Gilbert Pearson was instrumental in the establishment of the federal wildlife refuge system that was beginning to take shape as well. To achieve all these goals Pearson had worked closely with John B. Burnham, the man chosen in his place to head the American Game Protective Association, the organization founded by the gun makers after the NAAS rejected their largesse.

While the NAAS board vote was making headlines in New York newspapers, Rosalie Edge was not yet watching birds through the binoculars Charlie had given her. She had trained them on the Emerald Buddha in Bangkok and at such a remove knew nothing of the nascent NAAS. Who, then, besides hunters and avocational collectors were the society's members? There was a binoculars-wielding, sentimental variety attracted to the society, but as Pearson had pointed out, they were too insignificant in number and financially unremarkable to count on for much.

IN THE RELATIONSHIP between rapacious humans and endangered wildlife, it could be said of Gilbert Pearson what was biblically said of Noah: that compared to others of his generation he was a most righteous man; perhaps not even Noah included all breeding pairs on the ark. Thanks to Pearson many species of birds were preserved, and public awareness of the need to protect wildlife grew. Pearson must receive the credit due him, particularly in light of his contemporary Paul J. Rainey, the profligate son of a strict Presbyterian coal tycoon. Young Rainey inherited a smaller share of his father's $40 million fortune than his siblings did, as a paternal judgment against his life of moral dissipation.[40]

Paul still had millions with which to squire around beautiful women, go on African safaris, and acquire vast tracts of private hunting grounds. The rich playboy big-game hunter decorated his lodges with the skins and heads of exotic animals he had shot on all continents. After an Arctic expedition, Rainey returned with a live polar bear he had captured, and newspapers reported how he pulled it on a rope into its cage at the Bronx Zoo. His published account of Silver King, as he named the bear, was titled "Bagging

Arctic Monsters with Rope, Gun and Camera," all three of which he expertly wielded.[41]

Rainey also coursed the East African plains at breakneck speed on horseback with a pack of dogs he had bred to track lions. The combination proved so lethal that he boasted he once shot nine lions in thirty-five minutes. British game officials tried to limit his kills for fear there would be no lions left for anyone else to shoot. Rainey was so accomplished with a movie camera that in 1914 he made a silent film called *Rainey's African Hunt* in which he showcased both his daring and his filming capabilities. His exploits were reported in the newspapers under the broad heading of human interest, and Rosalie Edge was one of thousands who read about them.

In September 1923, Paul Rainey sailed from England to South Africa with his sister, Grace Rainey Rogers, for yet another big hunting expedition. One night aboard the ship, Rainey was reportedly offended by a dark man dancing with a white woman and demanded they stop. Legend has it that as the dark man left the dance floor, he was heard to whisper the curse that Rainey would not live to see the sun go down on his next birthday. Rainey died the next day and was buried at sea. It was his forty-sixth birthday.

One of the landholdings in Paul Rainey's estate was twenty-six thousand acres of coastal marsh in Louisiana, which his sister, Grace, inherited. In 1923 Paul and another wealthy young adventurer, Tabasco Sauce tycoon Edward Avery McIlhenny, who owned the adjacent pepper plantation, had been planning to turn the area into a private reserve for wealthy duck hunters they called the Vermilion Bay Hunt Club. It was expected to be a "monstrous club of 4,000 members to occupy some 80,000 acres of swamp lands" in the vicinity of three established bird sanctuaries.[42] The hunting club's location near the bird refuges increased the number of ducks that could be shot while flying to or from these feeding and resting places.

A club prospectus reached William Hornaday and NAAS member Henry W. de Forest, lawyer and executor for the adjacent sanctuaries. Both men were shocked to read Gilbert Pearson, "President of the National Association of Audubon Societies, Member Advisory Board, United States Biological Survey," listed as a member of the Vermilion's advisory committee. Hornaday brought the matter up with NAAS board president Theodore Palmer in August and demanded that Pearson withdraw from the proposed hunt club. Henry de Forest also vehemently opposed any NAAS involvement in it and interrogated Ed McIlhenny about Pearson's role. McIlhenny insisted that Pearson had indeed been a key player. De Forest demanded that Pearson clearly state once and for all whether he was more interested in hunting or in bird conservation.[43]

For three months Pearson's responses to the question of whether he had lent his name to the proposed Louisiana duck-hunting club resounded with obfuscation and ambiguity. He had been in Europe; the club did not have the NAAS board's approval because the board had not formally met to discuss it; in one tortuous sentence he explained that he had not replied one way or the other when McIlhenny asked him to participate.[44] None of these were the answers expected of someone who had absolutely refused to have anything to do with a shooting club's placement adjacent to a sanctuary.

Regardless of Pearson's genuine preferences, he again dodged a hail of bullets with remarkable aplomb. After learning that Rainey's Louisiana Gulf holding was home to more than 120 species of birds, Pearson persuaded Grace Rainey Rogers to deed her late brother's portion of the land to the NAAS. He promised that the society would establish a sanctuary for birds and wildlife and name it for Paul J. Rainey. After Grace Rainey agreed, Pearson asked her to fund an endowment for the sanctuary's perpetual maintenance. The terms of her gift to the NAAS stated that

> by "Sanctuary for Wildlife" is meant a place of refuge wherein the killing,
> trapping or destruction by any means of wild birds and wild mammals,
> shall not be permitted; provided, however, that if any form of such life, bird
> or otherwise, shall at any time be found by the said donee to be obnoxious
> and injurious and detrimental to other forms of animal life, whether bird
> or otherwise (and the donee's decision on this question shall be final and
> conclusive) the said donee shall have the right to grant hunting or trapping
> privileges or otherwise provide for the destruction of the aforesaid animal
> life. Any income derived from any such grant of hunting or trapping rights
> shall be applied exclusively for the benefit of said sanctuary.[45]

BY 1920 MORE than 4 million hunting licenses had been issued in the United States—up from 1.5 million licenses a decade earlier. The increase was attributed to postwar prosperity, a shorter work week, and the automobile. Cars enabled more hunters to head farther into the backcountry. As thousands of hunters went where few had gone before, the water fowl population in particular declined. But excessive hunting was not the only pressure on the birds' reproduction rates. After World War I, the economic boom dictated that thousands of square miles of swamplands that waterfowl depended on were drained. New towns sprawled over them as for the first time millions of Americans could afford homeownership.

Pearson—and the late Paul J. Rainey, for that matter—were the great rescuers of wildlife, heroes of the conservation movement. The movement in that postwar decade, however, was narrowly defined by the need to give hunters what they wanted—refuges where popular game birds could breed. The American Game Protective Association and other prohunting organizations argued that public shooting grounds and sanctuaries ought to be one and the same, or at least be in close proximity to each other.

Opponents to this idea wanted the shooting grounds located at a respectable distance from refuges, so that at first light the birds would not fly into bullet barrages. The federal system of refuges for which they argued incorporated the notion of "inviolability" so that hunting would be prohibited. Both sides agreed that the new system would be funded by the sale of duck stamps drawn by wildlife artists.

The fight between those who wanted to make refuges into public shooting grounds and those who wanted to prohibit all refuge hunting dragged on ten years. In conservation it was a bitter decade dominated by the ire of sportsmen and sentimentalists. The NAAS, the nation's largest, wealthiest, and most influential defender of birds, was again dodgy about which side of this argument it was on. An article in *Bird-Lore*, for example, failed to inform NAAS readers that the public shooting-grounds concept was winning strong support in Congress.[46]

Pearson's pronouncements on bag limits asserted that without free public shooting grounds "only the rich" could afford to hunt.[47] Although this was a justifiable concern, was it the one that should most trouble the NAAS? Indeed, the NAAS position was so similar to that of the American Game Protective Association that John Burnham quoted Pearson in his speeches. Pearson, according to his friend Burnham, had warned of the "mighty precarious situation" gun makers faced from "the landowners, women, and the sentimentalists" who showed an interest in birds. If this body continued to grow, summed up Burnham, "free shooting was doomed."[48]

In 1926 the NAAS published an educational bulletin called *Federal Power and Duck Bag Limits: Facts*. Bulletin no. 6, as it would become known, sought to spell out Pearson's stand on hunting controls. One need read no further than its cover to ascertain that the NAAS would not be elaborating on the harm done by overhunting. Instead Bulletin no. 6 declared that "the fundamental dangers that threaten our ducks are irresponsible criticism of governmental administration of wild fowl and attempts to curtail the powers of the government and to cripple its administrative capacity."[49]

The governmental administration to which Pearson alluded was none other than the Bureau of Biological Survey, which oversaw hunting regulations and was the agency that employed NAAS board member and cofounder Theodore Palmer. Bulletin no. 6 further stated that ducks were prolific, and the bag limit that stood at twenty-five birds a day was sustainable. Indeed, wild fowl numbers had increased so much in the previous thirteen years "as to astonish the country."[50]

There was, it claimed, "no present necessity . . . to further restrict the killing. . . . Decrease what sportsmen believe necessary and reasonable, and disregard of game laws will be general," Bulletin no. 6 warned. The right number of birds each hunter would be permitted to take ought to be left to individual "sportsmanship, taste, conduct." Pearson revealed his particular southern bias by claiming that the Bureau of Biological Survey's "only responsibility [was] to maintain a surplus of ducks and, so far as consistent, states' rights." He asserted, "This surplus must be delivered to the people. It can not issue regulations governing the ethical use of it. We would rebel against such a misuse of federal power. Each sportsman may decide this for himself. A majority in any state may, if they think it wise, attempt state regulation in this ethical field. The federal government, never."[51]

Bulletin no. 6's message, bolstered by full NAAS board support and Audubon staff visits to legislators in Washington, was apparently so effective that it was said to have put an end to congressional attempts to reduce bag limits.

In his speeches during that decade, Gilbert Pearson sounded jaded, a man who had rationalized away all the challenges civilization posed to wildlife. "When man cuts down a forest or drains a marsh, it does not necessarily follow that the resultant changes reduce the number of birds of the region," he told the National Conference of Outdoor Recreation in 1924. "Many species of birds thus profit by man's inroads on the wilderness," he argued. "A few others, for example the Ivory-billed Woodpecker, shrink from civilization and from causes difficult to determine, pass away." Meanwhile forests that were cleared for farmlands "provide congenial homes for the Quail."[52] This species, Pearson did not need to point out to this audience, was classified as a game bird, while the ivory-billed woodpecker was not. In 1927 Pearson, a thirty-year veteran of bird conservation, reflected cynically on his professional purpose: "How many people really care whether pelicans or herons or ducks live on? After all, why bother about such things? Speeding over miles of paved highways and drinking beer under shady arbors is so much more important anyway."[53]

After a decade of demoralizing disputes over bag limits, automatic weapons, public shooting grounds, and inviolate refuges, the Migratory Bird Conservation Act was finally passed in February 1929. Washington State senator Clarence Dill, who added an inviolability clause to federal refuge management, condemned the NAAS's part in getting the legislation passed: "The Bill that the Audubon Societies and affiliated organizations tried to cause Congress to pass would have made out of the refuges parks to be used for the slaughter of birds. I say this because I do not want any one to get the impression that the real migratory bird legislation that has passed Congress was due to the efforts of the Audubon Societies or those affiliated with them."[54]

After the bitter complaints about the NAAS's ambivalence toward refuges as public shooting grounds, however, it was the association's years of silence on the Alaskan bald eagle bounty that finally provoked Waldron DeWitt Miller, Willard Gibbs Van Name, and Davis Quinn to write the *Crisis in Conservation* pamphlet. Pearson's cynicism and his belief in states' rights were two possible explanations for the NAAS's refusal to oppose the Alaskan territorial government's bounty, in place since 1917.

But there was yet another explanation. It seemed that the Audubon president personally hated eagles and other birds of prey, an attitude ingrained in him as the son of farmers. Eagles had always posed a problem to the NAAS, as even the great John James Audubon had spoken ill of the bird: "For my part, I wish the Bald Eagle had not been chosen as the representative of our country. He is a bird of bad moral character, and does not make his living honestly."[55]

In one Audubon pamphlet meant to educate the public, Pearson quoted Benjamin Franklin's opinion that "the eagle is never a good case. But like those among men who live by sharping and robbing, he is generally poor." To strengthen the case against this race of bird, Pearson recalled the time he saw a bald eagle carry off a lamb. "It did not once pause and flutter its wings, as birds-of-prey sometimes do, in order to get a better hold of its burden, for it seemed to have seized the lamb securely when it first made its downward plunge." He watched the bird fly more than half a mile with its prey; he knew another ornithologist who claimed he had seen an eagle carry a lamb weighing more than itself for five miles over open water. Such presumably expert reports did nothing to convince the American public that the Alaskan eagle bounty ought to be halted.[56]

WHEN ROSALIE and the children returned to New York at the end of the summer of 1929, Peter and Margaret went back to school, and she resumed her morning walks in Central Park. She asked other birders if they had read the *Crisis* pamphlet or knew its authors. She was told that Waldron DeWitt Miller had died just a few weeks before when his motorcycle crashed into a bus.[57] Of the remaining two pamphleteers, she was advised that Willard Van Name, an invertebrate zoologist at the American Museum of Natural History, would be her best contact.

But since the pamphlet had appeared, Van Name had also been silenced, although not as dramatically as Miller had been. The American Museum of Natural History demanded that Van Name sign a new employment contract in which he agreed not to put his name on anything but articles about "ascidians and isopods" without the museum's prior approval.[58] Museum director George H. Sherwood distanced himself from the *Crisis in Conservation* message by denouncing it in an official statement: "The Museum not only does not approve of this pamphlet but believes that it will convey a wholly false impression of the existing state of affairs in the conservation of bird-life, and by discrediting the efforts of organizations whose records of achievement are unquestioned and worthy of all support, this pamphlet may do much harm."[59]

Sherwood's denunciation, however, best illustrated what the authors meant about the ambivalence entrenched among wildlife conservationists. "It is inevitable that some species of birds must vanish as the advance of increasing population demands for their haunts," Sherwood had further written.[60]

For years Willard Van Name had been complaining about the torpor that had immobilized the conservation movement. Van Name was judged to be an irritable fellow when it came to virtually any conservation question, so the *Crisis* pamphlet was only the latest and crankiest example of his tedious criticism. Van Name griped about his colleagues' indifference toward the extinction of the wild species they studied. He argued that scientists should do more than observe, measure, and record the various species as they declined and passed out of existence. When the preponderance of evidence pointed to humankind's role in a species' extinction, Van Name thought scientists ought to try to stop it.

But at fifty-seven, Willard Gibbs Van Name had made no progress in convincing the scientific community to rectify its pursuit of pure objectivity. NAAS board member George Bird Grinnell advised his colleagues to answer any of Van Name's diatribes with silence. It was best to leave the difficult man "severely alone," and the *Crisis* pamphlet was to be ignored as well.[61]

Yet something drew Rosalie Edge to Van Name's irascible brilliance as soon as she met him. As they talked, they walked in Central Park. She noticed that Van Name did not depend on binoculars for identification, but like her former mentor Ludlow Griscom, knew birds instantly by their call or momentary flash of pattern. "To Dr. Van Name I owe more than to anyone else my knowledge of birds, such as it is," Edge wrote years later. "He was a wonderful teacher, and took a little pride in his pupil, though a great deal of conscientious scolding accompanied the instruction."[62]

Willard Van Name replaced Ludlow Griscom as her mentor. Although they initially set out to watch birds, Rosalie discovered that of all nature's life forms, Van Name loved trees most. "Dr. Van Name's spirit rose in the presence of virgin forests," she wrote much later, perhaps not realizing quite yet that her own did as well, ever since the tree visitations with Grandmother Frances.[63]

But as a scientist Van Name understood before Edge did "that the world would need these forests as laboratories, if forestry were to be something better than the swinging of axes."[64] Much of what Van Name had written before she met him concerned the need to preserve virgin forests and stave off timber raids on the national parks. As usual, his warnings fell on deaf ears.

Edge marveled at what a consummate pessimist Van Name was about humanity and considered his unswerving commitment to wild creatures a "penance, or let us say a compensation, for his distrust of mankind."[65] He had what seemed an effeminate manner; he had never married and was described as a monastic bachelor in certain circles, which at the time was a veiled reference to his homosexuality. Van Name's sexual preference may have been why conventional scientists and manly sportsmen distrusted him and explains Grinnell's stern admonition to leave the scientist not merely alone but severely so. Rosalie Edge was one of the few who could appreciate the misanthropic Van Name's "sweet and gentle streak" during their tramps through woods and meadows. She was pleased that the scientist enjoyed her company, at least as much as it was possible for him to enjoy anybody's.[66]

WILLARD VAN NAME was, like Rosalie Barrow Edge, descended from a family that prized erudition.[67] In 1872 he was born in the house his grandfather Josiah Willard Gibbs had built near Yale University's campus. Josiah Gibbs was a scholar of biblical languages—as Rosalie's father, John Wylie Barrow, had been—and a language professor at Yale, which had bestowed an honorary degree on Barrow.

Another similarity between them was that Willard's father, Addison, was Yale's head librarian for forty years and had expanded the school's collection from 45,000 volumes to 500,000. In 1867 Addison Van Name married Julia Gibbs, the sister of his friend J. Willard Gibbs, a brilliant mathematical physicist and winner of the Copley, the highest prize in mathematics. Young Willard loved to join his Uncle Willard on walks through the rural countryside outside New Haven, "a most beautiful city" rimmed by "farms, woods, picturesque hills and winding often beautifully shaded country roads." No mention was made of the uncle and nephew going out to shoot, though they would have been the rare pair of appreciators had they not been armed and killed something to study or eat now and then.[68]

After Van Name received his doctorate in 1898, he went to work for the American Museum of Natural History as a curator of lower invertebrates. With no family of his own to support, much of his modest museum paycheck went to wildlife preservation causes, and he paid for the publication and mailing of the *Crisis* pamphlet.

On their walks, Van Name imparted much more than his bird knowledge to Edge. He also passed along his caustic views of bird protection societies. Although Rosalie had never attended an NAAS gathering, the opportunity to do so was coming up. The society's annual meeting was to be held on Tuesday, October 29. She decided she would attend and see if Van Name's descriptions of the organization were at all accurate.

THE WEEKEND BEFORE the Audubon meeting, the lights burned all night on Wall Street. Brokers, bankers, and clerks struggled to execute the deluge of sell orders at the New York Stock Exchange, and margin calls mounted every minute. Anxious crowds gathered outside. When the stock market opened on Monday, October 28, losses were staggering, but it was not until the gong sounded Tuesday morning that the stampede to sell swept the exchange and the street. The Great Crash of 1929 commenced.

That Tuesday morning as she headed to the Audubon annual meeting, Rosalie Edge was perhaps not yet aware of the chaos on Wall Street and how it might affect Charles's fortune and her own welfare. The fate of wild birds, not stock market doom, was much more palpable to her. A few miles away from the Wall Street frenzy, the scene she entered could not have been more different. In one of the tranquil chambers of the American Museum of Natural History, the twenty-fifth annual meeting of the NAAS was getting under way. Coincidentally the meeting must have started just as the stock exchange began its historic plunge, so news of it had no time to penetrate this calm, quiet sanctum.

Rosalie had birded across the familiar, beloved terrain of Central Park toward the museum. In the bird diary she now kept with greater regularity, she noted that she saw a robin, a starling, a grackle, a "hermit creeper," a junco, a fox sparrow, a white-throated sparrow, and a Savannah sparrow along the way. "Happy and relaxed" was how she described her mood, as, binoculars still in hand, she entered the small room where the Audubon meeting had begun. She was politely motioned to take a seat near the front. Outside a hermit thrush sat on the window ledge. Writing of that day more than twenty years later, Edge, perhaps for dramatic effect, recalled that her "entrance made a stir," because no newcomer was expected.[69]

Most of the others who were either presiding or sitting in the audience were people whose names she knew from Van Name's debriefing. A who's who of the bird world's supreme leadership was present: Gilbert Pearson, NAAS president; Theodore Palmer, assistant head of the Bureau of Biological Survey; Frank Chapman, American Museum of Natural History bird curator and publisher of *Bird-Lore*. Van Name had probably also mentioned Robert Cushman Murphy, a renowned Arctic naturalist and seabird curator at the museum, and William Wharton, one of Pearson's most dedicated supporters, who had donated $200,000 to the society's endowment fund.

A primly bearded gentleman, otherwise unidentified in Edge's memoir, was speaking when she entered. The speaker—apparently ignorant of what was happening on Wall Street at that instant—emphasized the society's sound financial position. "It was my first experience hearing the Audubon Society praise itself, and it impressed me to know how great and good it was," Edge wrote, looking back years later.[70]

Near the end of his report, the bearded gentleman noted that the Audubon

Association had "dignifiedly stepped aside"—his exact words, according to Edge—from responding to a pamphlet that was beneath referring to by its name or, for that matter, ever again. Edge was witnessing for the first time Big Conservation stuck in all its inertia.[71]

When she was recognized she rose, and in a voice that reminded those who heard it of Eleanor Roosevelt's, posed her first question.[72]

"What answer can a loyal member of the Society make to this pamphlet, 'A Crisis in Conservation'?" she asked. For emphasis she quickly added, "What are the answers?" Silence. A man sitting behind her stood up and "inveighed against the pamphlet, against its author, and against [her] for [her] temerity in asking [her] question." Another man stood and asked if she was a member.[73]

"Yes, a Life Member," Rosalie replied sprightly, perhaps for the first time relieved by her fear-driven generosity before Margaret's birth in 1915. A third man came over to her and whispered that if the Audubon directors responded to the charges in the offensive pamphlet, it would only generate publicity. Dr. William Hornaday might worsen the situation by taking "horrid" advantage of it.[74]

Undeterred, Edge proceeded, rising each time to ask a question, then taking her seat to await its answer "with all the friendliness possible." She feared she stood often. Finally she asked if the NAAS should "stand silent in the face of accusations" that it did little or nothing to save birds facing extinction, though it had ample means. "Was the Society alert in watching legislation? Did it press for the protection of rails, of the yellowlegs, or the Golden Plover? I begged that at least a notice should be inserted in *Bird-Lore*. A mere line would do, stating that all criticisms raised by the pamphlet would be answered in due course."[75]

NAAS president Gilbert Pearson addressed the newcomer. He told her she had spoiled the meeting with all her questions. She had used up the time scheduled to show the new moving picture on birds, and the lunch awaiting them in the museum's Bird Hall was getting cold. Before the meeting adjourned, however, the interloper won a small concession. The board passed a motion in favor of giving the offensive pamphlet its further attention. Rosalie Edge did not stay for lunch.

A FEW DAYS LATER the notorious Dr. William Hornaday called to invite her to dine with him. Hornaday. This was the man whose name had been whispered with such trepidation at the Audubon meeting, although she might also have heard it from Van Name, who considered Hornaday one of his rare allies. Hornaday had undoubtedly learned of Mrs. Charles Noel Edge from Van Name.

When the two met, Hornaday commended Edge for confronting the NAAS board. He also paid her the supreme compliment of treating her, she wrote, "as a fellow man." Despite his adversarial reputation, she found the famous naturalist to be a "kindly, generous, humorous, charming and learned old gentleman" of seventy-five. By the time Edge met him, he was "calm and judgmatical." Edge spent hours with him as his protégé as well as Van Name's. Hornaday added considerably to her knowledge of conservation history, which he of course knew firsthand.[76]

He intimated that Pearson's problems were not all in the past; that, indeed, the NAAS could still not bear close scrutiny. Offering Pearson's $14,000 annual salary as an example, Hornaday speculated that the Audubon president's income was funded by commissions he received on the donations he brought in, a portion of which came from the same hunters and gun makers who had previously tried to sway the NAAS political agenda. The allegation intrigued Edge.[77]

Nine days after the Audubon meeting, Edge followed up with a letter to T. Gilbert Pearson. She asked if there had been any action on the *Crisis* pamphlet, and she peppered him with more questions: What had the society done lately to reduce bag limits on waterfowl? Or to put an end to hawk trapping and the Alaskan bounty on bald eagles? Did it support state laws protecting snowy owls? Was it hiring enough wardens for its fifty-one bird sanctuaries? She concluded with "Awaiting with confidence your early reply, believe me, with every good wish for the Audubon Society, Sincerely Yours, Mrs. Charles Noel Edge."[78]

Pearson's answers to her litany of questions arrived three days later and spelled out the NAAS's hands-off approach to confronting powerful interests when it came to birds of prey. The farming element in most legislatures was too strong and opposed extending any form of protection to the birds, he explained. Snowy owls, which numbered in the millions, preyed on game that hunters also liked and therefore would be impossible to protect. As far as the Alaska eagle bounty was concerned, Pearson noted that public sentiment against the bird was so bitter it was best not to mention eagles to them at all.[79]

On the subject of bag limits in Bulletin no. 6, Pearson stood by his purpose, which was simply to state the facts as he knew them and not attempt to persuade any federal agency to reduce the number of birds hunters should be permitted to kill. Pearson ended by reminding Edge that the NAAS was but one of many organizations interested in the enthralling subject of wildlife conservation and could not be expected to do all that needed to be done. He also defended the Audubon board's desire to ignore the *Crisis* pamphlet because the organization had more constructive business to attend to. Edge was encouraged to read her *Bird-Lore,* or if she dropped by Pearson's office he could tell her which birds were protected in various states.

Rosalie's two preceptors had warned that Pearson's response would be bland and evasive. She was perhaps shocked to discover how bland and evasive, how altogether lacking in the spark of a fighting spirit, and how *compromised* the conservation movement had indeed become.

It was not a movement at all but a still life compared to the suffrage movement, which had displayed so much perseverance before women achieved the right to vote. Edge did not care about the farmers and the sportsmen, and she did not believe the NAAS should care so much about them either. She was committed to the survival of all birds, even Alaskan eagles, as the NAAS should be. Indeed, if the NAAS did not think all species were worth protecting, which of those many large conservation organizations that Pearson referred to would?

With her children nearly grown, too much time on her hands, and a heart not entirely mended, Rosalie Edge was finding a sense of purpose more powerful than any she had known since she campaigned for women's suffrage. She showed Pearson's letter to Van Name and talked about what to do next.

Edge's intelligence and sincerity gave Van Name an idea. "They can prevent me from signing them, but they can not prevent me from writing them," he told her.[80] Would Rosalie be willing to sign her name to the anti-Audubon screeds he wrote?

CHAPTER SIX

A Common Scold

Looking back years later on her entry into conservation, Rosalie Edge wrote of that fateful conversation with Willard Van Name:

> How could I know that this simple suggestion was to change my whole life, to absorb my attention almost daily for the next thirty years, and more, to force me to study in fields that I had never distantly approached? It is so that our lives are changed in one moment. We get up in the morning unable to foresee the immensity of the day's decisions and go to bed at night, our destiny directed in an opposite direction. Some people say that this is done by the hand of God. In my case, it was the hand of Willard Van Name.[1]

Truly, she was giving herself too little credit and Van Name too much. Had she not grown up in close proximity to a scientific library in her father's study that was one of the city's finest? Had not she accompanied her grandmother on visits to favorite trees and joined the Grace Church pastor in botanizing? Had she not loved the natural beauty of Scotland, the Dobšiná ice caves, Japan and Malaysia, trekking through Asian jungles? Had she not learned the names of birds? All of this she had closely approached. Whether she recognized it or not, all of this was preparation.

Partnership details had to be worked out. Anyone who read the criticisms Van Name penned would know that whoever this "Mrs. C. N. Edge" was, she was not the authority on the subjects

that appeared above her signature. She decided she needed a panel of recognized experts or a committee not only to shield the real author but also
to lend credibility to the articles that bore her name, while she protected
other sources of her information. The formation of a committee that would
produce educational pamphlets may have been an idea sparked by her stint
in the NYSWSP press and publicity office, where she had churned facts and
figures into persuasive arguments for women's suffrage.

She perhaps enjoyed the stealth and suggested insurrection this fictitious
"committee" provided. Van Name refused to let her name him as one of her
committee members but agreed to anonymously underwrite all costs for
printing the publications that Edge would edit, publish, and distribute. She
offered her spacious townhouse at East Seventy-second Street as committee
headquarters. Although she was not sure what her role would be, she was
quite clear from the start that she intended to be much more than a "mere
figurehead."[2]

With her NYSWSP Press and Publicity Council experience, Edge knew
how to develop stories from dry facts and enliven statistics—how to get
them to speak to ordinary people. She considered her own ignorance of
wild birds and animals and the dearth of information available to amateurs
like herself.

What was sorely needed was a "clearing-house" of publications with information about the natural world that would educate the silent constituency
whose bird appreciation did not come through the barrel of a gun. There
needed to be an alternative to the leaflets published by the NAAS, which
she dismissed as "inept and childish."[3] Dramatization of an issue was her
strength, and her love of language found a worthwhile release; Van Name
might have been surprised at how quickly she assumed the role not only of
editor but also of author, composing pamphlets in her emphatic style after
close consultation with him. The title Edge chose for one of the first they did
together trumpeted suffragette-style the moral indignation within: *Framing
the Birds of Prey: An Arraignment of the Fanatical and Economically Harmful Campaign of Extermination Being Waged against the Hawks and Owls.*[4]
This pamphlet went to six hundred people on Van Name's *Crisis* pamphlet
mailing list about a month after Edge received Pearson's dull letter.[5] *Framing the Birds of Prey* made no mention of Edge's committee, and for some
reason Van Name's young friend Davis Quinn, who had cosigned the *Crisis*
pamphlet, took credit as the writer.

That winter Van Name was a frequent guest at 113 East Seventy-second

Street. He was more at ease with young people than with his contemporaries, and at one dinner he instructed sixteen-year-old Peter in the precise art of carving the roast duck that the family's cook had prepared.[6] Even Margaret, who was an awkward fourteen, was comfortable enough to ask Van Name for help with her algebra. After dinner the Edges and Van Name retired to the library, where Peter and Margaret did homework. Willard smoked a cigar and fulminated for the rest of the evening against the conservation movement, debunking it one prominent man at a time.

This nightly indoctrination compelled Edge to type "fierce" letters to one or another of the delinquent conservationists that Van Name railed against.[7] Rosalie wistfully recalled these evenings as much perhaps for their cozy simulation of an intact family as for the vestigial committee that was taking shape.

Word of Edge's confrontation with the Audubon board quickly spread through the membership. As a rebuttal, American Museum of Natural History director George Sherwood asked the editor of *Forest and Stream* to reprint his original critique of the *Crisis* pamphlet in the next issue. William Bruette agreed, but only if Sherwood's statement was paired with the opposing viewpoint. Bruette hired a thirty-six-year-old freelance writer named Irving Brant to express it.

Brant's father owned the *Iowa City Republican*, where Irving had begun his newspaper career as a teenager.[8] The Brants lived on a farm and either raised their food or hunted it, much as Gilbert Pearson's family had. Young Irving quit hunting when he shot and killed a seagull, mistaking it for a duck. He soon joined the NAAS, and unlike Rosalie Edge he read *Bird-Lore* avidly.

In 1923 Brant decided to quit his editorial position with the *St. Louis Star* and move his young family to New York City, where he hoped to make a living as a freelance nature writer. He had been "appalled" by Audubon's Bulletin no. 6, but it was as a writer covering the hearings in Washington, D.C., on public shooting grounds that he discovered a greater betrayal by the organization.[9]

During one of the shooting grounds hearings, Gilbert Pearson testified against bag limit reductions and confessed he was not the author of Bulletin no. 6. To write what amounted to the NAAS's pro-hunting position, he had hired the late Charles Sheldon, chairman of a strong hunting consortium called American Wild Fowlers.[10] Brant's disillusionment with the Audubon

Society was still raw when Bruette asked him to write the piece opposing Sherwood's position.

Brant could not have wished for a better assignment, for it gave him the place to flog his concern about "the propriety of the activities of Dr. T. Gilbert Pearson on the most important conservation questions of the decade." Museum director Sherwood's easy capitulation to the notion that species extinction was the inevitable price of population growth was "not an answer that [would] raise hopes in the hearts of those who love[d] wild life or encourage them to further efforts in its defense."[11]

In his piece Brant questioned Sherwood's objectivity, since the NAAS and the American Museum of Natural History were so closely linked: "What appears on the surface to be a defense of the Audubon Society by the American Museum turns out to be a defense of the Audubon Society by the Audubon Society," Brant asserted, noting the museum's strong representation on the Audubon board.[12]

Edge phoned Brant after she read his *Forest and Stream* piece. She offered her Audubon annual meeting experience as a worthy follow-up story, and he agreed. The first time they met he was impressed by Edge's "keen mind, fighting spirit and devotion to conservation." But while Brant was writing Edge's story, *Forest and Stream* was put up for sale. Editor Bruette raised enough money to buy the magazine himself, but mysteriously its price shot up, and a better offer came in from a publication called *Field and Stream*, which was a pro-hunting magazine that spoke for higher bag limits, longer seasons, baiting, and live decoys. Bruette told Brant that he was certain "Audubon put up the money."[13]

Whether or not Bruette's suspicion was correct, the new editors killed Brant's follow-up story. Edge saw this move as part of a conspiracy to squash Audubon's opposition. The loss of *Forest and Stream*'s sympathetic voice strengthened her conviction that conservation needed an independent entity to publish pamphlets that would boldly expose all the "unpleasant facts" she was uncovering. Perhaps Brant would help her.

"Our need is a small committee to sponsor such pamphlets," Edge told him when they next spoke. "Would you like to be a member of such a committee?"[14] Brant was not sure what he could do, since he had been unable to support his family on his freelance writing career and had returned to his full-time newspaper job in St. Louis. She could still consult with him, she said. Having a veteran newsman to call on along with Van Name strengthened her ability to publish unpleasant facts in a way that was certain to grab the public's attention.

In the spring of 1930, Van Name covertly wrote the next pamphlet, *The Bald Eagle, Our National Emblem: Danger of Its Extinction by the Alaska Bounty*, following congressional hearings about whether the eagle ought to receive federal protection. The NAAS was still of the opinion that it should not.[15] Audubon's persistent opposition to bald eagle protection seemed to convince Edge that her committee's clearinghouse mission was an urgent one, and she hit upon an urgent-sounding name for it: the Emergency Conservation Committee (ECC), a name well suited to the times. There were plenty of emergencies during the Depression, and she insisted that the possibility of wildlife extinction be placed on an equal footing with the rest.

The choice of name may also suggest that Edge did not expect the ECC to last very long, since no state of emergency continued forever. The conservation emergency would end when the NAAS recovered its fighting spirit. "Emergency Conservation Committee" was, however, a catchy name for her little committee. On April 5, 1933, President Franklin Roosevelt would sign Executive Order 6101, establishing the similarly named Emergency Conservation Work Administration to employ young men in the restoration of the country's natural resources. Four years later the ECWA officially became the Civilian Conservation Corps.

During its first year, Rosalie Edge, under the auspices of the ECC, edited and distributed three more pamphlets written by Van Name and Brant. As intended, her titles got the attention of people who had never given such arcane matters as federally funded predator poisoning efforts a moment's thought: *The United States Bureau of Biological Survey: Destruction, Not Scientific Investigation and Conservation, Now Its Chief Activity* was one publication frequently requested; elaborating further on her antipoisoning theme, she produced *It's Alive! Kill It!* The ECC again hit its primary target within its first year, with *Compromised Conservation: Can the Audubon Society Explain?* Then *The Antelope's S.O.S.: The Extinction of the Pronghorn Antelope Is a Preventable Misfortune That We Are Neglecting to Prevent*, presumably authored by Van Name, focused public attention on still another issue, for perhaps the first time.

Edge's clearinghouse boomed. Pamphlets "went out, by request, singly, in dozens, by the hundreds, all free," thanks to Van Name's underwriting.[16] Three or four pamphlets lambasting all the Bureau of Biological Survey's predator and pest poisoning efforts remained in great demand. She edited all in the interrogatory style reminiscent of the NYSWSP Press and Publicity Council pamphlets she had written for the suffrage movement:

> Would the public approve or enjoy an attempt to rid the country of criminals and undesirable citizens by poisoning the food in the markets and grocery stores? That is the way the wild life of this country is being treated for reasons that *will not bear investigation.* The Biological Survey's demands for appropriations are based on figures implying that 2,000,000 young cattle, horses, sheep and hogs are killed by wolves, mountain lions, coyotes, etc., in the United States every year, or 5479 a day! DO YOU BELIEVE SUCH ABSURD NONSENSE![17]

She assured one western rancher who wrote her after reading this pamphlet that "the Emergency Conservation Committee [was] very far from denying the unfortunate necessity of controlling various species of animals under certain circumstances and in certain places where they are injurious." But her greatest concern rested with the "hundreds of millions of harmless and useful birds and animals destroyed in the unscrupulous campaigns carried on or encouraged and aided by the bureau."[18] Edge's vehement opposition to indiscriminate poisoning of predators and insect pests was a drumbeat she would keep up publicly and privately for thirty years.

While the upstart ECC was setting off all sorts of public alarms, the NAAS plodded along on bland pronouncements. The differences between the organizations—if the ECC could be called such—were easy to recognize for anyone familiar with both, but Edge described their difference best. "Fighting as scouts ahead of larger, more richly endowed but more cumbersome organizations, the Emergency Conservation Committee is stripped of all unnecessary impedimenta," she wrote.[19] The ECC could be likened to a fleet of well-provisioned first responders dispatched at a moment's notice.

Yet there was only Mrs. Charles Noel Edge shielding the zoologist Willard Van Name so that he would not lose his job, and in time she would offer other scientists the same sort of protection. Fearlessly she steered repudiated ideas about conservation straight into one confrontation after another.

DESPITE HIS stock-market losses, Charles Edge again managed to send his wife and children abroad during the Depression's first summer. They went to Vevey, Switzerland, where Rosalie and Peter spent their days on alpine bird outings. Margaret, who at sixteen preferred the company of dogs, volunteered at the "l'oeil qui voit" and was entrusted with the care of Seeing

Eye dogs that she would bring back to the United States for placement with blind clients.

Vevey was cool and exquisite, the ideal summer retreat for all three Edges. The Swiss mountain town was "seated," as Henry James had once written, "upon the edge of a remarkably blue lake." But James was not the writer who kept Edge in his thrall during those restful weeks; rather it was the French ornithologist Jacques Delamain, author of the lyrical book *Pourquois les Oiseaux Chantent* (*Why Birds Sing*). For an ornithologist, Delamain's sensitivity toward all birds seemed unusual to Edge.[20] Having steeped herself in the science of birds during the previous months, she now delved into their lyricism.

Each day after they had gone bird-watching, Rosalie claimed a chaise in the hotel garden and settled into her book, keeping at hand a French dictionary to translate the words she didn't understand. Bird song, according to Delamain, expressed human emotion emanating from the spirit of the flock: "The solidarity of hard times has united the birds, by species. Together they have flown to the feeding-territory, slept in the low brush-wood, or in the thick pine tree tops. The first ray of sunshine in the cold morning brings forth joyous notes from their throats: the sensation of well-being, of wings still moist from the bath spread out to the light; the joy of being together, of having the same plumage, the same life and the same soul."[21]

For Delamain during the Great War, as much as for Elliot Coues during the American Civil War, the eerie silence between deadly engagements afforded splendid bird-watching opportunities. In the trenches of Flanders, Soissonais, and Champagne, Delamain soothed the ravaged nerves of his comrades by peering through his army-issue field glasses and pointing out flocks headed for the peace of a distant continent, perhaps America. From his narrow slot in the ground, he was content to watch birds in "a little wood of pines . . . a branch, a strip of sky and a few vineyards."[22]

Rosalie admired Delamain's ability to find nature's beauty anywhere, as she had learned to do during her own personal war with Charlie. She also shared Delamain's love of *les tendres rapaces*, "tender birds of prey," as he referred to hawks and eagles.[23] Delamain's rare fondness for them had earned him a medal of honor from the League for the Protection of Birds in France, and Edge was perhaps struck by how this attitude toward these species and their defenders differed from that of the NAAS.

The summer in Vevey was a good one for Margaret, and a profoundly inspirational one for her mother. It would take a few more years before the silkiness of Delamain's prose affected Rosalie's personal writings, softening them.

In the fall of 1930 the Colony Club's doormen, uniformed in the Continental Army colors of blue and buff, greeted fewer women at the club's entrance. Membership had fallen as the Depression set in. The hush that normally pervaded the Colony Club's interior, a balm to "nerves shattered by the incessant, intrusive cacophony of [the] rude city," was now perhaps deeper than ever intended.[24]

Charles Edge continued to pay Colony dues for his wife in the sixth year of their estrangement. She made much use of her membership, going almost daily for a swim, lunch, and a bridge game after early mornings spent birding in Central Park and attending to the mounting ECC chores. Rosalie kept weekly appointments with the Colony's hairdresser and manicurist.[25] "Keep up appearances whatever you do" was a dictum of Cousin Charles in his novel *Martin Chuzzlewit*, and both Charlie and Rosalie seem determined to do so.

The Colony's rule that married women were to be addressed by their husband's name gave Rosalie a protective veneer. Perhaps card partners like Ruth Morgan or Margaret Norrie were privy to her marital secrets, but if conversation shifted to the forbidden topic of her marriage, Mrs. Charles Edge's witty banter changed to icy remonstrance accompanied by a piercing glance. Marriage was one of the two subjects she avoided speaking of at the Colony Club. Curiously, conservation was the other. Her card partners evinced little interest in birds or in nature preservation, and Edge seemed content with their indifference. Yet considering the Colony's history of suffrage activism, it would seem an ideal place for Edge to rally influential and generous advocates for conservation. But she did not. Besides, the Colony Club's reformist fires had cooled so much that in the late 1920s Colony governors expressed concern about the apathy of its members. "The average woman between thirty and forty refuses to allow the mantle of pioneer feminist to fall on her lazy shoulders; or to respond to the battle cries that got women into causes," one officer complained.[26]

Rosalie Edge uttered no rousing battle cry on club premises nor cared to enlist Colonists in her new causes. Her two controlling identities—as Colonist and conservationist—lived in separate worlds. Only in her memoirs did she mingle their distinct vocabularies, writing of herself as "a debutante woman conservationist" or referring to her first congressional wildlife hearing as her "coming-out party."[27] "We all have dual personalities I suppose—I know I have," she would write to a friend a few years later. "In my work, persons are nothing to me, and I work only for accomplishments."[28]

In 1930 Rosalie Edge found her closest confidante outside the Colony Club and on the periphery of conservation. Yet beautiful Julia Stubblefield, a willowy blond twenty-five-year-old, combined attributes of both of Rosalie's worlds and became her closest friend since Beautiful Louise Marston.

Julia descended from a bloodline sufficiently impressive to win her Colony Club consideration had she been inclined to seek membership, which she was not. A casual "birdite," as the young woman called herself, Julia had met Rosalie at the American Museum of Natural History, where she worked as Willard Van Name's secretary.[29] Gracious Julia tolerated Van Name's misanthropy and adored the imperious Mrs. Edge, who had befriended him.

Here too similarities may have promoted the friendship. Julia graduated from Cornell University in Ithaca, where Louise Marston was born and had died. Julia, who had received her degree in English literature, was honored to have a cousin of the great Charles Dickens become her good friend. Julia was almost as tall as Margaret Edge and gradually became the appreciative daughter to Rosalie that Margaret never was. Though Rosalie and Julia Stubblefield were twenty-eight years apart, the older woman shared her secrets with the younger. To this friend and proxy daughter, and possibly to no other, Rosalie spoke of Charles's infidelity and confessed she had always loved the Big Man more than he had loved her. She had pursued him relentlessly, following him even to the Orient when he refused to come to New York to marry her. She loved him still.

In the ninth year of their separation, Charles asked his wife for a divorce. It seems his Abnormal Distortion of Conscience had subsided. His conciliatory notes and gifts had ceased much earlier. Charles wanted to marry Ruth Johnston, the secretary his sister-in-law, Margaret Barrow, had hired for him.[30] Informed of her husband's wishes, Rosalie told Julia she could not bring herself to grant her husband a divorce so that he would be free to marry another. It was not sufficient that, as Edith Wharton had written in her short story "The Other Two," a New York divorce was a "diploma of virtue" for the aggrieved spouse. Still, Rosalie may have loved Charles, and her undying affection for him might be the real subject of the poem she wrote a few years later, called "Valentine."[31]

Nor pour for me prefabricated cocktails,
Martinis, side-cars, Manhattans, daiquiris,
Nor offer me canned orange juice or grape juice—

Bring perfumed fruits from the Hesperides.
With bread the color of the waving wheatfields.
Now would I taste the true, the absolute—
And know, when the heart is hungry for the loved one
there is in all the world no substitute.

ALMOST A YEAR had passed since Rosalie Edge asked Pearson for "a complete and frank reply" to the questions raised in the *Crisis* pamphlet. She
had received none. Another NAAS annual meeting was upon her, and as the
head of the ECC she was planning the next public confrontation. She knew
how to proceed by recalling what it took to win the right to vote: "When
we suffrage women attacked a political machine, languid with over-feeding,
slumbering in inaction, we called out its name, and the names of its officers,
so that all could hear. We got ourselves inside the recalcitrant organization
if possible, and stood up in meeting[s]. We gave the matter to the press, first
doing something about it that should *make news*."[32]

A few weeks before the NAAS meeting, Rosalie mailed out Brant's *Compromised Conservation* to "stimulate attendance and discussion."[33] The pamphlet set the combative tone that might draw reporters.

> Who stands on the new battle line? The National Association of Audubon
> Societies? Its members think so. They give their money to protect the birds.
> They assume that it is spent for that purpose. They are sincere as ever, de
> voted, hopeful. The Audubon Society! Why the very name has in the past
> inspired such confidence that it is almost sacrilege to question either its
> devotion to a trust or the effectiveness of its work.[34]

Brant recited each misstep the Audubon board had taken since Pearson's
retracted acceptance of the $125,000 contribution from gun makers nineteen years earlier. He noted the appearance of conflicts of interest among the
interlocked directorates of the NAAS with the Bureau of Biological Survey,
the American Game Protective Association, the American Forest Association, the American Wild Fowlers, the American Museum of Natural History, and the Boone and Crockett Club; he included excerpts from Bulletin
no. 6, "the deadliest document ever put forth in the name of conservation,"
along with excerpts from Pearson's wan presentations at the latest congressional hearings.[35]

When Pearson read the litany of charges against him, he was reportedly
stunned and wondered if "Brant" was Rosalie Edge's nom de plume, in the

belief that "'*Branta Canadensis minima*,' or cackling goose, would better have befitted the writer."[36] Understandably concerned about this goose's intentions at the annual meeting, Pearson asked Theodore Palmer to discreetly secure voting proxies from Audubon members living in Washington, D.C., just in case Edge demanded that a "no confidence" vote be called.[37]

As word spread of Edge's audacity, requests for ECC pamphlets poured in at such a rate that she needed help in mailing them all out before the meeting. She asked some of the young men she birded with in Central Park who were Audubon members and also belonged to the Bronx County Bird Club to help her. A few of those who admired her for taking a hard line came to East Seventy-second Street to address envelopes and stuff them with the ECC pamphlets piled on the dining table in the servants' quarters. The twenty-two-year-old birder and art student Roger Tory Peterson "sat with open mouth at these clandestine meetings" hearing bold Mrs. Edge plot her insurgency.[38]

As Edge had hoped, her ECC pamphlets stirred up the buried mistrust of the NAAS. Henry de Forest, who represented the Russell Sage bird refuges in Louisiana and had protested Pearson's involvement in the proposed Vermilion Bay duck hunting club, wrote Edge to encourage her tough stance.[39] De Forest still wondered if a portion of Pearson's $14,500 salary consisted of contributions from gun and ammunition makers, who might not have given so generously to the NAAS if they had not thought they would gain an advantage. De Forest wrote that the NAAS would be impotent until Pearson left.

Pearson's on-again, off-again rival William Temple Hornaday, who was not a member of the NAAS, joined a month before the meeting just to be able to attend and oppose the society's president in person.[40] The old gentleman gallantly agreed to escort Rosalie, since Van Name still refused to be seen in such a place.

ON THE MORNING of October 28, 1930, so many people showed up for the annual meeting of the NAAS that it had to be moved to a larger chamber at the American Museum of Natural History. The ECC's agitation may have succeeded in stimulating attendance, but the audience that turned out was not one that was largely sympathetic to Rosalie Edge or to William Temple Hornaday. Edge sensed the hostility seething around her as she took her seat at the front.

After the usual introductory remarks and committee reports, the meeting chair recognized Hornaday. The great zoologist wanted to read his seven points for "constructive conservation," to which he believed the NAAS should commit. With his usual rhetorical flourish, Hornaday offered to extend a "golden bridge over which the Audubon Society might pass to the side of conservation" across the "pestilential swamp" in which it "had been floundering." Not surprisingly, such a majestic offer dashed any hope of a reunion.[41]

Now the tension in the room was so thick it was almost tangible, but Edge ignored it. When she was recognized by the chair, she stood to read Henry de Forest's accusatory letter, which indelicately broached the subjects of Pearson's $14,500 salary and disloyalty. She finished the letter and offered a magnanimous resolution of her own requesting an inquiry into these matters. The verbal anarchy that erupted moments later made it difficult for her to give a clear account of what happened: "The room was in an uproar; one after another, various men rising to oppose the resolution, to inveigh against 'Compromised Conservation,' and to throw scorn at Dr. Hornaday and at me. Dr. Hornaday tried repeatedly to get the floor, but as he rose, there would be stamping and calling."[42]

"Who appointed you to inquire into such things?" somebody shouted at her. "We appointed ourselves," Edge haughtily retorted.[43] She thought she saw Theodore Palmer wink at each speaker in turn as if by prearranged cue, and the chaos mounted until she and Hornaday were driven out of the room. It required all the prestige and authority Connecticut senator Fredrick Walcott, an NAAS member, could muster to restore order. One woman who was distressed by the disintegration of decorum understatedly remarked that the meeting had "not been ideal" and called for a vote of confidence in Pearson and the Audubon board.[44] They won, handily.

Edge and Hornaday did not stay for the society's lunch in the Bird Hall. She had perhaps been unprepared for the vehemence of the opposition to them, since so many had been privately encouraging her to go forth into battle. But Hornaday's spirits were soon buoyant again. "Why bother with the Audubon Society?" he asked as he tucked into his entrée at a nearby restaurant, his appetite undiminished by the furor.[45] Edge was too distraught to eat. After she and the great Hornaday had been treated so contemptuously, there could be no amiable and reunifying resolution as she had said she wished. What conservation needed at that moment was not the ploughshare but the sword, or in her parlance, not the dove, but the serpent.[46]

In being driven out, Edge had proved her imperviousness to insult and retribution, and the prominent ornithologists and naturalists—some of whom had silently witnessed the debacle that morning—confidentially urged her to stay the course. These men, like Van Name, feared that if they said what Edge said in public, their careers at the Biological Survey or the Museum of Natural History or some prestigious university or prominent law firm would be ruined.[47]

They were content to let the lady fight alone if she was willing, and the lady, who was bruised but in no way beaten, was more than willing to battle on. The men behind her assayed her unique strength as an outsider and a woman of apparently independent means. She had nothing to lose, while they risked everything.

Edge drew upon her growing number of secret allies for moral as well as educational support. Van Name cheered her up when she told him about the latest rout, as did Irving Brant, one of the few who never feared to be identified with the ECC. Henry Carey, a lawyer and disgruntled bird-watcher from Philadelphia, said that her indignation was magnificent and her purpose sound. Henry de Forest, whose letter had sparked the near-riot, also praised her courage when he heard what had happened.[48]

Nearly lost in all the commotion was the fact that Edge had gained one important concession. The board of directors, having survived a no-confidence vote, did agree to appoint an impartial panel of experts to investigate all charges that the ECC had lodged against the NAAS. Three candidates whom Rosalie Edge suggested for this panel were rejected. Gilbert Pearson chose the two that would serve: Thomas Barbour, director of Harvard's Museum of Comparative Zoology, and Chauncey Hamlin, president of the Buffalo Museum of Science.

Carey, the prominent Philadelphia lawyer who was one of Edge's morale boosters, said that both men were Pearson's close friends. Barbour, a wealthy hunter, advocated bounties on hawks and owls, and it was Hamlin who had chosen Bulletin no. 6 author Charles Sheldon to head his duck-hunting club after the previous director backed bag reductions, according to Carey. Carey predicted these gentlemen would find nothing wrong at the NAAS and saw a whitewash coming.

Edge must carry her reform campaign to the entire Audubon membership, Carey told her, and suggested she ask for the Audubon Society's complete mailing list.[49] With it in her possession, she could send the ECC's pamphlets to all NAAS members and let them know what had transpired at the past two annual meetings. As a life member of the society, or corporation, as Carey saw it, Edge ought to have the right to communicate with other members—her fellow corporate stockholders—about NAAS management.

As Carey had suggested, Rosalie Edge strolled into Audubon's New York headquarters and requested its membership mailing list. Her simple request was icily rejected. Now she had two righteous purposes: to reform the NAAS and to fight for her right to free speech. And to whom would she turn for advice on the First Amendment? "To Roger Baldwin, of course," she noted sprightly.[50]

Roger Baldwin was no less than the cofounder and current director of the American Civil Liberties Union. He had imbued the ACLU with his "complex mixture of liberal social reform impulses and conservative reverence for the Bill of Rights," which were precisely what Edge was counting on.[51] Baldwin, like Edge in the Audubon situation, had a penchant for leading uphill battles.

During the Red scare of the 1920s, he defended the rights to free speech of Communists. He aided Clarence Darrow's defense of teacher John Scopes's right to teach evolution in Tennessee's infamous monkey trial. Baldwin's ACLU famously fought to end literary censorship in Boston after city fathers forbade the sale of Theodore Dreiser's *An American Tragedy* and Ernest Hemingway's *The Sun Also Rises*, along with about sixty other books in a case that gave rise to the "banned in Boston" slogan.

Roger Baldwin was also a member of the NAAS. Edge went to his office and was in the midst of stating her complaint against Audubon when he cut in with his own tirade against the society. She had caught the ACLU lawyer soon after he had read one of Pearson's "long letters saying nothing."[52]

What exercised Baldwin so greatly was the NAAS's refusal to do anything about the exploding population of feral cats in New York, which posed a grave threat to bird life. Pearson had responded to Baldwin's inquiry noncommittally and ended with the suggestion that Baldwin drop in for a chat.

"It was a technique of side-stepping in which Audubon executives were fairy-footed," Edge informed the ACLU's incensed chief.[53] Edge, who by this time had made a thorough study of Pearson's management style, told Baldwin that other Audubon members had resigned on account of the society's failure to take up the cat question. Then she returned to her particular complaint against the NAAS, and he agreed that she did indeed have a First Amendment case on her hands. He referred her to a young civil rights attorney on the ACLU board, Charles Dickerman Williams, who could ably represent her.

Williams found Edge's free-speech argument intriguing and agreed to take her as his client in the suit she wanted to bring against the society to obtain its entire mailing list. Van Name and Carey offered to cover Williams's legal fees.[54]

That June, Williams filed Edge's complaint in the New York Supreme Court. "The Matter of the Application of M. R. Edge, Petitioner, for a Peremptory Mandamus Order against the National Association of Audubon Societies for the Protection of Wild Birds and Animals" claimed, "[The] petitioner is a sincere woman, interested only in bird and animal protection, who desires to circularize her fellow-members in the Association in order to effect a change in administration, and totally without any selfish or ulterior aim on her part."[55]

Her suit shocked the conservation world. Although conservationists had bitterly quarreled over hunting limits and other issues, they had not sued anyone—certainly not one another—for the sake of their ideological positions. Among conservationists, going to court to save nature may have been a precedent set by Rosalie Edge. It was a "cause célèbre." Audubon's officers "appeared to be deeply wounded" by her tactic.[56] It necessitated their staying in the city during the summer to be deposed, while the plaintiff decamped to a cooler clime to await the New York Supreme Court's decision.

The NAAS hired the prestigious law firm of Charles Evans Hughes to represent Gilbert Pearson and Audubon officers Theodore Palmer, Frank Chapman, and Robert Cushman Murphy. Charles Evans Hughes Sr.—former New York governor, one-time U.S. secretary of state, and the presidential candidate narrowly defeated by Woodrow Wilson—had just been appointed chief justice of the United States Supreme Court when the Audubon case arrived at the firm. Charles Evans Hughes Jr., an Audubon member, would represent the society along with Samuel Carter, another firm attorney and longtime Audubon loyalist.

Edge's unusual suit made the news that she hoped it would, but it was the affidavits of the Audubon leaders that ultimately revealed the breadth of her reform effort. She was determined to shake up every major conservation body in the country, whether in the public sector or in the private one. In their statements the defendants denounced the plaintiff's "animosity and hostility" toward conservation's "organizations of unquestioned standing and repute."[57]

Edge's pamphlets, "as may be inferred from their titles, are attacks upon the sincerity and effectiveness of the bird protection associations, the Bureau of Biological Survey and other organizations," testified Gilbert Pearson. They were "replete with loose and general condemnations." They were nothing but "sweeping indictments of the various ornithological, scientific and bird protection societies of the country." Her vilification of these organizations must stop immediately, he demanded, also denying Edge's charge that the NAAS was heavily influenced by sportsmen's groups. There were not more than six such groups represented among the eleven thousand members of the NAAS, he asserted.[58]

Pearson marshaled an impressive defense of his leadership and read into the record letters of support from Gilbert Grosvenor, president of the National Geographic Society, and George D. Pratt, president of the American Forestry Association. Pratt's letter commiserated with Pearson, because he too had felt the lash of Edge's pen. She had written him to complain about the conduct of the Forestry Association, charging, "[It has not told] the public of the need to curtail the present prodigal consumption of our forests; that your Association has failed to protest against the Forest Service Policy of cutting from our forest reserves and the failure of your Society to oppose raids on the National Park System."[59]

Such an opinion "shows that Mrs. Edge has very little knowledge of any of these conditions," Pratt had written to Pearson. "The American Forestry Association is constantly on the watch for any attempt to encroach on the forest reserves," and such attempts "certainly do not come from the United States Forest Service" as Mrs. Edge alleged.[60]

The affidavit of Theodore Palmer, the Biological Survey's assistant director, denounced "the baseless nature of petitioner's attacks." If the NAAS addressed Edge's charges, "its work would be hampered and its resources depleted with no constructive result."[61] He quoted one of Edge's publications to show how offensive and wrong they were:

The Biological Survey is not being and has not been for years conducted according to scientific methods. Appropriations are all that it is interested in, and it seems to be quite willing to wipe out of existence the wild life, which it was established to protect, if it can get appropriations for doing so. The Bureau has the support of the powerful lobby of the sheep-raisers who are quite

willing to have the public expend millions and destroy all our wild creatures
if it will save them some insignificant losses or some trifling expense in caring for their flocks.[62]

It was Frank Chapman's testimony that perhaps was unintentionally
most helpful to Edge. He confirmed the hunting sector's influence on the
Audubon organization, stating, "Whether or not their motive be regarded
as praiseworthy, their interest is real. . . . Their contributions are very substantial and they are extremely active. The purpose of the Association could
not be adequately fulfilled against the opposition of this influential class of
people."[63]

The statement by Audubon treasurer Robert Cushman Murphy further
aided Edge's case by quantifying the sportsmen's influence. Pearson's annual
income of $14,500 "consists of $6,000 per year salary, the remainder being
commissions on contributions received."[64] For the first time the question-
able sources of Pearson's income, rumored for years, were confirmed.

Charles Dickerman Williams eloquently summed up his client's position:
"It is of course obvious that when the president of a bird protection society is
receiving a direct personal income from sportsmen his judgment as to when
the point is reached at which the interests of bird protection and bird shooting differ, may be affected." Wouldn't any concerned member of a private
group, he asked, have a duty to inform other members of that group of the
potential for conflicts of interest?[65]

NAAS attorney Samuel Carter summarized the problem Edge had raised
with a single epithet that would be a source of amusement to her ever afterward. The "petitioner is a common scold," he declared. Her response to the
insult is equally memorable. "Fancy how I trembled," she wrote, recalling
her reaction years later.[66]

Edge was relishing sea breezes at her hotel in Edgartown, Massachusetts,
when she received Williams's telegram containing the judge's decision in
its succinct entirety: "Motion granted. Settle Order."[67] Audubon's attorneys
threatened to appeal but decided not to go ahead when the judge ruled
that in the event of an appeal the 1931 annual meeting would have to be
delayed until the matter was decided. At the end of August, Edge was frost-
ily informed she would receive the NAAS mailing list of more than eleven
thousand names within the week.

THE TIMING of the judge's decision could not have been better from a
news-making standpoint. It coincided with the long-awaited release of the

report of the Thomas Barbour and Chauncey Hamlin investigation. In the ten months since their appointment, the men had met once at Audubon's headquarters. They took a statement from Pearson but refused to accept one from Edge. They read the ECC's pamphlets and many statements of glowing support that Pearson provided. Then they issued their findings in their "Report of the Special Committee Appointed to Investigate Charges Publicly Made against the National Association of Audubon Societies."[68]

> Most of the material presented is similar to that which everyone who has had any part in dealing with the activities of the so-called "zoo-phile cults" recognizes immediately. The zoophile may be defined as one whose arguments are always based on sentiment and not on reason, who with entire honesty believes that if a forest is to be protected and preserved, no tree should ever be cut down, and who believes that no species of bird or animal can be adequately protected if any individual of the species is ever killed. . . . After a full investigation we feel that the Society may be proud of a great record and that such trifling missteps as have possibly been made from time to time are due to the inevitable frailties of mere men.[69]

The Barbour and Hamlin report fully exonerated the NAAS leadership, refuting the complaints against it one by one. "The claim that the Audubon Society has an interlocking directorate merits no further consideration than to say that the type of person represented by the directors of the Association is inevitably interested in more than one good cause," the special committee report stated. "Hunting was a normal exercise of healthy and intelligent men, and has been so for all time and will continue to be; the conservation of wildlife was vitally dependent upon the interest of intelligent sportsmen more than any others."[70] Pearson's trademark "so-called" in reference to the ECC appeared so many times in the report that he might have written it himself.

Although the report's conclusions came as no surprise, there was something Edge had not expected. Henry de Forest, the Louisiana sanctuary trustee who had criticized Pearson's hunt club involvement, retracted his complaints and joined Audubon's side against her. He was angry that she had read the letter he sent her in the fall of 1930 at the annual meeting, since he had not given her permission to do so. He had intended it to be confidential.[71] It was a blow to lose such an important Audubon insider as de Forest as an ally. But this was politics, as Edge was learning.

Much more politics was hidden from view. The Barbour and Hamlin report's real truth was contained in a secret appendix given only to the NAAS board. Contrary to the public report's conclusions, the appendix stated that Pearson's salary must be fixed and his power trimmed.[72] Rosalie Edge was vindicated by Barbour and Hamlin's confidential judgments, but whether she ever learned this, we do not know.

EDGE REQUESTED two copies of the NAAS mailing list, valuing this new information so highly that she gave one copy to Williams to keep in his vault. She had only a few weeks to compose her circular to the entire Audubon membership and send it out. The earnest young men from the Bronx birding club—Roger Tory Peterson among them—reconvened at the servants' dining table to help her with the mass mailings.

They folded a four-page personal letter written and signed by none other than Mrs. Charles Noel Edge into envelopes and addressed them to the eleven thousand members on the Audubon list. The only other women present were Edge's cook and maid, whom she drafted to help speed the process; Peter came in from Harvard on weekends to join his mother's mailing brigade. Margaret did not attend these gatherings. It was at about this time that she decided she would rather live with her father than with her mother and moved permanently to Parsonage Point.

What might have made Margaret's departure particularly upsetting to Rosalie was that the girl also claimed to prefer the company of Charles's secretary and presumed lover Ruth Johnston, or "Johnny," to her mother's. When Margaret moved to Rye, she and her father anticipated a custody fight from Rosalie, but none came. Margaret regarded this failure to act as proof that her mother did not love her, had never loved her. Childless Aunt Margaret and Aunt Anna consoled their niece with their recollections of how spoiled her mother had been as a child and how she had mistreated them as "far back as the baby carriage."[73]

Margaret's break with her mother seems only to have strengthened Rosalie's bond with the adoring Julia Stubblefield, who was emotionally distanced from her own mother. Virtually motherless and daughterless, the two women filled a familial void for each other, and Rosalie played the maternal part in Julia's marriage to a young educator named Walter Langsam.[74]

As Edge prepared to carry trouble to Audubon's doorstep for the third annual meeting in a row, she needed to propose her own slate of candidates to run against Theodore Palmer and two other Audubon loyalists up for reelection. With the explanatory letter her mail brigade sent, a proxy was included with the request that each member return it to her so that she could cast their vote for her reform candidates. Absentee votes sent to her to cast would be "solely for the purpose of endeavoring to elect directors favorable to policies and methods that [would] insure honest and efficient conservation and to adopt measures to that end."[75]

It was an informative and gossipy package that Audubon members received from her, containing not only her complaints but the full text of the letter Henry de Forest had sent her the year before criticizing Pearson. De Forest may have switched sides, but Edge would not let his disavowal stand in her way. This was war, and she was ruthless in its conduct. She seems to have felt no qualms about publicizing the powerfully incriminating letter yet again. The heated battle for proxies, and for the hearts and minds of the NAAS membership, was on.

Signed forms began pouring through the letter slot of 113 East Seventy-second Street a few days later. One morning Edge gave her maid ten dollars to give the postman for return postage on proxies respondents mailed back. She thought that amount would cover whatever came in. She was in the bathtub when the maid knocked on the bathroom door and reported that the postman was waiting in the hallway downstairs, "demanding $47" for immediate payment. "Dripping wet I dealt with the situation," Edge wrote, noting that she eventually grew accustomed to such disruptions to deal with conservation crises as they arose.[76]

Notes included with the returned proxies were addressed to "Dear Sir," as if the honorific "Mrs." before the name Charles Noel Edge had been misread, or to "Dear Sirs," as if her effort could not be the work of one person. Many of those who wrote responses to her were horrified by her allegations. Though they might not have heard of Mrs. Edge or the ECC before, they sent small contributions so that she could continue the ECC's important work.

Edge had indeed touched a nerve; one writer felt so betrayed by the NAAS that he asserted the organization deserved to be dynamited. Another irate man sent her his vote though he predicted she would be defeated. The NAAS was too powerful to be overthrown by one person, he wrote. Although he did not approve of her guerrilla tactics, he was more disgusted with the Barbour and Hamlin report; he, a Harvard man, could not believe that any Harvard man would sign his name to such whitewash.[77]

THE ANNUAL business meeting of the NAAS was moved to a still larger room at the American Museum of Natural History. It was the society's largest annual meeting to date. Edge had alerted the press to the possibility of a successful insurrection, and reporters turned out to see which side would win the proxy vote. She also hired a transcriptionist to record the meeting's proceedings and asked her lawyer to be there to advise her.[78] Willard Van Name came as well, for not even he could bear to miss the excitement of this showdown.

The meeting was off to a lively start when Pearson called Edge "ridiculous," and she refused to allow the election of new board members to proceed until the proxies were counted. Williams then made a statement on behalf of his client, who it seemed had decided it was beneath her to be directly subjected to any more of the society's contempt:

> Certainly sportsmen have a great interest in birds and animals. However, there are also a great many people—I guess you could call them sentimentalists—who are primarily interested in bird protection and are not interested in preserving the birds so that they can be shot. There are probably two absolute legitimate points of view in this matter. However, it is quite possible that these points of view may come into conflict. There is no doubt but that it is entirely proper to have the point of view of sportsmen represented. . . . [T]he sentimentalists, who are interested in birds from the point of view of seeing them and studying them, have very few organizations. The principal one of the organizations which they have is this Association. Now, in Mrs. Edge's view and those who agree with her, it is very important that this Association preserve complete freedom of action so that whenever there is that conflict in interest . . . the Association can act according to the interests of the sentimentalists.[79]

After Williams completed his summation, his client threatened parliamentary mayhem again by using suffrage tactics of disruption. Edge interrupted Pearson as he was delivering the "Report of the President" to ask him how much Audubon paid its refuge wardens. Theodore Palmer, who chaired the meeting, instructed Edge to wait for the treasurer's report to be given for that information. She would not be silenced, however. "It will take only a second," she insisted, "and it will help you get to your—lunch on time. As I said, I asked the treasurer two years ago why the amounts paid to wardens were so small. Dr. Murphy said, 'For want of exact information, I will have to refer you to President Pearson for an answer, a detailed answer, to that question.' I don't know why the treasurer had to refer a question like that to the president, but that is his own affair."[80]

Edge spoke further, repeating her demand that the NAAS hire more game wardens and urging the board to pass a resolution that opposed the Biological Survey's ten-year plan to eradicate predators, chiefly with thallium. Palmer called her out of order several times. One reporter later noted that Mrs. Edge was "polite but spirited."[81] Halfway through the meeting, the proxies were counted and the winner of this breathlessly awaited contest was announced. Edge had submitted 1,646 absentee votes. Audubon supporters held on to 2,801.

The insurgency was defeated, but Edge and her backers had known that the proxy vote was a long shot. It had served well to generate publicity for the great moral victories the ECC was achieving. Meanwhile, the NAAS board voted to freeze Pearson's salary at $13,000 and disassociate his income from contributions he brought in. The newly elected board, which included none of Edge's candidates, voted to add more game wardens to its sanctuaries. Edge's resolution opposing the Biological Survey's use of thallium also passed unanimously.

"We are agreed on one thing," said Frank Chapman after this last vote was taken. The audience laughed, evidently in relief. "Naturally," Edge retorted, "when I was the one to move for that very thing, I am in favor of it."[82] One resolution that did not pass was her bid to ban Bureau of Biological Survey employees from serving as Audubon board members. Chapman defended the survey's place on the board with great passion: "The whole back bone of conservation in this country, conservation of bird life I refer to particularly, has been supplied by the researches of the Biological Survey," he declared. When he added that it would be "one of the most ungracious, untruthful, ungrateful acts of which bird conservationists could be guilty" to prohibit Survey participation, the audience of Audubon loyalists applauded.[83]

Though she had failed to change the board's makeup, Edge declared this annual meeting was an important victory for her side. She told a reporter from the *Herald Tribune* that she had proved that "a considerable element" in the conservation community was deeply dissatisfied with how the Audubon Society was being run, a point the ECC pamphlets had brought into sharpest focus.[84]

With the Audubon membership list in her possession, Edge had gained access to eleven thousand dues-paying conservationists around the country. Many, she suspected, were unrepresented zoophiles and sentimentalists. Her performance that day had impressed Roger Baldwin and Charles

Dickerman Williams so much that they both made donations to the ECC and asked if they could serve on her committee. Hundreds resigned from the NAAS in disgust, and many sent the ECC contributions.

Edge had, of course, alienated many. "I sometimes think I must seem very fierce to those who do not know how long it is since the Directors were first urged to make reforms," she wrote to one of her critics.[85]

Edge might have contented herself with what she had accomplished at the meeting and ended her crusade. The expansion of the ECC clearinghouse of conservation publications was enough to keep her busy. But she was not content. Something still troubled her about the Audubon refuge situation. She wondered what was meant by the line item "Rentals of Sanctuary" that had appeared in the NAAS budget during the last few years and that the NAAS had never bothered to adequately explain. Feeling perhaps invincible after acquiring the mailing list, she next decided to request an independent audit of Audubon's finances.

Willard Van Name didn't think it was worth bothering with the NAAS books, but if it made her feel better, he would pay for the audit. The NAAS board undoubtedly wished to avoid any more bad publicity and turned its books over to the accounting firm of Edge's choice.

IN DECEMBER Rosalie and Peter joined the nation's top bird scientists at the Wilson Ornithological Society meeting in New Orleans. Much to everyone's relief, she and Gilbert Pearson dropped their hostilities long enough to play parlor games in the evenings.

Perhaps an inordinate amount of politeness was called for at this particular ornithologists' meeting, for Louisiana naturalist Edward "Ned" McIlhenny, Tabasco Sauce tycoon and derailed business partner of the late Paul J. Rainey in the Vermilion Bay Hunt Club proposal, was also present. "M'sieu Ned" had implicated Pearson in the hunt club scheme that had gotten the Audubon president into so much trouble with his board. Though some five years had passed since Pearson had survived that scandal, it wasn't clear what sort of terms he and McIlhenny were on.

M'sieu Ned, apart from running the family pepper concern, had been an adventurer and trophy hunter before becoming a respected naturalist. He embodied Gilbert Pearson's creed that sportsmen were the only true saviors of wild creatures. As a teenager McIlhenny shot a nineteen-foot-long alligator on the pepper plantation, reputedly the biggest ever killed. After dropping out of college in 1894, he joined an Arctic expedition to study Arctic plants and animals and helped save a fleet of stranded Japanese whaling ships.[86]

When McIlhenny returned home a few years later, he was shocked to discover that the snowy egret rookeries of his native Avery Island had been plundered by plume hunters. Across the island's salt dome laced with swamps, McIlhenny searched for intact egret nests, thinking he might try to save any that remained. His search turned up two nests, and from the eight eggs they contained, he established his successful egret captive-breeding effort. McIlhenny's egrets increased so dramatically that in less than thirty years the offspring of his original birds had repopulated not only Louisiana's Gulf Coast but much of Florida's as well. Prospects for egret recovery were stronger on both supply and demand fronts, for McIlhenny's captive-breeding experiment coincided with the Audubon Societies' agreements with the milliners and the change in fashion that the agreements drove.

Rosalie was impressed by McIlhenny, whom she lauded as "the father of Louisiana Conservation." He was a rich, adventurous, and courtly southerner who spun good tales as well as she could and was as passionate about nature preservation as she was. Though he still hunted, he was "a true conservationist," she declared.[87] Like all the men to whom Edge was most powerfully drawn—men like John Wylie Barrow, Charles Noel Edge, and William Temple Hornaday—McIlhenny was a larger-than-life figure. Undoubtedly she flirted with him, but it seems there was nothing more.

M'sieu Ned invited her and Peter to visit Jungle Gardens, his private estate at Avery Island. Despite his involvement in the Vermilion Club and his reputation as a marksman, Edge's admiration of him was unconditional after she saw the perfect Eden he had created on his property.

At his invitation she returned in spring. Perhaps with a certain sad nostalgia for those recuperative days on the Malay Peninsula, Rosalie wandered through McIlhenny's dense bamboo forest. She marveled at the lake brimming with pink lotus, the elephantine trunks of the live oaks that cascaded gray green tatting, and the intoxicating hedges of gardenia flowers as big as headlights. She heard Carolina wrens, mockingbirds, and cardinals in fullthroated song, and through the tangle of woodlands "herons appeared like myriads of great white blossoms" on the water's edge. Slender-necked anhingas, or snakebirds, sat with their limp wings drying, "looking for all the world like the imprint of the fossil archeopterix."[88]

McIlhenny apparently admired Edge for her pluck, but he might have had an ulterior motive for befriending her. There might still have been a score to settle with Gilbert Pearson after the Vermilion Bay Hunt Club fell through and Audubon acquired a portion of the real estate to make into the Paul J. Rainey Refuge. Perhaps Rosalie Edge's reform campaign gave him the opportunity to get even. As one of the region's premier wildlife and habitat experts, McIlhenny knew some things about how the NAAS ran its refuge. Conceivably—even before he and Edge first met—he had been the one to suggest she look into the "Rentals of Sanctuary" wording in the Audubon financial statement.

Or perhaps while both attended the Wilson Ornithological Society meeting, she had been the one to raise the question of the curious item in the budget. One way or another, it seems McIlhenny was the secret partner who slipped Edge the Louisiana Department of Conservation's latest annual report, which she later opaquely wrote, "happened to fall into my hands."[89]

The annual conservation report listed fur trappers licensed in Louisiana. The NAAS was one of them. On further investigation Edge learned that since 1925, when the Audubon Society acquired the Rainey parcel, more than 300,000 muskrats, raccoons, minks, and opossums had been trapped within the sanctuary.[90] The society split the proceeds from the sale of pelts with the trappers it hired and had earned about $150,000 from its lucrative enterprise.

The animals were killed in the kind of steel traps that some states had outlawed because of the slow and painful death they inflicted. This was an unpleasant fact, and more piled up: Some trappers baited the steel jaws with birds they caught on the sanctuary to attract mink, whose fur fetched the highest price. Sometimes ducks, for which the preserve had been primarily created in the first place, were accidentally caught in the traps.

"It was horrid enough that the Audubon Society should kill animals it was pledged to protect, kill them on a sanctuary, and kill them in steel-traps," Edge wrote. "But that it should receive large sums of money for killing animals, and hide the transaction under a misleading entry on their books was intolerable."[91] Before the annual meeting of 1932, Edge had collected enough information to inform the NAAS membership about Audubon's profitable business dealings on its wildlife refuge.

IN THE WORLD of conservation, however, there was much else besides fur trapping on a Louisiana wildlife sanctuary to keep both Rosalie Edge and the ECC very busy. The matter of the Audubon Society's stand on live decoys, baiting, and automatic guns was still unsettled. There was also what

Edge considered the society's disregard for animals labeled "vermin," which she contended meant every type of predatory bird or mammal that hunted prey that humans also liked to eat.

Edge wanted to see and hear for herself how the NAAS claimed it protected wildlife in its presentations to Congress. In 1932 she began to regularly attend and testify at hearings on wildlife in Washington, D.C. Few if any other women were present in the often packed hearing rooms. Edge brought a cartoon drawn for her by Pulitzer Prize–winning cartoonist J. "Ding" Darling to serve as a visual aid in one of her early congressional presentations. Darling was one of her staunchest admirers and at her urging drew a cartoon of a wounded duck reading a dictionary's definition of the word *sportsman* as being one who was "fair and generous." During the hearings Darling's perplexed-looking duck was widely syndicated, increasing not only the hunting dispute's public visibility but also Mrs. Charles Edge's.

At another congressional hearing she attended with Willard Van Name, Gilbert Pearson and Robert Cushman Murphy testified that hawks needed no laws to protect them because they were common birds. "But the time to save a species is while it is still common," Van Name whispered to her. Ever the attentive student, she copied Van Name's retort in her notebook. After Murphy testified against granting federal protection to birds that were not rare, Van Name again leaned over to her and hissed, "Does he not know that the only way to save a species is to never let it become rare?"[92]

In those incredulously posed questions, Van Name had summed up what had become her own guiding principles. Edge excused herself and went to call her printer. Over the phone she read him the battle cry that would be included on all ECC publications from thence forward: "The time to save a species is while it is still common. The only way to save a species is to never let it become rare."

THAT SUMMER she had to keep "an appointment" in Mexico City but offered no further elaboration. Peter, who often served as his mother's escort, drove her from New York to Brownsville, Texas, stopping to visit M'sieu Ned at Jungle Garden along the way. In Brownsville the Edges planned to catch a plane to Mexico City, which itself was a bold decision for a casual traveler to make in 1932, but all the more so under the circumstances. A hurricane was brewing in the Gulf of Mexico. The flight was canceled, and Brownsville residents were told to move inland.[93]

The Edges considered evacuating, but with Rosalie's previous experience of sailing in and out of typhoons, she opted for hunkering down in their Brownsville hotel. "We have always found prudence to be a featherweight in the balance of our decisions," she wrote of the cocky decision to live with limited food, water, and electricity for a few days. But waiting out the storm in town gave them a chance to be on the plane for Mexico City whenever it was safe to take off.[94]

Rosalie was an expert in this sort of travel from her time in the Orient, and bravely observed: "Adventure weighs much heavier; and this rising sea, this rending wind, these torn clouds had a reality of craved experience from which we could not turn away."[95] When the electricity came back on, she listened absentmindedly to radio reports of a small fishing boat with a crew of three that had disappeared during the hurricane. Planes had been sent to search for it.

As the Edges' plane flew low along the Texas coast toward Mexico City, she sat with her eyes pinned to the window watching for white pelicans. Birding had given her a way to never be idle. The plane was passing a desolate spit of sand jutting into the Gulf when she noticed a man below waving something red. She told herself that "perhaps the man had some business on that lonely shore." But then she called the steward and told him she had to speak to the pilot. The steward refused to let her. "I could have a cheese sandwich with Apollonaris, White Rock or Gingerale; but the pilot was sacrosanct and not to be disturbed."[96] Undeterred, Rosalie scribbled, "I have seen a shipwrecked man" on a napkin and passed it forward to the airplane's radio operator.

That night at the Edges' hotel in Mexico City, the other guests talked of how three shipwrecked fishermen had been rescued after a passenger in a commercial plane spotted the men while looking for birds out the window. Rosalie did not identify herself as the observant passenger mentioned in the news accounts. One of the guests who knew her reputation as a conservationist turned to her for an explanation. "Mrs. Edge, you are an ornithologist, and a flyer, tell us why a person looking for birds should see what the eyes of an aviator missed." She politely declined to answer, and as the band struck up a marimba tune and couples got up to dance, she excused herself to go up to her room to sleep.[97]

The next summer and fall, both sides were preparing for yet another proxy battle at the next annual meeting of the NAAS. The society was taking Edge's latest challenge very seriously and was calling on its most august members to help defend against her. On October 1, 1932, Theodore Roosevelt's widow, Edith, sent a letter on her personal Sagamore Hill letterhead to the entire Audubon membership, emphasizing her unwavering support for the society and her strong opposition to a "small group of people" within the association who were making trouble. She did not wish to dignify said group by naming it and further denounced its members for "condemning the administration and practically accusing the Board of directors of misdirection of funds." Mrs. Roosevelt's letter included other impressive signatories: Mrs. John D. Rockefeller, Mrs. Thomas Edison, Paul Rainey's sister Grace Rainey Rogers, Connecticut senator Frederick Walcott, and Henry W. de Forest among them.[98]

Mrs. Roosevelt had a personal interest in matters pertaining to the NAAS board of directors because her son Kermit was its president-elect, and several of her late husband's close hunting friends still served on it. Though Senator Walcott added his name to Mrs. Roosevelt's letter, he may have had mixed feelings about doing so. Walcott chaired the Senate's wildlife committee hearings before which Edge had testified, and he was beginning to respect what she had to say.

E. W. Nelson, retired director of the Bureau of Biological Survey, was alarmed by the shift in the senator's sympathics and warned him not to be deluded by anything Edge had to say about conservation or by her wild accusations. Nelson assured Senator Walcott that "the entire barrage" of Edge's complaints was honeycombed with half-truths and ill-informed conclusions. If Mrs. Edge got her way with the Audubon Society, Nelson warned the senator, she would put an end to all meaningful bird conservation efforts for years to come.[99]

ROSALIE EDGE'S REFORM agenda had grown much broader than birds, however. It was as broad as nature itself. In 1932 another of the many professional conservationists she shielded leaked an internal memo to her that indicated even Yellowstone National Park was being managed according to the mind-set of the Bureau of Biological Survey. In the memo park administrators requested the survey to send agents to poison the pelicans on Yellowstone Lake because they competed with the anglers for the fish.[100]

An ECC pamphlet on the matter resulted, much to the embarrassment of National Park Service director Horace Albright, who denied the ECC's charges of poisoning. But then he learned that the documents Edge cited

were genuine and had been accurately quoted. She had obtained them illegally, however, and it was an outrage that she had run them. "The letters
were purloined," she admitted. "But the ends justified the means. Needs
must when the devil drives."[101]

With the ECC's *Slaughter of the Yellowstone Park Pelicans* distracting the
conservation community's attention away from the NAAS, Gilbert Pearson
seems not to have realized that the Rainey sanctuary trapping enterprise
bespoke his biggest trouble with Edge yet. She was combative on so many
issues at once it was hard to predict where, or on whom, she would inflict
the most damage. Her complaint about fur trapping on the Rainey, airing
concurrently with her exposé on pelican poisoning, was merely some scatter
shot in her entire barrage.

Besides, what Pearson had accomplished with the Rainey Refuge acquisition was a thing to be proud of, one of the crowning achievements of his
long career in wildlife preservation. From Gladys Rainey Rogers he not only
had secured a vast refuge diverse in species but had also established a rich
financial endowment to support the refuge's perpetual management. Edge
might try to make too much of her trapping charges, but Pearson had acted
well within the terms of Audubon's agreement with Gladys Rogers.

It was these points of pride that Pearson would emphasize at the
twenty-eighth annual meeting of the NAAS on the last Tuesday of October
1932. Setting that tone, the meeting opened with a glowing report by Ernest
Holt, Audubon's director of sanctuaries. All the societies' bird and wildlife
preserves were in excellent shape, the director declared. The transcriptionist Edge had hired that day noted that the audience applauded when Holt
finished.[102]

The chair recognized Rosalie Edge. All present had read or heard of her
latest broadside charging the NAAS with illegal trapping. This latest complaint had no doubt stimulated much of the attendance and again attracted
the press. But she would keep them in suspense. She asked, unexpectedly,
why there were no roseate spoonbills at Black Bayou in Louisiana.

"Certainly, because there are oil wells there and boats going up and down
there all the time," Holt replied.

"If that is one reason it isn't the only reason," Edge said slyly. "If I could
see you some other time—not to take the time of all these people—I will
tell you the other reason."

"I wonder if you yourself know," retorted the sanctuary director.[103]

She did indeed. Did Mr. Holt know that the esteemed Mr. Edward McIlhenny of nearby Avery Island had made a thorough field investigation? Poachers, not oil wells and boats, had wiped out the spoonbills, and he had informed the Audubon Society of this. The sanctuary director replied that Mr. McIlhenny was mistaken; an Audubon warden reported there was no poaching.

This gave Edge her opening. Had an Audubon warden given that report? Mr. McIlhenny had written in *Bird-Lore* that a Louisiana state game warden patrolled the area, and that the poaching occurred when he was off his watch. Holt responded that he did not see what difference the warden's affiliation made. "It is all right with me," he said testily. "What I am after is the protection of birds."[104]

"What I am after is to make the Audubon Society efficient," Edge interjected. In classic Edge style she had begun her presentation by playing the dove. Now as the serpent she struck. She would have to let Mr. McIlhenny know that the NAAS, and not the people of Louisiana, were paying for that game warden's services. "The Louisiana conservation department had jolly well got to take that back," she said, as a few supporters snickered and nervously applauded.[105]

"Now, there are two things," she proceeded. "You know—who was it? Some very intelligent gentleman—oh yes—Dr. Pearson," she said in self-mocking hauteur and dramatically paused for more laughter. "Dr. Pearson said there are all sorts of differences of opinion in conservation, that one person thought one thing and another person thought another thing."[106]

Ernest Holt did not seem to like Edge's new tack and stood up to speak. "I have the floor," Edge remonstrated. "You can sit down. You can sit right down." The audience tittered as she continued. Not only did some conservationists like Audubon's sanctuary director think it did not matter who footed the bill for a private refuge's wardens, Edge said. This sort of conservationist, like Mr. Pearson, also appeared to be indifferent to whether thousands of muskrats, raccoons, and minks in a wildlife sanctuary were trapped for profit by those entrusted with the sanctuary's protection.[107]

Edge had pounced at last on the subject everybody had come to hear about. She wanted to speak on behalf of conservationists who were different from the type that Gilbert Pearson and his supporters seemed to be: people who thought it was wrong if the nation's leading bird and wildlife protection society inhumanely trapped thousands of animals in its wildlife sanctuary, secretively and for profit.

Edge, fully engaged as citizen-scientist and citizen-advocate, delivered the lessons she had learned not only from Willard Van Name but also from Louisiana's Father of Conservation, Edward A. McIlhenny, who perhaps knew his native marshlands better than any.

It was true that muskrats ate the grass preferred by geese, but "they cannot be considered in any way a detriment to wild fowl or waders," she asserted. By eating this natural source of goose food—which grew in excess—muskrats opened places in the marsh for nutrient sources such as crustaceans and plants that ducks and other wading birds favored, thus maintaining a natural balance among all species. "This has been going on for a long, long period before even the oldest of us, and some of us are pretty old—so that if the muskrats didn't eat this grass and leave areas of shallow water the ducks would not have the water they dearly love, the duck food and the crustaceans," Edge said.[108]

It was an oversimplification perhaps, for even in refuges intended to be left in a natural state human stewards must decide how to accomplish this goal. But it was a startlingly ecological presentation to make in such a group. More important, Edge was urging people who called themselves conservationists to insist above all on maintaining nature's balance. She reminded them that conservationists were not the ones to seek short-term profits on a long-term refuge or to promote popular species of the day at the expense of unpopular ones.

What, she wondered, had Pearson meant by the word *sanctuary* if he was the one with the exclusive authority to determine which animals were obnoxious and targeted for elimination? And while Audubon officials had contended that muskrats were so numerous that 100,000 could be taken every year off the refuge with no fear of their disappearance, mink were more rare but were also trapped. Edge explained why they too were trapped. "Mink skins, mink especially, are very very valuable, and to kill mink when there are so few looks as if the Association were trying to make money out of it."[109]

Her ecologically based tutorial ended. When it was Pearson's turn, he justified Audubon's refuge trapping practices by quoting some of the largely anthropomorphic opinions of the day, including one held by William Temple Hornaday. Fur-bearers "are fiercely predatory and absolutely require the hand of the human killer to keep them from overrunning and destroying men, beasts and birds," the NAAS president said.[110]

"Fishers, martens, skunks, weasels, minks are merciless. . . . They were wholesale slaughterers who murder helpless birds by the dozen for the mere lust of murder." If muskrats are not "trapped off as soon as the season opens, they will soon clean this tract out and ruin the sanctuary for blue geese for at least two years," Pearson asserted. The same could be said of mink, which was "by nature a killer and lives largely on water fowl in marshes."[111]

On that day so full of rancor, Edge taught a lesson based on her emerging sense of ecology, a word that was seldom used at the time. Pearson's defense might have rested on the difficulty of all human decisions that concerned how best to leave a place wild, but this was not yet within the scope of the conservation debate. The simplistic dichotomy that ruled the Rainey universe, as Edge had pointed out, was that the NAAS could profit most from dead muskrats and minks and live geese. Not only had Pearson divided the animal kingdom into good and evil in his rebuttal to her arguments. He also had upheld conventional wisdom with well-oiled considerations of financial gain.

YEARS LATER Rosalie Edge would recall the competing viewpoints aired that day. It was, she said, "always a matter of wonder to me that even the most simple people should not see that the association of species and the ecology which worked successfully through the ages before Columbus discovered America will still continue to work."[112]

Edge never favored a ban on all killing of wild animals. Such a sweeping prohibition against the taking of animal lives did not fit the broad ecological scheme of her thinking. It had also been true long before Columbus that humans were predators and natural seekers of personal profit and consumptive pleasure. Indeed, these desires had their place; she would not deny her own pleasure in wearing fur, for example, although her conscience pricked her after the fur-trapping debate. She encouraged furriers to explore how they might make coats from humanely killed animals.[113]

The board of the NAAS did not vote to end fur trapping on the Rainey Refuge that day. Pearson read a letter of commendation from Gladys Rainey Rogers that put the matter to uneasy rest: "I am glad that because of a fortunate turn in the market in furs you have not been put to extra expense in controlling these destructive forms of wildlife of the region, but have actually received an income from the fur which has made it possible for you adequately to guard the territory and increase the endowment which I was pleased to present to the Association some time after giving you the land."[114]

The board also voted down Rosalie Edge's request to change "Rentals of

Sanctuary" to "Sale of Pelts." At the next two NAAS annual meetings, Edge would consider it her duty to stand after the treasurer's report was read and ask whether the term *rentals* in the annual financial statement referred to the sale of pelts on the Rainey Refuge, to which the answer would be a weary yes. Only after she made this clarification could the treasurer's report be approved.

Edge did not leave the 1932 meeting empty-handed. The board finally went on record against all baiting. It also agreed to study Audubon bylaws as she had demanded, although to her chagrin her ECC supporter Roger Baldwin was recruited to help rewrite them. The ACLU chief parted company with Edge and the ECC and joined the NAAS board of directors. Despite the liveliness and length of the fur-trapping debate, it was merely a prelude to what came next.

Alaska zoologist John Holzworth had come to the NAAS annual meeting to secure what he had assumed would be a mere formality: board ratification of its earlier vote favoring the creation of a national park or refuge on Admiralty Island in the Alaskan Territory to protect grizzly bears. But after consulting with Audubon board member George Pratt, the directors had cooled to the bear refuge idea and no longer cared to endorse it.

Pratt, who had come to Pearson's defense in Edge's suit for the NAAS mailing list, headed the American Forestry Association. He explained to his fellow board members that timber-rich Admiralty Island was dear to wood-pulpers and loggers, and foresters would not surrender their economic interest in very large trees for the sake of very large bears. When Holzworth was informed that the NAAS board had indefinitely tabled the bear refuge idea, he exploded, his patience with the organization perhaps taxed by Edge's exchanges with Holt and Pearson.

"So, some day—you are waiting for some day," Holzworth seethed. "If I ever saw a classic piece of lying that had more indecision and procrastination . . ." Chairman Palmer gaveled Holzworth out of order, which further enraged the bear man. Palmer banged the gavel so hard it shattered, and pandemonium again broke out in an Audubon meeting.[115]

"Throw him out!" several men in the audience shouted, and lunged toward Holzworth. "Who'll put me out, who'll put me out, come one, any three of you!" Holzworth screamed back at them menacingly. Edge watched in perhaps bemused, comradely admiration as yet another conservationist with guts to fight tilted against Audubon's armored inertia. When the room quieted, she offered a motion to support the bear refuge. It was tabled, as were her attempts to secure board support for the protection of all hawks and eagles. The board was in no mood to be bullied by sentimentalists.[116]

"Bear Panic at Bird Meeting" read the next day's headline for the *New York Sun*'s article about the Audubon meeting, upstaging Edge's trapping confrontation; "Audubonists' Feathers Are Ruffled and One Member Offers to Be Tossed Out," read the subhead. Buried in the story was a brief, facetious mention of "Mrs. C. N. Edge, famed for her feeling for muskrats."[117]

After this meeting Audubon members began resigning in great numbers. The NAAS attributed the decline to the Depression, although unsolicited donations to the ECC increased at the same time. Two-thirds of Audubon's members had quit since Edge's campaign against the NAAS began, making her active mailing list larger than theirs.[118]

Some of Edge's enemies became her admiring friends: Connecticut senator Walcott and (secretly) W. L. McAtee, a senior food biologist at the Bureau of Biological Survey, offered to be advisers to the ECC. Stealthily, key Audubon defectors like Frank Chapman and Robert Cushman Murphy also joined her side. A productive symbiosis evolved. By educating Edge, the progressive ornithologists, zoologists, and naturalists served the ECC's mission of public education. Meanwhile, she remained willing to take heat for any of the challenges they posed to the status quo.

Edge's war against Audubon spilled into the supposedly disinterested ranks of the American Ornithologists' Union, in which NAAS vice president Theodore Palmer also held office. When Mrs. Charles Noel Edge sent in her three dollars for membership, her check was cashed but full privileges of membership were being withheld, she was told.[119] Palmer threatened to resign from the AOU if Edge was permitted to attend its meetings and vote on any AOU matter. His rejection, he made clear, was not because she was a woman or an amateur in the field, since the AOU accepted both. Palmer's hostility was purely personal.

Within the AOU her league of admirers was growing. Each year more scientists signed the petition that requested Mrs. Charles Noel Edge be extended full rights of AOU membership. Six times Palmer threatened to resign if the petitioners succeeded. The petitioners backed down five times rather than lose Palmer. The sixth time the petition circulated, however, Palmer was the one to back down, and against his protest Edge finally became a voting member of the AOU.

EDGE'S COSTLY RELENTLESSNESS on behalf of conservation convinced her opponents that she was a "New York society woman of unlimited wealth who fed her vanity and her hot temper by dabbling in conservation."[120] Pearson and the others did not guess that this was far from the case. The ECC operated on a shoestring, and Rosalie Edge gave no money of her own to it. Willard Van Name, a man of slender means, kept the ECC propped up from one month to the next, aided by the small donations that steadily came in. As the ECC's sole worker, Edge was indefatigable and confided to Peter that she would not give a penny to the ECC because, she said, "I give all of myself to conservation." She could, she said, "do no more than that."[121]

During the winter of 1933, the woman whom Audubon leaders presumed was using her unlimited personal wealth to defeat them was, by her own financial estimation, wiped out. In public, conventional conservation was Rosalie Edge's great enemy. In private she was twelve years into the war against her estranged husband, and the situation had steadily gotten worse. Charles Edge had used Rosalie's East Seventy-second Street townhouse as collateral on his stock-market investments and lost it.[122]

To protect the rest of her household possessions from Charles and his creditors, Edge sold her home's rich contents for one dollar—at least on paper—to nineteen-year-old Peter.[123] In a revised legal separation agreement, Charles agreed to pay Rosalie a lump sum of forty thousand dollars if she surrendered her spousal claim to his mansion at Parsonage Point.

On January 20, 1933, Mabel Rosalie Edge conveyed the deed of her cherished East Seventy-second Street brownstone to the Bank for Savings in the City of New York. It had been home to her for almost fifty years, the place to which she always returned after her global migrations. By losing her house, Charles had betrayed her yet again, she confided to her young friend Julia Stubblefield Langsam.[124] Julia would register that betrayal was a recurring theme in her friend's life.

The irony of the situation could not have escaped Rosalie. Weeks after her effort to assure that a wildlife refuge would not be that in name only, she was left with no refuge of her own. Edge rented one apartment on Fifth Avenue and then found a preferable one in the Beaux Arts building on the same block. The second apartment offered the views of Central Park that she would enjoy from her living room for the rest of her life. When she did not dine at the Colony Club, she ate at the Chippendale table overlooking the trees. She told Irving Brant the vista made her "feel like a *bird*."[125]

Precious family heirlooms and marital acquisitions that had filled fifteen rooms were winnowed to furnish four. Rosalie gave some antique furniture to Julia and Walter Langsam. Edge wryly explained to Julia that after being forced to relinquish so many beloved possessions she had managed to hang on to her Oriental pearls and Oriental carpets, but she feared that neither was worth much. "Cultured pearls are now in fashion, and Oriental carpets have gone out of it," she said.[126]

Nevertheless, the unfashionable Oriental carpets, the French inlaid dressing table, the Chippendale table, the Whistler etchings, the Chinese silk embroidered coat she had purchased on the eve of the Chinese Revolution, and an impressive remnant of her father's prized library of leather-bound first editions were the rich detritus of her old life. Perhaps under the influence of the lyrical ornithologist Jacques Delamain, this traumatic juncture in her life would also be marked with a poem.

> I like the new arrangement of my books,
> Arrayed for height, not content, lined-up pell-mell—
> The Bible and Darwin, Punch, Conrad, Reineke, Fuchs,
> Moby Dick, the Rubaiyat, Hemingway's Tolling Bell. . .
> The Iliad my great-great-grandfather read,
> And logarithms, my Dad's idea of play,
> Hug cookery receipts for brides long dead,
> And flank this Simian World, by Clarence Day.
> So shelf by shelf. Gone is the ample space
> Where, catalogued and sorted for our learning
> Books drew aside, each subject in its place.
> New lights and old beliefs with wisdom burning,
> They live and let live now in easy reach.
> And is not this what comradeship can teach?[127]

Her new quarters could no longer house the ECC. Edge moved the committee's headquarters from the old servants' sitting room to a dingy pocket of an office on Lexington Avenue across from Bloomingdale's—ECC rent being another expense undoubtedly picked up by Van Name. A few months after she moved to a new address, rumors of improprieties in her marriage reached her. An Audubon loyalist wrote to object to her prior suffrage career, which he noted had been characterized by her unwomanly vehemence.[128] In light of her own compromised marital situation, he suggested Edge mind her own business and cease telling the NAAS what to do.

Edge forwarded the letter to Charles Dickerman Williams and instructed him to strike the proper legal tone with the offensive man. Mrs. Edge was "doubly aggrieved," Williams wrote back. "Any woman of honor resents scandalous gossip about herself, and, second, she realizes that her campaign for reform of the Audubon Society will be handicapped by such tactics, the gossip be as irrelevant as it is false."[129]

If the gentleman knew what was good for him, he would apologize to Mrs. Edge immediately, Williams warned, and sent him a suitable letter of apology to save him from having to compose his own. If the gentleman wished to avoid hearing from Mrs. Edge's lawyer again, he would sign the letter Williams provided and not speak of the matter ever.

Mrs. Charles Noel Edge's change of address had perhaps also caught the attention of the self-appointed arbiters of the Social Register. Her worthiness for continued inclusion on the exalted list was questioned; curiosity about her marital status was expressed.[130] She rebuked the inquirers for their impertinence and mentioned her lawyer might give them a call. Mr. and Mrs. Charles Noel Edge retained their standing as a married couple in the Social Register, which of course is what they were.

AS ROSALIE EDGE and the ECC were making news, her Colonist friends remained congenially disinterested in her work. "Dear Rosalie, she is so fond of the birds," she heard one woman murmur as she passed her. Another time she overheard, "You know, she *likes hawks*."[131] Colonists ascribed Edge's eccentric affections to her being "a conservationist," an explanation that seemed to satisfy her and them. Once, however, a puzzled club member pressed the matter further. "What do you do when you look at a bird?" the woman asked Rosalie.

"What do you do when you see a great painting?" Edge archly retorted. Expanding later on this response she wrote: "Sensitive, cultured, deeply religious, I can picture her enraptured before a great cartoon of Raphael, or an exquisite Memling. 'This artist,' she might say to herself, 'is inspired by God.' When we who have a feeling for birds observe a mighty eagle, or the perfection of a tiny warbler, we see, not the inspiration of God filtered through human agency, but the very handiwork of the Creator himself."[132]

Conservation and Colony Club membership were two distinct affirmations of Rosalie Edge's self-actualization and social elevation. She required both to feel secure in the world, alone.

Oil portraits of Rosalie Edge's parents, Harriet Bowen Barrow and John Wylie Barrow, painted in 1864 at the Gerrard Street flat in London where John Wylie grew up and his cousin Charles Dickens frequently visited. *Used by permission of Deborah Edge.*

The Noblest Girl—Mabel Rosalie Barrow at about age four, believed to have been taken at the Barrow family's West Forty-sixth Street home, ca. 1881. *Used by permission of Deborah Edge.*

Mabel Rosalie Barrow at about age twenty. *Used by permission of Deborah Edge.*

Charles Noel Edge and his bride, Mabel, on their wedding day, May 28, 1909, in a garden on The Bluff in Yokohama. *Used by permission of Deborah Edge.*

Charles and Rosalie on a steamship in 1909. The newlywed Edges "were in a chronic state of going on the next boat." *Used by permission of Deborah Edge.*

Peter Edge, at about age six, and his four-year old sister, Margaret, standing by a suffrage sign that their mother had posted. *Used by permission of Deborah Edge.*

Rosalie Edge walking between her "Baby Giants," Peter and Margaret, ca. 1937. *Used by permission of Deborah Edge.*

A display of the annual *sparebenbarich*, as the Kittatinny Ridge hawk slaughter was known in the local patois, prior to Edge's establishing the world's first hawk sanctuary at the site in 1934. *Used by permission of Hawk Mountain Sanctuary Archives.*

On one visit to the Kittatinny Ridge in the fall of 1932 Richard Pough and Henry Collins laid out the dead and dying hawks by age and type, assigning some order to the carnage. *Used by permission of Hawk Mountain Sanctuary Archives.*

In the fall of 1934 hunters protested their opposition to the new hawk sanctuary by nailing dead hawks to trees offsite and displaying them on the bridge over the Schuylkill River at Drehersville. *Used by permission of Hawk Mountain Sanctuary Archives.*

Maurice and Irma Broun in Schaumbach's with puppies, ca. 1938. *Used by permission of Hawk Mountain Sanctuary Archives.*

Rosalie Edge, center, standing near Maurice Broun beneath the sign indicating the sanctuary's North Lookout trailhead. Irma Broun, left, with Clayton Hoff, a Delaware Valley Ornithological Club member who made peace with Edge after "the Affair of the Supper Party," when the NAAS tried to claim Hawk Mountain Sanctuary. Photo ca. 1940. *Used by permission of Hawk Mountain Sanctuary Archives.*

A CRISIS IN CONSERVATION

Serious Danger of Extinction of Many North American Birds

If bird students and nature lovers are led by self-congratulatory reports of bird protection organizations or by the deplorable and astonishing indifference to bird destruction and extermination that scientific and ornithological associations exhibit, to suppose that all is going well with our native birds, they are due to get a rude awakening before many years have passed. Effective protection for our song and insectivorous birds against willful destruction may be nearly an accomplished fact, and the former wholesale sacrifice of bird life for millinery purposes has ended, permanently we hope, as far as this country is concerned. In all other cases our success is far from complete; in many cases there has been no success at all and no sincere effort is being made to achieve any. The results that we are paying for we do not get, and the outlook for the long survival of many of our most beautiful and most conspicuous and most interesting native birds has become a poor one. The earnestness, activity and efficiency which characterized our bird protection efforts and our organizations for that purpose during the early years of the present century has not been maintained.

LET US FACE THE FACTS NOW RATHER THAN ANNIHILATION OF MANY OF OUR NATIVE BIRDS LATER

Factors destructive to bird life increase almost from day to day, but appeals and protests many times repeated have not had the slightest effect on the complacent inertia and perfunctory routine of those to whom the public has been intrusting bird protection work and bird protection money, and what is vastly more serious, the responsibility for the future existence of a large part of our American bird fauna. This pamphlet has therefore been printed for distribution not to the public in general, but especially to those who are giving evidence of their interest in our native birds by membership in organizations for bird study, nature study and wild life protection and, most of all, to those who are making contributions for bird protection work. The remedy is in their hands.

THE SITUATION WITH WHICH WE HAVE TO DEAL

With the surprising increase of popular interest in nature study that the last few years have shown and with sums of money available that the pioneers in bird protection work of a generation ago did not ever hope for, results have grown less instead of greater. The expenditure of public funds

1

The pamphlet that sparked Edge's conservation activism. *Crisis in Conservation* was written by Willard Van Name, W. Dewitt Miller, and Davis Quinn. Edge received it in Paris in August 1929. *Used by permission of Hawk Mountain Sanctuary Archives.*

Opposite: Sampling of ECC pamphlets attacking the Bureau of Biological Survey for its poisoning policies, and conservationists who opposed bald eagle protection, 1930. Both subjects were ones Edge returned to repeatedly over the next thirty years. *Used by permission of Hawk Mountain Sanctuary Archives.*

THE UNITED STATES BUREAU OF DESTRUCTION AND EXTERMINATION

The Misnamed and Perverted "Biological Survey"

CONTENTS

"FRAMING" THE BIRDS OF PREY

An Arraignment of the Fanatical and Economically Harmful Campaign of Extermination Being Waged Against the Hawks and Owls

Its Motives not Conservation of Game, but to Sell Ammunition, and Stave off Reduction of Bag and Shortening of Open Seasons by Diverting Attention from the Real Cause of the Decrease of Game

Among all birds there are none more fascinating for the
more certain to arouse the interest and admiration of the
than the birds of prey—the hawks, eagles and owls. The
and beautiful plumage, in spite of the absence of bright
derful eyesight and powers of flight, and the activity and
many members of the group possess make them remarkable
birds, but among all living creatures. Taken as a whole
are of great economic usefulness, only a few of them
extent on birds, and to a still less extent on game
troublesome small rodents, such as field mice and
large insects such as grasshoppers and locusts, so that
dations are more than compensated for.

These beautiful birds will soon be largely
country if their wanton destruction continues
every species of such birds native of North A
diminished in numbers within the last few ye
of a hawk or other bird of prey even of the s
longer a frequent event in most places.

This is the result of nothing else than
vindictive persecution
fact that

THE BALD EAGLE, OUR NATIONAL EMBLEM

Danger of Its Extinction by the Alaska Bounty

A criticism of the United States Biological Survey which,
by its own admission, has for years been authorizing the
continuance of the Alaska bounty on eagles because of
"alleged" destructiveness to game, etc., without investigation and without proof of any necessity for it. Also an
.... for the passage of the bills to protect the Bald
Eagle now before Congress

.... matter of small consequence whether this magnificent bird, one
.... most beautiful, interesting and unique of North American
.... national emblem and the symbol of the power and authority
.... our government, passes out of existence or not?

.... introduced by Senator Peter S. Norbeck and H. R. 7994,
....gressman August H. Andresen, will afford the Bald Eagle
....ral government, which it should have, being a migra-
....ts of its range. These bills can hardly fail to force
....vey to take action to end the Alaska bounty on eagles.
....g this all the time, but has done nothing.
....ills in the form of letters or telegrams to Senators
....tly needed. See the last page of this pamphlet.

... PRESENT DESPERATE SITUATION

....tates proper, the Bald Eagle is rapidly dis-
....one its former nesting places, and deserting
....ne, in spite of the protection it receives in
....entiment, for it is by no means so wary
....nificent size and conspicuousness should
....ng people who never let an opportunity
....tiful creature. Throughout most of its
....in raising any young. Owing to the
....th of the young, about five months
....does not consists of more than two
....s full of peril for the parent birds
....d in a large tree, are conspicuous
....in a place safe enough for an
....to find every year. Year by
....dwindles. If a species cannot

ITS ALIVE!—KILL IT!

The Present Policy Toward Native Birds and Animals of North America

THE UNITED STATES BIOLOGICAL SURVEY IS NOW
EXTENDING ITS WHOLESALE POISONING
OPERATIONS TO THE SONG BIRDS

Tens of thousands of Redwings, Linnets or House Finches, (a bird similar to the Purple Finch of the eastern states), Song Sparrows and other
native Sparrows, and Horned Larks are poisoned by the Biological Survey
in California. Operations purposely conducted when the birds had young.
Thousands of nestlings left to perish of hunger and exposure. Biological
Survey Chief prides himself on the success of this "experimental work" to
develop effective methods for large scale destruction.

CLOSE TIE-UP OF NATIONAL ASSOCIATION OF AUDU-
BON SOCIETIES AND BIOLOGICAL SURVEY FUNCTIONING
WITH GREAT EFFICIENCY TO PREVENT EFFECTIVE OP-
POSITION BY THE AUDUBON ASSOCIATION AGAINST THE
POISONING, AND TO SUPPRESS ALL AVOIDABLE PUBLICITY
REGARDING IT.

SUBJECTS DEALT WITH IN THIS PAMPHLET

Hawk Mountain Sanctuary board members Joseph Taylor, Roger Tory Peterson, and Marion Ingersoll with sanctuary employees Francis Trembly and Maurice Broun posed with Peter Edge and Rosalie Edge on the North Lookout during the annual hawk migration. Photo ca. 1950. *Used by permission of Hawk Mountain Sanctuary Archives.*

Edge in Yosemite National Park in the summer of 1935, with park superintendent Col. Charles G. Thomson, left, and unidentified ranger. "Do you want to save the sugar pines?" she had come from New York to ask. *Used by permission of Deborah Edge.*

Edge displayed a photo of herself standing by a Douglas fir tree on the Olympic Peninsula during congressional hearings on the establishment of Olympic National Park, 1937. *Used by permission of Hawk Mountain Sanctuary Archives.*

Rachel Carson at Hawk Mountain Sanctuary's North Lookout, 1946.
Richard Pough introduced Carson to the sanctuary, and Carson later requested data
from Hawk Mountain on raptor migration that provided persuasive evidence of
DDT's effect on the birds' declining population. *Photo by Shirley Gibbs.*
Used by permission of Frances Collin, trustee.

RACHEL L. CARSON

11701 BERWICK ROAD, SILVER SPRING, MARYLAND

May 13, 1960

Mr. Maurice Broun
Hawk Mountain Sanctuary
Route #2
Kempton, Pennsylvania

Dear Mr. Broun:

As you may possibly have heard from some of our friends in the conservation world, I am at work on a book that will explore some of the effects of chemical pesticides, especially their ecological effects. In writing of what has happened to the birds, I am of course mentioning the problem of the eagles even though we cannot as yet pin it down specifically to pesticides. I have seen you quoted at various times to the effect that you now see very few immature eagles in fall migration over Hawk Mountain. Would you be good enough to write me your comments on this, with any details and figures you think significant.

As I understand it, ornithologists believe that the eagles passing over Hawk Mountain in September belong to the southern population which has wandered northward in the spring and summer. Do you also have a migration later in the fall or early winter of eagles that nest in the north? If so, have you seen any signs of a reduction in these northern populations?

You may be sure that anything you tell me will be most useful.

Sincerely yours,

Rachel Carson

C:D

Rachel Carson wrote to Maurice Broun several times while investigating the decline in hawk migration for *Silent Spring*. The sanctuary provided significant data that helped Carson prove her case against the pesticide DDT's damaging effect on bird populations. *Used by permission of Frances Collin, trustee.*

Rosalie Edge with a red-tailed hawk, ca. 1937. *Photo by Maurice Broun.*
Used by permission of Hawk Mountain Sanctuary Archives.

Edge at her ECC office
the summer of 1959. Photo
by Carsten Lien, who said
she had just ordered him
not to take her picture.
He took it anyway and
captured her visual
remonstrance. *Used by
permission of Carsten Lien.*

Willard Van Name, Edge's
most important mentor.
For years they refused
to speak to each other in
person. When Van Name
died in 1959, however,
Edge commissioned a
stained-glass window
in his honor and had
it installed in Hawk
Mountain's community
room. *Used by permission
of Hawk Mountain
Sanctuary Archives.*

Edge, even at Hawk Mountain dressed as if she were on Fifth
Avenue. The Native American silver dragonfly brooch was a
favorite piece of jewelry. *Used by permission of Hawk Mountain
Sanctuary Archives.*

CHAPTER SEVEN

Sweet Reasonableness

In the fall of 1927, George Miksch Sutton, a bird artist and ornithologist from Pennsylvania, accompanied the state's game
protector, Archie Smith, to a mountain ridge on the county
line between Berks and Schuylkill, hoping to see the impressive
hawk migration that had been rumored for several years. The
two men were not disappointed. "Several gunners accompanied
Mr. Smith to a point along the mountain past which the hawks
flew in numbers, and secured, in a remarkably short time, a total of ninety sharp-shins, sixteen Goshawks, eleven Cooper's
Hawks (*Accipter cooperi*), thirty-two Red-Tailed Hawks (*Buteo
borealis borealis*), and two Duck Hawks (*Rhynchodon peregrinus
anatum*)."[1]

Cars lined the rutted dirt road up to the Kittatinny Ridge's
craggy lookout, and hunters from the nearby towns of Pottsville and Reading piled out with guns and ammunition. It was
the season of the *sparebenbarich*, as the locals called the hawk-
killing spree in the patois of the Pennsylvania Dutch.[2] Within
a few October weekends, thousands of hawks and eagles were
"secured"—to use Sutton's word. Even ospreys, which the Pennsylvania Game Commission had determined were birds useful
to men and ought not be shot, wound up among the dead and
dying.

The Kittatinny's autumn hawk hunt depended on an anomaly of topography and weather. After the season's first blast of
cold air, dry winds from Canada blew south and struck the

Appalachian massif. The convergence of wind, mountain, and hawks mimicked on a grand scale the partnership of a whisk broom with a dustpan and their power over scattered crumbs. Thousands of hawks that had summered along the wide eastern continental flyway were brushed into the narrow seam along the mountain face to be swept by the winds on to their fall migration route.

The birds soared for miles on currents that rose from the warm land, catching each new thermal cell faster than the previous one cooled and sank to earth. Observing that raptors did not flap their wings the way other migratory birds did because of this ability to ride the rising warm air, Wilbur and Orville Wright applied the same principle to keep their first gliders aloft.[3]

Gliding from one thermal cell to the next gave the birds an opportunity to rest on their journey, which for some species was up to five thousand miles. Along the Kittatinny portion of this seasonal and geographical anomaly, however, hawks flew within yards of poised hunters, and at gun-sight level. For hunters the meeting of mountain and wind presented a different opportunity: the ability to shoot more hawks than anyone had ever seen in one place. This part of the annual anomaly was the only one subject to change. Since hawks and eagles were universally loathed, few thought any change necessary.

Heading to the Kittatinny in fall was an act that righted the many wrongs the birds did. For centuries human observers watched in moral horror as hawks snatched innocent birds from midair or skimmed the sky above a forest to drop with missile precision into the treed shadows. In the dark woods a darting rabbit might have caught a bird's penetrating eye from the sky and would be swiftly skewered.

Hawks killed their prey with feet and talons, pinning their meal to the ground as they devoured it or carrying it to a high perch to be shredded. They plucked out feathers or fur and swallowed them and tore with hooked beak into flesh, tendons, and bones. Some hawks landed on an animal with such force that it killed on impact and bloodlessly. Early twentieth-century ornithologists attributed the worst traits of humans to birds of prey. The diminutive sharp-shinned hawk was "the terror of all small birds and the audacious murderer of young chickens," according to the well-respected Arthur Cleveland Bent. Massachusetts field ornithologist Edward Forbush, another of the nation's best-known observers of bird behavior, divided hawks into two categories: the useful and the "pernicious." The Cooper's hawk, a pernicious type, was also "crafty," according to Bent.[4]

Forbush said the Cooper's hawk carried "terror to the hearts of weaker creatures." A "hush of death" fell over the woods after its loud call, as "all erstwhile cheerful thrushes and warblers become still and silent." Exiting the forest after feeding, the Cooper's hawk left a "trail of death and destruction." The duck hawk, or peregrine falcon, was "anathema to the poultryman or gamekeeper." Its only redeeming trait was that it hunted other hawks, jays, and crows, and might be worth preserving only as an example of "rapacious power."[5]

Forbush seemed slightly more forgiving of the eagle, the largest kind of hawk. "Our eagle may deserve some of the epithets that have been heaped upon him," he wrote. "He may be a robber, a skulker and a carrion feeder; nevertheless he is a powerful and noble bird and a master of the air." When Forbush watched a bald eagle wheel in the sky and climb to ten thousand feet above the earth, he could not help but admire the bird for the way it symbolized "a great country and a mighty people." The ornithologist noted that eagles had become rare in the continental United States and so posed fewer problems than previously.[6]

The goshawk, nicknamed goose hawk in Europe for its favorite domestic prey, was another hawk of the pernicious sort. A goshawk attack was "swift, furious and deadly," wrote Forbush in his seminal work *Birds of Massachusetts*. "In the death grapple it clings ferociously to its victim, careless of its own safety until the unfortunate creature succumbs in its steely grip. Its stroke is terrible." Slicing through the neck of a rabbit, a goshawk was as efficient as a guillotine. Forbush described a goshawk that pursued a hen into a farmer's house and "seized her on the kitchen floor in the very presence of an old man and his daughter." In the early 1900s he declared that the goshawk was a race of bird "not to be encouraged by the game keeper, the sportsman or the farmer."[7]

What prompted George Sutton to visit the Kittatinny Ridge in 1927 was an alarming invasion of goshawks.[8] They were competing with hunters for small game and preying on the young livestock roaming the sylvan farms of the Pennsylvania Dutch. The slate gray species rarely visited the state, yet in just two years four hundred severed goshawk heads had been turned in to game authorities for bounty payments. Twenty birds had been killed in the vicinity of the Berks-Schuylkill county line alone.

Goshawk populations fluctuated, from none to an invasion of hundreds, their number rapidly rising or falling in proportion to the quality of an area's food supply. The sudden increase of goshawks in Pennsylvania coincided with the state game commission's painstaking reintroduction of ruffed grouse. Meant for hunters, these birds were also a preferred food source of the "pernicious" visitors.

With so many varieties of dead hawks available at the Kittatinny Ridge, Sutton wanted to examine the contents of all the bird stomachs to see what they ate; to have so many goshawk innards available was a bonus. As a dedicated man of science, he had not come to question whether hunters should continue killing thousands of hawks every year or to ask what effect excessive hawk hunting within the Commonwealth of Pennsylvania might have on the larger scheme of natural things; nor was it his or any other ornithologist's job to posit that there was a larger scheme of natural things for Pennsylvanians to concern themselves about.

That October weekend Sutton quickly gathered 158 dead hawks of four different species and slit open their stomachs. Of the sixteen goshawk stomachs he examined, ten were empty, one contained a chicken, two contained squirrels, one a rabbit, and two held the remains of game-department grouse. He published his dietary findings on all 158 in the prestigious *Wilson Bulletin*.[9] Ornithology was served, and the annual slaughter proceeded.

TEN YEARS BEFORE the Pennsylvania Game Commission was established in 1895, the state had passed "An Act for the Destruction of Wolves, Wildcats, Foxes, Minks, Hawks, Weasels and Owls," bluntly known as the Scalp Act. The act spelled out the prevailing attitude in Pennsylvania and elsewhere toward birds and animals that killed to eat:

> For the benefit of agriculture and the protection of game, within the Commonwealth, there is hereby established the following premiums for the destruction of certain noxious animals and birds, to be paid by the respective counties, in which the same are slain, namely: for every wild cat two dollars, for every red or gray fox one dollar; for every mink fifty cents, for every weasel fifty cents, for every hawk fifty cents, and for every owl, except the Acadian screech or barn owl, which is hereby exempted from the provisions of this act, fifty cents.[10]

The Pennsylvania Game Commission was progressive in its restoration of some game species that had vanished due to excessive hunting or the loss of habitat from logging and farming. "Pennsylvania has been wide awake, and in advance of her time," remarked the hypercritical William Temple Hornaday in 1910 when the state's nascent wildlife refuge system gave deer, rabbits, and squirrels a chance to rebuild their populations.[11]

Pennsylvania's game restoration efforts were especially commendable because the state had been one from which the passenger pigeon had been entirely eliminated. Until the mid-1800s, witnesses marveled at the dense flocks blackening swaths of sky four miles long and one mile wide for entire afternoons. Easy to catch, the pigeons were netted and transported in the millions by rail to big-city restaurants, where they were served as the popular delicacy called squab. In 1914, when the last bird died in his cage at the Cincinnati zoo, the passenger pigeon became the most dramatic example of extinction in the entire country.

"The passenger pigeon millions were destroyed so quickly, and so thoroughly en masse, that the American people utterly failed to comprehend it, and for 30 years obstinately refused to believe that the species had been suddenly wiped off the map of North America," wrote Hornaday.[12] Despite this example of dramatic and contemporary extinction, few in Pennsylvania or elsewhere thought it necessary to accord birds of prey any sort of protection.

People had been critical of a recluse, J. Warren Jacobs, deemed crazy for trying to save wounded hawks.[13] In 1916 Jacobs, a Waynesburg, Pennsylvania, woodworker known for building elaborate birdhouses that were miniature versions of the White House or the U.S. Capitol, distributed a pamphlet that pled for the wanton *sparebenbarich* to stop. During World War I the hunting protests by Henry Shoemaker, a native Pennsylvanian who became ambassador to Bulgaria, aroused his neighbors' ire and called his patriotism into question. The ambassador was accused of depriving America's sons of live target practice before they were shipped off to fight.

Earl Poole, curator of the Reading, Pennsylvania, Public Museum, which housed a bird collection, was another who helplessly witnessed the slaughter year after year. "Twenty to 25 nimrods were stationed at strategic points along the ridge, and every time hawks drifted into sight, it sounded like a Fourth of July celebration," he wrote. The birds seemed confused by "cross currents that blew through the gap, and seem[ed] unable or unwilling to rise out of range, passing from 25 to 100 feet over the trees where they made easy targets."[14]

The late Waldron DeWitt Miller, coauthor, with Willard Van Name, of the infamous *Crisis in Conservation* pamphlet, received evidence of the Kittatinny hawk shoot from a friend who sent him bundles of hawk skins for the American Museum of Natural History's collection. The shoot had disturbed Miller, who was that rare ornithologist who did not find it "advisable to put a bird to death in order to know it better." Miller might have tried to do something about the hawk shoot had he lived.[15]

Locally the shoot was enthusiastically endorsed. In October 1929 the *Pottsville Journal* reported on the arrival of another season: "Chilled by the early October winds, many thousand hawks are sweeping past the mountain pinnacle, inviting extermination, a challenge that has been accepted by local sportsman and hunters who are shooting hundreds on a favorable day. Impressed by the unusual opportunity to wipe out thousands of enemies to bird and game life in the State, a Pottsville sportsman today urged local hunters to cooperate in killing hawks."[16]

The Pennsylvania legislature encouraged the sport by establishing a five-dollar bounty for goshawks. At the beginning of the Depression, bounties gave jobless coal miners a way to make extra money. Since few miners could distinguish a goshawk from any other kind, the bounty encouraged the shooting of more hawks of all species, even though the state only paid for verified goshawks. The *Lebanon Daily News* reported that in 1929 only seven of one hundred hawks turned in for bounty money were goshawks.[17]

Word of the hawk hunt had by this time trickled into the headquarters of the NAAS in New York. At an American Game Conference in New York City, Gilbert Pearson weighed in, tentatively:

> In the interests of the agricultural investments of the country, in consideration of feelings of bird-lovers, for the sake of these great, handsome birds themselves, in the spirit of fair play, will the game authorities not be willing to discourage statewide bounty systems on the killing of all kinds of hawks; and, will they not accept the offer of the National Association of Audubon Societies to assist in educating people of the country, so that they may be better able to distinguish those species protected by law?[18]

The Pennsylvania Game News did as Pearson had blandly counseled and ran an article in 1931 to help hunters distinguish a "good" hawk from a "pernicious" one; perhaps even this response had been sparked by Rosalie Edge's reform campaign. The *Game News* let its readers know that good hawks had short tails, long wings, and soared like turkey vultures. Bad hawks had the opposite configuration and hung in midair before plummeting at great speed.[19] Once this information was published, the public was served and so, it seemed, was conservation.

RICHARD POUGH, a twenty-four-year-old birder and Philadelphia photographer, read Sutton's hawk-shoot article in the *Wilson Bulletin*. In September 1932 he went to see the spectacle for himself. When he stopped to ask farmers if they knew a good place to shoot hawks, he was directed to the mountain ridge north of the tiny town of Drehersville. Dozens of cars were parked along the dirt road, the main route between Pennsylvania's picturesque farms and its grimy coal-mine towns.[20]

A well-worn path led to the summit, crowded with hunters. Pough watched as hawks streamed past at close range, while guns blasted away. He saw birds that had been hit tumble into the trees below or fall to the valley floor. Sometimes a hawk was only grazed by a shot and flew away. The hunters kidded each other about shooting too soon.

Pough returned the next weekend with his brother Harold and another birder named Henry Collins. The hawks weren't flying that day because there wasn't enough wind. The three visitors hiked down to the forest below the ridge and were sickened by what they saw: hundreds of rotting and dying hawks littered the ground. Hunters, it seemed, were unaccustomed to seeing such large birds at close range and often shot too soon, wounding many. The birds perished slowly of hunger and thirst if their injuries weren't mortal. Pough and his party ended their grisly inspection with mercy killings.

The men returned the following weekend when the winds were strong, and hunters again crowded the ridge. A small but lively industry had developed, as entrepreneurial-minded locals drove loads of cartridges up to the site to sell to those who ran out, and scrap dealers came up to shovel the spent brass into sacks and sell it in the nearby towns. Pough and Collins saw a wounded hawk tied to a log at the summit, and as other hawks approached, a man jabbed the captive with a stick. The hawk's shriek attracted the incoming birds' attention, and they too flew into harm's way to investigate possible prey. Nearby, blinded pigeons dangled from long poles, and their flopping movements lured more hawks into shooting range. A sharp-shin disappeared in a puff of feathers. The sound of carnage was unforgettable: a volley of gunfire followed by an ominous, six-second silence; then came a crackling noise like "a tropical deluge" as the struck birds hit the autumn-dry understory.[21]

These putrefying few acres of Pennsylvania woods littered with the dead and dying, spent shot, and spilled blood eerily recalled that most hallowed graveyard at Gettysburg, in the southern part of the state. Pough and Collins carried 230 limp hawks to a clearing. They laid the birds out by species and age, assigning some order to the slaughter. Now and then a quizzical hunter stopped to watch the young men at their gruesome task.[22]

AT FIRST THE ONLY thing the Pough brothers and Collins could think of doing was to appeal to the Pennsylvania Game Commission to enforce the blue law that made hunting illegal on Sundays.[23] When the state game commission showed no interest in doing this, Dick Pough appealed to the Lord's Day Alliance, which opposed hunting on Sundays, unless, he was told, the quarry was vermin, a category that included hawks. Finally, he and Collins urged the Society for the Prevention of Cruelty to Animals to do something. The SPCA posted two off-duty policemen for a few weekends. "We spent three nightmarish weeks on this mountain," one of the guards remembered. One day four hundred hunters showed up, and so many dead birds were left on the ground that a stench to make a person gag hung over the place. "We couldn't do anything about it," the guard said.[24]

Curiously, Dick Pough and Henry Collins did not immediately turn for assistance to the private bird organizations in the region, which were among the oldest and most prestigious in the nation. *The Auk*, published by the American Ornithologists' Union, came out of nearby Lancaster; the Wilson Ornithological Society's *Bulletin*, which ran Sutton's accounts of the slaughter, was based in Philadelphia, eighty miles away; and the sagacious Delaware Valley Ornithological Club, also in Philadelphia, had vowed its dedication to the welfare of birds in all of eastern Pennsylvania, New Jersey, and Delaware.

But it seemed that once again even the strongest bird lovers were conflicted when it came to birds of prey. Tiny Drehersville was a world away from where the wealthy urban birders lived, and they might have looked upon this part of Pennsylvania as they would have the distant frontier.

That December *Bird-Lore* ran Pough's letter about the "appalling slaughter," by which point the hawk migration and the shooting was done for the year. There was time to stop the hunt before it began the next fall, and Pough and Collins expected their exposés would mobilize the important bird protection organizations. But the autumn of 1932 came, and the killing resumed; Collins had gone to the NAAS annual meeting to discuss hawk protection, but met with resistance, no doubt strengthened by Rosalie Edge's attack on refuge fur trapping and John Holzworth's willingness to resort to a fistfight to defend bears.[25] The men next arranged meetings in Philadelphia and New York and invited members of the Hawk and Owl Society, the Linnaean Society, the National Association of Audubon Societies, and the Emergency Conservation Committee—meaning Rosalie Edge.

All present agreed that the best solution was for the NAAS to immediately buy the Blue Mountain ridge top and establish a hawk refuge on it, the first ever. Pearson committed Audubon to contributing key funds to accomplish this goal, and the meetings ended with a unified vision and an embracing sense of relief. "We rejoiced the more because we believed that the new sanctuary would be born with a silver spoon in its mouth, and that a ring of fairy godmothers would stand around its cradle," wrote Rosalie Edge.[26]

Pough contacted the ridge's owners and learned that the exhausted 1,398-acre parcel had been on the market for a long time and could be bought for the amount of back taxes owed. The property was desolate: virgin oaks had been logged off a century before, and chestnut blight had claimed the rest of the biggest trees. With the forest gone, the owners quarried the exposed sandstone for silicone they sold to glass manufacturers. Periodically trespassers burned off the undergrowth to clear the ground for bootleg wild blueberry crops, but the land was so barren that few native birds and wildlife lived there.[27]

People who could afford to buy such a parcel, even at the Depression-era price of about one dollar an acre, were scarce. The most likely prospect was a private gun club that considered buying it and charging hunters for their hawk-hunting pleasure. But the gun club hesitated; the members did not need to buy so much acreage for their narrow seasonal purpose, and the treasury lacked the funds to tender an offer. "We just left it go and left it go," one member explained.[28]

So, too, did the bird-protection organizations that had met in the fall and winter of 1933 and uttered their protective incantations. Audubon had gone so far as to create a twenty-eight-member hawk-and-owl task force, and in a peacemaking gesture, Willard Van Name was invited to serve on it with Pough and renowned wildlife biologists Aldo Leopold and Olaus Murie.

But still nothing changed. Thousands of hawks again tumbled lifelessly into the trees below the Blue Mountain promontories near Drehersville. Audubon's hawk-and-owl task force was impotent. Van Name fumed about "how effectively contrived the whole NAAS machinery was to prevent the accomplishment of any efficient work, or of doing anything whatever except after delays and red tape that would insure its being done too late."[29] The ring of fairy godmothers that Edge praised had fallen under a different spell, rendering it incapable of solutions either practical or magical.

MRS. CHARLES NOEL EDGE might be forgiven for her share of the neglect, even with all her vociferous doubts about the Audubon Societies' ability to act urgently on any matter. She too set aside the unpleasant facts of the Pennsylvania hawk shoot but was at least productively diverted by the ECC's many tasks. They had multiplied ecologically. She screeched her concerns—secretly influenced by career-conscious scientists—from each new ECC pamphlet she put out. The issues spanned the nation and covered far more than the Audubon Society or birds. Each pamphlet was considered "must reading" by a new generation of conservationists inspired by her activism.[30] They were "always useful," and "inspired all the conservationists of the day."[31]

The ECC's comprehensive conservation message was coming into vogue in Washington, D.C., with the change in the White House's occupant. Like his cousin Theodore thirty years earlier, Franklin Delano Roosevelt loved nature and was expected to take aggressive measures to integrate new federal protections of it. For this second President Roosevelt, the conservation gospel of utility embraced by Cousin Theodore's administration was tempered by Edge's message of interconnection. "A forest is not solely so many board feet of lumber to be logged when market conditions make it profitable," FDR had said. He spoke reverently of the incalculable balance between "the organic and inorganic worlds."[32]

The ECC had loyal friends who moved into influential positions in the new administration. Writer Irving Brant and cartoonist J. N. "Ding" Darling, both conservationists of the ECC stripe, had gained the confidence of their fellow midwestern progressives, Secretary of the Interior Harold Ickes and Secretary of Agriculture Henry Wallace. "Secretary Wallace and Secretary Ickes are with us," Edge trumpeted to a friend, after the men were sworn in.[33] Both President Roosevelt and Secretary Ickes, a passionate gardener, reminded her of trees, she said: "spreading trees that offer shade to the world weary, or trees hard and gnarled, but fine-grained and sound to the core."[34] Had she been on better terms with her co-Colonist Eleanor Roosevelt, she might have been treated to a private meeting with the president himself.

Secretary Ickes respected Irving Brant's ECC-informed stance on conservation so much that he offered him the position of National Park Service director not once but twice. Brant declined both times. He did not want to abandon his writing career and preferred to embark on the literary project that would consume much of the next twenty years, a five-volume biography of President James Madison. Brant did agree, however, to serve as Ickes's consultant on conservation issues and was paid forty-five dollars a day plus his expenses; Edge, who worked closely with him, received nothing and paid her own way.[35]

The cartoonist J. N. "Ding" Darling might seem as odd a choice to head the Bureau of Biological Survey as political outsider Irving Brant would have made as director of the National Park Service. But Secretary of Agriculture Wallace was also open to novel approaches at so dire a time in the nation's history, and Darling did come with some experience for the job. As well as being an artist, he had earned a college degree in biology and was a former director of Iowa's wildlife department.

The appointment of Darling, who had not been afraid to associate his name with the ECC, is one of the strongest indications that Edge's continuous barrages against the Bureau of Biological Survey had taken their toll. At one of many dinners with her comrade in arms, she continued to press him with her agenda; one night she and Darling stayed at a restaurant so late that its management threatened to turn off its lights. Edge had dominated the conversation with her instructions of what he needed to do. Darling had no chance to bring up "the anomalous position" in which he was left if she was "serious about the matter and intend to advocate the elimination of the Bureau of Biological Survey." He wrote to her afterward, "I can't very well continue as Chief of the Biological Survey and have my name appear as one of the Board of Directors of an organization which advocates the destruction of the Bureau of which I am chief."[36]

Darling quit the ECC's board of directors, as he called it for lack of a better term, and Rosalie retained frequent, needling access to him. She voiced her skepticism about her loyal ally's ability to do much about one of her chief campaigns: ending "the yearly appropriation of the United States Bureau of Biological Survey for the poisoning of mammals and certain insectivorous birds."[37]

She told Darling that game and ranch factions were too deeply entrenched in the agency he had inherited, and poisoning as a way to manage predators and insects was too much their conventional wisdom. "You should look to your laurels and go back to doing what you know how to do—incomparably well," Edge advised her friend and former ECC adviser, by which she meant cartooning.[38] She attempted to cut off the Survey's funding at the source, giving the Depression as a reason to House Appropriations Committee chairman Joseph Byrns: "While it is the patriotic duty of every citizen to make sacrifice, if need be, in order to reduce the expenses of government, it is of paramount importance to cut out of the Budget a needless expense for operations most harmful."[39] Perhaps this Congress would be an easier one to persuade to end blanket poisoning, by emphasizing its cost rather than the harm done.

Because Darling had accepted the position at the Survey without much power, Edge wrote him letters intended to prick his conscience.

Dear Mr. Darling,

I read with great interest the news item regarding your acceptance of the gift of $30,000 from a leading arms manufacturer and of the additional $42,000 of the tax payers' money which the Survey will contribute for courses in game management to be established in several universities. This is progress indeed. The amount offered to Pearson of the Audubon Association twenty years ago was only $20,000 [it was $25,000, but Edge wrote $20,000]. Accept our congratulations. May I offer you our Teaching units and all our free literature for the required reading of these courses? In frankness, however, I should state that our literature is for the preservation of all wild life and not merely for that small proportion of it known as "game." Perhaps your courses can be extended to cover the preservation of all our wildlife resources considering that your department represents the interests of all citizens.[40]

And another:

Dear Mr. Darling,

Will you kindly let me know which gull colonies of Maine are being visited by the Biological Survey for the purpose of puncturing eggs. I am particularly interested in this matter and would be glad to have all the information you can give me. I would like to know the name of the specific island or rocks.[41]

Darling implored her to show some "sweet reasonableness" now and then.[42] "You are always so full of such violent opinions regarding such surprisingly nice people that I am always somewhat surprised by your statements," he wrote in exasperation a few months later, after she accused the entire Survey staff of ineptitude. "Good heavens, Madam, didn't I jump in with all my clothes on in order to rescue the old ship which had been rammed and battered into an almost sinking condition and why shouldn't I think there were fine men among them?"[43] Darling stayed at the Survey less than a year. With new formulations and delivery methods, large-scale poisoning of predators and pests continued, as did Edge's opposition.

BY THE TIME her friends Brant and Darling made it to Washington, Edge was no longer as "green as any school boy" as she had been in 1931 when she first went to Capitol Hill as a lobbyist.[44] On that occasion she blithely asked North Dakota senator Gerald Nye to introduce a bill funding the purchase of eight thousand acres of virgin sugar pines on the border of Yosemite National Park in California. It was Edge's gratefulness to her anonymous benefactor Willard Van Name, who called sugar pines his favorite tree, that perhaps impelled her to act. With her mentor's help, she wrote the pamphlet *Save the Yosemite Sugar Pines* to alert the public to plans for logging the grove. Senator Nye did as Edge asked, and a bill was introduced. Nothing happened. This had been her first lesson in political advocacy.

It was, however, neither Darling nor Brant who provided Edge's introduction to Secretary of the Interior Harold Ickes. The ACLU's Roger Baldwin, a brief adherent of the ECC until he joined the NAAS board, opened that particular door for her. She walked through it soon after Ickes assumed his post, writing to him beforehand "on a matter of importance to [his] Department and of interest to this Committee."[45]

Her first meeting with the secretary happened to be on the day a large reception was held in his honor in his not-yet organized office. The new secretary of the interior knew of Mrs. Edge but did not yet know that she never came to Washington, D.C., for a mere hello and handshake. As always she had a conservation emergency to attend to—and now, so did the secretary. The matter on her mind that day dealt with the approved iniquity of a dam on Yellowstone Lake in Yellowstone National Park. The dam, intended to supply more water for Montana and Wyoming, would divert so much flow from magnificent Yellowstone Falls that it would flatten the park's dramatic chute to a trickle.

President Hoover had approved the water diversion several years earlier, and it seemed the sort of cause others gave up as lost, but that sparked Edge's desire to fight. The Yellowstone dam also gave her the first chance to impress upon an educable secretary of the interior the inviolability of the nation's natural patrimony, its national parks. Armed with maps of the park, Edge waited her turn to speak to Ickes during the party in his office.

She found herself standing among "the strangest assemblage of people" she had ever seen.[46]

There were black-robed priests of the Greek Orthodox Church and Buddhist monks in sandals. An Indian delegation in "magnificent war-bonnets of eagle feathers" waited to greet the new secretary of the interior, who as a Chicago attorney had prominently represented Indian causes. The guests bespoke the wide range of responsibilities that collected in the Department of the Interior, which Edge described as "the attic into which are thrown all the affairs that have not found a place in other Departments."[47]

When she at last moved into Ickes's greeting range, Edge introduced herself and immediately unfurled her maps onto his desk. The colorful assemblage pressed in around her. As she hurriedly explained the Yellowstone project that had been approved, "the Secretary looked appalled." He told her "he had no time to go into such a complicated matter. 'See the people waiting for me. I must talk to them all,'" he told her. Ickes told her to take her maps and explanations to his top aide, a young lawyer named Nathan Margold.[48]

Nathan Margold studied her maps and listened carefully to her explanation. He agreed that President Hoover's diversion order contradicted the laws governing the integrity of national parks and must be overturned.

The Yellowstone dam was not built. Rosalie Edge claimed it as her first victory in the new era of conservation that was dawning. It demonstrated that, as Brant had promised, this Department of the Interior would be vigilant in its protection of the nation's resources perhaps more than any previous Department of the Interior had been. From that point onward, Rosalie Edge would "turn up within the walls of the Department of the Interior" with great frequency.[49]

By 1934 she was busy shuttling by train back and forth to Washington, D.C., with her demands that the ECC's entire barrage of conservation emergencies be addressed, issues, she insisted, that neither Audubon nor any other organization had gotten around to representing. Secretary of the Interior Harold Ickes would prove as receptive to her agenda as she would be to his. Their relationship became as uniquely symbiotic as the one she had developed with scientists and bureaucrats reluctant to advocate publicly on behalf of their unpopular views, and sometimes as secretive. Edge understood that for conservation's new breed of national policy makers to stem the tide of nature's destruction, they needed the help of the ECC. Its pamphlets built "public support in advance of action," so that leaders could point to how they were fulfilling the informed will of the people.[50] The policy makers needed the fresh input from the policy shapers, and fresh input is what the ECC would give them, repeatedly.

In Ickes's first years as secretary of the interior, the ECC outlined its agenda through its must-read publications: *The Proposed Olympic National Park*, which called for the establishment of a national park on the Olympic Peninsula in the Northwest, was beginning to create quite a stir. But there was also *Montana's Sanctuary for Duck Killers* and *Disaster to the Yellowstone Park Elk Herds*. ECC literature was the first to announce a new issue necessitating conservation advocacy.

Edge's pamphlets protested that beaches were "defiled with oil and with dead and dying birds." They opposed the heavily subsidized ranchers in the West. They demanded international cooperation for the protection of the elephant, the rhinoceros, and the giraffe in Africa and federal protection for John Holzworth's grizzly bears in Alaska. ECC literature advocated for the protection of eagles, whales, sea lions, redwoods, and swamps.[51] The ECC provided the public with the most comprehensive blueprint for action of the day. All told, more than a million of its publications were mailed.

Edge went to Washington to speak—or sometimes to charmingly hector—lawmakers and bureaucrats, weaving instructive or entertaining excursions into her congressional testimony. "Ding" Darling's cartoon of a befuddled duck, which she had displayed during a wildlife hearing, was only one of the visual aids she used to make her point more colorfully.[52]

"Was it your organization that complained so bitterly about the so-called 'slaughter' of elk in the Teton forest region?" a hostile congressman once asked her during a hearing.[53]

"We have been complaining about it, yes," Edge replied, referring to the ECC's pamphlet demanding winter range in Wyoming's Jackson Hole. She offered to give the congressman "a little lecture on the elk." He declared he wanted none. That did not stop her: "Excuse me. What I want to say was that no matter how much you eat all summer, nor no matter how much I eat all summer, no matter how fat I might get in the summer, if I had nothing to eat in the winter I would starve. So with the elk. They have plenty to eat all summer; but being cut off of their food in winter, they starve, you see."[54]

Although the warm reception she received from Ickes and his Department of the Interior aides encouraged Edge to present her entire barrage, so too did the incontrovertible evidence of serious harm being done to the earth. On May 11, 1934, evidence of such damage blanketed the ivory keys of her grand piano, tables, and book shelves in grit. There was "dust, dust everywhere," Edge wrote. The Manhattan sky darkened hours before sunset. Streetlights went on, and people rushed inside buildings to get out of the strange, thick air. Edge was curious, went outside, and stood on Fifth Avenue to stare at the "billowing up, an ominous cloud that blackened the west." At first she thought there had been an explosion in New Jersey.[55]

It was the great dust storm packing the wind as it blew across the continent with tons of earth particles until it reached the East Coast and hurled its full freight at the complacent cities. The "life-essence of Oklahoma farms" settled on the furniture of the rich and poor alike in New York. For Edge the day marked "the beginning of integration in conservation." Plains topsoil was "a plaything of the winds, blown into the sea," and it struck her as perhaps never before that nothing less than the planet itself was at stake in her crusade for nature.[56]

Edge called the ailing William Hornaday, who also read the dirt in the air as a sign that nature was being destroyed by human rapaciousness and willful ignorance. "Thank God," he said. "Now the people have seen it, they will understand."[57] Or as Edge remembered her cousin Charles Dickens had written, we "almost die and learn, and learn sooner." Conservationists, she wrote,

> could no longer be content to work alone, each along the lines of his special interests, but must fit these into the pattern of the whole. The sanctuary for hawk protection could no longer be satisfied only to protect hawks, it must also teach forest protection and soil protection; the National Forests and National Parks must preserve watersheds; the birds and animals must be protected, not merely because this species or another is interesting to some group of biologists, but because each is a link in a living chain that leads back to the mother of every living thing on land, the living soil.[58]

Edge had not yet begun using the words *environment* and *ecology* in her pamphlets or speeches. But their meanings were implicit in what she said.

M. R. Edge, Lessee

With so many emergencies flying about her in the spring of 1934, Rosalie Edge allowed herself to believe that the NAAS was establishing the hawk sanctuary in Pennsylvania. About a month after the dust storm, her understanding of nature's interconnections was particularly keen, and she called Richard Pough for a progress report.

"What has Audubon done about the hawk shooting in Pennsylvania?" she asked him.[1] Audubon had done little, he told her. The NAAS had sent a man to scout the Kittatinny Ridge the previous fall, but there had been no wind the day he came and he saw neither hunters nor hawks. The society had decided that nothing needed to be done immediately.

Hearing this, Edge could not endure another hawk shooting season and one more degradation of nature. "It was no use to reason with myself, to try to persuade myself that this was the business of others," she wrote. "I was impelled to stop the killing."[2] As June's heat simmered in the city, she and Peter, home for the summer from Harvard, drove to tiny Drehersville. Richard Pough met them there and introduced them to the real-estate agent who represented the owner of the mountain property. Together they drove over the primitive bridge that crossed the Little Schuylkill River and lurched up the rocky and rutted two miles of switchbacks, virtually unchanged from a century before, when mule-drawn wagons crossed the mountain.

We can picture Edge alighting onto the miserable road dressed as though she were stepping from a cab at curbside on Fifth Avenue, her tailored suit accessorized with a large brooch, her cloche angled rakishly. It would have been too warm for gloves. She must have made one concession to the unaccommodating terrain by wearing sensible pumps. After tramping with Pough and Peter through spindly scrub-oak trees to the rock lookout the shooters used, Edge scanned the hot, empty sky. Peter noticed spent cartridges in the sandstone creases and pointed them out to his mother. Impulse, she would later assert, dictated her next action.

Edge turned to the real-estate agent and told him she wanted to lease the 1,398-acre mountain top for $500 with an option to buy it for about $2.50 an acre, or $3,000, within two years. There was no haggling. She rented the property as easily as she might have taken a cottage for the summer. "Practically everything in the world is rentable, from a dress suit to an ocean liner," she said later. "Why not a mountain?"[3]

Yet with her signature still wet on the contract, she wasn't sure where she would find the money for the mountain's lease and its purchase. She would solicit members of the Hawk and Owl Society, the Delaware Valley Ornithological Club (DVOC)—even the NAAS would have to contribute generously, she reasoned, having said as much publicly. She would personally bring DVOC members to the mountain top to see it and talk to them about sharing management responsibilities with the ECC.

But before she approached any of these potential backers, she needed five hundred dollars. Curmudgeonly Willard Van Name was the only source for that kind of money on such short notice. "Dear Will" marveled at her impetuousness when she told him what she had done and acted on his own impulse to write her a check for five hundred dollars on the spot. It was to be considered a loan, he emphasized, and of course to be kept confidential. She thanked him profusely.

Edge promised to ask the ring of fairy godmothers for the additional three thousand dollars and pay her anonymous benefactor back as soon as she had funds in hand. This would have to wait until September, however, when she returned from her trip with Peter to Panama, where they were going to look at birds.

One crucial detail remained that had to be addressed before Edge sailed. She needed to hire a caretaker for the property, and she knew just the man for the job. She had become a hero to a twenty-eight-year-old self-taught itinerant naturalist from Boston named Maurice Broun. Broun, though poor, periodically scraped together small donations that he sent to the ECC with notes of encouragement, for which she graciously thanked him each time. Edge had impressed him enormously. "Here was this woman in New York City who was doing things in conservation—very militant, very strident, very abrasive, but she was doing things," he said.[4] As far as Broun was concerned, Rosalie Edge was the only person succeeding on behalf of conservation.

Edge sensed that Maurice Broun, who built trails in Vermont and gave bird talks, would be the perfect caretaker for her hawk mountain property. He would have to live at the mountain and patrol it daily during the hunting season. She would ask him to post "No Trespassing" signs immediately around the property's perimeter when he arrived and have him notify local police of potentially dangerous confrontations with the hunters who would be turned away, at gunpoint if necessary.

In her August 21 letter to Broun, Edge outlined these responsibilities and warned, "It is a job that needs some courage." Was it possible that Maurice "would be available for a couple of months, say from the 15th of September?"[5]

MORRIS BROWNSTEIN—as Maurice Broun was known as a child—was not a person Rosalie Edge would have encountered in the society in which she felt most comfortable. A poor Jewish Romanian immigrant, he had arrived in the United States with his mother at about the age of four. Morris never knew his father, and his mother died of tuberculosis before he was ten. He spent his childhood moving from one orphanage or foster home to another, seeing his mother occasionally. Weekly beatings for small infractions were standard in each of the homes where he lived. The circumstances of his childhood were Dickensian, with many facts forgotten but with their wretchedness seared into the young man's psyche.[6]

A Jewish couple named Brownstein adopted Morris and moved their family to Boston from New York. Despite having a permanent family, Morris was hungry and lonely much of the time, and perhaps it was his need for food and companionship that sent him into the streets to snatch a roll from a bakery and run with other wayward boys. At thirteen while in the Boston Public Garden, Morris spotted the first beautiful creature he had ever seen in his life. A few people had stopped to stare at a tree. When he went to see what they were looking at, a tall woman handed him her binoculars and pointed where to focus them.

It was then that he spotted what the others saw. It was a bird "so graceful, so vivacious, so trim in its brilliant spring plumage of bright yellow, black and white," he wrote.[7] A magnolia warbler. Even its name was beautiful. From that moment Morris's life was altered. After finishing ninth grade, he refused to go back to school, an act of defiance that made life with the Brownsteins impossible for him. At fifteen he ran away and worked as a janitor, a delivery boy, a busboy, and a laundry attendant in a hospital, earning enough to pay one dollar a week for a room. His hospital job was a gruesome one. When he gathered the linens bloodied in surgery, he sometimes found amputated arms or legs wrapped in the sheets.[8]

In his time off from work, Morris educated himself in literature, philosophy, history, and music. He read about birds or went to look for them, and he could recognize two hundred species and mimic many of their calls. At the Boston Public Garden, Morris was considered a genius, and the adults he spoke to were as impressed with his self-acquired erudition as with his knowledge of birds. At nineteen Morris wrote his own guide to the birds of the Boston Garden.

The tall woman who had first handed him binoculars gave Morris's guide to a young ornithologist, John B. May. May, who assisted the famous ornithologist Edward Howe Forbush with his multivolume compendium of the birds of Massachusetts, recommended that Forbush hire young Morris as a field assistant. Before the third volume of Forbush's *Birds of Massachusetts* was published, the orphan who had been called Morris Brownstein started to call himself Maurice Broun, and it was by that name that he saw himself listed among the comprehensive text's contributors.

Although Maurice had barely enough money to live on, his earnings were at least derived from his devout love of birds, one of the two things that mattered to him most. The second was to be able to live and work far from any city. This desire led him to leave Forbush's employ and take a job as a naturalist for Pleasant Valley, a private nature preserve in the Berkshire Mountains. Once out of Boston, Maurice could satisfy his need to live in the wilds as simply as his hero, Henry David Thoreau, had done at Walden Pond.

Maurice grew into a lean, handsome man of a spare and retiring elegance. He spoke quietly but rendered his opinions with force. One of these opinions put him at odds with his Pleasant Valley employers, who ran a tea house on the preserve. Maurice did not approve of distracting visitors with such amenities as tea houses, common enough in the cities they had left behind for the day.

One Pleasant Valley visitor who might have appreciated both the tea house and the wild was the famous conservation activist Rosalie Edge, who ran the ECC to which Broun donated. Edge, aware that the young naturalist shared her opinions about the NAAS and the sorry state of conservation, asked him to speak on her behalf to Pleasant Valley guests. Broun's former mentor John May advised him to stay out of matters that did not concern him if he wanted to keep his job. Unfazed by the admonition, Broun passionately defended Edge's committee:

> Those people have the courage of their convictions and demand attention, and that speaks more for Mrs. Edge than for a lot of your so-called conservationists who may give money, but are too dull to see beneath the surface, who never raise a voice of objection or inquiry or anything else. In my estimation they are mostly a pack of hypocrites. They'll always fawn upon their superiors, and let the people with money do as they please. And it's about time someone fashioned a committee to thoroughly investigate the present conditions, which are too often accepted with complacency or indifference. Your Bureau of Biological Survey is Mammon—controlled, buttonholed by wealthy, killing clubs and ranchmen. . . . As for your National Association of Audubon Societies, the sooner there is a turnover and washout, the better.[9]

Broun found a new job at the Austin Ornithological Research Station on Cape Cod, where he banded and released wild birds with the aid of a bird-loving Boy Scout, Roland C. Clement. One Saturday morning Emma Knowles, who also volunteered at the Austin research station, brought her cousin Irma Penniman along on bird-banding rounds. When the tour was over, Irma thanked the tall, handsome bird expert named Maurice and blurted, "I think it would be wonderful to be married to an ornithologist."[10]

Irma's family lived in the Penniman Mansion, an ornate French Second Empire mansion overlooking the austere Massachusetts coastline. The mansion stood not far from where Broun's beloved Thoreau had paused to observe, "A man may stand there and put all America behind him." Irma's grandfather Edward Penniman had been a rich whaling captain who had sailed around the world seven times, taking his wife, Augusta, on some voyages along with one or more of the couple's three children.[11]

As a couple Maurice Broun and Irma Penniman were a study in the meeting of social contrasts that America made possible. The Romanian Jewish immigrant did not know his own father's name or that of the boat that had transported his family from Europe scarcely twenty-five years earlier.

Irma traced her lineage back to her forebears' arrival in the New World in the 1600s, and any school child had heard of the boat that she believed carried one or two of her ancestors to the bleak New England shore: the *Mayflower*.

On January 19, 1934, the penniless Jewish immigrant married the Puritan heiress in a New York City clerk's office. One of the first people he wanted his new wife to meet was Mrs. Charles Noel Edge, the most inspiring woman Maurice Broun knew. She invited the couple to lunch at the Colony Club, where for three hours she and Maurice talked of nothing but conservation. "Mrs. Edge is a woman of rare charm, brilliance and attractiveness," Broun wrote in the daily journal he would keep every day for the rest of his life.[12] Afterward Maurice Broun and Rosalie Edge stayed in touch.

Seven months later Edge confided to Broun that she had acquired a lease and option to buy "Hawk Mt." Despite financial uncertainties, she hoped to "get immediate possession and stop the slaughter of hawks on the mountain [that] autumn." Edge asked Broun to keep the news a secret so that "the gunners of Pennsylvania who [had] made this place a witches' holiday" would have no time to organize local opposition or make a counteroffer. She also did not want Gilbert Pearson to find out about her purchase before the deal closed. The Audubon president had "double crossed the Hawk and Owl Society and pussy-footed in this matter," she wrote, but she nonetheless feared that if the NAAS knew what she was up to, it might be "shamed to going into the market for it and would raise the price."[13]

Maurice and Irma, whose summer employment in Vermont ended in September, were available. In response to Mrs. Edge's query, Maurice wrote: "I think it is simply wonderful the way you go at things. Here's to your Hawk Mountain idea!" He was, he wrote, "wholeheartedly with the cause and with you." Mrs. Edge would deliver "a right proper knock-out" to the Audubon Society, he wrote.[14]

Knowing that the ECC operated on a shoestring, Maurice refused to take a salary, asking only that his and Irma's living expenses be covered. It was, he expected, a job of only two or three months' duration at most. "Let me post, patrol and otherwise guard that sanctuary and you'll never regret it," he wrote, as if he had been the one to apply to her for the job in the first place.[15]

In light of her employee's generous offer, the timing of Rosalie Edge's two-week birding vacation in Panama seemed awkward. But her mind was at ease knowing the Brouns would be guarding her mountain before cold winds began to blow from the north. A day or two before Rosalie and Peter were scheduled to sail, she stopped by Charles Dickerman Williams's office to draw up a power of attorney giving Maurice Broun authorization to represent her on the property in her absence.

Her last instructions to Maurice were to post the property line with signs that read "No Trespassing, M. R. Edge, Lessee" and to count and record every kind of bird that flew by the rocky lookout each day. She asked him to send his reports to her at least once a week, establishing a tradition that would last as long as she lived, and beyond. Although she didn't know quite how, she was certain the flight data would be useful someday. Rosalie Edge warned her new caretaker once more to mind his and his wife's personal safety. But even with the dangers to be faced, she predicted, "We will all get a lot of fun out of this."[16]

ON SEPTEMBER 10, 1934, Maurice and Irma Broun made the dismal drive through "murky, foggy, dusty, gloomy" Pennsylvania coal country on "god-awful nightmare roads."[17] Maurice did not describe how the anthracite coal mined in the region turned the Little Schuylkill River into a sludge dark as ink. Edge had warned them that the road worsened as it climbed up from Drehersville to the whitewashed stone cottage where she thought they might find lodging. Built in 1756 by the only survivor of a Delaware Indian massacre, the small cottage was an isolated outpost still. Jacob Gerhardt had been a child when his parents and five brothers and sisters were murdered in a cabin on the site, and when he grew up he had moved back to the place of his family's tragic end.[18] The cottage was bought by Matthias Shaumbacher a century later and run as an inn and tavern until it was sold to William Turner, who owned it when the Brouns arrived at its forlorn threshold.

Schaumbach's, as the stone cottage would remain known, had not been improved in more than seventy years. The haggard woman who was its caretaker told the Brouns in broken English that they could sleep in the attic. She sold them a lunch of turnips, bread, and jam. In the following torrid days, Maurice did everything Edge had asked of him. Following Edge's directions to count the number of birds that flew every day, Maurice was soon surprised to see fifty hawks flying at once, including three peregrine falcons and three bald eagles. Every time the "M. R. Edge, Lessee" and "No Trespassing" signs went up and were ripped down, Maurice put up new ones.

An article in the *Pottsville Evening Republican* responding to Broun's letter to the editor advised locals that the Emergency Conservation Committee of New York City had acquired control of the mountain near Drehersville. There would be no more hawk hunting on it, or hunting of any sort. The *Pottsville Evening Republican* responded: "While it may be true that examination of the stomach contents of thousands of hawks has proved that they feed for the greater part on mice and snakes and other vermin, hunters would like to see any species of hawks pass up a nice juicy grouse or quail for a mouse or other lowly creature. Hunters ask if the Emergency Conservation Committee has ever witnessed the inroads a hawk will make on a covey of quail after it has located them."[19]

As expected, hunters showed up anyway. Maurice and petite Irma were all that stood between the rough men and the well-worn trail that led to the shooting lookouts. On the Brouns' third night at Schaumbach's, three drunk, armed men knocked at the door. They spoke angrily to the frightened caretaker in Pennsylvania Dutch, then one man turned to the Brouns. "This ain't a healthy place. You'd better leave the mountain soon or we might have to shoot you off."[20]

The next morning the caretaker told Maurice and Irma they would have to leave. "All Pennsylvania is heaping curses on us," Broun wrote to Edge. "Fireworks soon." It was a good thing Mrs. Edge had hired the Brouns and brought them in from elsewhere. A local would have had his house and grounds torched; "that's how much sympathy natives have for hawks and people who protect them!" Maurice wrote. Maurice and Irma moved to a farm where the residents were more amenable to their purpose.[21]

Broun's request for state police protection reached the office of Governor Gifford Pinchot, former chief forester of the United States Forest Service, who had criticized Gilbert Pearson's acceptance of the gun makers' contribution to the NAAS more than twenty years earlier. But Pinchot was not in agreement with the radical notion that there ought to be a hawk refuge in his state, and no protection was provided.[22] Maurice hired a former policeman for twenty-five dollars a week who packed a .38 and could order locals off the mountain in the vernacular during the ten-week hunting season.

The Edges returned to Hawk Mountain in mid-September. Irma demonstrated how she stationed herself at the trail's entrance each day to turn away hunters. With Maurice, mother and son walked up to the old shooting site. Below them spread a discreet pattern of the wild and the tame, a patchwork of forests and farms, and the odd white intrusion of boulders as big as cars left by the last Ice Age.

Maurice amused Rosalie with the rumors he had heard about her: that she was a crazy, rich old woman who had come all the way from New York City to stop the hawk shoot. The locals could not believe that anyone would buy such a beaten-up piece of land for such a purpose and hire a guard to keep others from shooting hawks. Broun also heard that fourteen thousand hunters in the Schuylkill gun club were still determined to buy the mountain when Edge's lease was up and were asking its members to ante up fifty cents a piece.

Rosalie, Peter, and Maurice sat at the lookout enjoying the silence and the panorama that had been purchased in the name of hawk preservation. To the southeast eight hundred feet below the ridge was a potlike depression surrounded by low hills called "der Kessel" in Pennsylvania's German. The thermals that formed in this hollow sometimes caught hundreds of soaring broadwings at a time in their currents. The three who sat surveying the scene bestowed names on the places: their perch became the Lookout; the white boulders below them, the River of Rocks; the hollow to the southeast, the Kettle. The pattern of hawks in the sky above that hollow took its name from that place as well, and *kettling* entered the lexicon peculiar to those who would watch birds of prey not only at Hawk Mountain but anywhere in the world.[23]

On the first bright Saturday in October, Maurice turned away thirty-two hunters. Two openly defied him by sitting in one of the trees posted with a "No Trespassing" sign as they shot at hawks. Maurice approached cautiously while eight more hunters stood by to see what would happen.

"Well what'cha goin' to do about it?" snarled one of the men in the tree. "Just stay here and see what you fellows might do," Maurice replied. The man climbed down and advanced menacingly toward Broun. For a moment it looked as if there would be a fight. But rather than throw the first punch, the hunter stopped himself. "You damn hawk lovers," he muttered. "You're just a bunch of barbarians."[24]

Maurice laughed at this, and the tension eased. Another time a hunter put down his gun and walked up to the Lookout to see what its other attraction might be. When he came down, he was converted to the new way of appreciation. "A fellow doesn't want a gun up there; he should bring a pair of field glasses and a camera," he remarked. Reeducation, courtesy of Maurice Broun, had begun.[25]

Irma, "the keeper of the gate," as her husband called her, collected fifteen cents from each person who wished to go to the Lookout—an admission charge to it might cover the amount due in taxes, Edge had reasoned. On bright days when the wind blew from the north, more locals showed up to do nothing more than sit silently and watch the drama in the sky as though it were something that had never before occurred there.

One weekend the contingent Edge had invited from the Philadelphia-based Delaware Valley Ornithological Club came. The bird counts she had been relaying to her potential benefactors astounded them. On a cold, windy November 2, the day before Edge's fifty-seventh birthday, Broun counted 1,013 birds of prey: 853 red-tailed hawks, 128 sharp-shinned hawks, 8 Cooper's hawks, 2 goshawks, 6 marsh hawks, 1 rare white gyrfalcon, and a turkey vulture.[26] He had recorded 3,757 red-tails to date; he had not believed there were so many in existence.

That first fall when the guns fell silent on the Kittatinny Ridge, Henry Shoemaker, the former U.S. ambassador to Bulgaria whose opposition to the hawk shoot had put his patriotism in question, wrote stirringly of how Rosalie Edge had finally saved Hawk Mountain:

> There have been Audubon Societies and Linnaean Leagues and Bird Study Clubs, well-meaning and sincerely managed, but in a short time they have all joined that doleful category which recites the passing of first one then another species of American bird life into the realms of oblivion. Not so that intensively alive and virile organization known as the Emergency Conservation Committee headed by Mrs. C. N. Edge. On top of having performed prodigies for wild life protection in a span of existence of less than ten years, the committee has now put across the greatest accomplishment in bird conservation for all time.[27]

BETWEEN WEEKENDS spent at Hawk Mountain, Edge was back in New York confronting other conservation emergencies and dispatching the remarkable reports of Maurice's hawk tallies. Though she again attended Audubon's annual meeting and voiced the usual protest against fur-trapping and the other policies of which she disapproved, Rosalie was far too engaged in the work of conservation to mount another Audubon takeover battle.

Besides, she had won. Though the NAAS was not about to acknowledge her victory over their leadership, Audubon was changing. A few days after the 1934 annual meeting, Edge sent a telegram to Irving Brant with news she had been expecting: Gilbert Pearson had resigned. On the Audubon board, those who had been among Pearson's staunchest allies now openly came over to Rosalie Edge's side. John Baker, a gruff investment banker and amateur birder who had replaced Theodore Palmer as board chairman in the first wave of reform, took over Pearson's position. Pearson had been removed from the Audubon leadership, but he had not gone far. As president emeritus, he kept an office at NAAS headquarters until his death in 1943.

Though former board opponents Frank Chapman and Robert Cushman Murphy now backed reforms that Rosalie Edge had introduced, she suspected they were still in the minority on the board. Kermit Roosevelt, a wilderness explorer and trophy hunter like his father, Theodore, was named the NAAS's chairman. With Kermit at the head of the NAAS, its identification with big game hunters did not end, nor did its tradition of interlocking directorates loosen.

Kermit's grandfather James Roosevelt, father of Theodore, had been a founder of the American Museum of Natural History, where the Audubon annual meetings continued to be held. Kermit was no model of the new kind of conservation activist. Although he had shown great leadership potential as a youth, addiction to alcohol subverted his businesses and ruined his marriage. When Edge read that Kermit had gone to Alaska to hunt brown bears a few weeks after he was named Audubon's board chairman, she could not help but be amused at what counted as the NAAS's new image. Kermit Roosevelt ascended to the Audubon chairmanship in 1934, a deeply troubled man who would take his own life nine years later.[28]

On the same day Pearson submitted his resignation, the Audubon board also considered Edge's new project in Pennsylvania. One of Pearson's last acts as president was a peacemaking gesture; he moved that the Audubon directors commend the ECC for buying Hawk Mountain. The motion passed unanimously. And as one of Baker's first acts as the NAAS's new executive director, he sent a letter to Edge informing her of the board's action. As if Baker still believed there was a so-called committee backing the woman, his salutation was addressed to the "Gentlemen" of the ECC.[29]

Baker was conciliatory toward Edge, and she received his initial overtures with due courtesy. She wondered about his limited experience in conservation, which seems a hypocritical criticism coming from someone who had none when she began her conservation efforts. But she tried to be charitable and acknowledged what had also applied equally to her: a person "who knows nothing of a subject will make an unbiased research, and accomplish a better job of reform than one with preconceived opinions and prejudices."[30]

Edge invited Baker to tea at the Colony Club and to dinner at her home, and graciously offered to open the ECC files to him. She implored him to stop the steel-trapping on the Rainey Refuge, and he gave her his word that he would.[31]

Edge had challenged the NAAS to fight "its way back toward the high standards of its founders," and she had won, Irving Brant wrote. "At last a miracle, physiologically impossible, was achieved in the field of morality," he said. The Audubon Society had "recovered its virginity."[32]

In the weeks that the NAAS was concluding its first major personnel shakeup since its founding thirty years earlier, 10,776 hawks flew safely past the Lookout on Kittatinny Ridge. Maurice Broun identified fifteen kinds of birds of prey that fall: goshawks; sharp-shinned, Cooper's, and red-shouldered hawks; golden eagles and bald eagles; ospreys; turkey vultures; and a single white gyrfalcon streamed past, sometimes forming rivers of raptors, a thing he had never dreamed possible.

WILLARD VAN NAME was apoplectic over Rosalie Edge's latest request. She had asked him to call John Baker and personally explain the details of her Hawk Mountain lease-purchase. "I do not think it courteous to Mr. Baker's office as Chairman for us to have this matter go before him merely in the form of messages," she told Van Name imperiously.[33] She also asked Van Name to remind Baker of the society's offer to contribute one thousand dollars for operating expenses, as it had promised during the fairy-godmother meetings a year before. Confident that Hawk Mountain was secure in her own name, Rosalie seemed willing to play the dove rather than the serpent this time.

Van Name responded as if the warrior-queen were suffering battle fatigue. He was astonished at how callow his prize student seemed and how careless of the ECC's independence she had suddenly become. Audubon directors would only try to get "a strangled hold" on her and on Hawk Mountain if she got too close to them, he warned, scribbling his angry sentiments in the margins of the letter she had written to him.[34] Edge's attorney, Charles Dickerman Williams, agreed. She could not criticize the Audubon Societies one moment and accept its money the next.[35] Edge replied as one accustomed to extending noblesse oblige:

> It has been our policy, more especially during the past year, to invite the Audubon Association to join us in every endeavour for conservation. We have in this way been successful in obtaining many reforms and in inducing

them to do a certain amount of conservation work. Most recent examples are their call to members to protest to the Secretary of Agriculture against baiting and the recommendation of their Hawk and Owl Committee to prepare Teaching Units similar to those of the E.C.C. I consider that it would be harmful to conservation to reverse our present policy to invite cooperation of the Audubon Association in every conservation effort.[36]

Edge was no longer concerned about the NAAS. Several Delaware Valley Ornithological Club members told her they would contribute money for Hawk Mountain's purchase and discussed the creation of a twenty-thousand-dollar endowment fund to pay for ongoing expenses. "Hawk Mt. will be safer in the hands of five trustees devoted to its welfare than in the hands of any rich established organization with many other affairs to look after," she wrote. She envisioned a trusteeship formed with one or two members of the DVOC and the Hawk and Owl Society and one or two strong ECC supporters of her choosing, who would govern hawk sanctuary affairs.[37] She, of course, would be the head. A wealthy Pennsylvanian whose name she would not reveal had agreed to provide a large donation that would get the organization started.

But some of the rich Philadelphia birders she had invited to Hawk Mountain doubted Broun's daily hawk counts. There were, they said, far too many goshawks in the mix. When Edge dispatched news that Broun had counted fifty bald eagles and golden eagles in a single day, the DVOC birders responded contemptuously.[38] Even Richard Pough had scorned Broun's bird identifications, and he had done so in front of potential supporters.

Broun was incensed by Pough's "unkind, obnoxious doubts and criticisms of [his] observations" that he dared to air in the presence of others. Edge calmed Broun and attributed Pough's behavior to jealousy. "Rival organizations are *very sore* over my buying Hawk Mountain," she wrote comfortingly. "We have rocked the foundations of the Audubon Association."[39]

Yet despite initial pledges of financial support that Edge received and the Audubon board's commendation of her, by November she began to sense that something was wrong. When the DVOC board met, it did not vote to contribute any money to Hawk Mountain, though it knew how urgently she needed it. Her great secret patron was suddenly unavailable. "I think I see the fine hand of Baker in the DVOC situation," Edge told Broun.[40] The next day John Baker called to tell her that he had $1,500 in hand to buy Hawk Mountain, given to him by the same people who had promised they would back her.

The important donors had changed their minds. It seemed they had become convinced that the experienced NAAS would be a better refuge keeper
than the green Mrs. C. N. Edge. Van Name had called the situation correctly, while she had either been overconfident or too idealistic. Dropping
her guard, she had put aside her distrust of the NAAS. After the phone call
from Baker, Rosalie Edge trembled with rage, the earthquake this time
rather than the survivor of it.

This latest betrayal ripped her apart as Charles's unfaithfulness had fourteen years earlier. And it was a betrayal, one that had been carefully orches-
trated behind her back. At a secret supper that Baker attended in Philadelphia with Edge's key benefactors, he had persuaded them that the hawk
sanctuary ought to be owned and managed by the NAAS, not the ECC. At
least one person present at what Edge would call "the Affair of the Supper
Party" was also her informant. The pitch to the donors was so persuasive
that some wrote checks to the NAAS at the table and gave them to Baker
that night.

Why had the society suddenly decided to grab the hawk sanctuary idea?
Edge wondered. Her anonymous informant supplied an answer: "They just
busted in when they saw R. Edge had started things, and as usual, wanted
the credit for the enterprise!"[41]

Baker notified Edge that the donors had authorized him to assume her
Hawk Mountain lease and asked her to give it to him. She refused. He called
her attorney to obtain a copy of it, but she had instructed Williams not to
provide it. ACLU founder Roger Baldwin and other Audubon board members called her daily, insisting she turn Hawk Mountain over to the NAAS.
It was a well-orchestrated "third degree of persecution," she wrote. She felt
"harried and pursued."[42] "The pressure on me during the past week to force
me to sell Hawk Mt. to the Audubon Association is more than anyone would
believe," Edge complained to Maurice Broun. "They wish me to assign my
option at once. I have not the least intention in the world of handing Hawk
Mountain over to an association which steel-traps on its chief sanctuary. I
consider it hostile and unsportsmanlike of Baker to divert to the Audubon
Assoc. gifts from the DVOC which were, informally, promised to me."[43]

The betrayal was worse than she had expected. Richard Pough, who had
been with her when she signed the lease agreement and knew who her biggest donors were, had arranged the supper party without her knowledge.
Edge had asked Pough, who belonged to the DVOC and Audubon, to canvass
the "more prosperous Quaker members" about funding her sanctuary. But

the gentlemen had seemed reluctant to put up the money they had promised, according to Pough. "They had heard unfavorable reports about Mrs.
Edge, and wondered if it would not be better if Audubon bought the property." At their urging Pough called John Baker, and the Philadelphia supper
party was hastily arranged. "All went well and the full $3,000 was pledged
around the table," Pough would recollect some seventy years later. Rosalie
Edge "was left out in the cold."[44]

The truce that had been struck between Rosalie Edge and the NAAS was
scarcely a week old when open warfare broke out again. Now bitterness was
not only organizational but deeply personal, and "from that day on they
were mortal enemies," Pough wrote.[45]

From Edge's standpoint Richard Pough, as well as the NAAS, was her mortal enemy. "We worked together at every step," she wrote, still trying to make
sense of how Pough could have betrayed her. Pough "lunched with me the
day of the Audubon annual meeting and knew how indignant I was at
the chicanery and insincerity of the Association," she wrote.[46] Two days later
he was arranging the supper with Baker. Not long afterward Pough closed
his photography studio in Philadelphia and went to work for the NAAS.

ALL THE PAIN and anger she had held inside when she discovered Charlie's
unfaithfulness she now unleashed on John Baker and the NAAS. Even her
relations with Gilbert Pearson were good natured compared to those with
Baker. This time there would be no pleasantries and parlor games between
the head of the ECC and the head of the NAAS. Her fury at how completely
the new Audubon executive director had cut the ground out from under
her did not abate. She told everyone she knew that he was unkind, unethi-
cal, and vindictive. "High-handed, tactless, uncooperative. . . . No child of
12 would have asked money for the purchase of a piece of property and
have accepted cheques toward that end without first ascertaining whether
the property could be acquired," she wrote to one friend. Since Gilbert
Pearson's departure, the NAAS had become even more "indifferent and
neglectful."[47]

It dawned on Edge that the plan to seize Hawk Mountain had been in the
works almost from the start, just as Van Name had warned. When Baker
had visited in the fall, he was overheard talking to Pough about what it
might cost to run the sanctuary.[48] Another of Edge's informants told her
that he had seen a map at the NAAS headquarters showing Hawk Mountain
labeled as an Audubon sanctuary.

After her donors turned away, some of the scientists who had secretly supported her also distanced themselves from her. One tried to encourage her to turn Hawk Mountain over to those more experienced in such matters than she was. Reforming the NAAS was one kind of skill, he wrote. Running a bird sanctuary was quite another. The ECC, which had been so successful in some ways, should not hold on to Hawk Mountain, the friend advised.[49]

When the 1934 hunting season ended, Maurice and Irma Broun drove away from Hawk Mountain with the sad certainty that the NAAS would acquire the property and hire their own people to run the sanctuary. Edge's refuge had been an exciting, courageous experiment but appeared doomed for want of funds if she insisted on holding on to it herself. Broun resignedly wrote in his journal: "I feel honored to have had the opportunity to work with and for Mrs. Edge."[50]

Smug with the swift vindication of his intuition about the NAAS, Willard Van Name was among the few who stood by her. He had never seen Rosalie so demoralized. Seeing her desperation, he turned his $500 loan into a donation and then gave her another $250 along with some stern advice: "You own the Hawk Mtn. option. Do not let anybody boss you."[51]

AS HAWK MOUNTAIN lay silently mantled in snow during the winter of 1935, Rosalie Edge withstood the pressure to surrender her deed to the NAAS. She started to build a new base of financial support, convinced that her hawk sanctuary, if realized in her way, was too powerful an idea to be defeated. Modest checks toward Hawk Mountain's purchase arrived in the mail with reaffirming regularity. In April she wrote, "It is very touching to me the small donations that are coming in, often sent with fine letters in illiterate writing. These represent a very real sacrifice on the part of the givers."[52]

In Hawk Mountain's first year, Audubon contributed the $1,200 that had been initially promised—and that Edge had accepted before the Affair of the Supper Party. But its financial support dwindled considerably after that. Baker wrote to Edge that the NAAS board, with Richard Pough's counsel, decided it could not afford to contribute more than $25 to a non-Audubon organization. She composed a note steeped in sarcasm. It thanked Baker ever so "sincerely for the Association's generous donation" and his "gesture of cooperation" with Hawk Mountain's vital work. She did not sign this letter of gratitude, however. Instead, she asked Van Name's friend and *Crisis* pamphlet coauthor Davis Quinn to sign his name to it, suggesting perhaps that it was beneath her to respond directly to anything Baker wrote.[53]

Rosalie Edge soldiered on. "I cannot conceive that the nature-minded public will let our Hawk Mountain project fail," she wrote.[54] The following September, Maurice and Irma Broun returned to the Kittatinny Ridge, and Rosalie Edge, in full command, was there to ebulliently greet them. Hundreds of others soon followed. "Store-clerks and scientists, teachers and farmers, Boy Scouts and Camp Fire Girls, housewives and their children" assembled at the Lookout to see the birds fly. "When a group of boys charters a bus, paying $2.00 each for transportation from the metropolis to see the birds, we may feel certain that here are the much needed conservationists of the future," Edge wrote victoriously in 1935.[55]

"My brain-child" was how Edge described the Hawk Mountain Sanctuary decades later. It was a creation that arose "without conscious reflection."[56] Yet the subconscious portion of this reflection rises before us. Let us recall the day Rosalie was sitting with Charles in an elegant suite at the Peak Hotel in Hong Kong. A stiff gale blows open the windows, and startled by the sound, she looks up to see a large bird flutter into the room.

A "wee one" follows. She summons her Chinese servant to drive the birds out. But the winds persist and so do the birds. After the wee bird flutters back inside, the servant chases it out again and bolts the windows against both wind and irregular visitants. "The birds were taking refuge wherever they could," she explains in the letter to her mother.[57] Perhaps she remembered. At Hawk Mountain a quarter of a century later, Mrs. Charles Noel Edge opened a refuge to all birds that rode the wind.

Part Three

CHAPTER NINE

Canadian Spy

Relying on fifteen-cent admission fees to the Lookout and small contributions, the sanctuary took hold. Hawk Mountain became the platform on which Rosalie Edge stood to deliver her blistering conservation messages and was the place that best represented what an amateur nature lover could do. The David-and-Goliath story of Hawk Mountain inspired a generation. Curious to see what a hawk migration looked like, many sanctuary visitors might not have considered themselves conservationists when they arrived. But most left the Lookout having been awakened to the problems they posed for nature and inspired to do something about them.

Edge urged Maurice Broun to talk to visitors about more than hawk migration; people ought to make the preservation of watersheds, forests, soil, and all living species their personal responsibility, she insisted, because all led to "the mother of every living thing," the earth.[1] Maurice's Lookout tutorials to the public became known as "the school in the clouds." Within a few years students of personal conservation gathered on the Lookout by the dozens, then by the hundreds, and eventually by the thousands. The people exhausted the Brouns, but each fall the sight of the hawk migration renewed them.

Word of Hawk Mountain's autumnal spectacle was spread not only by those who witnessed it but also by its connection to the ecc, which played an increasingly visible role in important conservation issues in the country. Edge's ability to arouse the public to more than one conservation emergency at a time was particularly impressive in 1934—the year it seemed Hawk Mountain would go under and take her with it. But Edge did not require much to survive or to prevail. "Apart from the personality of Mrs. Edge, the small size of the Emergency Conservation Committee was its greatest asset," Irving Brant wrote glowingly years later.[2]

> The ECC could strike hard on any issue without being toned down by the conflicting interests of a large board of directors or a diverse membership. That was particularly valuable at a time when almost every nationally organized conservation body was in the paralyzing grip of wealthy sportsmen, gun companies, or lumbermen who were devastating whole states with their "cut and run" methods of operations. Usually there was a potential for actual conflict in such organizations between a deluded or dissatisfied membership and subversive directorates. Some avoided controversies to preserve income tax exemptions.[3]

Edge was amazed at how often ECC pamphlets were used in high school civics classes not to teach about conservation but "to show students how democracy works, to encourage them to interest themselves in public affairs, to show them how they may participate in government, and not be helpless bystanders."[4] Being "small" meant that Edge could offer the following evasive response to a dubious congressman who during a hearing inquired about the unpredictability of ECC campaigns: "We cannot announce our campaigns of the future," she said in what may have been an arrogant tone. "Our committee is organized to meet emergencies." The intentional vagueness of the pronoun *we* allowed Edge to shift the ECC's composition as needed from the sturdy troika consisting of herself, Irving Brant, and Willard Van Name in the shadowy background, to herself, Brant—and Secretary of the Interior Harold Ickes in the darkest shadows.[5]

The secretary remained, as she proclaimed when he took office, "with" her, and she with him. She was present—"of course"—at one meeting Ickes called to discuss an irrigation tunnel proposed for Rocky Mountain National Park. It was another holdover from the Hoover era that Ickes opposed. "Who of you will be crucified with me, if I try to reopen this subject?" he asked at the meeting to discuss the issue. "I immediately raised my hand," Edge wrote. "The Secretary saw me. 'Oh, you, of course, *you would*,' and a faint smile lightened the secretary's usual grimace."[6]

"WE APPEARED IN the '30s to be in the business of defending and creating National Parks," Edge noted breezily when she looked back on that decade in her memoirs.[7] This time the plural pronoun very pointedly included the secretary of the interior. In 1934 Edge published what could be considered the committee's most influential pamphlet, *The Proposed Olympic National Park: The Last Chance for a Magnificent and Unique National Park*, covertly written by Van Name but attributed to Edge. In characteristic overstatement the title's use of the word *proposed* suggested that a national park plan for Washington State was at that moment under active consideration.

But it was not. Establishment of a national park on the Olympic Peninsula had been attempted years before, had encountered insurmountable obstacles, and was then dropped. The ECC's pamphlet put the Olympic park idea squarely before those in Washington State who hoped it had died and for the first time placed it before the entire nation. The pamphlet informed the public that the continent's last virgin stands of majestic Douglas fir, red cedar, Sitka spruce, and hemlock were targeted for logging. The survival of the region's indigenous *Cervus elaphus roosevelti*, or Roosevelt elk, the largest subspecies of wapiti in the United States, was also perilously compromised.

What made this ECC pamphlet unique was its photos of the fir, cedar, and spruce, highly marketable trees—trees intended for cutting. The great sequoia groves of California had been set aside as one of the nation's first national parks in 1890, and a sequoia tree had become the National Park Service emblem. But the species *sequoia giganteum* simply had no better use than to be gaped at in awe. The enormity of these trees made them too costly to fell, while their wood was too brittle to use for anything but fence posts and pencils. Elsewhere in the country, not trees but either the deep red canyons of the Southwest or the Rockies' lofty ice- and snow-clad mountains above the tree line were the scenic standard for western national parks. What these natural wonders had in common was the perception of their economic worthlessness.

The ECC pamphlet proposed that the area of primeval forest stretching down the mountain flanks outside the existing boundaries of Mount Olympus National Monument on the west side—all the way from the glaciers to the sea—be protected in perpetuity. The ECC's map was audacious in its oblique-lined assertion that national park status ought to be conveyed to many square miles of virgin forest—precisely so that it would never be cut. In other national parks, boundaries were carefully drawn to avoid just such conflicts as those the ECC was deliberately creating.

The Olympic park pamphlet was particularly galling to those who read it in the state of Washington because it came from an organization—or perhaps from just a woman—3,700 miles away in New York. Previous efforts to establish national parks had been mounted by people who lived in the vicinity of the site they wanted to preserve or who knew its special qualities intimately. Mrs. Charles Noel Edge was an outsider. She had not yet even set foot on the peninsula and was insisting that a national park be carved out of it.

Whoever this Mrs. C. N. Edge, chairman of the ECC, was, she had the means to mail thousands of Olympic park pamphlets to U.S. congressmen, Washington State legislators, federal bureaucrats, newspapers, and ordinary citizens. And she had done it all from faraway New York—during the deepest Depression in the history of the United States. What Washingtonians did not realize was that at the same time Edge was fighting for the survival of a place called Hawk Mountain, she was opening a second major front in her assault on conservation's status quo. This battle would be truly national in its scope.

As was typical, the ECC's latest barrage stemmed from Willard Van Name's seething sense of the injustice done to nature, in this instance by bureaucrats who did not take into account the whole ecological picture when they concentrated on one or two natural resources. Van Name's perennial complaint about the United States Forest Service's mismanagement of the Mount Olympus National Monument was a perfect case in point. Theodore Roosevelt had established the national monument in 1909 by executive order to protect the habitat of the Roosevelt elk in the United States. The herd had fallen to less than five hundred because of poachers, who killed them for their incisor teeth, which were popular as watch fobs. Elk carcasses were left to rot on the mossy forest floor.

Granting national monument status by presidential executive order kept out the hunters but also the loggers and miners. In 1915 the U.S. Forest Service, which administered the monument, succeeded in having the 600,000-acre protected area cut in half by President Woodrow Wilson's revised order. The lower slopes with their old growth trees were to be opened to the timber interests, and miners could explore for mineral sites. More than one thousand sheep, which had not been allowed to graze within the monument's larger boundaries, were admitted to areas that had previously been reserved as winter feeding grounds for the elk.

The elk were confined to a much-reduced winter range, forcing them to overgraze on surrounding ranches or starve. Since the Bureau of Biological Survey had by this point exterminated the cougars, they left the elk with no natural predators besides the human hunter. To cull the herd, the Washington Game Commission declared a short bull-hunting season in 1933. Through this vicious circle of administrative reasoning, the Mount Olympus National Monument's Roosevelt elk protection purpose was essentially eliminated.

When Van Name heard rumors that the U.S. Forest Service permitted logging and hunting around Mount Olympus, he went to Washington State to investigate.[8] Van Name informed Irving Brant of what he had found, and Brant relayed the dire report to Secretary of the Interior Ickes. The Olympic Peninsula forest was under the jurisdiction of the Department of Agriculture, not the Interior, but Ickes wanted to change that. He told President Franklin Roosevelt that the eponymous elk would be better protected if Mount Olympus National Monument's management was transferred from the Department of Agriculture's Forest Service to the Department of the Interior's National Park Service.

At headquarters in Washington, D.C., Secretary of the Interior Ickes and Secretary of Agriculture Wallace feuded incessantly over their jurisdictions, and the competition between the chiefs of the nation's two resource-managing agencies permeated the ranks of both. But on the distant Olympic Peninsula, where local timber interests spoke loudest of all, these two federal agencies had developed a strange kind of simpatico.

National-park managers had cozy ties not only with tourism concessionaires, which the ECC had previously complained of, but also with logging entities. This realization was made abundantly clear to Brant, who wrote to National Park Service director Horace Albright asking for his support against the logging of Mount Olympus's virgin forests. Albright wrote back: "We cannot make a move that would be detrimental to the policies and interests of the Forest Service, a sister bureau of the Government."[9] It seemed that without the strongest kind of redirection, the National Park Service was no more inclined to protect the national monument's forest from loggers than the U.S. Forest Service was. As long as Mount Olympus remained a national monument, it would be subject to the administrative whims of either agency or to further reduction by a future president.

The ECC's solution was simple: raise Mount Olympus's level of protection from national monument to national park to remove any ambiguity about its purpose. Although the dire situation of the Roosevelt elk prompted Van Name's Olympic Peninsula investigation, the ultimate fate of the trees angered him most. Edge knew that big trees were what her most loyal supporter, Willard Van Name, loved above all else, and perhaps so did she. In 1934 the time to save one of the greatest forests in the world was quickly running out. An ECC pamphlet on the subject might help.

IN THE MID-1800s, while multitalented John Wylie Barrow was in New York becoming an importer of Europe's finest wares, other ambitious young men chased their economic destiny to the opposite side of the American continent. There they toiled at extracting their fortunes from material in its rawest forms. Gold and silver ore. And trees.

The United States had acquired six thousand square miles on the Olympic Peninsula in its settlement of a boundary dispute with Great Britain over where Canada ought to begin. The United States had really only wanted to acquire the Puget Sound for maritime and national security purposes, for the water more than the land seemed the key to the region's prosperity. Since the 1780s otter trapping in the kelp beds along the Puget shore had been the main commercial enterprise among the peninsula's indigenous coastal tribes such as the Quinault, the Quillayute, the Clalam, the Ozette, and the Makah and for the few whites. After the otter were gone in the 1840s, the white tribe still looked to the sound and the sea beyond for wealth. Whale oil and seal skins were the major currencies of trade.

The land that came with this vast territory of water was not, at first, considered advantageous. It was as sopping wet as a sponge, the wettest part of the United States of America. In some places on the Olympic Peninsula 250 inches of rain fell annually, and the trees dripped even when it was not raining. The climate made the peninsula's interior a difficult place for non-natives to live. The area, according to a Lieutenant Joseph O' Neil in 1890, "was useless for all practical purposes."[10] The land was so densely covered with three-hundred-foot-tall trees, the likes of which the white tribe had never seen, that it was considered uninhabitable and unexploitable. The newcomers commented on the forest's depressing silence. One woman forlornly complained she hadn't heard a bird sing for more than six months.[11]

But the perception of the forest's uselessness did not last long. As forests were stripped from New England and the Midwest, western gold rushes demanded new and nearer sources of lumber. In the late 1850s men from Maine with ten-foot-long crosscut saws and the largest circular saws—the best talent and technology available—arrived on the peninsula to cut logs at mills that were sprouting up along the shore. The massive Douglas fir that was the peninsula's dominant tree proved to be an astonishingly rich source of construction lumber.

Thick trunks reached to branchless heights of one hundred feet or more, and the grain of the wood ran straight and strong, making it a superior product for building houses and ships and shoring up mines. "The urge to cut virgin trees comes from the great profits to be gathered in from the huge trunks," Edge wrote in her memoir years later. "When the bark is sliced away and the enormous logs are squared, wide boards are sawed as a knife cuts cheese, with the minimum expense and the maximum of profit."[12]

Every day thousands of board feet were felled into water, which in the form of rivers, lakes, and the sound, functioned as the region's highways. Logs were pushed and poled until they floated to the mills for processing and were loaded onto schooners to be shipped to distant ports. So many trees were dropped that the loggers yelled, "Timber! Timber till you can't sleep."[13]

To encourage timber farming by individual homesteaders, the U.S. government passed the Timber and Stone Act in 1878, enabling a citizen to buy 160 acres of timberland at $2.50 an acre. Before that time a man could use his military scrip to purchase a homestead at a discount. But these timbered homesteads, which were sold by the newly created Department of the Interior's General Land Office, did not stay in the hands of the many. The act, according to historian Ray Allen Billington, "invited corruption. . . . Any timber magnate could use dummy entrymen to engross the nation's richest forest lands at trifling cost. Company agents rounded up gangs of alien seamen in waterfront boarding houses, marched them to the courthouse to file their first papers, then to the land office to claim their quarter section, then to a notary public to sign over their deeds to the corporation, and back to the boarding houses to be paid off."[14]

The wages for such service were low. Fifty dollars was the fee in the beginning, but eventually the land could be acquired for "the price of a glass of beer."[15] In this way thousands of acres of trees in the public domain were transferred into the ownership of the few. In 1892 Puget Mills alone owned 186,000 acres of land containing more than 1.5 billion feet of timber. By 1900, 3.6 million acres of timberlands had slipped into private ownership.

The logging outfits cut deeper into the interior with the help of powerful machines called by animal names: the donkey engine and the iron horse, which was the logging railroad.

As the cutting and hauling became more mechanized, the tree line fell back from the sound, leaving an ugly foreground of waste and stumpage that receded into the distance. Loggers had come to resemble crack infantry, and the industry in which they served was like a war. The forest was an enemy to be attacked again and again, until it was driven back and destroyed, and thereby conquered.[16] With so many new mills opening every year, the forests were no longer silent. They roared with the processing. There were so many machines and men that the forests were what logging historian Stewart Holbrooke described as a factory without a roof.

Yet if a logger on the Olympic Peninsula in the 1880s had been told that the big trees could run out in his lifetime, it would have strained his imagination, such little faith did he have in human perseverance and ingenuity. The roofless factory was not an economical one, for it cut so many trees that lumber prices fell and the mills closed, making the timber industry another of the West's boom-or-bust industries.

CARL SCHURZ, first secretary of the interior, implored Congress to do something before all the wood disappeared, but to no avail. He condemned the nation for "looking with indifference on this wanton, barbarous, disgraceful vandalism; a spendthrift people recklessly wasting its heritage; a government careless of the future and unmindful of a pressing duty."[17] By 1891 the rapacious consequences of the Timber and Stone Act were so undeniable that the law was repealed. A rider attached to the rescinding legislation retreated far in the opposite direction, though few noticed it at the time. The Forest Reserve Clause, as this rider was called, stated that "the President of the United States may, from time to time, set apart and reserve, in any state or territory having public lands wholly or in part covered with timber or undergrowth, whether of commercial value or not, as public reservations, and the President shall by public proclamation, declare the establishment of such reservations and the limits thereof."[18]

Presidentially ordained forest reserves were not new. In 1801 John Adams established government reserves to assure a supply of good oak for the Navy, but when shipbuilding practices changed, other uses were found for the oak trees. This new forest reserve authority was different from the previous one in its sheer breadth and vagueness.

In 1891 President Benjamin Harrison transferred 13 million acres of western forests from General Land Office administration into the presidential reservations. Six years later President Grover Cleveland removed another 21 million acres of western real estate from sale by the Land Office and added it to the forest reserves. The largest reserve created by presidential order was the 2.2 million acre tract on the Olympic Peninsula, which was the area that had not yet been transferred into private hands under the Timber and Stone Act.

Westerners were understandably livid over this sweeping exercise of executive prerogative, which seemed to grant a democratically elected president the power once vested in a king. One who found the forest reserve act incomplete as written was a young forester named Gifford Pinchot. Pinchot, the same who would in 1911 criticize Gilbert Pearson for accepting large donations from gun makers, had gone to Ecole Nationale Forestière in France to study the scientific method of growing trees like crops.

It was not the idea of government-regulated forest reserves that Pinchot objected to; on the need for this he was in agreement with John Muir, the naturalist of California's High Sierras and the wilderness sage of the Yosemite Valley. Where Pinchot famously differed from Muir was in the underlying purpose of the forest reserves. Muir believed trees in the reserves ought to be preserved or selectively cut. When he learned that the Olympic Forest Reserve had been established, Muir predicted, "The Olympic will surely be attacked again and again for its timber."[19]

Pinchot declared that the trees and other reserve natural resources were for economic use. Pinchot's utilitarian doctrine of forest stewardship was based on his conviction that trees had no higher use than to be turned into lumber, animals no higher use than to be hunted, and water no higher use than to be, in a word, used. In 1905 Theodore Roosevelt appointed Pinchot head of a new agency, the United States Forest Service, to regulate the cutting of the nation's publicly owned forests.

Pinchot hired a scientifically educated cadre of foresters from America's recently established forestry schools. Progress was made. Timber companies would no longer have the ability to cut wherever or whatever they wanted on the public domain. But they would certainly be permitted to cut, as long as they paid the U.S. Treasury the going price for the privilege. With Pinchot's help, President Roosevelt added some 150 million acres to the new national forest system. Since trees were to be grown and harvested like crops, the lands were transferred from the Department of the Interior to the Department of Agriculture. It was as tree farmers that Pinchot and his enlightened, scientifically trained cadre of young foresters would thereby assure the nation's continuing supply of timber.

Meanwhile, the Olympic Peninsula Douglas firs in private ownership continued to fall at a dizzying rate. In 1926 the mills in Grays Harbor cut 1.6 billion board feet, which was a record. But the special saws that had been designed to cut trees like cheese were running out of the tall, big-girthed trees.[20] By 1926 the end of such timber stands on private land was an unpleasant fact that everyone could see. The timber interests saw their future in their expectation that the U.S. Forest Service would put the virgin trees of the Olympic National Forest up for sale when their private reserves were exhausted.

Eight years later, the ECC's *Proposed Olympic National Park* landed on the desks of congressmen from the Pacific Northwest and from every other state in the union.

For Rosalie Edge, raising her committee's political visibility with its Olympic National Park campaign was a logical if dramatic extension of her fight with the NAAS. The dynamics were the same whether on the local or the national stage. As an Audubon member she had demanded protection for birds of prey and their habitat, and failing to receive satisfaction, she had created Hawk Mountain Sanctuary. As a conservation activist of national stature, she was concerned about Roosevelt elk and their habitat, and the establishment of a national park could save both.

As an Audubon member Edge protested the undue influence of special interest groups such as bird hunters on a bird protection society. As a conservation activist she opposed the timber industry's influence on the U.S. Forest Service and the National Park Service. As an Audubon member she spoke up for people like Willard Van Name and herself, a tiny constituency who loved to look at birds and not kill them. As a conservation activist she championed a powerless constituency who loved to look at trees on the public lands and not have them cut down.

As an Audubon member Edge argued that bird and wildlife preservation ought not be dictated by which species were popular or profitable at a given time, but rather by the overarching principle of keeping all species in balance within their natural habitat. As a conservation activist she argued that the price of a single kind of timber ought not dictate the fate of a public forest's other species of trees and dependent wildlife. All this she credited Willard Van Name for teaching her.

But Rosalie Edge had not been immune to a forest's intrinsic values; she just had not recognized its formidable power over her own psyche. Beyond this subconscious drive, she contributed something unique to both her NAAS and federal conservation reform campaigns: her literary sensibility ingrained as a child and practiced as a suffrage publicist. She cared to ignite her fellow Audubon members' or the American public's desire for sweeping conservation change. From the start the ECC's success derived from both Van Name's unorthodox ideas about the natural world and Edge's conviction that she could do something to implement them. She gave her mentor's cloistered opinions the viability they had never attained previously. Her pamphleteering and speaking style radicalized armies of amateurs and dilettantes who would push the politicians and professionals forward. And these were energized by the passions that had lain dormant within her—and not Van Name.[21]

U.S. REPRESENTATIVE Martin Smith from the mill town of Grays Harbor in Washington asked for an additional thousand copies of the ECC's Olympic park pamphlet. Edge filled his order, though given his district's dependence on logging, she joked that he wanted that many so he could put them in the trash.[22]

In the nation's capital the U.S. Forest Service and the National Park Service drafted park proposals to counter what the ECC pamphlet laid out before them. The Forest Service criticized the ECC's grand scheme in terms that Edge had heard before in her Audubon confrontations. The pamphlet, one official statement noted, "was an appeal to the ultra sentimental and emotional elements."[23] The Olympic National Forest supervisor traveled to towns on the peninsula and opposed the ECC plan. If the park this little committee wanted was created, millions of dollars in local revenue—funds for schools and roads—would be lost, he said. The region would be thrown into economic turmoil from which it might never recover.

The supervisor reminded his audiences that "forestry is the growing of trees for human use. . . . Trees reach maturity the same as any other crop and if not harvested will die and rot," he declared. This opinion was what one expected to hear from an employee of the U.S. Forest Service, an agency of the Department of Agriculture. The supervisor of Mount Olympus National Monument also spoke in the timber towns and decried "a certain pamphlet published by the Emergency Conservation Committee of New York." He reassured business and civic leaders that the federal government should never be "suspected of any desire to seriously effect the industrial well being of any community or state by locking up in a National Park a large and important natural resource."[24]

When the Forest Service and the Park Service each released their department proposals for a park, the area was smaller than the ECC had requested, and the big trees again lay outside the park boundaries in both proposals. The two agency counterproposals were so similar in their intent to keep virgin forests outside national park boundaries that Edge wryly observed that with the U.S. Forest Service already speaking so strongly on behalf of the timber interests, perhaps the Park Service could find another constituency to represent—say, the preservationists. Or more to the point, the ECC, which was nature preservation's dominant organization.

Secretary Ickes had left the drafting of the National Park Service's counterproposal entirely up to his agency and had signed off on the recommendations it made. A copy of the lackluster plan with Ickes's signature was leaked to Van Name before it was made public. He was so upset by its deliberate removal of the forests from protection that he left his office at the Museum of Natural History early, took a cab to Penn Station, and caught the next train to Washington, D.C., to have a chat with the interior secretary, whom he had never met. When Van Name arrived at Ickes's office, the secretary, who knew of the zoologist from Brant and Edge, agreed to receive him.[25]

Van Name delivered an emotional but cogent explanation of how the National Park Service had come under the sway of the U.S. Forest Service on the matter of Olympic National Park's creation. Van Name had reached the ardent conservationist Ickes where he was perhaps most vulnerable: in the interior secretary's desire for more power at the expense of the agriculture secretary.

Ickes listened carefully to Van Name and then picked up the telephone. He called National Park Service director Arno Cammerer and within Van Name's hearing rescinded his approval of the agency's plan for a much smaller Olympic park. When Ickes hung up, he asked Van Name to draw the boundaries that the national park should have. Van Name did so, going beyond those proposed by the ECC pamphlet by including more of the low-lying rainforest of the Bogachiel and Hoh valleys. Van Name also inserted a wilderness stipulation. He wanted to prevent the National Park Service from following its tendency to approve roads, hotels, stores, and entertainment concessions, which he found so at odds with the agency's primary mission of preserving natural values. It was an objection similar to the one

Maurice Broun had brought against the teahouse at Pleasant Valley, in the Berkshires.

Now two Olympic proposals—the first by the National Park Service staff and the second outlined by Dr. Willard Van Name in Secretary Ickes's office—were released. Park Service leaders in Washington, D.C., were bewildered by how their boss had arrived at a proposal at such variance from the one they had submitted, and that he had initially approved. Despite much internal consternation and Park Service opposition, Van Name's proposal went forward. In March 1935, H.R. 7086 was introduced by Washington congressman Mon Wallgren, requesting that the 730,000 acres in the uncut Mount Olympus National Monument, along with an additional 400,000 acres of surrounding Olympic National Forest, be designated the Olympic National Park.

As the battle for the Olympic forests commenced, the ECC found that despite its having the interior secretary's strong support, it was fighting both the U.S. Forest Service and the National Park Service. "The Park Service had . . . declared war on the Emergency Conservation Committee, the only group that was fighting to create Olympic National Park," wrote historian Carsten Lien.[26]

Edge's weapon of choice was endless advocacy through writing letters, newspaper articles, and editorials, and meetings in Washington, D.C., coupled with more letters, newspaper articles, and meetings in Washington State. In the summer of 1935, Rosalie and Peter visited the Olympic Peninsula for the first time and saw the majestic forests for themselves. Seeing them and smelling their moist fragrance, she might have recalled Japan, which the Pacific Northwest resembled in its intensely green expanses and pearl gray skies swathed in cloud ribbons. While on her fact-finding mission in Washington State, Edge was tethered to the other conservation work she had left behind in New York. "The ECC goes to bed with me wherever I am," she assured J. "Ding" Darling, who finally reached her to discuss another matter. "Motoring, riding, climbing and running the ECC makes a great life if you don't weaken."[27]

Edge too rode the speaking circuit, encountering much stony resistance in the timber towns. It did not help that she was from New York. It was rumored that she was also an agent of the Canadian government, "engaged to help lock up the Olympic forests, so as to raise the price of Canadian timber," she wrote.[28] Lending credence to this story was the fact that Edge had entered Washington by way of Victoria, British Columbia. No one knew that she had cousins on the Charles Dickens side of her family living in BC whom she wanted Peter to meet. While Edge was thrilled by the denunciations of her, as both a New Yorker and a Canadian spy, neither perception helped her cause.

The ECC needed local grounding, but given the timber industry's hold on the state, it could not hope for much; a smattering of tree preservationists kept their antilogging opinions to themselves. With Edge's encouragement, residents of Port Angeles raised enough money to send four people from Washington State to Washington, D.C., to testify at upcoming congressional hearings in favor of the ECC's large national park proposal. It was a costly sacrifice to make during the Depression for the sake of trees.

But politically speaking the ECC still needed a local grassroots partner with a somewhat higher profile. Seattle's leading outdoor recreation group, the Mountaineers, was the only prospect. The Mountaineers were as adamantly opposed to the timber industry as the ECC was. The Mountaineers, however, had become so distrustful of Park Service management at Mount Rainier that they vehemently opposed the ECC's Olympic park proposal for fear of more bureaucratic mismanagement over a larger area. Van Name, continuing to work behind the scrim the ECC provided, convinced a Mountaineers officer, Irving Clark, to back the committee's park position. Although he obviously shared Clark's hatred of the National Park Service's attachment to some of the tawdry aspects of tourism promotion, Van Name saw this federal agency as "the best that [could] be had." If the ECC failed "to work for them and fight for their protection we shall save nothing at all," Van Name wrote to Clark.[29] With Clark as the ECC's Washington State operative, Edge's outsider status became somewhat less of a flash point.

AS EDGE STRUGGLED in 1935 to keep Hawk Mountain going and the campaign to create Olympic National Park grew increasingly complicated, each effort seemed so consuming a task there could be no room for her to respond to yet another conservation emergency. But room for another there was. Van Name's old concern about the eight thousand acres of virgin sugar pines along Yosemite National Park's major entrance on its northwest side and near the Tuolumne sequoia grove also demanded immediate attention. The fate of the 250-foot-tall sugar pines, second only to the sequoias in size, was the reason Edge had paid her first visit to Capitol Hill on conservation's behalf, when she called on Senator Gerald Nye. In 1932 her pamphlet *Save the Yosemite Sugar Pines!* had portrayed the beauty of the grove as "ONE OF THE IMPORTANT SCENIC FEATURES OF THE YOSEMITE PARK," an exaggeration, given the competition from so many stunning natural features in the area. But of course she hadn't been to Yosemite to see this for herself. The pamphlet railed, "Immediate action is urgently needed. . . . The logging railroad of the Yosemite (Sugar Pine) Lumber Company already approaches close to it; cutting may begin at any time, and the terribly rapid and destructive methods of modern logging will strip the area before the public realizes what is going on."[30]

Nevertheless, it was a rescue mission launched to right an old wrong. The fifteen-thousand-acre grove of sweet-sapped trees had been included within Yosemite National Park when it was established in 1890. In the early 1900s, during a corruption-riddled era of the Department of the Interior, the tract of sugar pines was illegally sold. Before the Depression, John D. Rockefeller and Congress split the $3.2 million cost of buying back the grove on one side of the Big Oak Flat Road and restored it to the park's protection. The sugar pines on both sides of the road were identically sensational, engulfing park visitors in their perfumed, midnight green majesty. But the sugar pines on the other side of Big Oak Flat were still very much at risk.

Rosalie Edge may have been hasty in broadcasting her 1932 message of the trees' impending doom, for just as the Depression prevented Congress from authorizing their purchase, the abysmal economic conditions spared the Yosemite sugar pines from any loggers. In 1935 the Depression had eased enough, however, for the Yosemite Sugar Pine Lumber Company to announce that cutting would begin the following year. So perhaps the ECC sugar-pines pamphlet published three years earlier had not been premature after all, for it had started to raise public and political awareness before it was too late to act. Among those the ECC had begun to persuade to its point of view were the great lovers of trees Secretary Harold Ickes and President Franklin Roosevelt. The secretary wondered if the ECC might further "arouse public interest in this atrocity."[31]

Edge for the moment put aside the campaign to save the big trees of the Olympic Peninsula for the more urgent task of saving the big trees that had once belonged to Yosemite National Park. *Save the Yosemite Sugar Pines!* was reissued and was distributed more widely than the first time. The ECC's next challenge was, as in the Olympic campaign, to cultivate the grassroots.

But who might they be? The U.S. Forest Service in California adamantly opposed the ECC's attempts to restore the sugar pines to Yosemite National Park. In 1932 the officials of Tuolumne, Alpine, Amador, Calaveras, San Joaquin, and Stanislaus counties had gone on record opposing the trees' preservation because it would reduce their tax base. The California State Chamber of Commerce representing the Central Valley denounced "the activities of the Emergency Conservation Committee with headquarters at 113 East Seventy-second Street, New York City," and flatly opposed any extension of national parks in the state.[32] Meanwhile, the National Park Service had remained unfathomably silent for three years.

As the ECC had also learned in its Olympic campaign, Park Service support of tree preservation was not something that could be assumed. Van Name declared that the ECC would get no help from the Park Service on the Yosemite matter either, and that it ought to stay away from its bureaucrats. Edge refused to be put off by Van Name or by the Yosemite National Park Service superintendent Charles G. Thomson, who had never answered her letters or calls. In the summer of 1935 the trip to the Olympic Peninsula would have to include a stop at Yosemite National Park, where Edge intended to meet with the elusive Colonel Thomson face to face.

AT THE AGE of fifty-eight, Rosalie Edge visited Yosemite for the first time. The national park on the eastern flank of California's High Sierras, with its wild, cataclysmic grandeur spreading over a region the size of Rhode Island, could not have been more unlike the 1.3-square-mile greensward she went to almost every day of her life in New York. There was, however, one strong connection between Manhattan's midsection and the fabled Yosemite; Fredrick Law Olmsted was the man hired to envision the public parks in both places.

In 1864 President Abraham Lincoln was diverted from the grim prosecution of the Civil War to sign the Yosemite Valley Grant, a most optimistic piece of legislation given the times. Preserving only the valley—a chasm one mile wide by ten miles long—was but the first step toward the eventual establishment of a vast national park. The grant conveyed to California the Yosemite "upon the express conditions the premises shall be held for public use, resort and recreation."[33]

After completing his Central Park commission, Olmsted went to Yosemite to ascertain how this might be done without destroying the beauty that had merited Lincoln's precious attention in the first place. Olmsted noted,

There are falls of water elsewhere finer, there are more stupendous rocks, more beetling cliffs, there are deeper and more awful chasms, there may be as beautiful streams, as lovely meadows, there are larger trees. It is in no scene or scenes the charm consists, but in the miles of scenery where cliffs of awful height and rocks of vast magnitude and of varied and exquisite coloring, are banked and fringed and draped and shadowed by the tender foliage of noble and lovely trees and bushes, reflected from the most placid pools, and associated with the most tranquil meadows, the most playful streams, and every variety of soft and peaceful pastoral beauty.[34]

Central Park's makeover of an insignificant slab of granite had been radical. Olmsted's overarching concept for the vistas of Yosemite Valley's high temples of granite was equally so: in this case, he recommended doing nothing to alter the natural state. All incursions of "false taste" into the valley were to be prohibited, he counseled in his preliminary report. He had further remarked that the "temptation to cut down [the valley's] groves should be avoided."[35]

When John Muir saw Yosemite Valley in the 1870s, he shared Olmsted's sentiments, for unlike Central Park, which men had made, Yosemite's landscape was "fresh from God's hand."[36] Like Olmsted, Muir was partial to the groves of big trees, but particularly to the sugar pines. He praised the graceful asymmetry of their long limbs reaching eastward to avoid prevailing winds, with their immense cones swinging like bells in the slightest tug of breeze. In Crane Flat, perhaps within the site targeted for logging in the 1930s, Muir had built his sugar-pine cabin some sixty years earlier.[37]

Without leaving her apartment, Rosalie Edge could appreciate what Frederick Law Olmsted and Calvert Vaux had wrought in Central Park. But to finish what Muir had not quite succeeded in doing where the largest grove of sugar pines was concerned, she had to travel all the way to Yosemite, and she had to go there against Willard Van Name's expressed wishes. Yet when she and Peter arrived in Yosemite, she wasted no time in asking a park ranger to track down Superintendent Thomson so that she could meet with him.

The next morning Edge and a ranger drove and then hiked out to the threatened grove to see Thomson. Edge in her city clothes was breathless from the physical exertion, but the moment she met Thomson "a spark of confidence and mutual liking flashed" between them. The superintendent invited her to sit down and rest. She demurred. "I have come from New York to ask you one question," she later wrote, with characteristic drama. *"Do you want to save these Sugar Pines?"*[38]

"With all my heart," Thomson replied. Hearing this, Edge finally sat. She asked why, then, the superintendent had done nothing a few years earlier to advance Senator Nye's original sugar-pine preservation bill. Because he had been instructed during Herbert Hoover's administration to say and do nothing, Thomson replied. But then why hadn't he spoken up when Secretary Ickes came in? Because he had been insulted by Dr. Willard Van Name, he said. Perhaps Superintendent Thomson knew of Van Name's intense loathing of all Park Service personnel; the scientist's denunciation of the agency as "miserably weak and craven" was not intended to win friends within it.[39]

But Thomson had his own reasons to be offended by Van Name, he told Edge. Van Name had spent several weeks at Yosemite studying the sugar pines and making maps of the area. During this time the superintendent was surprised to read letters in the local newspapers calling for the trees' preservation. The letters were signed not by Willard Van Name, however, but rather by the young man who was his traveling companion, and not a scientist or any sort of expert on the subject. At no point during Van Name's fact-gathering mission did he contact the superintendent of Yosemite National Park to let him know what he was up to. Thomson said he had felt slighted by such an intentional discourtesy. And this was a shame, because he would have been most eager to help the ECC once he was permitted to speak up.[40]

Sitting with Rosalie Edge in the grove, Superintendent Thomson said he had learned that the logging railroad would reach the heart of the grove by the time the snow melted in 1938, and cutting would immediately commence. That meant something must be done to save the trees before Congress ended its session in 1937, just two years away.[41] The two strategized together. Senator Nye's bill needed to be amended to counter Forest Service opposition based on its predictions of dire economic consequences if logging was prohibited.

When Edge returned to New York and reported her good news to Van Name, he was not happy to hear it. Not only had Edge allied with Thomson, but she had also, by her own admission, told Thomson that Willard Van Name was no longer interested in fighting for the trees. "I have put a tremendous amount of work on the Sugar Pines and the Bill," she wrote to him, including the formation of a powerful alliance with Colonel Thomson. But Edge seemed to have poisoned it for Van Name by getting on so well with the Yosemite superintendent.[42]

He refused to cooperate with her. Van Name was so infuriated with Edge that he paid a young freelance writer, William Schulz, to represent the ECC in California on the matter. He further instructed Schulz to have nothing to do with Edge, which, given that she was the ECC's only permanent member, created an impossible and potentially embarrassing situation.

It required all of Irving Brant's diplomacy and Schulz's respect for both Van Name and Edge to keep the sugar-pine preservation effort moving ahead. Edge felt cast out of her own committee. Schulz had to help the former suffragist cultivate the support of California women's groups, which she had ignored in her fury toward Van Name. Thanks to Schulz, the American Jugo-Slav Women's Club, American War Mothers, California Daughters of the American Revolution, Madrone Social and Improvement Club, and a dozen or more garden clubs wrote letters to legislators in support of the revised sugar-pine bill. In California women who grew roses confronted men who cut big trees.

The ECC—as represented by Schulz or Edge—also forged strong support from the San Francisco-based Sierra Club, which John Muir had founded, and California's Save-the-Redwoods League. Apart from the need for the majority of Californians to support the trees' preservation, Secretary of Agriculture Henry Wallace had to agree on the sugar-pine grove's transfer from Stanislaus National Forest jurisdiction to Yosemite National Park jurisdiction. As Californians increasingly spoke in favor of the trees' preservation, Wallace consented to surrender another piece of the Department of Agriculture's territory to its rival, the Department of the Interior.

The bifurcated ECC—meaning perhaps Brant and Van Name, or Brant and Edge, but never the three together—knew that winning a Depression-era congressional appropriation for the purchase was at best a hopeless case. In his role as consultant, however, Brant had learned that the Department of the Interior still had Depression relief funds that it had not spent. Ickes would need President Roosevelt's approval to use a portion of the money to purchase the trees. The secretary dispatched Brant to make the request of the president.

Roosevelt wanted to know how much the sugar-pine grove would cost. Brant answered that $1 million would go "a long way," at which point Roosevelt gave the go-ahead. When Ickes heard Roosevelt's response, he wondered if $1 million was really enough. "I think we'd better make it two million," he told Brant. Brant reported these highest-level conversations to Edge, who seemed to take a proprietary joy in them. She wanted to share the news of the progress made with her readers and perhaps assure them that the ECC was extremely well connected.[43]

"Finally, the people of California were awakened to the fact that one of the state's grandest possession was being destroyed," Edge wrote in a proud summary of the rapid developments.[44] She urged her readers to write to the Department of the Interior and members of Congress, and thousands responded. She also reported that the secretary of the interior had sent her a telegram asking for copies of all letters of support.

While Ickes may indeed have made such a request, Edge committed a major political blunder by saying so publicly. Like Henry de Forest's letter denouncing Gilbert Pearson, Ickes's request for copies of supporting letters was meant to be kept confidential. The ECC's additional report that both the president and the secretary of the interior wholeheartedly endorsed the purchase of the sugar pines for up to $2 million made matters even worse, for this figure was not supposed to have been made public. Publicizing the amount the Department of the Interior was willing to spend caused the price for the grove to shoot up to $1.9 million. The irate secretary is said to have written Edge a stinging reprimand, which cannot be found among her carefully kept correspondence. Ickes ordered her to never speak for him again without his authorization. She in turn was shocked at the interior secretary's "rudeness" toward her.[45]

Although Roosevelt had approved Ickes's use of Department of the Interior funds to buy the sugar pines, the ECC next learned that it might still be impossible for Ickes to do so without congressional approval. In 1937 hearings on the Yosemite sugar pines were needed on the Hill after all.

During the hearings on the revised Nye bill, U.S. Congressman Harry Englebright, who represented the Yosemite district and strongly favored logging the sugar pines, expressed his distaste for the ECC's bountiful influence on Californians. He attributed the one thousand letters he had received in favor of purchasing the sugar pines to the committee's "well-laid plan of propaganda."[46] Edge responded charmingly.

As long as he had Mrs. Edge under oath, Representative Englebright wanted to know about the composition of the ECC. He asked her how its officers were elected.

"We reelect ourselves," Edge replied. "We have no membership to stop it."

"I see," the congressman said. "You are just a private organization."

"Just as private as can be," she answered. "There is no one who can control us. Might I just say about our committee, we have only one controlling thing. We take a vow. I don't know whether the gentlemen ever take a vow, but we have a vow that we will tell the truth, no matter how disagreeable. I tell the truth, no matter how disagreeable, you cannot hold a political position. Of course you all know that. (laughter) You cannot get advancement in civil service, and you practically cannot have a position in any public institution, museum or college, or anything like that. Not one of us [in the ECC] can be controlled."[47]

"THE SUGAR PINES ARE SAVED, definitely and finally," Edge wrote to Van Name's sister Theodora on September 9, 1937. He still refused to speak to his protégé in a civil tone. "The story of the Sugar Pines grew positively dramatic at the end," Edge wrote, in the hope that Theodora would pass word of the victory along to Willard, who, she was told, had refused to believe it. The bill approving Ickes's expenditure for trees passed just one hour before Congress adjourned in September 1937 and required a hasty amendment to make it through.[48]

All in all, it had been a more bruising campaign for Edge than the one against the Audubon Society, for this time her most ardent supporters had turned against her. Secretary Harold Ickes still needed her publicity efforts to secure the rest of his conservation agenda and accepted her back into his good graces. But not so Willard Van Name. "He never forgave me that I had asked for and accepted the cooperation of a man with whom he had had disagreement," Edge wrote years later.[49]

The Thomson incident permanently spoiled the congeniality among Edge, Brant, and Van Name. As Edge acted with increasing independence of Van Name, their dinners of roast duck and tramps in the woods were things of the past. "Mrs. Edge had an element of spitefulness in her makeup and Dr. Van Name—invariably right on conservation issues—believed that everybody who disagreed with him had evil motives," Brant wrote.[50]

Edge and Van Name quarreled so interminably that by 1936 Brant had to navigate ever so gingerly between them. The scientist declared that Edge was "certainly not competent to head an important conservation organization in her present mental condition." Meanwhile, Rosalie told Brant, "Friends of calm judgment exacted a promise from me that I would not see him [Van Name] alone." After one of Van Name's frequent tirades against

Edge, Brant told him, "I have concluded that most people who do things worthwhile have both temper and egotism." He warned that the committee's long-term chances of success depended on keeping those traits "under control."[51]

Rosalie Edge's break with Willard Van Name seemed to cause almost as much pain as her break with Charlie had. At almost sixty years old, Rosalie Edge was a battle-scarred veteran, and she was not up to continuing the conservation struggle. "I love my ECC, and I love conservation work," she told Brant. "But the whole Committee was started for V.n. [sic] and belonged to him. Now that he hates it, and has knifed it, why should I go on? I have a revulsion of feeling about myself. I no longer see myself as big and magnanimous, enduring all things, etc., etc. I only see myself as ridiculous to have endured all I have gone through."[52]

Although Van Name and Edge could no longer tolerate speaking to each other, Van Name never withdrew his support from the ECC, "the only conservation agency in the country that [was] worth its board and lodging," he conceded.[53] He also continued to contribute to Hawk Mountain Sanctuary; Edge directed Maurice Broun to thank him each time, for Van Name would not read a letter of gratitude if it came from her.

Willard Van Name "had slipped out from under his share of the work the ECC carried, and left it very heavy on my shoulders," Edge later wrote.[54] At the beginning of 1937, she asked Brant if he thought she should dissolve the ECC. He did not reply, and after some time she wrote to him again: "You are the finest man I know except in just one way, . . . you haven't given me the help I need in deciding whether the ECC shall go on."[55]

But it seems she had already gotten an answer to the question from someone else: "Very strong pressure has been brought on me that the committee is too vital to die a natural death, and that if I kill it, it is murder."[56] Heading back into the battle for the establishment of a park on the Olympic Peninsula, Edge went without Willard Van Name as her guide or as her friend.

IN THE MIDST of the ECC's campaigns to save the sugar pines and a large area of the Olympic Peninsula, the committee's dominance over the awakened conservation community was suddenly challenged in a new way. Her friend Robert Marshall, a socialist-minded forester and strong wilderness advocate who had backed the ECC, was forming a rival organization called the Wilderness Society. Edge asked Marshall why she had not been asked to join the group, since she knew all eight of its founders, and several of them had quietly supported the ECC in the past. "I cannot say why Andy Anderson, Harvey Broome, Bernard Frank, Aldo Leopold, Benton Mac-Kaye, Ernest Oberholzer or Bob Yard did not invite you to join," Marshall wrote back. "The reason I did not invite you was because of my unsystematic thinking of names, I did not happen to think of yours. Had I thought so, I would probably have suggested you."[57]

What may have crossed the minds of all the men was that none wished to be ruled by Edge. They may have intentionally rejected her as a cofounder, but they did appropriate their mission statement from Edge's ECC: "The Wilderness Society is born of an emergency in conservation which admits of no delay," this new manifesto declared.[58]

In April 1936 the Wilderness Society was but a babe in the woods. As congressional hearings on the establishment of an Olympic National Park got under way, the ECC was still the undisputed leader of the campaign.

DURING HER VISIT to the Olympic Peninsula in the summer she drove west with Peter, Edge encountered the roaring fear of joblessness. It was a fear that was not premised on the Depression but extended well into the future. It was also a fear fueled by the U.S. Forest Service as much as by the timber companies. She noticed that when she spoke to audiences where foresters and timber representatives were present, people said little in favor of Congressman Mon Wallgren's Olympic National Park proposal. But after the meetings these people would take her aside and quietly thank her for her courage. "You are right, absolutely right," one man said to her in private. "I absolutely agree with you, but we dare not say this out where people can hear us."[59] At the congressional hearings in April, Edge spoke to the entire country, not just to the beleaguered counties of the Olympic forests:

It seems to me that no one has made enough of the fact that the whole Nation is involved. . . . Now, the Forest Service has logged off very much of this bottom portion and . . . we ask as a restitution that we shall be given the forest to the west, and I really think there is not enough made of that, that it is the right of the people of the whole United States to have given back to them the equivalent of land that was cut out in the hysteria of war time, because that is what it really amounted to.[60]

This time her visual aid was a photograph of herself standing beneath a Douglas fir. She declared that the tree was part of a rainforest like no other she had seen, and she had seen many rainforests around the world. She had also seen the great devastation of rainforests—albeit when she was less conscious of it, on the Malay Peninsula's rubber plantations in Southeast Asia more than thirty years before her visit to the Olympic Peninsula. In Washington, in places where the trees had all been logged off, she pronounced the landscape "ugly to a degree." But the American landscape also had a historic element that was being wantonly destroyed. "Here we are asking to save just one little compact piece of this marvelous forest of the Northwest. It is the forest of Lewis and Clark that children read about in their books."[61]

Representative Martin Smith, the congressman from Grays Harbor, questioned Edge in a way that seemed more like an inquisition, but she gave as good as she got. The congressman must have sized up Edge's age and her fine clothes and ascertained, correctly it turned out, that she had not ventured beyond that tree she stood beside in her photo.

He grilled her as Congressman Englebright had during the Yosemite sugar-pine hearings about the size and composition of her "so-called conservation committee"; Smith also wanted to know who contributed the money for "the propagandizing" that it carried on. She explained that she often received contributions as small as twenty cents for postage. "I am more interested in the large contributions," Rep. Smith said, impatiently.[62]

"I am sorry, but there are no large contributions," Edge responded.

"Do you ever receive any contributions from any Canadian timber interests?" he asked.

"Never, no tainted money, but if you would like to contribute we would be glad to have your money," she replied, and stretched out her palm as if to receive it from him. Edge was famous for making the audience laugh during dry congressional hearings, but some dismissed her antics as those of a foolish old woman.[63]

"If you are going to wait until I contribute, you will be without funds a very long time," Smith replied, so savagely that Public Lands Chairman Rene De Rouen of Louisiana remonstrated.[64]

Representative Smith asked Edge about outlandish predictions she had published stating that tourism would become a better base for the local economy than timber had been if the virgin forest remained intact. She replied that all the big old trees that had stood for hundreds of years could be logged in three or five or ten years, and what jobs would there be for the people of the Olympic Peninsula then? Smith answered her:

There are only about 25, I think, on the regular pay roll of Mount Rainier National Park, and your parks do not give a great deal of employment, and that is why the laboring people and the farmers and the civic organizations out here are very much opposed to this bill, because we know we cannot get any help from you in New York or your conservation committee. If your expectations in regard to this wonderful development that will result from the tourist travel do not occur, what will happen to us out there after you bottle up the Olympic Peninsula and remove 17 billion feet of timber and tie it up?[65]

Edge might have responded by citing her own Hawk Mountain as an example of how a shift from one economic base to another that had been unimaginable happens. Such was the case at the three-year-old sanctuary in Pennsylvania, where all kinds of people were coming by the hundreds to watch hawks rather than shoot them. Instead she painted a larger picture. "The only knowledge in the world is the knowledge deduced from past experience," Edge said. "Now, if in past experience every park in the United States, in Canada and in Africa, have [sic] brought in great streams of tourists, it is reasonable to say that this one other park will do the same."[66]

Opposition to the national park's establishment, as expressed at the Public Land hearings, was so strong that there was considerable doubt the ECC-backed bill would find the supporters it required to pass. Despite Ickes's surreptitious switch to the acreage Van Name had mapped in his office, the Department of the Interior remained ambivalent. The National Park Service still openly sympathized with the Forest Service's loss of board feet.

Yet oddly, a bigger rift that the ECC had exposed was the one between the U.S. Forest Service's top officials in Washington, D.C., and the managing foresters on the ground in Washington State. Secretary Wallace and Chief Forester Ferdinand Silcox had come around to supporting the idea that the virgin timber should not be logged, although they insisted the trees remain under Forest Service jurisdiction. They argued justifiably that the tourism-development mentality of the Park Service rendered it incapable of protecting the land's pristine character.

The ECC appreciated Chief Forester Silcox's change of heart about the need to preserve such forests. But it nevertheless refused to allow the forests to remain under his agency's administration. "Mr. Silcox is not immortal," Edge had testified at the hearing. "If Mr. Silcox, with that opinion that the trees should not be cut, was going to live on for ever and ever, like the

Douglas fir, we would be glad to leave the trees in the Forest Service, but Mr. Silcox, I regret to say, will be cut down in the course of time and his successor may not agree."[67]

By this Edge understood that in the timbered principality of the Olympic Peninsula, the dogma that old-growth forest was decadent forest would prevail over dictates from the nation's Capitol. Ranks of foresters trained in the silvicultural methods that applied to French or German forests could not let trees simply rot and go to waste as an unused commercial product. Confronted with eight-hundred-year-old trees, the foresters of the Pacific Northwest still applied principles they had learned concerning eighty-year-old trees. The Douglas firs that had been growing for four hundred years may have been decadent by U.S. Forest Service thinking; according to the ECC's understanding of the primeval tree lifecycle, they were middle-aged. Conceivably some trees, like the two-thousand-year-old giant sequoias of northern California, might never die.[68]

That year, the U.S. congressional session ended with no Olympic National Park bill's emergence. Asahel Curtis, the head of the Seattle Chamber of Commerce, had strengthened both Forest Service and Park Service leaders' resolve not to preserve a square foot more than necessary. Curtis had represented the timber industry when the Mount Olympus National Monument was cut in half in 1915, and his influence still counted. Representative Wallgren, whose name was on the park bill that Van Name had crafted in Ickes's office, went home to face what seemed uncertain reelection.

Yet Wallgren's three-to-one margin of victory indicated that his park bill had acquired a surprising mass of local support. When he returned to Congress in early 1937, he introduced a new bill, meant to please the National Park Service as well as the people of his district so that it might finally pass. But the congressman's new bill proposed a national park that was 100,000 acres smaller than the previous bill's.

The ECC was furious. "The power of the Forest Service over the Park Service is clearly demonstrated by the introduction of this new bill of Congressman Wallgren," Edge told Ickes, deliberately prodding the interior secretary in the territorial part of his nature. Gone from Wallgren's new bill were the wild and primitive Hoh and Bogachiel river valleys, removed after the congressman's consultation with the very agency that should have been the ECC's chief ally in preserving them. Now the deeper the wedge the ECC could drive between Ickes and his own National Park Service, "the greater the potential for success for the Emergency Conservation Committee in getting the park they wanted."[69]

To help the secretary regain command of his agency's direction, Edge prepared another pamphlet to incite the public. She bestowed on it a most provocative title: *Double Crossing the Project for the Proposed Mount Olympus National Park: No Economic Need, but Only Commercial Greed, the Obstacle to the Mount Olympus Park.*

> DO NOT FORGET THAT THIS IS THE LAST CHANCE FOR A PARK WHICH WILL PRESERVE ANY OF THE SPLENDID FORESTS OF THE NORTHWEST. DO NOT FORGET THAT IT IS TO THE NATION—INCLUDING YOURSELF—THAT THESE WONDERFUL TREES BELONG. DO YOU WANT THEM USED TO MAKE SMALL BOARDS, BOXES OR SHINGLES WHEN WE HAVE PLENTY OF SMALL TREES FOR THESE PURPOSES?[70]

The pamphlet's "value was that it told the truth, and told it with emphasis," Edge later wrote.[71] *Double Crossing* recounted the dramatic story of how a few timber-based communities on the Olympic Peninsula were intent on preventing the rest of the nation from ever knowing its ancient forests and river valleys draped in moss and fern like no other river valleys in the world. The ECC strategy had been to sow seeds of distrust everywhere: between Secretary Ickes and the National Park Service that reported to him; between Ickes and Secretary of Agriculture Henry Wallace; between those who ran the U.S. Forest Service office in Washington State and those who ran it from Washington, D.C.; and now, between those who cut trees for a living and those who had naively entrusted the cutting to them. The latter were all the people who consumed wood products without considering what was destroyed in the process. Once they were confronted with the alternative of preserving timeless beauty, they formed an enormous new constituency with a compelling interest in the future of the Olympic forests.

By the fall of 1937, the ECC had stirred up so much divisiveness that at Irving Brant's urging President Roosevelt decided to go see these highly contested forests for himself. The presidential visit began at a lodge on Lake Crescent, which had been cut out of the proposed park but according to the ECC belonged within it. From there the Roosevelt entourage proceeded into the heart of the timber-cutting region. As if to guarantee that President Roosevelt heard only one message, regional U.S. forester C. J. Buck scarcely left his side and eliminated any escort who did not speak for the timber industry.[72]

Since the ECC was unable to get one of its own representatives close to the president, Brant had made sure ahead of time that Roosevelt received facts about timber employment and economics that refuted anything Forester Buck told him. The ECC's grassroots-building efforts on the peninsula had much to do with the scene that greeted the presidential motorcade as it drove through Port Angeles. About three thousand school children lined the streets in the rain. Their banner read: "Please Mr. President, we children need your help. Give us our Olympic National Park." When Roosevelt spoke, he told the children he intended to do that, adding that it would be the largest national park possible.

The Regional Office of the U.S. Forest Service had not been able to control the dramatic demonstration of the Port Angeles school children. Nor could it keep the president's procession away from one area of utter destruction along his route, although it did the next best thing. The U.S. Forest boundary sign was deliberately moved to make the denuded wasteland look as if it lay on private land outside the national forest.

"I hope the lumberman who is responsible for this is roasting in hell," Roosevelt was heard to say as his limousine drove slowly through it.[73] Yet despite the president's public pronouncements, Edge understood that Harold Ickes's internal opposition to the National Park Service might not be politically sustainable. It did not seem that the secretary could remain on the same side of the issue as the ECC, against the insistent stand his own agency had taken. "What I want most to know is: Is Ickes with us on the Olympic matter?" she wrote to Brant.[74]

Ickes was with them on the Olympic matter, and despite the Park Service's continued opposition, everything seemed to be proceeding toward the ECC-backed reintroduction of a third bill calling for a park of almost 900,000 acres. This acreage was indeed a bold reach beyond the grasp. It included not only the Bogachiel and Hoh valleys as before, but also the rainforest valleys of Elwha, Quinalt, and Skokomish and a strip of land leading from the forested interior to the sandy coast that President Roosevelt had specifically requested. If passed, Olympic National Park would be the first in the nation to include ecosystems ranging from snow-clad peaks to ocean shore.

But then a casual remark made on the campaign trail by the president threatened to derail everything. Roosevelt observed that while he very much wanted a large park on the Olympic Peninsula, he also appreciated the beauty of the manicured Black Forests of Germany and wondered if the selective cutting methods practiced there might be permissible in the Olympic forests.[75] With such an offhand presidential endorsement, the hopes of pro-timber forces revived, and they seized his remark to push for the addition of a selective-cutting measure to the Olympic parks bill. The Seattle Chamber of Commerce's Asahel Curtis praised the president for his understanding of forestry, that commercial logging could indeed proceed in peaceful coexistence with scenery, as in Germany.

Significantly, this stance, which was so unacceptable to the ECC, was backed by two enemies whom Edge had faced before. First was the millionaire William Wharton, vice president of the NAAS board, who was also president of the National Parks Association. At NAAS meetings Wharton had, for the sake of timber, opposed the protection of Admiralty Island brown bears and had spoken against hawk protection.[76] Wharton's personal views had not changed, and his leadership of an organization that sounded as if it supported park preservation was most puzzling. On the question of selective cutting in the proposed national park, he was very much in line with the position of the American Forestry Association, which was also still represented on the NAAS board.

In January 1938, Edge sent out eleven thousand copies of the twenty-two-page ECC pamphlet that Brant had written to combat the selective-cutting compromise. He also attacked the Forest Service's projections of timber-based employment, which assumed that the peninsula could employ 1 million and support a population four times that, "all living on the products and by-products of sustained yield lumbering."[77]

Once exposed by the ECC, the Forest Service could not realistically support the data on which its economic projections were based. Nor by this point could the public's clamoring for a large park that included virgin forests be denied. The American people, supported by President Roosevelt, had made it clear that nothing less than the creation of a national park rolling from shining mountains to misty sea would do.

Legislative intricacies remained; the full vision of the national park would not be realized until several distinct and complicated measures received congressional approval. Only then was the "Emergency Conservation Committee's triumph over the Forest Service, the Park Service and the timber industry" confirmed.[78]

The day the final bill came up for a vote, Edge pulled one last publicity stunt. She distributed to each member of Congress a cartoon from the *New Yorker* that she had used in Brant's pamphlet. It showed two men surrounded by tree stumps. The caption read: "Well, I still claim it was a good site for a saw mill when we moved here." The cartoon, she said, was a coup. It expressed "the reality that most everyone has experienced with his own eyes and gets him in touch with his feelings about it."[79]

"YOU ARE the master strategist," Edge told Brant exultantly, when it was all over. Willard Van Name may have lit the initial spark, but it was Edge who had fanned the campaign into full flame through her tireless advocacy and dramatic pamphleteering. "Rosalie Edge brought not only a sharp mind, acid tongue and quick wit to the fight, but also organizational skills without which the whole effort would have failed," asserted Seattle historian Carsten Lien years later.[80] The ECC had won its most difficult campaign to date by standing in public opposition to two powerful federal agencies and the Washington State timber industry, challenging the predominant culture of the state by introducing an ecologically based ethic and economy, the only sustainable kind. For the first time Edge gave amateurs and dilettantes a strong voice in how the nation's forests would be managed.

Secretary Ickes sent letters thanking Brant, Edge, and presumably Van Name, his three indispensable partners in conservation. To Edge, Ickes wrote: "I wish to express my appreciation and to thank you for your faithful service, your loyal support, and the splendid work which you rendered during the trying period before the establishment of the Olympic National Park. Your sincerity of purpose as Chairman of the Emergency Conservation Committee is widely recognized as being largely responsible for the creation of the park, and I realize that no one gave more generously of his [*sic*] time . . . than you."[81]

Connecticut senator Frederic C. Walcott, a former opponent who had become an avid admirer of Edge, also wrote to commend her on the "splendid piece of work" she had done. "I doubt very much that the great system of forests, with its sanctuary for the Roosevelt elk and the mountain lion, could have been saved inviolate without your help," he wrote.[82]

Such accolades undoubtedly prompted Edge to boast that Olympic National Park "was [her] most scenic accomplishment," though she happily shared the credit for it with Brant. But when Brant wrote that "Willard Van Name" deserved to be carved into the new park's tallest tree, she bristled. She would not yield an Olympic Peninsula tree's worth of credit to

"V.N." When, years later, she felt more charitable toward her former mentor, Edge would bestow the title of "Dr. Van Name's Sugar Pines" on the eight-thousand-acre Yosemite grove that had undone their conservation partnership.[83]

When Van Name died in 1959, she honored his memory by ordering a stained-glass portrait of him to be installed at Hawk Mountain Sanctuary. It is the only material artifact anywhere that acknowledges Willard Van Name's contribution to her and to the nation.

CHAPTER TEN

Hawk of Mercy

Rosalie Edge's simultaneous associations with the ECC, Hawk Mountain Sanctuary, Yosemite National Park, Olympic National Park, and the ongoing campaign to end federally funded poisoning gave her a position of unprecedented visibility for a woman in the conservation movement. Indeed, the old wildlife crusader William Temple Hornaday proclaimed her "the only woman in conservation."[1] Some years after the Olympic National Park victory, one small Baltimore publication acknowledged her ubiquity by declaring, "Rosalie Edge has a Continent for a Garden."[2] Considering how she had abandoned her flowerbeds the night she fled from Charlie almost twenty-five years earlier, this description seems unusually perceptive and tender.

In the autumn of 1938, Hawk Mountain Sanctuary miraculously reached its fifth anniversary. Maurice Broun counted more than seventeen thousand birds of prey of fourteen different species, and Irma collected admissions to the Lookout from 4,200 visitors.[3] The Brouns no longer extended casual dinner invitations to random visitors or offered them the floor to sleep on at Schaumbach's. The hawk watchers had grown too numerous. They arrived by the hundreds on weekends during the migration, pitching tents in the sanctuary's dog-hair woods since there were no nearby lodgings in which to stay.

Edge's office on Lexington Avenue was the pulse point for both Hawk Mountain and the ECC. Somehow she managed to keep the two organizations' affairs separate, if only by inches, stacking Hawk Mountain papers on one side of her desk and ECC papers on the other. Hawk Mountain had its own set of publications for her to compose and mail; in addition to the sanctuary newsletter, there were her letters soliciting funds and her steady stream of appeals to Pennsylvania legislators requesting changes in state laws concerning hawks.

Edge visited the sanctuary frequently but entrusted a great deal to Maurice and Irma, who cared for her mountain and its mission as their own. To provide a permanent home for the Brouns, Edge decided that Schaumbach's must be bought by the sanctuary along with adjacent property. Her intentions meant that unlike the ECC, Hawk Mountain needed to become a proper legal entity with a board of directors and tax-exempt status. Also, unlike the ECC it would encourage membership in addition to donations. Hawk Mountain membership cost two dollars a year, a sum many could afford even during the Depression.

Papers for the incorporation of the Hawk Mountain Sanctuary Association were drawn up. Marion Crary Ingersoll, a former suffragist and NAAS member, bought Schaumbach's along with the land Edge wanted to preserve on the perimeter. The sanctuary grew to two square miles of meadow and regrown woodland. Edge asked Marion to join the Hawk Mountain board in return for her generosity. Marion was the elegant and socially progressive wife of Brooklyn borough president Raymond V. Ingersoll. She had joined with Margaret Sanger to establish the country's first birth control provider in Brooklyn, which would later be known as Planned Parenthood.[4]

Marion Ingersoll's life was the sort Rosalie Edge might have envied. In addition to the Ingersolls' luxurious apartment at Beekman Place in Manhattan, they owned a seaside estate framed by resplendent gardens on Duck Island in Northport, New York. Marion's life was a contented one, inside the bosom of her family and in the outside world.

The Ingersolls' daughter Asho attended Bennington, where Margaret Edge had gone to college. When the two mothers went together to visit their girls at school, the deep fissures in the Edge family could not be hidden.[5] Margaret was aloof and was clearly unhappy to see her mother. Afterward it was Hawk Mountain, rather than personal friendship, that bonded Rosalie and Marion Ingersoll. Marion shared Rosalie's vision of the sanctuary and the commitment to build a "large and democratic following" of people who wanted to protect all birds of prey, everywhere.[6]

Ingersoll's generosity notwithstanding, Edge's Audubon experience had alerted her to how easily any well-meaning organization could be manipulated by a few rich donors, and she was determined to build a wide base of support with the sanctuary's two-dollar annual dues. No additional contribution received was too small to be acknowledged in Hawk Mountain's first annual report: A pair of binoculars. A rocking chair. Margaret Edge had given her college furniture to Schaumbach's, despite the young woman's "real affection" for the items.[7]

But Margaret's greater affection lay with a law student named Eric. She quit Bennington and eloped that December, keeping the marriage a secret from her parents for six weeks. Her mother may have found some vindication in her daughter's rash act when she learned that her new son-in-law's last name was Nightingale.

ROSALIE ALMOST ALWAYS got along better with young men than with young women, and she hit it off so well with Eric Nightingale that together they enrolled in creative-writing classes at Columbia University. She hoped to improve her pamphleteering style, and Eric simply liked to write.

"You really should join us," Edge entreated her daughter. "It is not fair, I think, for you to hold yourself in a position of superiority—the pedestal of the critic—when Eric and I have rolled back our cuffs so determinedly."[8]

Rosalie, the oldest student by far in the classes that she took, developed her latent talent for composing poems, several of which were published in the school's annual poetry anthology. Her poem "O Hawk of Mercy" would have been awarded Columbia's prestigious Van Rensselaer Prize but was disqualified because Edge was not enrolled in a degree-granting program.[9] "I do not aspire to literary fame except for my work," she wrote, though no doubt pleased by the fact that the judges would have awarded her hawk poem the top prize if they could have.[10]

> O clear-eyed hawk
> Against the zenith poised
> Black scimitar of steel the Huntsman swings
> Who rides the rushing stallion of the winds;
> Now, as he sweeps his arm
> in one swift strike
> I see the lightening plunge,
> Thy clement death
> That strikes to earth the gold-plumaged bird
> The one of all the covey too weak and slow

To fly for cover.
Not knowing, he is dead,
Dead in the midst of sunlight without fear.
O Hawk of mercy, spiraling to the clouds
To rest again upon the Huntsman's wrist,
Plead with Him for me, that He send me death
With wings like thine to overtake my pain;
That I may die unknowing in the sun,
That I be saved from cowering in the dark,
Listening, fearful
To the laggard tramp of time.

Her poems depicted the fragile beauty of birds and trees, and the puz-zling relationship between people and nature. Many were published; her exceedingly modest earnings from them—payments of five or ten dollars a piece—were more than she had ever earned as a conservationist. In the po-ems she wrote and kept for herself, she expressed her life's greatest sources of pain and joy.

Edge had taken writing classes to improve her conservation pamphlets and seems to have been surprised that, at the age of sixty, the talent that emerged was a poetic one, since she had always preferred telling stories. Although her poetry flourished, she told Margaret that she still could not write a story in its proper sequence. It was an inability that characterized her whole existence, she said resignedly, for she was "learning to write at the wrong end of it" and had begun while knowing "nothing of the preface" that should tell her what life is "all about." To never let the truth spoil a good story seemed to be as far as she ever got with her prose.[11]

IN JANUARY 1939 the Redwood Mountain and Redwood Canyon groves of giant sequoias outside Sequoia National Park in California were in dan-ger of being blasted to smithereens. Together these adjacent sequoia groves covered five square miles. They were not only the last groves of big trees in private ownership but also the largest area with such trees left in the world. Although many sequoia groves had been cut down, the remainder had been saved in 1890 with the establishment of both Sequoia and Yosemite National Parks.[12]

Compared to the furor surrounding Olympic National Park's creation, opposition to Sequoia's establishment had been negligible. Loggers had tired of the novelty of cutting the big trees down and sending sections of them to circus freak shows for the public's amusement. The trees were difficult to log in conventional ways, and their timber proved too brittle to be used for construction.

But if the gigantic two-thousand-year-old trees that were left unprotected were dynamited, they could be flayed into fragments to make pencils, fence posts, and the grapevine stakes that California's wineries needed. The more accessible Converse Sequoia Grove had met such a fate in the early 1900s. No logging railway or road ran close enough to the Redwood Mountain and Redwood Canyon trees to make them an economical resource for manufacturing pencils and fence posts. The completion of a highway built with Depression relief funds changed that. The groves' owners did not want to destroy their magnificent trees, but they had bills to pay and back taxes due, and they were running out of time. The government was the only possible purchaser of the sequoia groves and the only entity that could assure they would be protected.

The Redwood Mountain sequoias were unusual in that they grew on top of a mountain rather than in a sheltered valley, and their broccoli-headed tops made a bulbous rather than pointy outline against the open sky. Lower down the Redwood Canyon grove included the fabled Hart Tree, which at its base was said to measure thirty-six feet across. At a height equal to nine stories off the ground, the tree's trunk was said to narrow to twenty feet. Impressed by reports of the Hart Tree's girth, Secretary Harold Ickes asked an elevator manufacturer how many people would fit in an elevator of the tree's upper dimension. More than 150, he was told.[13]

If ever there was an example of Rosalie Edge's dictum to never let the truth spoil a good story, it was this often repeated tale of the Hart Tree. The tree was enormous, as is any mature sequoia, but in truth it was not large enough to make the top ten in the sequoia record book, which included the General Sherman and General Grant monarchs. Ickes had been misinformed, perhaps deliberately; whether by Mrs. Edge or someone else is not known. The more important truth was that seven thousand sequoias in private hands were soon to be turned into fence posts unless something was done. If it took an exaggeration of the Hart Tree's dimensions to change that fate, so be it.[14]

In the region of the Sierra Nevada of California, much more was at stake than the Redwood Mountain and Canyon sequoias. Water, and who would use it, complicated the situation enormously. Sequoias had no compelling economic benefit as lumber, but the value of water throughout the arid West was virtually incalculable.

A short distance from the threatened sequoias and bordering Sequoia National Park on the north lay 440,000 acres of the rugged Kings Canyon region of the High Sierras. In 1806 a group of Spanish explorers had discovered its major river. They called it El Rio de Los Santos Reyes—River of the Holy Kings—because they had first seen it on the Catholic holy day of Epiphany. White trappers and explorers came next, and the 1849 gold rush drew thousands of speculators.

But the Kings Canyon area was too rugged a place for the white people to settle. The Kings was a wild river that during spring runoff churned into speeding, blinding whiteness of wicked rapids. In this precipitous country, sheer granite walls rose more than eight thousand feet from riverbed to ridgetop, forming a geologic cut deeper than Yosemite Valley; the floor of Tehipite Canyon (later called Zumwalt Meadow) lay a mile below the highest mountain summits, which crested at 14,494-foot-tall Mount Whitney, the tallest mountain in the continental United States.

In the 1870s John Muir meticulously explored the Kings Canyon country and the three forks of the Kings River. He came to know the area better than most, perhaps as well as the indigenous Monache tribe did, which had lived there since prehistoric times. Muir ascertained that the mountains of the Kings River region held few mineral deposits, were too rugged for grazing, and contained little timber of value. But the beauty of Kings Canyon, particularly in Cedar Grove and Tehipite Canyon, was as deserving as his beloved Yosemite of being accorded national-park stature.

"Let our law-givers then make haste before it is too late to set apart this surpassingly glorious region," Muir wrote in 1891. He was flush with his victories of persuading Congress to establish both Yosemite and Sequoia National Parks south of the Kings Canyon region. These two preserved areas, according to Muir, were incomplete without the third—the lofty peaks, crashing rivers, and big trees of Kings Canyon. The entire area needed to be "comprehended in one grand national park."[15]

Muir's recommendation for yet a third national park in the Sierra Nevada was deemed excessive. When the U.S. Forest Service was formed in 1905, Chief Forester Gifford Pinchot opposed preservation of any additional acreage in either the Sequoia or the Sierra National Forest, even though the

Kings Canyon timber values were admittedly low. The young agency still wanted to make the land available to Californians for grazing, hydropower, and mining on whatever scale possible. At nearby Yosemite National Park, however, this was turning out to be on the scale of grand national development. With the grand national-park scheme that Muir had in mind, none of these uses would have been permitted.

In 1913 Congress approved the flooding of the Hetch Hetchy Valley. The decision that turned the magnificent valley into a reservoir for San Francisco is said to have ruined Muir's health, and he died on Christmas Eve in 1914.

The bitter fight that Muir led against the Hetch Hetchy Reservoir's construction reached its fever pitch not long after the NAAS agreed to take large donations from gun makers. Curiously, Chief Forester Pinchot's important opinions figured prominently in both controversies, though he seemed to be on different sides of the ethical issues in each. Pinchot's vocal opposition to the gun maker's gift was in large part what forced the NAAS to ultimately reject it. At the same time, the chief forester had no qualms about actively supporting the O'Shaughnessy Dam's construction within a national park, though such utilitarian projects clearly violated the national park concept of "the preservation by the Government in all its original beauty of a region like this."[16]

From one end of the nation to the other, on issues small and large, the moral principles of conservation were increasingly muddied. As the waters of the Tuolumne River rose above the Hetch Hetchy Valley floor, this was literally the case. These principles would still be mired in a slough of despond when Edge encountered them sixteen years later.

As it turned out, the new reservoir proved of little value to San Franciscans. By the time the reservoir was filled in the late 1920s, the city had found better and cheaper sources of water and means to electrify its homes and enterprises. But the flooding of Hetch Hetchy demonstrated more than anything else that national parks needed their own supervisory agency dedicated to their protection to prevent future travesties from occurring.

Stephen Mather, a native Californian and heir to the Borax fortune, had fought Yosemite Park's desecration as ardently as John Muir had. The loss of Hetch Hetchy may have hastened Muir's decline, and it was so painful to Mather that in 1916 he accepted the low-paying job as founding director of the National Park Service. The new service's placement within the Department of the Interior would trigger the recurring turf war with the

Department of Agriculture's U.S. Forest Service, which was eleven years older.

For the next fourteen years, Park Service director Mather made the preservation of Kings Canyon, Muir's other beloved region of the Sierra Nevada, a priority. Mather failed, even though he had the backing of the prestigious Sierra Club, which Muir had founded in 1892 specifically to preserve the area's wild beauty.

California's chambers of commerce wanted no more national parks; they were perceived as limiting economic growth. Meanwhile, the U.S. Forest Service, which administered the Kings Canyon region, continued to permit below-cost logging, overgrazing, overhunting, diversionary irrigation by farmers, and private construction of summer cabins. "I wish John Muir were alive now to help," wistfully remarked William Colby, a Sierra Club officer who had known Muir personally.[17] In 1929 when NPS director Mather died, the dream of permanent protection for Kings Canyon looked as hopeless as ever.

Mather learned the hard lesson that Muir had: in California, where there were steeply plunging rivers in the mountains and burgeoning cities downstream, municipal governments, chambers of commerce, and hydroelectric power companies were powerful foes of national parks. San Francisco had laid claim to a portion of Yosemite; Los Angeles visionaries predicted their city would need dams in the Kings Canyon country to realize its urban destiny. Though San Francisco's experience with the Hetch Hetchy Reservoir made Los Angeles's assumption a dubious one, it endured. For the next forty years, it seemed impossible that Los Angeles's dreams of growth and Muir's dreams of preservation could both come true.

BUT SHORTLY AFTER President Franklin Delano Roosevelt was elected, some of the prerequisites necessary to establish a national park in the Kings Canyon region sputtered to life. Miraculously the Los Angeles Bureau of Power and Light withdrew its decades-long reservations for high-country dam sites. City water developers had by this time learned that it cost too much to build large storage facilities in such rugged terrain and in a place where river flows fluctuated too widely from one season to the next. With the completion of the federally funded Hoover Dam on the Nevada border, Los Angeles was assured of cheap hydropower for years to come. It had time to find a new site for one large dam on a different river with a possibly more-reliable flow than the Kings, to meet needs beyond that.

But the High Sierras were still in California, where no water flowed without a thirsty claimant. Central Valley irrigation districts were eager to acquire the water rights that Los Angeles had vacated, particularly in the Cedar Grove Valley and Tehipite Canyon. Each time the Department of the Interior backed a Kings Canyon park bill, it was defeated by San Joaquin growers, chambers of commerce, power companies, hunting organizations—and the U.S. Forest Service. "The water must be impounded back in the mountains," insisted S. Bevier Show, the Forest Service's regional director. "Many reservoirs, not a single one, will be required to fully regulate and use the water."[18]

The iron determination of the new interior secretary to add a national park was, of course, another Kings Canyon national park prerequisite. Year after year Harold Ickes listed the establishment of a third national park in the High Sierras among his department goals. As the Olympic park victory loomed, Ickes seemed confident that a national park could be made out of Kings Canyon as well. At the interior secretary's request in the summer of 1938, his consultant Irving Brant packed into the High Sierras to scout the area before launching the next major national park campaign.[19]

Publicly, the three-year-old Wilderness Society, and not the ECC, was the national conservation organization that declared its intention to lead in the campaign for the long-overdue national park in Kings Canyon. True to its name, the Wilderness Society demanded that the National Park Service manage Kings as a wilderness park. This was a new concept. Although the agency's Organic Act stated that protected natural areas were to be left "unimpaired," this had never prevented the Park Service from encouraging all manner of developments to draw tourists. The resulting close relations of park managers with the profit-oriented concessions within the national parks were vehemently protested by the ECC and, now, the Wilderness Society.

Robert Marshall and other Wilderness Society founders generally preferred U.S. Forest Service management over that of the amenity-prone National Park Service, but Kings Canyon might be different. With its precipitous terrain and lack of roads, Kings Canyon presented an ideal opportunity to try wilderness preservation in John Muir's pristine sense of the word, which meant that none of the ring roads or souvenir shops found in other national parks would be permitted. As long as safeguards were in place, the Park Service could perhaps do a better job of protecting Kings Canyon as wilderness.[20]

Marshall, though himself an employee of the U.S. Forest Service, was concerned that if the area remained under his agency's management its wilderness stipulation was more likely to be administratively altered. He was willing to give the National Park Service a chance. Back in Washington, D.C., Secretary Ickes liked Marshall's idea of a national park wilderness. The top U.S. Forest Service officials were in rare agreement with the top National Park Service officials that Kings Canyon's scenic values outweighed the market values of its timber, grazing, and mineral resources. A Kings Canyon national park was something the National Park Service had wanted since its inception. Given the cost of making the rugged landscape hospitable with roads and hotels, the Park Service could accept the wilderness status that Secretary Ickes backed.

Then a second water miracle occurred. The powerful San Joaquin irrigation districts withdrew their opposition to a Kings Canyon park after the Bureau of Reclamation identified a much better storage site for their future water needs than either Cedar Grove or Tehipite Canyon. The new Pine Flat site was twenty-five miles downstream from the proposed national park's boundary. Secretary Ickes promised that in return for the irrigationists' support for the new park, the government would spend $25 million to build their water-storage facilities as soon as possible. With Irving Brant's assistance, Congressman Bernard W. Gearhart of Fresno drafted the most promising Kings Canyon park bill yet.[21]

Gearhart's bill depended on the support of the Sierra Club, which, after Muir died, had not fought much to preserve the wild region for which it was named. The organization had become more of a social club for mountaineers, "snobbish and smug" and perhaps not unlike what had become of the NAAS before Rosalie Edge tore into it.[22]

To spark Sierra Club fervor, Representative Gearhart's bill called for the establishment of the John Muir–Kings Canyon National Park, after the club's founder. With the bill's wilderness provision and Muir's name on it, the Sierra Club could not resist taking a lead role in getting the national park established. As if to fend off the New York-based ECC's habit of invading distant territories, Sierra Club secretary William Colby informed Edge of his club's commitment to cosponsor the necessary national park legislation.[23]

What the Sierra Club needed most from the ECC was some of its park advocacy literature, he said, until the Sierra Club produced its own. Neither the Sierra Club nor the Wilderness Society had what it took to blanket the continent with the rousing and instructive pamphlets for which the ECC was famous. The two larger organizations lacked the infrastructure and national recognition of the little ECC. Nor did they have the experience to mount a national-park campaign and succeed. At the Sierra Club's San Francisco office, a young man named David Brower wrote the club's newsletter. Sixty years later Brower, who became the key firebrand of his conservation generation, would recall that Rosalie Edge had been the leading model of conservation advocacy of his youth.[24]

BUT EDGE HAD BEEN reluctant to enter the Kings Canyon fray. Gearhart's park bill provided for the preservation of the imminently endangered Redwood Mountain and Redwood Canyon sequoia groves; here were more trees that Willard Van Name loved and wanted saved. She did not care to get involved with any more of Van Name's favorite projects, she told Brant. If Willard decided to join the effort, she would be "more of a stumbling block than a help," she said, putting the matter rather delicately.[25]

Irving Brant, at the behest of the interior secretary, continued to urge her to join the Kings Canyon battle, for thus far it had lacked her ability to build the essential "public support in advance of action."[26] To a large extent a Kings Canyon park had never gained the momentum it needed because it had never aroused sufficient national interest to combat the dominant California water interests. Combating strong local imperatives was just the sort of thing the ECC did so well.

"It is time that the whole people of California be awakened—and the whole people of America," wrote William Schulz, the former ECC operative Van Name had hired. Secretary of the Interior Ickes had been so impressed by Schulz during the Olympic Park and Yosemite sugar-pine campaigns that he hired him as a field representative for his department. Schulz, sounding very much like the ECC, wrote to Ickes: "I believe this awakening will soon become a fact for Mrs. C. N. Edge, Chairman of the Emergency Conservation Committee, will shortly have out a pamphlet on the John Muir National Park."[27]

That pamphlet was no. 74, *The Proposed John Muir–Kings Canyon National Park*, written by Brant and distributed four years after Secretary Ickes had first made known his desire for such a park. It was timed to be released, however, within days of Gearhart's introduction of H.R. 3794. Edge was again taking charge; at the Department of the Interior, Schulz wrote glowingly of her reputation as "America's first-rank conservationist."[28] In the spirit that had evidently been lacking from earlier Kings Canyon park efforts, she exultantly announced her entry to ECC readers: "I give you a name to conjure with! . . . There can be no more fitting memorial to the great American Mountaineer than the reservation of this area of the grandest mountain scenery in America, and its great sequoia belt, the most verdant grove of the ancient trees in existence."[29]

The Proposed John Muir–Kings Canyon National Park pamphlet included artful photos of John Muir and Brant's toned-down prose. The pamphlet was the ECC's most graphically and editorially sophisticated piece of literature to date. "I have worked like the elephant who has but one aim, to please / His ivory tusks he gladly gives to make piano keys," Edge joked in a letter to Brant, proud that this publication was better than anything she had done with Van Name.[30]

The pamphlet made its national debut not a moment too soon, for the Redwood Mountain and Redwood Canyon sequoias were scheduled for dynamite at the end of 1938 unless the government agreed to purchase them from their tax-delinquent owners. Edge next set to work saturating California newspapers with guest editorials and articles and building grassroots support throughout the state. As usual, she did it all from her Lexington Avenue office in New York. This time she did not go out to visit, professing to be too much of "a tenderfoot" to properly appreciate any portion of the Kings Canyon region.[31] She depended on others for eyewitness reports of its grandeur.

Edge recalled one special informant. "One day my office door opened, and there entered a venerable gentleman, then in his ninetieth year. He seated himself in an old high-backed Dutch armchair. He held his fur cap, and his open fur-lined coat fell loosely around him. I wondered whether I dreamed. It was as though a Rembrandt portrait had come to life. He introduced himself, Dr. Gustavus Eisen."[32] Eisen had stopped by her office because he had read ECC pamphlet no. 74 and wanted to heartily thank its publisher in person. The Swedish-born botanist lived in New York but had spent years exploring the Sierra Nevada in the 1870s, arriving there before John Muir. Eisen had been one of the earliest advocates for the establishment of a Kings Canyon national park. With both Hornaday and Van Name out of reach, Edge welcomed into her life another idealistic scientist—another father figure perhaps—who loved nature and who would cheer her on if her confidence flagged.

EVEN FOR THOSE who were eager to support the creation of a wilderness park in the High Sierras, Congressman Bernard Gearhart's bill was hard to fully grasp. The Redwood Mountain and Redwood Canyon sequoia groves were not contiguous to the vast body of the proposed park, making John Muir-Kings Canyon's key scenic components not only varied but dispersed. There was, however, a much greater problem with the Gearhart bill. Buried in it was a threat to inundate Cedar Grove and Tehipite Canyon, which Muir had said were as exquisite as Hetch Hetchy and Yosemite.

The California growers, skittish in their support of the bill, still worried that the promised Pine Flat reservoir would not meet their irrigation needs. To assure this most important group did not bolt from the fragile coalition of park supporters, the Gearhart park bill *excluded* Cedar Grove and Tehipite Canyon. The Wilderness Society's board of directors was stunned. They knew well Muir's love of these particular areas. Without Cedar Grove and Tehipite, John Muir-Kings Canyon was a grand sellout to the water power and irrigation interests, not a grand national park for all Americans.[33]

The Wilderness Society directors voted not to support the Gearhart bill unless Cedar Grove and the granite Tehipite Dome and Canyon were included; William Wharton's National Park Association, which had opposed Olympic National Park's establishment and refuges for grizzly bears and birds of prey, also demanded these areas be made part of the proposed park. A third organization, the California Mountaineers, joined them. Only the ECC, the Sierra Club, and the John Muir Association stood by Representative Gearhart's John Muir–Kings Canyon park bill as it was written.

It is cause for wonder: what were these latter groups thinking?

While Rosalie Edge was raising awareness about the John Muir–Kings Canyon National Park bill, ECC master strategist Irving Brant was reviewing hydrologic studies. Another water-engineering report was due to appear, and its preliminary findings confirmed the previous ones. Cedar Grove and Tehipite Canyon would never serve the growers' water storage needs. The two sites were deemed so poor for this purpose they were not even mentioned in the region's biggest irrigation and power project bill then under consideration by Congress.

Brant was certain that when the California growers reviewed the final reports they would uncategorically reject Cedar Grove and Tehipite just as the Los Angeles water developers already had. The problem was that not all the hydrologic evidence would be available until it was too late to save the Redwood Mountain and Redwood Canyon sequoias. It was their preservation that made John Muir-Kings Canyon's establishment an urgent matter and not just an important one.

As Brant and Edge saw things, the great moral principle underlying the national park system itself was at stake. Brant had reasoned that keeping Cedar Grove and Tehipite Canyon within the boundaries of the Gearhart bill would have lost the support of the San Joaquin water developers unless they secretly entertained the hope of being able to flood these valleys for future development. Hetch Hetchy Valley had been inside Yosemite's boundaries when it was flooded and still stood as the destructive precedent.[34]

On the potential danger of repeating a Hetch Hetchy atrocity, Brant and Edge were in complete agreement with the Wilderness Society. It was a risk but a carefully calculated one. But the fact that Hetch Hetchy had been dammed in spite of its location led Brant to seek a solution that would strengthen the underlying national-park principle: lands were to be left "unimpaired for the enjoyment of future generations." The Gearhart bill also gave the president the authority to include Cedar Grove and Tehipite *unharmed* once the hydrologic studies were completed.

The lands would then be forever preserved in their wilderness condition, and the public would have a stronger precedent embedded in the national-park psyche. The Sierra Club appreciated Brant's convoluted though shrewd reasoning, judging it a master stroke rather than a sellout.

It was then up to Rosalie Edge to hammer the convoluted point home after the Wilderness Society withdrew its support. She put it into words better than Brant the journalist and strategist could. Tehipite and Cedar Grove were "symbols of cheap power to the irrigationists," Edge wrote. "It would be fatal to ignore this psychological fact. . . . It is better to eliminate Cedar Grove and Tehipite altogether from the Gearhart bill, rather than to bring them in now, before the irrigationists get their cheap power on the North Fork. When this power is assured, the irrigationists will never lift a finger against the two beautiful canyons."[35]

Edge's previous confrontations with William Wharton's National Parks Association also enabled the ECC to expose a conspiracy by park opponents. She was happy to report everything to Secretary Ickes. By its name the National Parks Association allowed itself to be mistakenly identified as a pro-park organization or perhaps a quasi-government agency of the Department of the Interior. From her previous dealings, however, Edge knew it as a private organization heavily funded and influenced by the American Forestry Association.

Under this cover, Edge charged, the Forestry Association was "pursuing its familiar system of sabotage."[36] With the information Edge gave Ickes, the Department of the Interior dissociated from the National Parks

Association, and in a press release Secretary Ickes colorfully denounced it as "a stooge for lumber interests."[37] Edge and Brant further alleged that the group called California Mountaineers also pretended to be a friend of the proposed John Muir–Kings Canyon National Park. The Mountaineers had been formed by California chambers of commerce that had strongly opposed the national-park proposal in the past and in a new guise were intent on defeating it again.[38]

Edge's prominence in the John Muir–Kings Canyon National Park campaign earned her the private derision of retired chief forester and former Pennsylvania governor Gifford Pinchot. A mutual friend of hers and Pinchot's naively asked if he would speak in favor of Kings Canyon's transfer from the Forest Service to the National Park Service. Pinchot would do no such thing. He was, in fact, "heartily and vigorously against" the transfer. "Furthermore, there is nobody of my acquaintance who goes off half cock with greater regularity than Mrs. Edge," he wrote.[39]

Mrs. Edge was amused. "Some historian may look over when Mr. Pinchot and I and even you . . . are dead and gone," she wrote to her informant, and decide who was right and who was wrong. "Mr. Pinchot has never been able to realize that a tree or a forest has any other function than the production of board feet. I really have no personal feeling against him on account of his stupid opposition to the preservation of virgin forests. His mind is blind in one eye—that's all."[40]

Before a national park in Kings Canyon would come into being, the Gearhart bill would endure a great deal that was out of the ordinary: Forest Service and Park Service allegations and counterallegations of insanity, burglary, and illegal wiretapping; the addition by park opponents of water storage facilities; the removal of its wilderness provision. It would lose its hyphenated tribute to John Muir after a rumor of the naturalist's marital infidelity resurfaced and made him unworthy of having a national park named in his honor.[41]

But the most dramatic defamations were aired in Congress. Representative Alfred Elliott, a Democrat, represented the district that overlapped with the proposed park. Unlike his colleague Republican Representative Gearhart, who sponsored the Kings Canyon bill, Representative Elliott was bitterly opposed to a third national park in his backyard. His opposition gave rise to what Irving Brant described as "one of the most bizarre, laughably idiotic, yet most damnable incidents in congressional history."[42]

The incident began when Representative Elliott received a one-hundred-dollar check in the mail made out to Representative Bernard Gearhart. An elderly Sierra Club member, Gertrude Achilles, had mistakenly sent her contribution to Gearhart instead of to the Sierra Club. Achilles compounded her error of writing her check to Representative Gearhart instead of the Sierra Club by addressing it to Representative Elliott. With this check in hand, Elliott devised a trap for Gearhart.

He photostated the check made out to Gearhart and sent it to J. Edgar Hoover, telling the FBI chief it was evidence of a vote-buying scheme. Charles Dunwoody, a member of the California Mountaineers, which the ECC had discredited, then took Achilles' original check, put it in a new envelope, and typed Representative Gearhart's Washington office address on it. He mailed this envelope from a town in California near Achilles' home. Representatives Elliott and Dunwoody then waited for Gearhart to cash the check.

When Gearhart received the check, he immediately returned it to Achilles with a note saying she should send her donation to the Sierra Club rather than to him. As far as Gearhart was concerned, that was the end of the matter. A short while later an anonymous informant called Gearhart to tell him that Elliott was publicly accusing him of taking a bribe. Elliott had made the charge while holding up the copy of Achilles' check at a meeting with voters in his district. "He is out to frame you, Buddy," the caller told Gearhart.[43]

Gearhart, a former Fresno district attorney, gathered proof that he was innocent. It was an easy case to win. Achilles had never owned a typewriter nor learned to type, so she could not have typed the address on the envelope addressed to Gearhart. Gearhart asked if he could speak on a point of personal privilege on the floor of the House of Representatives. Irving Brant was on Capitol Hill that day when word of a showdown between two congressmen spread. Dozens crammed the gallery to hear the floor exchange.[44]

Gearhart outlined the plot against him, and Elliott was given forty minutes to respond and answer questions. Brant recalled one of the comical moments. "Elliott was asked if he had given Charles Dunwoody the letter 'with instructions to mail it from ... Fresno.'" "'No,'" replied Elliott. Then Elliott was asked, "'What were the gentleman's instructions'"? "'[To mail it] From San Jose,'" the flustered congressman blurted.[45]

Not long after the scandal, Congress voted to establish the 460,000-acre Kings Canyon National Park—partly it seems, out of disgust for the lengths to which one of its own was willing to go to keep the park from winning approval. In the end, water storage facilities were out. The wilderness mandate was in. The Redwood Mountain and Redwood Canyon sequoia groves were saved. As promised, pristine Cedar Grove and Tehipite Canyon were included after the hydrological studies were released. The combined, grand national Sequoia–Kings Canyon park area would cover more than 800,000 acres.

The ECC's master strategist, Irving Brant, was always generous in his praise of Rosalie Edge. "It may be fairly said that in the 1930s and 1940s, Mrs. Edge's committee was to conservation in general what Harold L. Ickes was to conservation in the federal government," he wrote. "Again and again, when Secretary Ickes was faced with some issue, he would say to me: 'Won't you ask Mrs. Edge to put out something on this?' And she always did, for in forest and wildlife conservation an Ickes objective was practically certain to be a natural objective of the committee."[46]

Gustavus Eisen, the ninety-two-year-old visitor who had dropped by the ECC office to thank Edge for the Kings Canyon pamphlet, lived to see the national park's creation. He asked that when he died his ashes be scattered from the 12,160-foot-tall mountain along the Sierras' Great Western Divide that was named in his honor.[47]

CHAPTER ELEVEN

Hellcat

Even in the grim weeks before and after Pearl Harbor, Rosalie Edge could be found at her post on the conservation front. The nation was in no position to consider new national parks, but she continued her fight for unpopular causes of nature. At the end of 1941, Edge went to a congressional hearing to oppose the eradication of livestock tick infestations in parts of Florida using insecticides; she feared what wide applications of the poison might do to deer and other wild creatures. She suggested that the livestock owners dip their cattle rather than expose all wildlife to toxic substances.

In 1939 Secretary Ickes had finally dismantled the Bureau of Biological Survey, no doubt under Edge's influence. Certain Biological Survey functions were retained and combined with elements of the Bureau of Fisheries that the empire-building interior secretary had acquired from the Department of Commerce. The Fish and Wildlife Service formed from this union was presumably more to the secretary's liking and to Rosalie Edge's. Its mission focused on the management of federal wildlife refuges, a more life-affirming emphasis than that of the old Biological Survey.

But ingrained practices died slowly, and livestock interests still requested federal expenditures for the eradication of one nuisance species or another. Edge's testimony regarding the cattle-tick issue did not make headlines the way her national-park testimony had. Yet lawmakers now respected her peculiar credentials to address ecological esoterica. "I am not myself a scientist," Edge began, although by this time this fact was well known to the congressmen. "The men in the museums and in universities have not the time, and they have not often the political acumen that is necessary to express themselves. They express themselves through me, and through my committee, and I pass on information to bodies such as this." It was her duty to educate the senators since they obviously knew nothing of "sciences, entomology, ticks, and mammals."[1]

"Please do not limit it to that," interjected Senator James O'Connor. "We are all human, Mr. Chairman," she offered magnanimously.[2]

In the fall of 1941, with war fever high, Edge learned from Fish and Wildlife director Ira Gabrielson that the army planned to use the short flyway of the few remaining trumpeter swans near Yellowstone National Park as a practice artillery range. The extinction of the largest native bird in the lower forty-eight states was virtually guaranteed if their flyway was used in this manner. Her request for the range to be relocated was rejected by the War Department. At the Colony Club, friends thought she was joking when she told them over bridge one day what she was trying to do.[3]

Edge attempted to rally conservationist opposition, but she was considered unpatriotic by everyone but her old ally Irving Brant, who egged her on. At Brant's urging she sent copies of her correspondence with the army to President Roosevelt, Vice President Harry Truman, and Secretary of War Stimson. Brant notified Ickes, who also sent a memo to Roosevelt repeating Edge's arguments for moving the artillery range out of the trumpeters' flight path. Four days before the attack on Pearl Harbor, Edge received a letter from Major General E. S. Adams stating that "appropriate steps [were] being taken to discontinue all planning activities in connection with that site."[4]

The Colony Club ladies were impressed, or so Edge wrote later of the episode. "Fancy the War Department changing its plans for *swans*!" the doubters marveled over their next bridge game.

Edge then presented the perilous circumstances of the trumpeter swan to Ira Gabrielson, the director of the new Fish and Wildlife Service of whom she had approved. Gabrielson had been a strong backer of the ECC. Captive breeding of trumpeter swans had worked elsewhere, she told him. Might the service institute such a program? Fish and Wildlife began to breed captive trumpeters and saved the big birds.

WHEN THE UNITED STATES entered the war, twenty-eight-year-old Peter Edge sought a coast guard commission, and thirty-seven-year-old Maurice Broun enlisted in the navy. Irma moved back with her family at the Penniman mansion on Cape Cod for the duration. Rosalie refused to leave Hawk Mountain Sanctuary unguarded and hired a local man, Fran Trembly, to regularly check the grounds and count the birds.[5] Maurice had grown to be so much like a son to her that when she received a letter from him and from Peter on the same day, she did not know which to open first.

Peter, on a ship in the South Pacific, and Maurice, in a trench in the Philippines, spent their idle hours as the ornithologist-soldiers Elliott Coues and Jacques Delamain had in previous wars: They calmed their jittery nerves and chased away boredom by watching birds. They sent Edge descriptions of birds they did not know.[6] She consulted her bird guides to determine what they had seen and sometimes enclosed pages torn from her guidebooks in the V-mail she returned to them.

Perhaps to still her own nerves or chase boredom, Edge wrote a poem, marking yet another time when feelings of loss engulfed her. "To Peter and Other Storm Petrels" was a tribute to all the nation's sons who had gone off to war:

Not all the flares and bombs and guns of hate
Can halt the spring along your northern ways
Whose hours of sun in splendor far outrate
The stripes of day and dark in palm-girt bays.
Nor are the birds concerned with strife of man,
That navigate their course from pole to pole,
The skies and seas one vast blueprint whose plan
Is but a small-scale section of the whole.
You have their compass in your heart, and know
The will that rules their flight.
Northward you go where waves are harmony to wild bird cries.
And when on island rocks the gold light dulls,
I'll wait your coming with the Goldeneyes,
And know your voice among the Laughing Gulls.[7]

At Hawk Mountain, Edge had gotten to know many conservation-minded boys. In the autumn before the war, at what Maurice called his "pre-induction camp," they gathered at Schaumbach's. She remembered leaving

the old stone cottage for what would be the last time for several years. The
boys had gathered around the wood stove for one of Broun's inspiring talks
that mingled love of birds with love of country.[8]

How odd to recall that when the previous generation had gone off to war,
shooting hawks from the Kittatinny Ridge was considered patriotic preparation, but under Maurice's guidance, the freedom of hawks to fly unharmed
was one of the things for which these soldiers would risk their lives.

On that somber, rainy December weekend in 1941, Edge drove back to
New York with Beethoven's Fifth Symphony pounding in her head, the fer-
vent music Broun blared on the record player after his farewell tutorial.
She was determined that the beauty, the solace of Hawk Mountain, and the
tender birds of prey that flew over it would "outlive wars."[9]

Soldiers and civilians responded to her wartime requests for donations,
though she was criticized for asking for money at such a time. Remarkably,
sanctuary memberships increased.[10] One airman sent his donation while
thinking of his next bombing mission. Edge received it after she got word
that he had not returned. Letters filled with Hawk Mountain remembrances
came from men waiting in foxholes. One soldier who came home on leave
used his gas ration to drive to Hawk Mountain with his injured brother. He
carried him to the Lookout so they could watch the hawk flight together.
Such devotion touched Edge profoundly, and she reciprocated by keeping
the sanctuary alive.

In 1943 Margaret and Eric Nightingale had a son. Rosalie's relations with
her daughter had deteriorated to the point that she was not invited to baby
Eric's baptism. She went anyway, hugging the shadows of St. Bartholomew's
chapel, away from the marble altar donated by her parents, John Wylie and
Harriet Barrow, decades before. Her husband, Charles, and his companion,
Ruth Johnston, sat with Margaret and Eric in the front.

Rosalie celebrated the baby's arrival with a poem:

Appearances too often blur
The Truth. Not fish the whale.
The platypus, though wrapped in fur,
Lays eggs like any rail.
Asserting she is avian,
Whatever says her male.
So Eric, longed-for, tiny man,
Wee fledgling Nightingale,

Appeared bachtrachian,
Till, feasting at his mother's breast,
He slept, the very happiest
Two-legged mammalian.
But weaned, with yells exuberant,
In ritual robes most elegant,
Hungry, he is a Protestant
Episcopalian.[11]

The shattering news that reached her on June 29, 1944, came not from any theater of war but from Parsonage Point. Charles was the fatality. It seems he had again been mending the bridge that spanned the narrow channel between the shore and the islet Rosalie used to visit at low tide. He had fallen on the rocks, and though his injuries had not seemed critical, he died a few days later.[12] Charles Noel Edge's obituary in the *New York Times* noted that he was survived by a son and a daughter but made no mention of a wife.[13]

Peter came home on leave. Rosalie, Charles's estranged wife for twenty-four of the thirty-five years they were married, did not attend the small ceremony that Margaret and Ruth Johnston held at his cremation. Rosalie again carried her grief to her daughter-substitute, Julia Langsam. She reminisced about how as a bride she had paddled after Charlie through Asia. In those distant days the hardships of sickness and incessant travel brought them as close to happiness as they ever came, together.

Rosalie told Julia about the time in 1911 when she and Charlie had stayed in Moscow as they traveled home from China. It was when, after long days on the Trans-Siberian Railroad, they had lost their heads and made extravagant purchases. They attended the ballet and went to a ball in a room that glittered like a scene in a fairy tale. As they waltzed, Charles had leaned down to whisper to her, "My dear, see how everyone is admiring you in your lovely new dress!" Rosalie told Julia that even then, in perhaps the most beautiful gown she had ever worn, she suspected she was not the one whom people noticed. With his handsome looks and astonishing height, Charles was the one who attracted so much frank attention that night, as on many others.[14]

Rosalie received more devastating news when Peter arrived. In the last will Charles wrote two years before he died, he had drastically reduced Rosalie's portion of his estate, and he had done so in an unusually vindictive manner.[15] "It is my intention . . . to give my wife Mabel R. Edge, the least portion of my estate, and the least income to which she may be entitled by the laws of the State of New York."[16]

The harshness was compounded by another provision: Peter was to receive nothing from his father's estate until after his mother's death. The will gave Ruth a share of Charles's estate equal to Margaret's. In 1932 Rosalie had artificially sold all her household possessions to Peter to keep them out of the hands of Charles's creditors after he had used her family home as collateral and lost it. Charles may have discovered this and reciprocated by putting all his possessions in a trust created in 1934 for Margaret and Ruth.

But when he paid Rosalie forty thousand dollars in stock during the Depression, she had agreed only to relinquish her share of the market value of the house and land at Parsonage Point. She had never surrendered her financial interest in Treasure Island's costly, museum-quality contents; the typed inventory of Charles's treasures filled twenty-one single-spaced legal-sized pages.[17] At auction the items would fetch as much as or more than the real estate.

In the almost tropical heat of a gas-rationed August afternoon, Edge was trapped in New York. She wrote candidly to Maurice that her life was "all a mess. . . . [Charles] was supposed to be a rich man, but has left very little, and I receive the minimum under the law."[18] For the second time she threatened to give up her conservation work. Rosalie had been fighting to save wild species since 1929. Now she had to save herself.

She contested Charles's will. After a vicious legal fight that lasted almost a year, Rosalie Edge regained her share of her husband's estate. Margaret and Ruth reluctantly agreed to a three-way split of the proceeds from Charles's estate, which was sold at auction. The cost of winning included more than what Rosalie Edge paid her lawyer, the aptly named George Battle. She and Margaret never spoke again. Though Edge had glimpsed little Eric at his baptism, she never would see him again or meet her other two Nightingale grandsons, Charles and Trevor. Mention of Margaret Nightingale's name was forbidden in Rosalie's presence.

Margaret Nightingale never stopped hating her mother for "breaking the will." If they happened to pass each other on a Manhattan sidewalk, the daughter looked the mother in the eye and then with slow deliberation crossed to the other side of the street.[19]

THE BROUNS RETURNED to Hawk Mountain after the war, and the sanctuary began to receive thousands of visitors year-round, as many as five thousand visitors on a perfect fall weekend. Even when the Canadian winds did not usher in one cast of hawks after another, the mountain's serene beauty was a constant reward. Hikers diverted from their 2,175-mile-long journey on the nearby Appalachian Trail to rest and attend Maurice's School in the Clouds. The road to the sanctuary, now paved, was more clogged with cars than it had ever been when the Lookout was a hunter's paradise. Edge's request for the state of Pennsylvania to widen the highway was granted, for hawk watchers were good for the local economy.

By the early 1950s, the Brouns were worn out by the year-round stream of visitors. "When you get ready to write a book about Hawk Mountain, I suggest the title: Hawk Mountain, the Snowball that Grew into an Avalanche," Broun wrote to Edge. "Hawk Mountain should be a decent job, not slavery."[20] The Brouns had been stretched too thin by the demands placed on them. Maurice, of a solitary nature, had wanted to live like Thoreau, in the woods away from crowds. But the crowds kept coming to the Brouns' woods.

The sanctuary had become famous as "the cross-roads of naturalists," proclaimed Hawk Mountain board member Roger Tory Peterson, the phenomenally successful bird-guide author who had listened in amazement while Edge plotted against the Audubon Society. Peterson would credit Hawk Mountain Sanctuary with shaping "the ecological thinking of our time."[21]

Even Gilbert Pearson made a pilgrimage to the Kittatinny's crossroads of naturalists and wrote to tell Edge how much he admired what she had achieved.[22] Hawk Mountain drew prominent nature writers like William Vogt, Edwin Way Teale, Sigurd Olson, O. S. Pettingill, Joseph Wood Krutch, Florence Page Jaques, and Rachel Carson. All visitors approached the lookouts through the rustic entry into the woods, the sanctuary's own version of a torii gate.[23]

The unassuming Carson, a marine biologist as well as a bird-watcher, had worked for the Bureau of Fisheries until Secretary Ickes acquired it and combined it with the salvageable parts of the Bureau of Biological Survey. Carson wrote public information releases for the Fish and Wildlife Service before establishing herself as an author. In 1946 one memo Carson wrote noted the growing use of a synthetic insecticide called dichlorodiphenyltrichloroethane, or DDT.[24] Edge put the item in her "Poison" file, which went back twenty years to the days of strychnine and thallium and contained the earliest reports of DDT's ominous effects.

Oddly, with all the colleagues and conservation concerns that Rosalie Edge and Rachel Carson shared, the older woman, who had been acclaimed the only woman in conservation, would never meet the younger woman, who would soon eclipse her. Their mutual acquaintance, Richard Pough, could easily have introduced them, since he had first led Edge to Hawk Mountain in 1934 and had brought Carson to it twelve years later. But Edge refused to speak to Richard Pough. Despite her success at Hawk Mountain, she had never forgiven him for his part in the Affair of the Supper Party, which had tried to take Hawk Mountain from her.

John Baker's underestimation of the abilities of both Edge and Carson was something else the women shared. The president of the NAAS—renamed the National Audubon Society in 1940—had not only tried to stop Edge from running Hawk Mountain. He had also rejected Rachel Carson as the staff writer Pough recommended for *Audubon Magazine*, the new title chosen for Frank Chapman's restyled *Bird-Lore*.[25]

Rosalie Edge's park-making prominence faded when Harold Ickes left President Harry Truman's administration in 1946, ending his thirteen-year tenure as secretary of the interior, the longest in the department's history. Irving Brant was perhaps correct in his observation that Edge and Ickes needed each other to further their aggressively shared agenda of national park establishment and bird and wildlife protection. Nevertheless, Edge found other sugar pines and sequoias in California to save, on land owned by the Pickering Timber Company adjacent to Calaveras Big Trees State Park.

The ECC published Brant's *Protect the South Calaveras Sequoia Grove* just six months after the bombing of Pearl Harbor; Van Name, it seems, anonymously came through one last time to underwrite a big-tree project.[26] "WHEN OUR COUNTRY HAS SURVIVED ITS PRESENT PERILS WE SHALL WANT THIS BEAUTIFUL PARK," Edge added to the pamphlet, in her usual upper-case alarm. "We must not, in the excitement of war, neglect this important duty to the present and future generations of Americans."[27] It was a complicated piece of work and took twelve years to assure that the big trees would never wind up as timber. Ultimately a welter of federal and state land exchanges and matching funds needed to be structured, under the orchestration of the New York-based ECC.

After the war Rosalie Edge fought closer to her home more frequently, responding in person to emergencies in conservation that erupted around

New York. Nothing had been too large for her to take on, nor was anything too small. In 1946 Edge organized the rescue of three peregrine chicks from their nest on a cornice of the St. Regis Hotel, outside actress Olivia de Havilland's penthouse.[28] With pigeons abundant in Manhattan's sheer canyons of concrete, glass, and steel, peregrine falcons found man-made ledges and crannies suitable for raising their young.

Although Manhattanite Rosalie Edge had done more than anyone to enlighten the nation about the need to protect birds of prey, many New Yorkers were still revolted by the peregrines' shrill screams and violent feedings, observable from high apartments and offices. Miss de Havilland had not complained, but the nestlings had gotten on the nerves of another St. Regis guest. Edge was notified that something had to be done to silence these wee ones permanently.

Edge assembled a chick rescue crew and led them to Miss de Havilland's terrace. Across the street the mother peregrine screeched from a ledge of the Gotham Hotel. The actress wanted to cuddle the chicks before they were taken away, but Edge bade her not to touch them. "Here were creatures that did not appreciate the attentions of Olivia de Havilland," she chided her gently.[29]

The peregrines were moved, banded, and raised in rural Pennsylvania until they could fly and hunt for themselves. The female was named Olivia. Edge never had the heart to tell Miss de Havilland, who joined Hawk Mountain Sanctuary and came up to visit, that all three birds were killed a year or two after their rescue. Two had been shot; the peregrine named Olivia was electrocuted when she flew into a power line.

On one of Rosalie's city walks she saw a manacled golden eagle for sale in a pet-shop window and forced the owner to surrender the bird to wildlife authorities. The sight must have affected her deeply, for she marked the occasion with a poem, which *Nature Magazine* published.[30]

"A MOST SERIOUS situation arises in Westchester County, New York, one which is probably repeated in many places," Rosalie Edge wrote to the director of the New York State Division of Fish and Game in the spring of 1948.[31] One of her anonymous scientist-informants told her that country clubs were using the chemical pesticide DDT to eradicate mosquitoes and other insects. This inexpensive and easy-to-use synthetic compound had been invented for military use during World War II but had fast become the weapon of choice in the ongoing war against bugs, as Rachel Carson had reported in her 1946 Fish and Wildlife press release. To New York's Fish and Game Department Edge wrote:

> The golf clubs of Westchester are using a 50% solution of DDT on the golf courses. I understand that no solution stronger than 10% is advisable for fear of killing the birds. As a result of this 50% solution, the destruction of birds is appalling. For example, in the immediate vicinity of the Gedney Farms Golf Course, nineteen robins were found dead on a small lawn. At another place three orioles were found dead, in spite of the arboreal habits of the oriole. I might go on giving you many examples. I beg that you will get in touch with your Warden and investigate.[32]

The Department of the Interior dispatched a field agent, who confirmed Edge's report. But in 1948 such examples of harm found in the wake of DDT's application were anecdotal and therefore insufficient. The Bureau of Biological Survey no longer existed to pose an institutional threat to the nation's wildlife, but Rosalie Edge kept her "Poison" file open.

Edge continued to steer Hawk Mountain Sanctuary's course from her Lexington Avenue office, but when she came to the mountain it was as if the queen were in residence. Late one afternoon the writer Florence Page Jaques observed Edge, "the Boadicea of conservation," at the Lookout attended by "a small bodyguard" of awestruck young men; at Hawk Mountain, Boy Scouts and young men followed her everywhere.[33]

Her royal expectations sorely taxed Maurice and Irma. Though she claimed to love Maurice like a son, she sometimes treated him as her personal chauffeur, groundskeeper, and errand boy and Irma as her cook and housekeeper.[34] Had Maurice bought stamps? Repaired the boundary fence? Hired that young man she had recommended? Written to thank Dr. Van Name for his latest donation? Had Maurice gone to testify in Harrisburg on that hawk protection bill she had drafted? Changed the tires on the sanctuary's only car? And by the way she was arriving in Hamburg that Friday and he should meet her train there at three o'clock. She would, as usual, be staying with them at Schaumbach's for the weekend.

"If I'm not sweating at hard labor on the grounds, I'm glued to the desk, or chinning with the public," Maurice vented in one letter to Edge. He then had the temerity to say that her twenty-year-old "prejudice against the Audubon Society amount[ed] to a mania."[35] She shot back a sharp rebuke: "I did not like your letter of the—. It was not the way to address the President of the Association, and your senior by many years."[36]

It infuriated Irma to hear Edge refer to Maurice as "my curator." "Maurice may be your curator, but he's my husband!" Irma finally screamed at her imposing houseguest. Edge stalked out of the tiny kitchen. The next morning she demanded that Maurice take her to the train station.[37] The rift deepened in 1949 with the publication of Broun's book *Hawks Aloft*.[38] More than anyone else, Edge had changed the public perception of birds of prey, one of her greatest achievements. But Broun acknowledged Edge only for reading his manuscript and dedicated the book to Edith McLellan Hale, the tall woman at the Boston Public Garden who had pointed out the magnolia warbler to him when he was thirteen.

A fourteen-page profile of Rosalie Edge in the *New Yorker* reasserted her supremacy in the broader world of conservation. "Rosalie Barrow Edge, an elderly, implacable widow, is the chairman of the Emergency Conservation Committee, an organization that favors conserving, in the wildlife line, everything," the profile began.[39] It ended with a quote from Willard Van Name.

"We quarrel a good deal," Van Name had said, perhaps in answer to a question about how he got along with Edge. He may have paused to find words that best described the woman he admired most and perhaps despised to the same degree: "She's unique in the field. She's the only honest, unselfish, indomitable hellcat in the history of conservation."[40]

CHAPTER TWELVE

Implacable

Friends urged Rosalie Edge to write her memoirs, and at the age of seventy-four she began to compose them, ultimately completing 230 pages of manuscript, which she called "Good Companions in Conservation: Annals of an Implacable Widow." The *New Yorker* article's opening characterization had evidently appealed to her; the words "implacable" and "widow" summed up her essence.

But publishers rejected her memoirs.[1] One objected to the title "Implacable Widow" and found her prose to be all parry and thrust, with no personal revelations and little of the literary grace found in her poetry and articles or the penetrating wit of her testimony and speeches. As she revised her memoir in the late 1950s, she wrote as a spectator of the conservation movement rather than as its spearhead, proud that "an army of conservationists had come into being."[2]

In that decade the gentlemanly Sierra Club was being radicalized by David Brower, who perhaps more than any other conservationist of his generation had assumed Edge's combative mantle. When Brower opposed building a dam within Colorado's Dinosaur National Monument, Edge sent circulars to her enormous mailing list and wrote dozens of letters to high government officials. But this time it was she who joined the fight led by both Brower's Sierra Club and the Wilderness Society. Pulitzer Prize–winning author Bernard DeVoto's pugnacious articles, rather than Edge's ECC pamphlets, put the unpleasant facts of the water storage project before the public.

Edge watched proudly as conservation's advocates gained "force and momentum year by year." She seemed confident that what she had begun twenty-five years earlier would result in the saving of "our wild life and its environment." New federal legislation would be "the most powerful means of promoting conservation," she predicted, and so it would become.[3]

Perhaps Edge was still feeling too proprietary of the conservation movement to name a successor. The Wilderness Society emerged first from her committee's long shadow, although she clearly admired the Sierra Club's Brower. The ECC's spawn would rapidly multiply and take various approaches to the challenge of bringing humanity and nature into sustainable balance. One way or another, in their professions or their personal lives or both, these conservationists had been touched by Rosalie Edge's spirit of informed activism.

Edge's purchase of Hawk Mountain to save it was Richard Pough's model for the Nature Conservancy, which he cofounded in 1951.[4] Roland C. Clement, who had met Edge when he was a Boy Scout and was one of the respectful young men who absorbed her pronouncements at Hawk Mountain, became a crusading biologist at, of all places, the National Audubon Society. When he could not persuade the Audubon Society to do everything he wished to halt the use of DDT, Clement did not give up. He remained at Audubon but became the quiet force behind the formation of a new organization, the Environmental Defense Fund.[5]

The most famous woman of this post-ECC generation would be the Fish and Wildlife biologist Rachel Carson. Her 1962 book, *Silent Spring*, about the hazards of DDT is commonly considered the starting point for the environmental movement. But people brought up on the battles defined by Rosalie Edge's ECC might beg to differ; like Edge they thought the movement had begun twenty-five years earlier and that they had been part of it.

In 1960 Rachel Carson's research on DDT led her back to Hawk Mountain Sanctuary, which she called one of the most "famous vantage points" for watching birds of prey.[6] "As you may possibly have heard from some of our friends in the conservation world," Carson had written to Edge's curator, Maurice Broun, "I am at work on a book that will explore some of the effects of chemical pesticides, especially their ecological effects." The decades of data that Broun had given Carson on immature hawk and eagle migration would prove "especially significant" to her.[7]

If so, then Rosalie Edge's role was also especially significant. Hawk Mountain was her brainchild. She had been the one to insist that Broun count the birds of prey every day of the autumn migration. And fourteen years before

Silent Spring's publication, Edge, as citizen-scientist, offered the government proof that high concentrations of DDT had killed songbirds at a Westchester golf course.

Though the ECC was superseded by much larger conservation organizations, Edge in her eighties did not relinquish any authority over Hawk Mountain Sanctuary. She ran it with the same white-gloved iron hand as she always had. She was mentally alert and physically strong. In New York she swam almost daily at the Colony Club and birded in Central Park or in whichever cooler clime she traveled to in summer. Her world bird list numbered a respectable eight hundred or so species. A week or two before she turned eighty-four, she hiked to the Lookout, accompanied by her usual phalanx of young men. She was still the "grand dame" of conservation.[8]

IT WAS AS A grand dame that she presided over people's lives, even among those who were like family to her, as Julia and Walter Langsam had become. After Walter was appointed president of Gettysburg College and then the University of Cincinnati, Edge spent a week each Christmas at the Langsams' home. She permitted the young Langsam boys, Walter and Geoffrey, to address her as "Aunt Rosalie," though they were never comfortable doing so. They remained terrified by her sheer majesty and the breadth of topics on which she could vividly discourse: Birds and classical music. Her world travels. Sequoias and Renaissance masterpieces. Asian art and history. The latest ECC pamphlet and great literature. Stories of her life and travels could fill the night, though she insisted on telling each one only once.[9]

Young Walter Langsam's awe of Aunt Rosalie did not keep him from staying with her when he returned to New York City to look for a job after he graduated from college. One day while perusing the old books that had been in her father's library almost a century before, he picked up a volume of Thomas Bewick's *Birds*. Inside Walter noticed a bookplate engraved with the words *John Ruskin Brantwood*.

"Who was Mr. Brantwood?" Walter innocently asked his hostess. Aunt Rosalie looked at the young man in confusion and then skewered him with one of her raptorial glances. "Why, they were John Ruskin's own set," she replied, undoubtedly aggrieved that Walter, a lover of the arts and a recent graduate of a fine liberal arts college, had not recognized the name of the nineteenth-century British art critic. Indeed, it may have been the name of the volumes' previous owner, more than their subject, that compelled John Wylie Barrow to purchase them. In 1877 John Ruskin was sued by Barrow's

near cousin James McNeill Whistler for libeling his art. The sensational-
ized case bankrupted the contentious painter. Didn't her young guest know
this? To the abashed Walter Langsam, Aunt Rosalie explained, in a tone
that rendered such ignorance impermissible, that John Ruskin had "*lived
at Brantwood.*"[10]

   She spent less time with her natural grandchildren Deborah, David, and
Stephen Edge than she had with the Langsam boys. Peter married a woman
named Mary Kerr, whom his mother did not like. They settled in Winnetka,
a town of charming amplitude north of Chicago. Rosalie came for brief visits to admire her own descendants but was not the sort of grandmother who
could be asked to babysit them.[11] After birding in the morning, she took the
train to the Chicago Art Institute.

   A certain Chinese artifact at the institute touched her soul, just as the
silk embroidered robes of overthrown Mandarins had touched it fifty years
earlier. She told Peter she liked to sit in the institute's Asian Hall in sight of
an intricately carved eleventh-century wooden statue of a seated Kwan Yin,
or Kanon, as the deity was known in Japanese. It was the Buddhist goddess
of mercy. When Edge had lived in Asia, she had seen hundreds approach
such statues to ask for forgiveness of their misdeeds. The goddess's palm
extended as delicately as a leaf.[12] The Kwan Yin's half-lidded gaze surveyed
all, bathing supplicants in mercy. Mercy, and even peace, for Rosalie Edge.

   Keeping peace at Hawk Mountain was another matter. The breach between Broun and "Madame Edge," as he called her in his journal, remained.
After each argument Maurice tendered his resignation, and Edge, softening,
coaxed him to stay. "You and I have been friends for 30 years—before you
married and were still a boy," she wrote after one of their later disagree-
ments. "I cannot think that you should fail me now that I am at the close of
my career and of my life."[13]

   Perhaps considering him her own son, Edge insisted on loaning Maurice
and Irma eight thousand dollars to pay off debts on the Penniman mansion
at Cape Cod, which Irma had inherited. Through Edge's National Park Service connections, she may have been privy to the agency's wish to eventually include the Penniman mansion in the proposed Cape Cod National
Seashore.[14] She advised the Brouns to hang on to the property so they could
sell it to the National Park Service at a profit.

   Edge may have intended her loan to the Brouns to be on the same terms
as those of Willard Van Name's loan to her to buy Hawk Mountain. She had
never stinted on giving all of herself to conservation. But if, as it appears, the

money she lent the Brouns was not repaid, it was the only financial contribution she ever made to her conservation cause.

In 1962 Julia Langsam's son Walter bumped into Edge in Manhattan. She
clutched the young man tightly in greeting. Walter expected to be impaled
by her hawkish glare or a sharp word. Instead Rosalie Edge spoke with
surprising gentleness. "Tell your mother I love her," she said, and walked
away.[15]

AT THE FIFTY-EIGHTH Annual Meeting of the National Audubon Society
in Corpus Christi, Texas, in November that year, Roger Tory Peterson was
among the first to greet Rosalie Edge in the lobby of the Robert Driscoll Hotel. She was in a conciliatory mood. "Roger," she said, "I think I would have
gotten further with the Audubon if I had been more moderate."[16] She had
heard that the new Audubon president, Carl Bucheister, was doing a good
job, and that many of the reforms she had demanded thirty years earlier
were finally in place.

Peterson went to find Bucheister to tell him what Edge had said. He perhaps found the Audubon president in the midst of reviewing the history
of mutual hatred between the Audubon Society and Rosalie Edge and still
wondering whether that history had changed.

After talking to Peterson, Bucheister knew what to do. He invited the old
woman to sit on the dais with him and the other dignitaries at the society
banquet the next night. Edge promptly said yes, even when told that her old
foe John Baker would be at the table.[17]

The night of the banquet, the Audubon faithful packed the ballroom.
Bucheister guided the frail Mrs. Edge to her place. In the moments before
he introduced her, it was uncertain whether the audience would politely
applaud or remain awkwardly silent. Might some boo? Then he spoke her
name. The Audubon crowd came out of their seats. The room filled with a
thunderous ovation. As a standing army of twelve hundred conservationists
stood before her, Rosalie Edge's pale eyes surveyed the former enemy and
perceived that final triumph was hers. She phoned Peter afterward to report
her latest conservation feat. "I have made peace with the National Audubon
Society," she proclaimed.[18]

EDGE'S DAYS at this stage of her life were orderly and purposeful. She decided that the ECC's work had come to an end and closed the Lexington
Avenue office, packing more than thirty years' worth of committee files into

boxes. In her memoir she had commended volunteerism as the most mean-ingful way to bring about change. "I beg each one to keep conservation as his hobby, to keep his independence, his freedom to speak his mind," she had written years before. She had seen too many professionals become jaded or fall captive to special interests. She, on the other hand, had spoken freely. There would always be a need for those who could do that, she warned.[19] As she prepared to send the boxes across country to the new Conservation Collection at the Denver Public Library, Rachel Carson's book *Silent Spring* was sounding the shrill alarm awakening the public to the latest crisis in na-ture. Edge had read Carson's book. She heard the nationwide commotion it was causing; the Hawk Mountain board had proudly spoken of *Silent Spring* because of the sanctuary's role in providing Carson with her migration data. Requests for Maurice to speak flowed in.

Two weeks after Rosalie Edge's reconciliation with the Audubon Society, Richard Pough called to ask if she wanted to drive to Hawk Mountain with him. To this former enemy she also said yes without a moment's hesitation. "It was a lovely weekend," Pough wrote years later. "All bitterness was gone and we had a great time on the drive talking over old times—all the fights the Emergency Conservation Committee had with the Biological Survey, U.S. Forest Service, Audubon and others were forgotten."[20]

She went out most nights to dine with friends, regaling the company with her stories until late.[21] Eighteen days after the Audubon reconciliation, Ro-salie Edge woke in the night with crushing chest pains. She summoned her housekeeper, who called an ambulance and then rang Peter in Chicago. The housekeeper bid him come to Manhattan as quickly as possible. Before he arrived on the morning of Friday, November 30, his mother had died.[22]

Peter phoned Maurice to tell him the news and let him know the memo-rial service would be held at St. Bartholomew's on Monday. The Brouns were stunned. Mrs. Charles Noel Edge had dominated their lives for so long, they could not believe her fierce governance over them had finally ended. She had been a queen and at times "a battle-axe," but Maurice's admiration for her diluted the bitterness. "The obituaries will eulogize her," he wrote in his journal. "The grand old dame will be elevated no doubt, among the immor-tals among conservationists." Publicly Broun said that Edge was "without question the foremost woman conservationist of the twentieth century."[23]

Dick Pough, fresh from mending relations with Edge, mourned her passing unequivocally. "I am so glad that I drove Mrs. Edge back to Hawk Mountain that weekend before she died," Pough would say. "I may not have agreed with how much she fought with everybody, but I never stopped thinking about her or admiring her enormously for all she did for conservation. When I began the Nature Conservancy, it was, I think, because of what she did, because she had shown better than anybody how you could buy land to save it and the wildlife from harm."[24]

In the damp Pacific Northwest, virgin forests of Douglas fir, Sitka spruce, cedar, and western hemlock grow older. In California's arid High Sierras, sugar pine and giant sequoia pierce the sky. All these trees, spreading their perfumed green dominion over a total of 1.5 million acres, are of a size and age that still stagger the imagination and preserve essential habitat for wildlife.

In Pennsylvania every autumn thousands of tender birds of prey are swept by Canadian winds past the Kittatinny Ridge. They fly unharmed and are daily counted as they coast down one thermal cell to ride the next. Hawk Mountain Sanctuary is the best-known monument to Rosalie Edge.

The least known monument to her stands in the Newburgh cemetery, where she is buried near her parents and infant son. The epitaph she instructed Peter to inscribe on her gravestone does not encourage her immortalization as a conservationist as Maurice Broun predicted.

MABEL ROSALIE EDGE

1877–1962

DAUGHTER OF

JOHN WYLIE BARROW AND HARRIET BOWEN BARROW

WIDOW OF

CHARLES NOEL EDGE

It is with these last five words that our story began. Coming at the end of Edge's life, they make a curious epitaph, yet they hold the promise of another tale. But it would take too long to tell.

Afterword

The early twentieth-century conservation movement was an attempt to find ways of balancing resource demands without undue conflict. Rosalie Edge was one of the most forceful conservation activists who led the way by emphasizing the conflicts. For her they had to be faced because the protection of wildlife and the safeguarding of lovely places and unique forests were fundamental to a wholehearted humanity.

It was my good fortune to meet this elegant lady when she came to visit Maurice Broun at the O. L. Austin Ornithological Research Station on Cape Cod in the 1930s. Mrs. Edge was keen, intense, utterly devoted to her cause.

Over the years I spoke with Mrs. Edge when I saw her at Hawk Mountain Sanctuary and knew her, of course, as founder and director of the Emergency Conservation Committee, whose reports I read. ECC publications provided an important education to conservationists of that time. They were essential reading for anyone who wanted to be informed about the movement's pressing issues.

Perhaps the most memorable conversation I had with Mrs. Edge was at a Linnaean Society dinner at the American Museum of Natural History in 1962. We spoke of the National Audubon Society, which I thought had made promising changes, and I invited her to the next Audubon convention in Corpus Christi, Texas, to see for herself, which she did.

It is tragic, but all too characteristic of the 1930s and for too many subsequent decades, that Rosalie Edge's challenges to the officers of the Audubon movement and many of the federal conservation agencies were taken so negatively. Instead of listening to her, they sought to ostracize her. How naive of these otherwise distinguished men not to have recognized her stature, her prescience, and the reasonableness of her concerns. Wildlife science of the day was on the men's side, but this woman knew her holistic view was the correct one, and she refused to be silenced.

The conservation movement of the 1960s is attributed to Rachel Carson's prophetic warnings that we were poisoning the world, the atomic threat, early space shots, and television. But Rosalie Edge had been sounding educated warnings for years about how we were harming the natural world, and until the end of her life she dedicated herself to saving that world. Many of us paid heed to her warnings. Many of us built our environmental careers with her work at Hawk Mountain Sanctuary and the national parks as models.

Now as I look back over the twentieth century, I recall a few of the great people whose generational imprint has been eclipsed. Rosalie Edge is certainly one of them. Many know Rachel Carson, but few today remember Mrs. Edge, who animated the conservation movement for three decades before it seemed to suddenly burst out in the 1960s. In a similar vein, I suppose, everyone has heard of the scientist Albert Einstein, but far fewer know of the philosopher Alfred North Whitehead, who had equally important things to tell us about the processes of existence.

Just as the environmentalists of the 1970s were parvenus, mostly ignorant and heedless of the struggles and the leaders who preceded them, so it seems today, with the many people who talk as if the environmental movement were new, rising out of the threat of global warming. But forgetting those who went before us and all the battles they fought will not speed our progress in finding solutions. What is the value of any legacy if those who created it are forgotten? A legacy, it seems to me, is mostly measured by our recognition of the passionate and truthful expression of the earlier ideals and the implementation of them. They are what we ought to build on. If we fail to know what came before, then the heroes of each generation will vanish in the seeming chaos of the passing aeons, and their vision will be lost.

It is my pleasure to write this reminder that it is important to learn about Rosalie Edge's career as an activist and to appreciate the many ways she saved the natural world for generations to come. After a long period of public unawareness about Mrs. Edge's role in bringing us to where we are today, it is another generation's turn to be inspired by her example and to continue her valuable work.

Roland C. Clement

Notes

RE   Rosalie Edge
REPDPL   Rosalie Edge Papers, CONS29, Conservation Collection, Denver
            Public Library, Denver, Colorado
SSC   Sophia Smith Collection of Woman's History Manuscripts,
            William Allan Neilson Library, Smith College, Northampton,
            Massachusetts
WVN   Willard Van Name

INTRODUCTION

1. Official program of the National Audubon Society, "A Texas Notebook Annual Convention," Corpus Christi, November 10–14, 1962, NAS-NYPL. For Edge's unexpected appearance, see Graham, *Audubon Ark*, 201.

2. Roger Tory Peterson, Sixtieth Anniversary Address at Hawk Mountain Sanctuary, and interview with author, October 1994.

3. Interviews with Richard Pough (October 1990) and Roland C. Clement (July 1990, May 2007, November 2007) confirmed that they spoke with RE at the NAS convention.

4. For Edge's resemblance to Queen Mary and a pointer, see Robert Lewis Taylor, "Oh, Hawk of Mercy!" *New Yorker*, April 17, 1948, 31. The size of the ECC was five according to Bainbridge, "Origins," 184. The testimony given by RE at the House of Representatives Public Lands Committee Hearing on Mount Olympus National Park, April 27, 1936, 78, stated there were twelve members.

5. *New Yorker*, April 17, 1948, 31. See RE's unpublished memoir "Good Companions in Conservation: Annals of an Implacable Widow" for her preference for a broad approach to conservation.

6. IW 1, 84.

7. Marjorie Shuler, *Christian Science Monitor*, October 2, 1938; *Brooklyn Daily Eagle*, April 17, 1938; *Altoona (Pa.) Tribune*; *Time Magazine*, October 11, 1937; Jaques, *Birds across the Sky*, 188.

8. *New Yorker*, April 17, 1948, 46.

9. RE, ECC pamphlets against Bureau of Biological Survey poisoning programs date to 1930, opposing strychnine and thallium.

10. RE testimony at Senate Hearing of Committee on Indian Affairs, 77th Cong., 1st sess., *A Bill Providing for Federal Assistance in Eradicating the Cattle Tick in the Seminole Indian Reservation in Florida*, S. 1476, November 5, 1941, February 25, 1942, 118.

11. Shuler, *Christian Science Monitor*.

12. Graham, *Audubon Ark*, 201.

13. RE's appearance is drawn from the last known photo taken of her by friend Margaret Raymond in the summer of 1962 and from the Carsten Lien photo, 1959.

14. Roland C. Clement, the conference organizer, provided number attending.

CHAPTER ONE: Noblest Girl

1. RE lived at 1200 Fifth Avenue in 1933, before moving to 1215 Fifth Avenue, where she lived until 1962.

2. IW, 223.

3. Ibid.

4. Ibid., 63.

5. Ibid., 9.

6. Original handwritten letter from H. R. Barrow to MRB, April 13, 1909, PEPLD.

7. RE, "Coquette," 1939, 3, PEPLD.

8. RE, "Letter to My Daughter," February 2, 1941, PEPLD.

9. RE, "Coquette," 13–14.

10. Ibid.

11. RE, "Coquette," 3.

12. "Noble Girl" or "Noblest Girl" in original handwritten letters from JWB to MRB, September 30, 1883; from JWB to MRB, November 16, 1884; from JWB to HBB, December 19, 1884. Reference to siblings as "subordinates" in letter from JWB to MRB, June 5, 1883, PEPLD.

13. Original handwritten letters from JWB to MRB, May 26, 1882; from JWB to MRB, November 16, 1884, PEPLD.

14. Letter from JWB to MRB, June 5, 1883, PEPLD.

15. Original handwritten letter from JWB to MRB, June 1883, PEPLD.

16. Woodward genealogy from published but unidentifiable genealogy text with chapter written by Mary Nicoll Putnam and William Amos Woodward, late 1800s, 131–62, PEPLD.

17. Washburn, "From Puritan, Huguenot, and Patroon," 413.

18. Typed copy of original letter signed "Harriet B. Barrow," addressed "Dear Children," May 25, 1899, PEPLD.

19. RE, "Date with Cousin Charles"; also in "Shadow of the Photograph," 2, PEPLD.

20. Copies of JWB's original notes and charts titled "Jan Hendrik Van Bael," written 1879. "The Macleans of Karrow, Islay," unpublished narrative of the Barrow lineage, provides Revolutionary War background and links to James McNeill Whistler. JWB June 18, 1828, birth date in his handwriting on the Van Bael chart and on back of JWB's oil portrait in the Edge family possession. Regarding Whistler as a near relative, see "Catalogue of the Books," viii, PEPLD.

21. Interview with PE.

22. See Kaplan, *Dickens*, 34–37. Also MacKenzie, *Dickens*, 5; Johnson, *Charles Dickens*, 7; Ackroyd, *Dickens*. Quotation from JWB's obituary, *New York Times*, April 28, 1885.

23. Kaplan, *Dickens*, 21.

24. Ibid., 58.

25. See Ackroyd, *Dickens*, 899. 10 Gerrard Street is the address of JWB's birthplace and written on the back of the 1864 oil portrait in the Edge family's possession.

26. Ackroyd, *Dickens*, 61.

27. "Catalogue of the Books." JWB was commended for his language ability in "Proceedings of American Oriental Soc.," on stationary from Semitic Languages Department of Columbia University, 1889, PEPLD.

28. Interviews with PE, and PE's "Kyrie Eleison," 3–5, mention JWB's codex role; in an 1899 letter HBB also mentions Codex Sinaiticus in the family possession. Codex background from Bentley, *Secrets of Mount Sinai*, 41.

29. "Catalogue of the Books," vi; PE, "Kyrie Eleison," 2.

30. Interview with PE.

31. Interview with PE; the "arithmometer" is mentioned in "Catalogue of the Books," vii.

32. James T. Anyon, *Recollections of the Early Days of American Accountancy, 1883–1893* (New York: James Anyon, 1925), 3, 11.

33. RE, "Shadow of the Photograph," 1.

34. "Catalogue of the Books," viii.

35. Original handwritten letter from JWB to HBB, December 14, 1884, PEPLD.

36. RE, "Shadow of the Photograph," 1–4.

37. Ibid.

38. JWB obituary, *New York Times*, April 28, 1885; eulogy from American Orientalist Society, Columbia University.

39. RE, "Coquette," 18.

40. Interview with PE.

41. See Bainbridge, "Origins," 14.

42. Wharton, *Backward Glance*, 5.

43. Interview with PE.

44. Interviews with Archibald Barrow's granddaughter Elizabeth Barrow Doering. See also a letter signed by Louise Carnegie, June 11, 1931, available at http://www.historyforsale.com (accessed December 2006).

45. RE noted Margaret's appearance in "Date with Cousin Charles," 2, and family letters.

46. RE, "Coquette," 1.

47. Copy of handwritten grade report from "English Class," PEPLD.

48. Letter from Francis Evertson Woodward to MRB, October 17, 1893. PE told the author that RE worked with the church choir.

49. RE, "Rose in the Snow."

50. The *New York Times* obituary gives March 15, 1899, as the date of Frances Woodward's death. Inheritance information from interview with PE.

51. RE, "Coquette," 3.

52. Ibid.; interviews with Walter E. Langsam and Irma Broun Kahn. Quotation from RE, "Shadow of the Photograph," 2.

53. Von Harten and Macleod, *Man of Wolverhampton*; interviews with Melissa Marston Macleod, 1990.

54. Von Harten and Macleod, *Man of Wolverhampton*, 18.

55. Ibid. In an interview Melissa Marston Macleod confirmed that MRB was one.

56. Interviews with PE and Elizabeth Barrow Doering, November 1994.

57. Nasaw, *Andrew Carnegie*, 564, 656, 678, 698–99.

58. Ibid., 627, 698–699.

59. Von Harten and Macleod, *Man of Wolverhampton*, 37.

60. Interviews with PE.

61. Macleod, "Family of Charles Edge," PEPLD.

62. Interview with PE.

63. Von Harten and Macleod, *Man of Wolverhampton*, 9.

64. Original handwritten letter from MDB to HBB, May 29, 1909, PEPLD.

65. Interview with PE.

66. Original handwritten letter from CNE to HBB, March 15, 1909, PEPLD.

67. Original handwritten letter from RE to HBB, December 17, 1912, PEPLD.

68. *New York Times*, January 8, 1908, 1.

69. Ibid., May 10, 1908.

70. Interview with PE; also "The Count and Countess Are Very Happy," *New York Times*, August 8, 1908, C1.

71. Interview with PE; also photos provided by Elizabeth Barrow Doering place RE at Skibo. Family letters, circumstances confirm MRB in England and Europe in fall 1908.

72. Original handwritten letter from Cyril Edge to MRB, October 1908, PEPLD.

73. Original handwritten letter from Louise Johnson Marston to MRB, February 28, 1909, PEPLD.

74. Original letter from Countess Széchenyi to RE, April 28, 1909, PEPLD. MRB saved about sixty original congratulatory letters written January–April 1909, PEPLD.

75. Ball, *Things Chinese*, 717–20.

76. MRB's original notebook listed wedding gifts, PEPLD.

77. Original handwritten letter from CNE to HBB, May 9, 1909, PEPLD.

78. Original handwritten letter from MRB to HBB, May 18, 1909, PEPLD.

79. Ibid.

80. Ibid.

81. Original handwritten letter from MDB to HBB, May 29, 1909, PEPLD.

82. Ibid.

83. Ibid.

84. Ibid.

85. Ibid.

86. Ibid.

CHAPTER TWO: Wife of Charles Noel Edge

1. Manthorpe, *Travels*, 51.

2. Original handwritten letter from RE to HBB, June 1, 1909, PEPLD.

3. Ibid.

4. Ibid.

5. Original handwritten letter from CNE to HBB, November 29, 1909, PEPLD.

6. Original handwritten letter from MDB to HBB, June 11, 1909, PEPLD; original wedding invitation, PEPLD.

7. Original handwritten letter from CNE to HBB, June 18, 1909, PEPLD.

8. Ibid.

9. Original handwritten letter from RE to HBB, June 13, 1909, PEPLD.

10. Ibid.

11. Original handwritten letter from RE to MDB, June 11, 1909, PEPLD.

12. Ibid.

13. Original handwritten letter from RE to HBB, June 18, 1909, PEPLD.

14. Ibid.

15. Ibid.

16. Ibid.

17. Ibid.

18. Original handwritten letter from RE to HBB, June 13, 1909, PEPLD.

19. Ibid.

20. Kirtland, *Finding the Worth While*, 175.

21. Ibid., 178.

22. Background from Clark, *Story of China and Japan*. See also New's historical novel *Shanghai* for descriptions of Shanghai street scenes circa 1909.

23. Original handwritten letter from RE to HBB, June 22, 1909; comment on needlework in original handwritten letter from RE to HBB, March 10, 1910, PEPLD.

24. Kirtland, *Finding the Worth While*, 178.

25. Ball, *Things Chinese*, 376.

26. Ibid., 181–82.

27. Original handwritten letter from RE to HBB, July 7, 1909, PEPLD.

28. Ball, *Things Chinese*, 590. For general background on China's industrialization in the early 1900s, see Spence, *Search for Modern China*, 245–68.

29. Original handwritten letter from RE to HBB, July 13, 1909, PEPLD.

30. Ibid.

31. Ibid.

32. Ibid.

33. Original handwritten letter from RE to HBB, August 9, 1909, PEPLD. Yangtze River description from original handwritten letter from RE to HBB, July 18, 1909. Destinations from letters written by RE to family members July 1909–December 1912, PEPLD.

34. Original handwritten letter from RE to HBB, July 24, 1909, PEPLD.

35. Ibid.

36. Ibid.

37. Ibid.

38. Ibid.

39. Original handwritten letter from RE to HBB, September 19, 1909, PEPLD. For descriptions of the tram and Victoria Peak, see Morris, *Hong Kong*.

40. Quotations courtesy of Phillip Bruce, Peak Lookout Restaurant, where the Peak Hotel had stood.

41. Original handwritten letter from RE to HBB, September 19, 1909, PEPLD.

42. Ibid.

43. Ibid.

44. Ibid.

45. Ibid., emphasis added.

46. Ibid.

47. Original handwritten letter from RE to MDB, October 6, 1909, PEPLD.

48. Ibid.

49. Ibid.

50. Ibid.

51. Ibid.

52. Ibid.

53. Ibid.

54. Original handwritten letter from Louise Schanck to HBB, October 20, 1909, PEPLD.

55. Ibid.

56. Original handwritten letter from RE to HBB, November 18, 1909, PEPLD.

57. Ibid.

58. Ibid.

59. Original handwritten letter from RE to HBB, October 30, 1909, PEPLD. According to PE, A. Gordon Norrie and his wife, Margaret, whom RE worked with in suffrage, were probably the couple visited in Tientsin.

60. Ibid.

61. Original handwritten letter from RE to HBB, November 18, 1909, PEPLD.

62. Ibid.

63. Ibid.

64. Handwritten letter from RE to HBB, October 30, 1909, PEPLD.

65. Original handwritten letter from RE to HBB, January 19, 1910, PEPLD.

66. Original handwritten letter from RE to HBB, January 27, 1910, PEPLD.

67. Original handwritten letter from RE to HBB, March 12, 1910, PEPLD.

68. Ibid.

69. Original handwritten letter from RE to HBB, April 8, 1910, PEPLD.

70. Original handwritten letter from RE to HBB, May 16, 1910, PEPLD.

71. Ibid.

72. Ibid.

CHAPTER THREE: First Awakening

1. Original handwritten letter from RE to HBB, March 21, 1911, PEPLD.

2. Original handwritten letter from RE to HBB, March 24, 1911, PEPLD.

3. Original handwritten letter from RE to HBB, May 21, 1911, PEPLD.

4. Original handwritten letter from CNE to HBB, October 13, 1910, PEPLD.

5. Ibid.

6. Ibid.

7. Ibid.

8. Original handwritten letter from RE to HBB, November 17, 1910, PEPLD.

9. Original handwritten letters from RE to HBB, March 16, 1911, March 24, 1911, PEPLD.

10. Original handwritten letter from RE to HBB, March 24, 1911, PEPLD.

11. Original handwritten letter from RE to HBB, May 21, 1911, PEPLD.

12. Original handwritten letter from RE to HBB, March 21, 1911, PEPLD.

13. Original handwritten letter from RE to HBB, March 16, 1911, PEPLD.

14. Original handwritten letter from RE to HBB, March 24, 1911, PEPLD.

15. Ibid.

16. Original handwritten letter from RE to HBB, April 19, 1911, PEPLD.

17. Ibid.

18. Original handwritten letter from RE to HBB, October 9, 1911, PEPLD.

19. Interview with PE.

20. Original handwritten letter from RE to HBB, December 11, 1911, PEPLD.

21. Ibid.

22. Ibid.

23. Original handwritten letter from RE to HBB, November 17, 1912, PEPLD, emphasis in the original.

24. Ibid.

25. Original handwritten letter from RE to HBB, December 17, 1912, PEPLD.

26. Ibid., emphasis in the original.

27. Original handwritten letter from RE to HBB, December 1912, PEPLD.

28. Interview with PE.

29. Background on D. A. Thomas from the National Archives, http://www.learning curve.gov.uk. (accessed January 23, 2007).

30. Beddoe, "Woman and Politics in 20th Century Wales," 18th Annual Lecture of the Welsh Political Archive at the National Library of Wales, November 5, 2004.

31. Lady Margaret Mackworth, the Lusitania Resource, http://web.rmlusitania.info (accessed October 24, 2006); quotation from Lady Mackworth's memoir, *This Was My World* (1933), at the National Archives, http://www.learningcurve.gov.uk. RE told writer Robert Lewis Taylor that Margaret Mackworth's imprisonment kept her from making the trip with her parents. Mackworth's case is well documented in histories of the British suffrage movement, and she was in prison at about the time of RE's friendship with Lady Rhondda. See Robert Lewis Taylor, "Oh, Hawk of Mercy!" *New Yorker*, April 17, 1948; this item is one of the few mentioned in the article that PE confirmed.

32. Norquay, *Voices and Votes*, 256–57.

33. Ibid.

34. The Hyde Park march numbers are disputed. See Wingerden, *Women's Suffrage Movement in Britain*, 83; Smith, *British Women's Suffrage Campaign*, 35. Wingerden puts the figure at 500,000; Norquay, *Voices and Votes*, gives the date as June 29.

35. Norquay, *Voices and Votes*, 256.

36. John Stuart Mill, "The Subjection of Women," ebooks@Adelaide (Australia), 2004, recorded into HTML May 24, 2003 by Steve Thomas, University of Adelaide Library Electronic Texts Collection, based on 1929 Everyman's Library edition.

37. R. Strachey, *Cause*, 79.

38. Smith, *British Women's Suffrage Campaign*, 36.

39. Norquay, *Voices and Votes*, x.

40. Taylor, "Oh, Hawk of Mercy!" 34.

41. Original handwritten letter from CNE to RE, July 7, 1914, PEPLD.

42. Inventory from CNE's will, 1944, and RE's list of furnishings, 1932.

43. RE, "Good Companions in Conservation," 5.

44. Ibid., 6.

45. Preston, *Lusitania*, 91.

46. Lady Mackworth's memoir, *This Was My World* (1933), at the National Archives, http://www.learningcurve.gov.uk (accessed September 7, 2002).

47. Preston, *Lusitania*, 267.

48. IW, 6.

49. RE's banner and pamphlets published by the New York State Woman Suffrage Party are in PEPLD.

50. R. Strachey, *Cause*, 41.

51. Gurko, *Ladies of Seneca Falls*, 310.

52. Bainbridge, "Origins," 19.

53. Adickes, *To Be Young*, 93.

54. Wheeler, *One Woman, One Vote*, 298.

55. Taylor, "Oh, Hawk of Mercy!" 34. An example of a "blistering" speech is "Abstract of Address by Mrs. Charles Noel Edge," dated 1916, PEPLD.

56. Interview with PE; see also IW, 6.

57. Interview with PE. For the Norries' residence and their friendship with the Roosevelts, see Cook, *Eleanor Roosevelt*, 292, 321, 339.

58. IW, 6.

59. *Better Babies*, PEPLD.

60. *Why Not?* PEPLD.

61. "Woman Suffrage, a War Measure," PEPLD.

62. Bainbridge, "Origins," 21.

63. Crystal Eastman, *Christian Science Monitor*, March 8, 1920.

64. IW, 9.

65. For Ruth Morgan presidency and Colony Club background, see Cox, *History of the Colony Club*, 12, 85. The Colony Club will not confirm past or current membership. Simultaneous admission of RE and Eleanor Roosevelt noted in interview with PE.

66. RE, "Winged Friendships," 2, PEPLD.

67. Ibid.

68. Ibid.

69. Ibid.

70. Ibid.

71. Ibid., 4.

72. IW, 9–10.

73. Ibid., 3.

74. I am grateful to Mr. and Mrs. Jules Krol for a tour of the Parsonage Point grounds and home, originally built by CNE, in October 2003. Property features are from "Real Estate Proceedings 1945" documents pertaining to CNE's last will and testament filed in Surrogate's Court of Westchester County, White Plains, N.Y.

75. Interview with PE.

76. Ibid.

77. Interview with PE provided details of his parents' argument and his nine-year-old's recollection that his mother's arm was disabled as a result.

78. RE, "Winged Friendships," 5.

79. Excerpt from "Storm," by RE, PEPLD.

80. Original handwritten letter from CNE to unknown recipient, PEPLD. Interviews with both PE and MEN regarding parents' separation places it in the spring of 1921.

CHAPTER FOUR: Amateur and Dilettante

1. RE, "Winged Friendships," 5.

2. Ibid.

3. Vanderbilt, *Fortune's Children*, 255.

4. Court documents concerning CNE's 1944 give the date of the couple's separation, filed in Surrogate's Court, Westchester County. For a discussion of early New York divorce laws, see Vernier, *American Family Laws*, 341.

5. Excerpts from original handwritten letters in PEPLD: from CNE to RE, December 28, 1922; from CNE to RE, "Ap 24"; from CNE to RE, January 3, 1925; from CNE to RE, June 7 (no year); from CNE to RE, February 4 (no year); from CNE to RE, May 1922.

6. Original letter from CNE to RE, June 7 (no year), PEPLD.

7. Original letter from RE to CNE, "23 january," PEPLD.

8. Interview with PE.

9. Interview with Melissa Marston Macleod, October 1990.

10. RE's earliest bird notations and complete bird life lists are at JHMA-HMSA.

11. RE, "Winged Friendships," 5.

12. IW, 9A

13. "Winged Friendships," 6.

14. IW, 10.

15. RE, "Winged Friendships." 7.

16. Ibid., 8.

17. Ibid., 9

18. RE's calendar with partial life list, JHMA-HMSA.

19. Interview with MEN, October 1990.

20. IW, 12, and interview with PE.

21. IW, 13

22. Roger Tory Peterson, "In Memoriam," *The Auk* 82 (October 1965): 603.

23. IW, 14.

24. Peterson, "In Memoriam," 600–601.

25. Coues, *Field Ornithology*, 21.

26. Ibid., 15.

27. Orr, *Saving America's Birds*, 52.

28. Chapman, *Autobiography of a Bird-Lover*, 66–67.

29. Bainbridge, "Origins," 63–64, 129.

30. Joseph Grinnell, "Conserve the Collector," *Science* (February 12, 1915): 229–32.

31. IW, 14.

32. Ibid., 13.

CHAPTER FIVE: Like a Man

1. Willard Gibbs Van Name, Waldron Dewitt Miller, and Davis Quinn, *Crisis in Conservation*, June 1929, REPDPL; also available at the University of Washington Library, Seattle, Carsten Lien MS, and the Peabody Museum of Comparative Zoology, Harvard University, Cambridge, Mass.

2. Ibid.

3. Ibid.

4. IW, 6–7.

5. Ibid., 6.

6. Quotation from Henry James, *The Outcry* (New York: New York Review Books, 2002), 74. Edge describes contemplative states aboard ship and elsewhere for dramatic effect; see IW.

7. AOU estimate in Graham, *Audubon Ark*, 25; quotation from Trefethen, *Crusade for Wildlife*, 129.

8. Orr, *Saving America's Birds*, 31.

9. Graham, *Audubon Ark*, 9–13, quotation on 9–10.

10. Ibid., 13.

11. Trefethen, *Crusade for Wildlife*, 89.

12. Graham, *Audubon Ark*, 13.

13. Chapman, *Autobiography of a Bird-Lover*, 23.

14. Ibid., 65.

15. Graham, *Audubon Ark*, 38–39, 61; Orr, *Saving America's Birds*, 37.

16. Graham, *Audubon Ark*, 45–46.

17. For Willcox's stipulations regarding NAAS goals, see Trefethen, *Crusade for Wildlife*, 135. Willcox referred to protection of "useful mammals," meaning game, reflecting the dominant thinking at the Bureau of Biological Survey.

18. Orr, *Saving America's Birds*, 19, 89, 141.

19. Graham, *Audubon Ark*, 61.

20. Orr, *Saving America's Birds*, 1.

21. Ibid., 10.

22. Ibid., 129.

23. Graham, *Audubon Ark*, 62.

24. Fox, *John Muir and His Legacy*, 155.

25. Bainbridge, "Origins," 252n.

26. G. O. Shields, "Pearson and Pump Guns: Believes Audubon Society's Secretary Really Favored Them," *New York Times*, July 3, 1911, REPDPL.

27. Fox, *John Muir and His Legacy*, 155.

28. Ibid., 155–59; Orr, *Saving America's Birds*, 222–23; Graham, *Audubon Ark*, 74–82; Bainbridge, "Origins," 68–73. Quotation from Trefethen, *Crusade for Wildlife*, 150.

29. Orr, *Saving America's Birds*, 224.

30. Ibid.

31. Bainbridge, "Origins," 67; quotation from Orr, *Saving America's Birds*, 224.

32. For NAAS board vote, see Bainbridge, "Origins," 69. Quotation from Fox, *John Muir and His Legacy*, 156.

33. "Winchester," *New York Herald*, June 3, 1911, REPDPL.

34. William Temple Hornaday, *Two Years in the Jungle: The Experience of a Hunter and Naturalist in India, Ceylon, the Malay Peninsula and Borneo* (New York: Charles Scribner's Sons, 1885), 370.

35. Orr, *Saving America's Birds*, 226.

36. Catherine Dutcher's letter to Gifford Pinchot entered by Sen. William H. King, in 69th Congress, 1st Session, *Congressional Record* (May 24 1926), p. 14; copy in REPDPL.

37. G. O. Shields, *New York Times*, July 3, 1911, REPDPL.

38. Orr, *Saving America's Birds*, 230.

39. Ibid., 231.

40. Graham, *Audubon Ark*, 102–5; "Paul's Great Adventure," *Commercial Appeal*, September 20, 1923, http://prb.datalane.net/prbhis.htm (accessed February 28, 2006); Paul J. Rainey Estate—Tippah Lodge, http://www.rootsweb.com/mstippah/Raineyestate.html (accessed February 28, 2006); Danny Murry, "The Amazing Paul J. Rainey," http://prb.datalane.net/prbamaz.htm (accessed February 26, 2006). RE also mentions Rainey in IW, 59.

41. "Bagging Arctic Monsters with Rope, Gun, and Camera," *Cosmopolitan*, December 1910–May 1911.

42. Letter from Henry W. de Forest, later included in "Report of the Special Committee Appointed to Investigate Charges Publicly Made against the National Association of Audubon Societies," August 19, 1931, REPDPL.

43. Hornaday protested to T. S. Palmer in an August 2, 1923, letter and to Bureau of Biological Survey chief E. W. Nelson in a memo, "The Part of the Audubon Society of Neutrality toward the McIlhenny Club of 4,000 Duck Hunters," both in REPDPL. Henry de Forest's 1923 letter is reprinted in "Report of the Special Committee," REPDPL.

44. "Report of the Special Committee," REPDPL.

45. Graham, *Audubon Ark*, 104.

46. *Bird-Lore*, March–April 1925.

47. T. G. Pearson, speech to the National Conference on Outdoor Recreation, *Is American Game Protection a Success?* circular no. 8 (May 23, 1924), REPDPL.

48. Letter from John Burnham to DuPont Powder Company, July 16, 1924, cited in 69th Congress, 1st session, *Congressional Record* (May 21, 1926), p. 16, copy in REPDPL.

49. *Federal Power and Duck Bag Limits: Facts*, NAAS Bulletin no. 6, p. 1, REPDPL.

50. Ibid., 8.

51. Ibid., 11.

52. Pearson, *Is American Game Protection a Success?* REPDPL.

53. Fox, *John Muir and His Legacy*, 173.

54. Irving Brant, *Forest and Stream*, November 1929, 822–23, REPDPL.

55. Gilbert Pearson, *The Bald Eagle Educational Leaflet no. 82*, REPDPL.

56. Ibid.

57. James P. Chapin, "In Memoriam," *The Auk* (January 1932): 3.

58. Bainbridge, "Origins," 182. RE mentions WVN's employment situation in IW (25), and it remained a key motivation for her role as an independent advocate.

59. George H. Sherwood, "Statement of the American Museum of Natural History in Regard to a Pamphlet Entitled 'A Crisis in Conservation,'" July 23, 1929, reprinted in *Forest and Stream*, November 29, 1929, 822, REPDPL.

60. Ibid.

61. Fox, *John Muir and His Legacy*, 174.

62. IW, 29.

63. Ibid., 102.

64. Ibid.

65. Ibid., 27.

66. Ibid., 28. WVN's homosexuality was noted by PE and Walter E. Langsam in interviews with the author.

67. Bainbridge, "Origins," 129–33.

68. Ibid., 136.

69. IW, 15–19, quotation on 15; bird lists are in JHMA-HMSA.

70. Ibid., 174. Bainbridge states: "Annual reports showed the NAAS had received over $2.3 million from 1917 to 1927" ("Origins," 174).

71. IW, 15.

72. Comparison to Eleanor Roosevelt made by Robert Lewis Taylor in "Oh, Hawk of Mercy!" *New Yorker*, April 17, 1948. JHMA-HMSA also has a recording of RE's voice.

73. IW, 15.

74. Ibid., 16.

75. Ibid.

76. Ibid., 27, 19, 20.

77. RE mentioned Pearson's salary in IW, 23. Graham writes that Pearson's salary was a percentage of NAAS annual income (*Audubon Ark*, 114).

78. Letter from RE to T. Gilbert Pearson, November 8, 1929, REPDPL.

79. Letter from T. Gilbert Pearson to RE, November 11, 1929, REPDPL.

80. IW, 26.

CHAPTER SIX: A Common Scold

1. IW, 26.

2. Ibid.

3. Ibid., 26, 170.

4. Original ECC pamphlets in REPDPL.

5. Clark Bainbridge, "Rosalie Edge Chronology, 1877–1963," prepared for the JHMA-HMSA, March 2001.

6. Interview with PE. See also IW, 28.

7. Ibid.

8. Bainbridge, "Origins," 153–64.

9. Brant, *Adventures in Conservation*, 4.

10. Ibid., 12.

11. Irving Brant, *Forest and Stream*, November 1929, 823.

12. Ibid.

13. Brant, *Adventures in Conservation*, 18. RE's reaction to *Forest and Stream*'s purchase is noted in IW.

14. Brant, *Adventures in Conservation*, 5.

15. Ibid., 12.

16. IW, 29.

17. ECC pamphlet *The United States Biological Survey: Destruction, Not Scientific Investigation and Conservation, Now Its Chief Activity*, May 1930, REPDPL, italics in original.

18. Letter from RE to C. L. Jamison, April 25, 1935, JHMA-HMSA.

19. ECC pamphlet *The Advance of Conservation*, 1, REPDPL.

20. Interview with PE. PE also gave the author RE's copy of the book in French, with her handwritten notes.

21. Delamain, *Why Birds Sing*, 44.

22. Ibid., xx.

23. Ibid., 229.

24. Cox, *History of the Colony Club*, 80.

25. Interview with PE.

26. Cox, *History of the Colony Club*, 55.

27. IW, 54a.

28. Letter from RE to JDD, August 5, 1934, JHMA-HMSA.

29. Correspondence and telephone interviews with Walter E. Langsam, 2002–6; also Langsam's presentation to the Literary Club of Cincinnati, January 27, 2003, "Oh Happy Hawk: The Ultimate Tale of Passionate Renunciation."

30. In an interview with the author, PE noted CNE's wish to marry Ruth Johnston, the secretary to whom MDB had introduced him.

31. RE, "Valentine," PEPLD.

32. IW, 7.

33. Ibid., 35.

34. Irving Brant, *Compromised Conservation: Can the Audubon Society Explain?* ECC publication, 1930, REPDPL.

35. Ibid.

36. IW, 32.

37. Fox, *John Muir and His Legacy*, 178.

38. Roger Tory Peterson, foreword to Brett, *Mountain and the Migration*, 6.

39. Letters from H. W. de Forest to RE, October 17, 1930, October 20, 1930, REPDPL.

40. Hornaday prepared to give his "Resolution for Constructive Conservation," REPDPL.

41. For "golden bridge," see IW, 37. Other quotations from deposition by Robert Cushman Murphy affidavit, 4, "In the Matter of the Application of M. R. Edge, Petitioner, for a Peremptory Mandamus Order," Supreme Court of New York County, July 13, 1931, REPDPL.

42. IW, 37.

43. Theodore Palmer affidavit, 2, for "In the Matter of the Application of M. R. Edge, Petitioner, for a Peremptory Mandamus Order," Supreme Court of New York County, July 13, 1931, REPDPL.

44. Fox, *John Muir and His Legacy*, 178.

45. IW, 38.

46. For "dove-serpent" terminology, see original letter from RE to HBB, March 24, 1911, PEPLD.

47. Numerous private letters to RE from various professionals support this view; see REPDPL.

48. Letter from H. W. de Forest to RE, October 29, 1930, REPDPL.

49. Carey as the source of RE's mailing list request; see letter from Henry Carey to RE, November ?, 1930, REPDPL.

50. IW, 39.

51. Walker, *In Defense of American Liberties*, 30.

52. IW, 40.

53. Ibid.

54. Interview with PE; see also letter from Henry R. Carey to RE, October 31, 1930, REPDPL.

55. Charles Dickerman Williams, "Statement of Facts." Documents associated with the "Peremptory Mandamus Order" including attorney arguments and depositions are in REPDPL.

56. IW, 42.

57. Pearson affidavit, 25, REPDPL.

58. Ibid., 24, 23; regarding Pearson's assertion of six groups out of eleven thousand, see p. 3. Pearson's defenders are mentioned in his affidavit, with letters of support.

59. Letter from George Pratt to T. Gilbert Pearson, read into the affidavit, ibid., 13.

60. Ibid.

61. Theodore Palmer affidavit, 5, REPDPL.

62. Excerpted from *The United States Biological Survey: Destruction, Not Scientific Investigation and Conservation, Now Its Chief Activity*, in Palmer affidavit, 3.

63. Frank Chapman affidavit, 2, REPDPL.

64. Robert Cushman Murphy affidavit, 8, REPDPL.

65. C. D. Williams's "Statement of Facts," REPDPL.

66. Samuel T. Carter Jr., "Memorandum on Behalf of Defendants in Opposition," 25, REPDPL; IW, 43.

67. Letter from CDW to RE, August 4, 1931, REPDPL.

68. Conduct of investigation cited in several letters, REPDPL.

69. "Report of the Special Committee," REPDPL.

70. Ibid.

71. Regarding de Forest's complaint, see "Special Committee" report; letters from Henry de Forest to RE, October 3, 1930, and October 20, 1930; and subsequent NAAS official correspondence, REPDPL.

72. Secret appendix noted by Fox, in *John Muir and His Legacy*, 179.

73. Interview with MEN.

74. Author interviews and correspondence with Walter E. Langsam regarding his mother, Julia Stubblefield Langsam's, relations with RE.

75. Official letter from Mrs. Charles Noel Edge to NAAS members, n.d., REPDPL.

76. IW, 48.

77. See letter from W. V. Field to "Dear Sirs," October 17, 1931, REPDPL; also letter from A. K. Fisher to "Gentlemen," May 21, 1933, JHMA-HMSA.

78. According to PE, Willard Van Name paid for the transcription. All direct quotes and the description of the meeting are from the transcript, "Proceedings of Twenty-seventh Annual Business Meeting of the National Association of Audubon Societies," October 27, 1931, REPDPL.

79. Ibid., 14.

80. Ibid., 21.

81. "Audubon Societies Uphold Pearson in Convention Test," *New York Herald Tribune*, October 28, 1931, REPDPL.

82. "Proceedings of Twenty-seventh Annual Business Meeting," 45.

83. Ibid., 46.

84. "Audubon Societies Uphold Pearson."

85. Letter from RE to Floyd M. Shoemaker, December 8, 1931, REPDPL.

86. McIlhenny background from IW; Roger M. Grace, "Edward McIlhenny: Businessman, Naturalist, Author . . . Fibber," 15, Metropolitan News Enterprise, http://www .metnews.com/articles/2004; and "To See a World: Spotlight Avery Island," http:// www.marin.cc.ca.us.

87. IW, 61.

88. Ibid.

89. IW, 68b.

90. Three hundred thousand total comes from ECC pamphlet *Steel Trapping by*

the Audubon Association, September 1932, REPDPL. In IW RE writes that in 1929–31, 103,000 animals had been trapped, for $100,000, split between the NAAS and contracted trappers (70).

91. IW, 51.

92. Ibid.

93. For an account of the trip, see RE, "An Appointment in Mexico," *Blackwood's Magazine,* no. 165 (August 1953): 129–36, PEPLD.

94. Ibid., 131.

95. Ibid.

96. Ibid.

97. Ibid.

98. Letter from Edith Roosevelt to the NAAS membership, October 1, 1932, REPDPL.

99. Letter from E. W. Nelson to "Dear Fred," possibly Connecticut senator Frederic C. Walcott, October 24, 1932, REPDPL.

100. RE's involvement in ending pelican poisoning is noted in Lien, *Olympic Battleground,* 109; and in ECC pamphlet *The Slaughter of Yellowstone Park Pelicans.*

101. Lien, *Olympic Battleground,* 110.

102. "Proceedings," Annual Meeting of the National Association of Audubon Societies, October 25, 1932, American Museum of Natural History, is the source of the meeting account, REPDPL.

103. Exchange between Holt and Edge in "Proceedings," October 25, 1932, 3–12.

104. Ibid., 4.

105. Ibid., 9.

106. Ibid., 9–10.

107. Ibid., 10.

108. Ibid., 12.

109. Ibid., 23.

110. Ibid., 23–24.

111. Ibid., 3–24, quotations on 18.

112. IW, 71.

113. See letter from RE to R. H. Macy, JHMA-HMSA.

114. "Proceedings," October 25, 1932, 20.

115. Ibid., 57.

116. Ibid., 67.

117. *New York Sun,* October 25, 1932.

118. Graham writes that NAAS membership dwindled from 8,400 in 1921 to 3,400 in 1933 (*Audubon Ark,* 117).

119. IW 173; circumstances of AOU membership are confirmed in personal letters between Francis Harper and RE. Regarding the AOU membership dispute, see letters

from W. L. McAtee to RE, October 20, 1934, and October 26, 1938; from Francis Harper to Dr. T. S. Palmer, November 9, 1934; from Francis Harper to RE, November 9, 1934, and October 27, 1938, JHMA-HMSA.

120. Brant, *Adventures in Conservation*, 22.

121. Interview with PE.

122. Interview with PE. According to PE, RE lost her house due to CNE's market losses, possibly on a margin call.

123. One-page legal document transferring household items, PEPLD.

124. In an interview, Walter E. Langsam recounted that RE spoke to Julia Langsam about how CNE lost her property.

125. Letter from RE to IB October 20, 1937, IBC.

126. Interview with Walter Langsam, who recalled what his mother, Julia Langsam, had told him.

127. RE, "Moving to Smaller Quarters," 1937, PEPLD.

128. Letter from J. Allen Wiley to RE, February 28, 1933, REPDPL.

129. Letter from CDW to J. Allen Wiley, March 15, 1933, REPDPL.

130. Interview with PE.

131. IW, 217.

132. Ibid., 9.

CHAPTER SEVEN: Sweet Reasonableness

1. George Miksch Sutton, "Notes on a Collection of Hawks from Schuylkill County, Pennsylvania," *Wilson Bulletin* (June 1928): 84, JHMA-HMSA.

2. "Hawk Mountain Sanctuary 1938 Report," JHMA-HMSA.

3. "Soaring the Ridges," Pennsylvania Bureau of Topographic and Geologic Survey, posted at Acopian Center for Conservation Learning of Hawk Mountain Sanctuary, Orwigsberg, Pennsylvania.

4. Bent, *Life Histories*, 95, 117; Forbush, *Useful Birds and Their Protection*, 86.

5. Forbush, *Birds of Massachusetts*, 113, 172, 118.

6. Ibid., 151.

7. Ibid., 118, 121, 123.

8. See George Miksch Sutton, "The Status of the Goshawk in Pennsylvania," *Wilson Bulletin*, June 1931, 108–13.

9. Ibid.

10. Nancy J. Keeler, "Soaring above 'This School in The Clouds,'" *Pennsylvania Heritage*, Summer 2004, 27.

11. Kosack, *Pennsylvania Game Commission*, 34.

12. Ibid., 19.

13. Keeler, "Soaring above 'This School,'" 41.

14. William D. Uhrich, ed., *A Century of Bird Life in Berks County, Pennsylvania* (Reading, Pa.: Reading Public Museum, 1997), 6.

15. Broun, *Hawks Aloft!* 6. See also Miller's obituary, "Waldron DeWitt Miller: Always Respectful of Their Rights," *The Auk* (January 1932): 3.

16. *Pottsville (Pa.) Journal*, October 1929 [day not visible], copy of article displayed at JHMA-HMSA.

17. Kosack, *Pennsylvania Game Commission*, 68.

18. Ibid.

19. Ibid., 78.

20. Richard Pough's unpublished memoir, "My Life," JHMA-HMSA, used with permission. The description of the hawk-hunting scene is based on an interview with Richard Pough in November 1990 and on accounts in numerous sources.

21. Harwood, *View from Hawk Mountain*, 50–53; Broun, *Hawks Aloft!* 6–14; Henry H. Collins Jr., "Hawk Slaughter at Drehersville," *Hawk and Owl Society Bulletin* no. 3 (1933): 10–18. Comparison to "tropical deluge" from Julian W. Hill, "Reminiscences of Hawk Mountain," *Delmarva Ornithologist* 18 (1985), JHMA-HMSA.

22. Collins, "Hawk Slaughter at Drehersville," and photo in Broun, *Hawks Aloft!* 7.

23. Pough, "My Life," 43–44.

24. Broun, *Hawks Aloft!* 10–11.

25. Regarding Collins's resolution to protect hawks at the 1932 NAAS annual meeting, see "Proceedings of Annual Meeting of the National Association of Audubon Societies," 81–82, REPDPL.

26. Harwood, *View from Hawk Mountain*, 64–65.

27. Brett, *Mountain and the Migration*, 16–20; Maurice Broun, "Hawk Migration in Pennsylvania during Fall of 1934," *The Auk* 52 (1935): 235. Keith L. Bildstein, PhD, Sarkis Acopian Director of Conservation Science at Hawk Mountain Sanctuary, noted blueberry crops in an interview with the author during an August 2006 visit.

28. Harwood, *View from Hawk Mountain*, 65.

29. Letter from WVN to IB, date not available, JHMA-HMSA.

30. Interview with Roland C. Clement, retired National Audubon Society senior biologist.

31. Author interview with naturalists Sylvia and Winston William Brockner, who consider RE a lifelong role model in their activism in Evergreen, Colorado, July 2008.

32. Watkins *Righteous Pilgrim*, 469.

33. Letter from RE to Helen G. Thompson, December 13, 1933, REPDPL.

34. IW, 34.

35. Brant, *Adventures in Conservation*, 116.

36. Letter from JDD to RE, August 2, 1934, JHMA-HMSA.

37. Letter from RE to Congressman Joseph W. Byrns, chairman, House Appropriations Committee, April 1, 1933, JHMA-HMSA.

38. Letter from RE to JDD, August 5, 1934, JHMA-HMSA.

39. Letter from RE to the House Appropriations Committee, April 1, 1933, JHMA-HMSA.

40. Letter from RE to JDD, June 21, 1935, JHMA-HMSA.

41. Letter from RE to JDD, July 6, 1935, JHMA-HMSA.

42. Letter from JDD to RE, May 5, 1934, JHMA-HMSA.

43. Letter from JDD to RE, July 24, 1934, JHMA-HMSA.

44. IW, 91.

45. Letter from RE to Harold Ickes, April 23, 1933, IBC.

46. IW, 97–101, quotation on 97.

47. Ibid., 98.

48. Ibid.

49. Ibid., 110.

50. Letter from IB to PE, January 20, 1963, JHMA-HMSA.

51. For an outline of ECC causes, see RE, *Fighting the Good Fight*, 3–7.

52. The cartoon appeared in *Field Ornithology* 1, no. 7 (June 1939), "drawn at the suggestion of Mrs. C. N. Edge," JHMA-HMSA.

53. House of Representatives Public Lands Hearings on Acquisitions of Lands for Yosemite National Park, April 21, 1937, 30, Denver Public Library Government Publications.

54. Ibid.

55. IW, 216–18, quotations on 217. RE noted her observations on May 15 in IW, but a *New York Times* front-page article on the subject ran on May 12.

56. IW, 217.

57. IW, 216.

58. IW, 217.

CHAPTER EIGHT: M. R. Edge, Lessee

1. Richard Pough's unpublished memoir, "My Life," 44, JHMA-HMSA, used with permission.

2. IW, 188.

3. RE, Twentieth Anniversary Celebration Speech, October 31, 1954, JHMA-HMSA.

4. Harwood, *View from Hawk Mountain*, 69.

5. Letter from RE to MB, August 21, 1934, JHMA-HMSA.

6. Details of Maurice Broun's life drawn from interviews with Irma Broun Kahn, January 1992, and "Keeper of the Kittatinny," unpublished autobiography of MB by Kenneth Kranick, written ca. 1981, used with permission. Broun's letters and journals are used with the permission of MBLAC.

7. Broun, *Hawks Aloft!* 3.

8. MB's hospital job was described by Irma Broun Kahn in an interview, January 1992.

9. Quoted in Kranick's unpublished biography; original letter at MBLAC.

10. Kranick, unpublished biography. Interview with Irma Broun Kahn, January 1992, confirmed impression of MB. Interview with Roland C. Clement, November 2007, noted meeting RE at Austin Research Station in Cape Cod.

11. Thoreau quote from CCNS Web site. Penniman history from "The Penniman House: A Whaling Story," Teaching with Historic Places Lesson Plans, CCNS Collection, http://www.cr.nps.gov.

12. MB's journal, January 1934, MBLAC, used with permission. Copies of MB's journal also at JHMA-HMSA.

13. Letter from RE to MB, August 21, 1934, JHMA-HMSA.

14. Letter from MB to RE, August 23, 1934, JHMA-HMSA.

15. Ibid.

16. Power of attorney authorization letter from RE to MB, August 29, 1934, JHMA-HMSA.

17. MB's journal, MBLAC and JHMA-HMSA. An account of the Brouns' arrival also appears in Broun, *Hawks Aloft!* 15–25.

18. See Broun, *Hawks Aloft!* 86; also Brett, *Mountain and the Migration.*

19. *Pottsville (Pa.)Evening Republican*, September 15, 1934.

20. Broun, *Hawks Aloft!* 22–23.

21. Letter from MB to RE, September 11, 1934, JHMA-HMSA.

22. The request placed with Governor Pinchot is noted in a letter from Col. Henry W. Shoemaker to RE, October 3, 1934, JHMA-HMSA.

23. Bildstein, *Migrating Raptors of the World*, 76.

24. Broun, *Hawks Aloft!* 34.

25. Ibid.

26. Bird count entry in MB's journal, November 2, 1934, MBLAC and JHMA-HMSA.

27. The Hon. Henry W. Shoemaker, "The Greatest Step Forward in Bird Protection," *Altoona (Pa.)Tribune*, September 28, 1934, JHMA-HMSA.

28. Background on Kermit Roosevelt from Candice Millard, *The River of Doubt: Theodore's Darkest Journey* (New York: Broadway Books, 2005), 346–49.

29. Letter from John H. Baker to ECC, November 9, 1934; a four-hundred-dollar donation was included with a letter from John H. Baker to RE, October 7, 1935, both in JHMA-HMSA.

30. IW, 77.

31. RE mentions tea with Baker in her letter to JDD, July 27, 1935, JHMA-HMSA.

32. Brant, *Adventures in Conservation*, 22.

33. Letter from RE to WVN, September 28, 1934; in a July 27, 1935, letter from RE to JDD, she talked about making peace with the NAAS, JHMA-HMSA.

34. Letter from WVN to RE, September 28, 1934; letter from RE to unknown correspondent, October 10, 1935, JHMA-HMSA.

35. Letter from CDW to RE, November 26, 1934, JHMA-HMSA.

36. Letter from RE to CDW, December 2, 1934, JHMA-HMSA.

37. Quotation from letter from RE to Richard Wood, *Nature Magazine* editor, January 8, 1935; in a February 5, 1935, letter to Witmer Stone, member of the Academy of Sciences and editor of *The Auk*, RE described the sanctuary she wanted to establish, JHMA-HMSA.

38. Letter from RE to MB, October 25, 1934, JHMA-HMSA.

39. Letter from MB to RE, February 5, 1935; letter from RE to MB, October 25, 1934, emphasis in the original, JHMA-HMSA.

40. Letter from RE to MB, November 8, 1934; see also letter from RE to MB, November 10, 1934 JHMA-HMSA.

41. Undated handwritten letter from anonymous correspondent to RE, JHMA-HMSA.

42. Letter from RE to Richard Wood, January 8, 1935, JHMA-HMSA.

43. Letter from RE to MB, November 10, 1934, JHMA-HMSA.

44. Pough, "My Life," 44, 45. Pough described his role in an interview with the author in 1991.

45. Pough, "My Life," 45.

46. Letter from RE to A. Brazier Howell, April 4, 1935, JHMA-HMSA.

47. Quotations from letter from RE to Julian Hill, March 21, 1935, and letter from RE to Edward S. Weyl, August 3, 1935. Examples of RE's anti-Baker comments are numerous: see letter from RE to Witmer Stone, February 11, 1935; letter from RE to Brazier Howell, April 4, 1935; letter from RE to JDD, July 27, 1935. All letters in JHMA-HMSA.

48. Letter from Bob Kramer to MB, December 16, 1934, JHMA-HMSA.

49. Advice in a letter from RE to A. Brazier Howell, April 4, 1935, JHMA-HMSA.

50. MB journal, November 14, 1934, MBLAC and JHMA-HMSA.

51. Letter from WVN to RE, May 27, 1935, JHMA-HMSA.

52. Letter from RE to A. Brazier Howell, April 4, 1935, JHMA-HMSA.

53. Letter signed by Davis Quinn to John Baker, November 11, 1936, JHMA-HMSA. For the NAAS's tone, see letter from John Baker to RE, November 5, 1936, JHMA-HMSA.

54. Letter from RE to A. Brazier Howell, April 4, 1935, JHMA-HMSA.

55. RE, *Forward into Battle: Yearbook of the Emergency Conservation Committee*, 1935, 8, JHMA-HMSA.

56. IW, 188.

57. Original handwritten letter from RE to HBB, September 19, 1909, PEPLD.

CHAPTER NINE: Canadian Spy

1. IW, 217.

2. Brant, *Adventure in Conservation*, 17.

3. Ibid.

4. IW, 198.

5. For public recognition of Ickes's quiet backing of the ECC, see Morgan, *Last Wilderness*, 181.

6. IW, 101, emphasis in original.

7. Ibid., 102.

8. Regarding Van Name's concern about Roosevelt elk, see IW, 106; also in Lien, *Olympic Battleground*, 112.

9. Lien, *Olympic Battleground*, 113.

10. "The Report of Lieut. Joseph O'Neil, Fourteenth Infantry, of His Exploration of the Olympic Mountains, Washington, from June to October, 1890," U.S. Senate, 54th Cong., 1st session, 1895–96, serial 3349, 20.

11. Morgan, *Last Wilderness* 7.

12. IW, 109.

13. Williams, *Loggers*, 48.

14. Watkins, *Righteous Pilgrim*, 309; see also regarding private ownership of forests. Regarding mill ownership, see Morgan, *Last Wilderness*, 78.

15. Watkins, *Righteous Pilgrim*, 309.

16. Morgan, *Last Wilderness*, 130.

17. Watkins, *Righteous Pilgrim*, 310.

18. Ibid.

19. Lien, *Olympic Battleground*, 17.

20. Morgan, *Last Wilderness*, 181.

21. For RE's radical conservationist role, see Fox, *John Muir and His Legacy*, 175–82.

22. Regarding Smith's request, see Lien *Olympic Battleground*, 123.

23. Ibid., 127.

24. Ibid., 127, 126.

25. Ibid., 129.

26. Ibid.

27. Letter from RE to JDD, July 27, 1935, JHMA-HMSA.

28. IW, 110.

29. Lien, *Olympic Battleground*, 126.

30. *Save The Yosemite Sugar Pines!* ECC pamphlet, October 1932, REPDPL.

31. Brant, *Adventures in Conservation*, 57.

32. Letter from Chairman, Central Valley Council, to Sen. Samuel M. Shortridge, reprinted in ECC's *Save the Yosemite Sugar Pines!* 7.

33. See http://www.nps.gov/history/historyonline_books/runte2/chap2.html.

34. Frederick Law Olmstead, "Draft of Preliminary Report upon the Yosemite and The Big Tree Grove," 1865, http://www.yosemite.ca.us/library/olmsted/report.html.

35. Ibid.

36. Fox, *John Muir and His Legacy*, 21.

37. See http://www.yosemite.ca.us/library/yosemites_pioneer_cabins.

38. IW, 93.

39. Ibid.; Lien, *Olympic Battleground*, 184.

40. For Edge's account of what happened between WVN and Thomson, see IW, 91–96. See also Brant, *Adventures in Conservation*, 59.

41. Brant, *Adventures in Conservation*, 60.

42. See letter from RE to WVN, December 1, 1935, for an explanation of the dispute, JHMA-HMSA.

43. Brant, *Adventures in Conservation*, 62.

44. *The Advance of Conservation*, ECC publication, 1938, 3, REPDPL.

45. For an account of Ickes's anger, see Brant, *Adventures in Conservation*; quotation from 64.

46. Transcript of hearings on the "Acquisition of Certain Lands for, and Addition thereof to the Yosemite National Park in the State of California, and for Other Purposes," April 20–23, 1937, House Committee on Public Lands, 75-1, p. 27.

47. Exchange between Edge and Englebright in transcript of hearings, 31.

48. Letter from RE to Theodora Van Name, September 9, 1937, emphasis in original, JHMA-HMSA.

49. IW, 95; see also Brant, *Adventures in Conservation*, 59; and Lien, *Olympic Battleground*, 182.

50. Brant, *Adventures in Conservation*, 59. Brant also attributed the break between RE and WVN to the disagreement over Thomson.

51. Lien, *Olympic Battleground*, 182.

52. Letter from RE to IB, October 20, 1937, IBC.

53. Letter from WVN to RE, January 3, 1936, JHMA-HMSA.

54. IW, 95.

55. Letter from RE to IB, November 11, 1937, IBC.

56. Ibid.

57. See letter from Robert Marshall to RE, October 11, 1935, JHMA-HMSA.

58. Zaslowsky and Watkins, *These American Lands*, 205.

59. Public Hearing on Mount Olympus National Park, House Committee on Public Lands, H.R. 7086, 74th Cong., 2nd sess., April 27, 1936, 76–77, quote on 77.

60. Ibid., 76.

61. Ibid., 77.

62. Ibid., 78–79, quote on 79.

63. Lien notes that RE reached out to Smith (*Olympic Battleground*, 139).

64. Public Hearing on Mount Olympus National Park, 79.

65. Ibid.

66. Ibid.

67. Ibid., 78.

68. Both Carsten Lien and Irving Brant address at great depth the Washington State Forest Service's independence from its U.S. headquarters.

69. Lien, *Olympic Battleground*, 157, 169.

70. *Double Crossing the Project*, REPDPL.

71. IW, 111.

72. For a full account of Roosevelt's visit, see Lien's *Olympic Battleground*, 171–78.

73. Brant, *Adventures in Conservation*, 89.

74. Letter from RE to IB, October 20, 1937, IBC.

75. Brant, *Adventures in Conservation*, 77.

76. For William Wharton's opposition, see "Proceedings of Annual Meeting of the National Association of Audubon Societies," October 1932, 75, REPDPL.

77. ECC pamphlet *The Olympic Forests for a National Park*, January 1938, REPDPL.

78. Lien, *Olympic Battleground*, 175.

79. Ibid., 193.

80. Ibid., 198, 339.

81. IW, 117.

82. Letter from Senator Frederic C. Walcott to RE, April 12, 1939, REPDPL.

83. IW, 96. Brant's comment about Van Name appears in Lien, *Olympic Battleground*, 198.

CHAPTER TEN: Hawk of Mercy

1. IW, 27. For other women in conservation, see Merchant "Women of the Progressive Conservation Movement."

2. *Humane Society of Baltimore Newsletter*, January 1944, 8, REPDPL.

3. The Brouns' data are from Hawk Mountain Sanctuary Annual Report, December 1938, JHMA-HMSA.

4. Marion Ingersoll's background from the Marion Ingersoll Collection, SSC.

5. Margaret Edge Nightingale spoke of her mother's visit in an interview with the author, October 1990. Asho Ingersoll Crain also noted the Bennington visit in an interview with the author, January 2006.

6. Hawk Mountain Sanctuary Annual Report, 1938.

7. Ibid.

8. Letter from RE to MEN, February 2, 1941, PEPLD.

9. Letter from Donald L. Cook to RE, April 10, 1940, PEPLD.

10. Letter from RE to MEN, February 2, 1941, PEPLD.

11. Ibid.

12. Background for Sequoia and Kings Canyon National Parks from Fox, *John Muir and His Legacy*, 212–17; Watkins, *Righteous Pilgrim*, 569–91; Stacey Wells, *Frommer's Yosemite and Sequoia/Kings Canyon National Parks* (New York: Macmillan, 1998); William Brewer, *Such a Landscape! A Narrative of the 1864 California Geological Survey Exploration of Yosemite, Sequoia and Kings Canyon from the Diary, Field Notes, Letters and Reports of William Henry Brewer* (Yosemite National Park, Calif.: Yosemite

Association, 1999); Orsi, Runte, and Smith-Barzini, *Yosemite and Sequoia*; Strong, *From Pioneers to Preservationists*; Wilkins, *John Muir*; Dilsaver and Tweed, *Challenge of the Big Trees*.

13. Hart Tree size mentioned in speech by Secretary Ickes to the Commonwealth Club, San Francisco, February 15, 1939, also broadcast on NBC, copy in REPDPL.

14. For Hart Tree misrepresentation, see Flint, *To Find the Biggest Tree*, 33–35.

15. Fox, *John Muir and His Legacy*, 213.

16. Worster, *A Passion for Nature*, 320.

17. Fox, *John Muir and His Legacy*, 213.

18. Watkins, *Righteous Pilgrim*, 572.

19. Ibid., 570–71.

20. Ibid., 571.

21. Ibid., 573.

22. Fox, *John Muir and His Legacy*, 215.

23. Letter from William Colby to RE, January 26, 1939, REPDPL.

24. Message from David Brower to the author, October 1998.

25. Letter from RE to IB, October 20, 1934, IBC.

26. Letter from IB to PE, January 20, 1963, JHMA-HMSA.

27. Department of the Interior memo from William Schulz to Harold Ickes, January 24 1939, REPDPL. Brant notes that WVN paid for the brochure's publication (*Adventures in Conservation,* 158).

28. Letter from William Schulz to William Wallace Chapin, April 26, 1939, REPDPL.

29. Undated ECC flyer, REPDPL.

30. Letter from RE to IB, January 20, 1939, REPDPL.

31. Edge turned down a pack trip, saying she was "too much of a tenderfoot"; see letter from RE to Richard Leonard, Chairman, Sierra Club Outing Committee, May 24, 1940, REPDPL.

32. IW, 124.

33. See "The Problem of the Kings Canyon Wilderness," *Wilderness News*, no. 9, February 20, 1939, REPDPL.

34. For Brant's complicated reasoning, see his *Adventures in Conservation*, 151–59. See also the ECC pamphlet *The Proposed John–Muir Kings Canyon National Park*.

35. Undated ECC publication *Stand by the John-Muir–Kings Park Bill: The Gearhart Bill Should Pass without Amendment*, REPDPL.

36. Ibid., 2.

37. U.S. Department of the Interior Memorandum for the Press, n.d., REPDPL.

38. For the alleged plot against the parks, see *Stand by the John-Muir–Kings Park Bill* and the U.S. Department of the Interior Memorandum for the Press, undated.

39. Letter from Gifford Pinchot to Howard Cleaves, May 23, 1939, REPDPL, used with permission of Peter Pinchot.

40. Letter from RE to Howard Cleaves, July 6, 1939, REPDPL.

41. See Lary M. Dilsaver, "Conservation Conflict and Kings Canyon," in Orsi, Runte, and Smith-Barzini, *Yosemite and Sequoia*, 117. See also Fox, *John Muir and His Legacy*, 216.

42. Brant, *Adventures in Conservation*, 203.

43. Ibid., 204.

44. Gearhart's remarks appear in *Congressional Record* 84 (May 5 1939), 5033–45, and are referenced in *Cong. Rec.* appendix 15473 (August 4, 1939).

45. Brant, *Adventures in Conservation*, 203–5.

46. Letter from IB to PE, 1962, PEPLD. Copy possibly in JHMA-HMSA.

47. IW, 129. Maps of Kings Canyon indicate that Mount Eisen sits along the Divide.

CHAPTER ELEVEN: Hellcat

1. Hearing before the Committee on Indian Affairs House of Representatives, *A Bill Providing for Federal Assistance in Eradicating the Cattle Tick in the Seminole Indian Reservation in Florida*, S.1476, 77th Cong., 1st sess., November 5, 1941, February 25, 1942, S. 1476, 118.

2. Ibid.

3. IW, 165–66. See also the ECC pamphlet on the subject, *To Save the Trumpeter Swan*.

4. Clark Bainbridge, "Rosalie Edge Chronology, 1877–1963," March 14, 2001, JHMA-HMSA.

5. Alex Nagy also assisted Maurice Broun at the sanctuary for many years after the war.

6. V-mail from PE and MB include bird descriptions. The letter from MB to RE, April 18, 1944, is an example of communications about birds, JHMA-HMSA. Irma Broun Kahn recalled that RE sent MB guidebook pages during the war (interview, January 1992).

7. "To Peter and Other Storm Petrels," PEPLD. A version titled "Sonnet for a Navigator" was published in the *Bulletin of Massachusetts Audubon Society* (1944).

8. Description of the last evening at Hawk Mountain drawn from IW, 194–96.

9. IW, 194.

10. Wartime newsletters of Hawk Mountain Sanctuary report donations and include letters from soldiers, JHMA-HMSA. RE includes letters from soldiers in IW, 191.

11. "Ode to Eric Nightingale," PEPLD.

12. The circumstances of CNE's death were provided by PE and MEN in interviews with the author, 1990.

13. CNE obituary, *New York Times*, June 30, 1944.

14. Information regarding RE sharing confidences with Julia Langsam from interviews and e-mail correspondence with Walter E. Langsam in spring and fall of 2004.

15. Michael Gilbert, Esq., of Denver, who specializes in estate law, provided his expert opinion on CNE's will, July 2006.

16. Last will and testament included in documents of Surrogate's Court, White Plains, Westchester County, "In the Matter of the Application of Mabel R. Edge, for a determination as to the effect of her election as surviving spouse, to take her intestate share against the provisions of the Last Will and Testament of Charles N. Edge," 1945.

17. Inventory included in legal documents of "In the Matter of the Application of Mabel R. Edge."

18. V-mail from RE to MB, August 13, 1944, JHMA-HMSA.

19. Interview with MEN, October 1990.

20. Undated letter from MB to RE, JHMA-HMSA.

21. Roger Tory Peterson, Hawk Mountain Sanctuary sixtieth anniversary speech, October 1994.

22. Letter from Gilbert Pearson to RE, October 21, 1940, JHMA-HMSA.

23. Teale's *Autumn across America* mentions Hawk Mountain. Carson's visits noted in Lear, *Rachel Carson*, 126–27.

24. Rachel Carson's DDT press release from the Department of the Interior, Information Service, Fish and Wildlife Service, May 18, 1946, in RE's file labeled "Poison" at JHMA-HMSA. It begins: "A warning must be taken in applying DDT." The "Poison" file is also mentioned in John K. Terres, "Dynamite in DDT," *New Republic*, February 25, 1946.

25. Lear, *Rachel Carson*, 117.

26. See Clark Bainbridge, "Rosalie Edge Chronology, 1877–1963," March 14, 2001, JHMA-HMSA.

27. ECC pamphlet *Protect the South Calaveras Sequoia Grove*. 9.

28. For the circumstances of the peregrine rescue, see IW, 176.

29. Ibid.

30. The incident occurred in the 1930s. RE's poem "To a Golden Eagle in a Pet Shop Window" appeared in *Nature Magazine*, June–July 1938, 369.

31. Letter from RE to William C. Adams, Director, Division of Fish and Game, Conservation Department, Albany, New York, May 12, 1948, JHMA-HMSA.

32. Ibid. A federal Fish and Wildlife memo responding to RE's complaint noted a "50% solution" had been applied, May 19, 1948, JHMA-HMSA.

33. Jaques, *Birds across the Sky*, 188. Former HMSA curator James Brett also noted the young men who attended RE on Hawk Mountain visits.

34. Letters from MB to RE and HMSA board members complain about the relationship with Edge after 1951. Also MB's journal notes tensions, MBLAC and JHMA-HMSA.

35. Letter from MB to RE, Wednesday evening (January 1950?), JHMA-HMSA.

36. Letter from RE to MB, January 14, 1950, JHMA-HMSA.

37. Interview with Irma Broun Kahn, January 1991.

38. Ibid.

39. "Rosalie Barrow Edge," from "Oh, Hawk of Mercy!" by Robert Lewis Taylor, *New Yorker*, April 17, 1948, 31.

40. Ibid., 44.

CHAPTER TWELVE: Implacable

1. Memoir rejection letters from publishers are at JHMA-HMSA.

2. IW, 230.

3. Ibid., 2.

4. In a 1990 interview with the author, Richard Pough said that Edge's example at Hawk Mountain was important to him in establishing the Nature Conservancy in 1951.

5. Roland C. Clement acknowledged RE's influence in interviews with the author, July 1991 and May and November 2007. Clement refers to himself as the "midwife" of the Environmental Defense Fund, and the organization's cofounder, Charles Wurster, concurred in an interview with the author, November 2007.

6. Carson, *Silent Spring*, 118.

7. Letter from Rachel Carson to MB regarding Hawk Mountain Sanctuary migration data, May 17, 1960, MBLAC; Carson, *Silent Spring*, 119.

8. MB uses the term *grand dame* in his journal entry of November 30, 1962, JHMA-HMSA and MBLAC.

9. Interview with and e-mails from Walter E. Langsam, March 2004.

10. The author is grateful to Walter E. Langsam for permission to use "Oh, Happy Hawk: The Ultimate Tale of Ultimate Renunciation," speech given at the Literary Club of Cincinnati, January 27, 2003.

11. Interview with Deborah Edge, August 2006.

12. Interview with PE, and Kwan Yin postcard given him by RE, PEPLD.

13. Letter from RE to MB, November 9, 1960, JHMA-HMSA.

14. MB's journal in 1959–60 notes Irma's Cape Cod property inheritance; also letters from RE to MB strongly suggest that RE lent the Brouns $8,000 to pay off liens on the Penniman property and hold on to the mansion until the National Park Service acquired it in 1962: "If the payment of the mortgage or interest is an embarrassment to you, it can be extended," RE remarked in a letter to MB, August 30, 1960. "I do not give it a thought and you need not to either." In a March 22, 1959, letter from RE to MB, she states that the proposed National Park (at Cape Cod Seashore) "should increase the value of Irma's property." Letters at JHMA-HMSA. A document from CCNS confirms purchase of the Penniman mansion for $27,000 in 1962. The sale to the National Park Service gave the Brouns their retirement fund, according to Irma Broun Kahn in an interview with the author, January 1991.

15. Walter Langsam, "Oh, Happy Hawk"; also e-mail from Walter Langsam to author, March 2004.

16. Roger Tory Peterson, sixtieth anniversary speech at Hawk Mountain Sanctuary, October 1994.

17. Graham, *Audubon Ark*, 201.

18. Interview with PE; Graham, *Audubon Ark*, 201.

19. IW, 230.

20. Richard Pough's unpublished memoir, "My Life," 45, JHMA-HMSA.

21. Interview with RE's friend Margaret Raymond, 1992.

22. Interview with PE.

23. MB's journal entry of November 30, 1962, JHMA-HMSA and MBLAC; concluding quotation from untitled written statement by Maurice and Irma Broun, believed to have been delivered in 1963 or 1964, JHMA-HMSA.

24. Telephone interview with Richard Pough, December 1991.

Bibliography

Archives and Collections

Cape Cod National Seashore, Edgartown, Massachusetts.

Hawk Mountain Sanctuary Papers, Julian Hill Memorial Archive-Hawk Mountain Sanctuary Archives, Acopian Center for Conservation Learning, Orwigsburg, Pennsylvania (collection was not cataloged prior to 1999, when author conducted most of her research in it).

Hong Kong Museum of History, Kowloon.

Irving Brant Collection, box 18, Manuscript Division, Library of Congress.

Maurice Broun Library, Acopian Center for Ornithology, Muhlenberg College, Allentown, Pennsylvania.

National Audubon Society Collection, New York Public Library.

Peter Edge private letters and documents (uncataloged; currently in author's possession).

Rosalie Edge Papers, CONS29, Conservation Collection, Denver Public Library, Denver, Colorado.

Sophia Smith Collection of Woman's History Manuscripts, William Allan Neilson Library, Smith College, Northampton, Massachusetts.

ECC Pamphlets

For a complete list of ECC publications, see Lien's *Olympic Battleground*, 418–22. The complete set is available at the Special Collections Division, University of Washington, Seattle, and at the Peabody Museum of Comparative Zoology, Harvard University, Cambridge, Massachusetts; a partial set is at REPDPL. Those listed below were referred to or consulted in this work.

The Advance of Conservation. March 1938.

The Antelope's S.O.S.: The Extinction of the Pronghorn Antelope Is a Preventable Misfortune That We Are Neglecting to Prevent. October 1930.

The Audubon Steel-Trapping Sanctuary. September 1934.

The Bald Eagle, Our National Emblem: Danger of Its Extinction by the Alaska Bounty. April 1930.

Blood Money for the Audubon Associations, Anti-Steel Trap League News (ECC reprint), December 1932.

Compromised Conservation: Can the Audubon Society Explain? October 1930, September 1931.

Conservation—Come and Get It. March 1939.

Crisis in Conservation: Serious Danger of Extinction of Many North American Birds. New York, June 1929. (pre-ECC)

Disaster to the Yellowstone Park Elk Herds. December 1933.

Double Crossing the Project for the Proposed Mount Olympus National Park: No Economic Need, but Only Commercial Greed, the Obstacle to the Mount Olympus Park. March 1937.

Fighting the Good Fight: Progress for Conservation Advance in Five Years. Report for 1934, published February 1935.

Forward into Battle. January 1936.

Framing the Birds of Prey: An Arraignment of the Fanatical and Economically Harmful Campaign of Extermination Being Waged against Hawks and Owls. December 1929.

The Impending Ruin of Kings Canyon. June 1939.

It's Alive! Kill It! The Present Policy toward Native Birds and Animals of North America. April 1932, May 1932.

Live and Let Live. August 1934.

Montana's Sanctuary for Duck Killers. April 1934.

The Olympic Forests for a National Park. January 1938, February 1938.

Poison for Our Wildlife: An Answer to the Biological Survey. May 1931.

The Proposed John Muir–Kings Canyon National Park. January 1939.

The Proposed Olympic National Park. April 1934, June 1934.

Protect the Roosevelt Elk. March 1938.

Protect the South Calaveras Sequoia Grove. June 1942.

Save the Bald Eagle! Shall We Allow Our National Emblem to Become Extinct? January 1935.

Save the Yosemite Sugar Pines! October 1932.

The Slaughter of the Yellowstone Park Pelicans. September 1932.

Steel-Trapping by the Audubon Association: The National Association of Audubon Societies Continues to Use Steel-Traps on Its Rainey Wild Life Sanctuary for Wild Birds and Wild Mammals. November 1933.

To the Members of the National Association of Audubon Societies. August 1932,
    September 1932 (with Roger Baldwin), October 1933.
To Save the Trumpeter Swan. February 1941.
The Tragic Truth about the Elk. April 1934.
Twelve Immediately Important Problems of the National Parks and Wildlife
    Conservation. May 1935.
The United States Biological Survey: Destruction, Not Scientific Investigation and
    Conservation, Now Its Chief Activity. May 1930.
The Waterfowl Get a Raw Deal. April 1934.
The United States Bureau of Destruction and Extermination: The Misnamed and
    Perverted "Biological Survey." September 1934.

Unpublished Memoirs and Documents

Edge, Peter. "A Determined Lady." PEPLD.
Edge, Rosalie. "Coquette." Ca. 1939. PEPLD.
———. "A Date with Cousin Charles." Ca. 1940. PEPLD.
———. "Good Companions in Conservation: Annals of an Implacable Widow."
    Ca. 1950. PEPLD.
———. "A Rose in the Snow." 1940. PEPLD.
———. "The Shadow of the Photograph." Ca. 1940. PEPLD.
———. "Winged Friendships." Ca. 1944. PEPLD.
Kranick, Kenneth. "Keeper of the Kittatinny." 1981. JHMA-HMSA.
Macleod, J. Keith, MBE. "The Family of Charles Edge and Ellen Allarton." Surrey,
    England, July 1985. PEPLD.
Pough, Richard. "My Life." 2002. JHMA-HMSA.
"Soaring above the Ridges." Poster by the Pennsylvania Bureau of Topographic and
    Geologic Survey, displayed at Hawk Mountain Sanctuary.

Catalogs, Newsletters, Meeting Transcriptions, Legal Briefs, and
Special Reports

Barbour, Thomas, and Chauncey Hamlin. "Report of the Special Committee
    Appointed to Investigate Charges Publicly Made against the National Association
    of Audubon Societies." August 1931. REPDPL.
"Catalogue of the Books Contained in the Barrow Library to Be Sold at Private Sale."
    New York City, 1888. PEPLD.
Edge, Peter. "Kyrie Eleison: St. Catherine, The Holy Mountain and the Child in the
    Raspberry Bush." Chicago Literary Club, 1981.
Felder, Raoul. "From Make Room for Daddy to Three Men and a Baby." *New York*
    Law Journal 199 (May 31, 1988): 103.

Langsam, Walter E. "Oh, Happy Hawk: The Ultimate Tale of Passionate
   Renunciation." Address to the Literary Club of Cincinnati, January 27, 2003.
Moyer, Ben. *Pennsylvania's Wildlife and Wild Places: Our Outdoor Heritage in Peril.*
   Pennsylvania Wild Resource Conservation Fund, August 2003.
"Petitioner's Brief," atty. Charles Dickerman Williams, and "Memorandum On behalf
   of Defendants in Opposition," atty. Samuel T. Carter, 1–24. REPDPL.
"Proceedings of the Twenty-Seventh Annual Business Meeting of the National
   Association of Audubon Societies," October 27, 1931, American Museum of
   Natural History. REPDPL.
"Proceedings of the Annual Meeting of the National Association of Audubon
   Societies" October 25, 1932, American Museum of Natural History. REPDPL.
Walcott, Frederick C. "The Necessity of Free Shooting Grounds." *Bulletin of the
   American Game Protective Association*, April 10, 1921. REPDPL.
Washburn, Mabel Thacher Rosemary. "From Puritan, Hugenot, and Patroon: An
   American Lineage in the Families of Van Rennselaer, Van Cortlandt, Floyd,
   Holland, Boudinot, Evertsen, Teller, Woodward, Nicolls, Bailey, Park, and Erdfyne
   with Allied Descents." *Journal of American History* 12, no. 3 (July–September 1918).
   PEPLD.
Wheeler, Everett P. *The Influence of Christianity upon the Condition of Woman.* Man-
   Suffrage Association Publication no. 13. New York, n.d.

Newspapers and Periodicals

Altoona (Pa.) Tribune (September 28,
   1934).
The Auk (1932–66, January 1990).
B International, Tokyo (March 1995).
Bird-Lore (1924–34).
Brooklyn (N.Y.) Daily Eagle (1931–38).
Cassinia (1932).
Century Magazine (1891).
Christian Science Monitor (1938–40).
Evening Republican, Pottsville, Pa.
   (1928–34).
Fresno (Calif.) Bee (1937–39).
Hawk and Owl Society (1933).
Japan Gazette, Yokohama (May 28, 1909).
Lebanon (Pa.) Daily News (1929).
Louisville (Ky.) Times (March 6, 1948).
NAAS Bulletin no. 6 (May 1926).

New Yorker (April 17, 1948).
New York Herald Tribune (1911, 1931–33).
New York Times (1885, 1908, 1911,
   1931–38, 1944).
Pennsylvania Heritage (Summer 2004)
Puget Sounder, Bellingham, Wash.
   (1936–38).
Scribners (April 1903).
Time (October 11, 1937).
Wilson Bulletin (1927–32).

Author Interviews

Family

Elizabeth Barrow Doering
Charleen Edge
Deborah Edge
Peter Edge
Alice Nightingale
Charles Nightingale
Eric Nightingale
Margaret Edge Nightingale
Trevor Nightingale

Friends and Acquaintances

Asho Ingersoll Crain
Walter E. Langsam
Anna Lea Lelli
Melissa Marston Macleod
Margaret Raymond

Conservationists

Keith Bildstein, PhD
James Brett
Sylvia Brockner
William W. Brockner
David Brower
Roland C. Clement
Irma Broun Kahn
Nancy Keeler

Kenneth Kranick
Carsten Lien
John B. Oakes
Roger Tory Peterson
Richard Pough
Joseph Taylor

Other Sources

Ackroyd, Peter. *Dickens*. New York: HarperCollins, 1990.

Adickes, Sandra. *To Be Young Was Very Heaven*. New York: St. Martin's Press, 1997.

Allen, Armin Brand. *The Cornelius Vanderbilts of the Breakers: A Family Retrospective*. Newport, R.I.: Preservation Society of Newport County, 1995.

Allen, Fredrick Lewis. *Only Yesterday: An Informal History of the 1920s*. New York: Harper & Row, 1931.

Amory, Cleveland. *Last Resorts*. New York: Harper & Brothers, 1948.

Bainbridge, Clark. "The Origins of Rosalie Edge's Emergency Conservation Committee, 1930–1962: A Historical Analysis." PhD diss., University of Idaho, December 1992.

Ball, J. Dyer. *Things Chinese*. London: John Murray, 1904.

Barrow, Mark V., Jr. *A Passion for Birds: American Ornithology after Audubon*. Princeton, N.J.: Princeton University Press, 1998.

Bean, Michael J. *The Evolution of National Wildlife Law*. Revised and expanded edition. New York: Praeger, 1983.

Bent, Arthur Cleveland. *Life Histories of North American Birds of Prey*. New York: Dover, 1937.

Bentley, James. *Secrets of Mount Sinai: The Story of Finding the World's Oldest Bible—Codex Sinaiticus*. Garden City, N.Y.: Doubleday, 1986.

Bildstein, Keith L. *Migrating Raptors of the World: Their Ecology and Conservation*. Ithaca, N.Y.: Cornell University Press, 2006.

Blakeslee, George H. *Recent Developments in China*. New York: G. E. Stechert, 1913.

Brant, Irving. *Adventures in Conservation with Franklin D. Roosevelt*. Flagstaff, Ariz.: Northland, 1988.

Brett, James J. *The Mountain and the Migration: A Guide to Hawk Mountain*. Kempton, Pa.: Hawk Mountain Sanctuary Association, 1986.

Brooks, Paul. *The House of Life*. Boston: Houghton Mifflin, 1972.

Broun, Maurice. *Hawks Aloft! The Story of Hawk Mountain*. New York: Dodd, Mead, 1948. Fiftieth Anniversary Edition published by Hawk Mountain Sanctuary Association.

Carnegie, Andrew. *The Autobiography of Andrew Carnegie*. Boston: Northeastern University Press, 1986.

Carson, Rachel. *Silent Spring*. Boston: Houghton Mifflin, 1962. Twenty-Fifth Anniversary Edition, 1987.

Chapman, Frank M. *Autobiography of a Bird-Lover*. New York: D. Appleton-Century, 1935.

Clark, James Hyde. *Story of China and Japan*. Philadelphia: Oriental, 1894.

Cook, Blanche Wiesen. *Eleanor Roosevelt*. Vol. 1, *1884–1933*. New York: Viking, 1992.

Coues, Elliott. *Field Ornithology: Comprising a Manual of Instruction for Procuring, Preparing and Preserving Birds, and a Check List of North American Birds*. Salem, Mass.: Naturalists' Legacy, 1874.

Cox, Anne. F. *The History of the Colony Club*. New York: privately printed for the Colony Club, 1984.

Cronon, William. *Changes in the Land: Indians, Colonists, and the Ecology of New England*. New York: Hill & Wang, 1985.

Delamain, Jacques. *Why Birds Sing*. London: Camelot Press, n.d. Originally published as *Pourquoi Les Oiseaux Chantent* (Paris: Librairie Stock, 1930).

Dickens, Charles. *Great Expectations*. Edited by Janice Carlisle. Case Studies in Contemporary Criticism. Boston: Bedford Books of St. Martin's Press, 1996.

——— . *Martin Chuzzlewit*. Wordsworth Classics. Hertfordshire, England: Wordsworth Editions, 1997.

——— . *The Pickwick Papers*. London: Bantam, 1983.

Dillard, Annie. *The Living*. New York: HarperCollins, 1992.

Dilsaver, Lary M., and William C. Tweed. *Challenge of the Big Trees*. Three Rivers, Calif.: Sequoia Natural History Association, 1990.

Dunlap, Thomas R. DDT: *Scientists, Citizens and Public Policy.* Princeton, N.J.:
Princeton University Press, 1981.

———. *Saving America's Wildlife: Ecology and the American Mind, 1850–1990.*
Princeton, N.J.: Princeton University Press, 1991.

Dunne, Pete, Debbie Keller, and Rene Kochenberger. *Hawk Watch: A Guide for
Beginners.* Cape May, N.J.: Cape May Bird Observatory/New Jersey Audubon
Society, 1984.

Fleming, G. H. *James Abbott McNeill Whistler: A Life.* New York: St. Martin's Press,
1991.

Flint, Wendell D. *To Find the Biggest Tree.* Three Rivers, Calif.: Sequoia Natural
History Association, 2002.

Forbush, Edward Howe. *Birds of Massachusetts, and Other New England States.*
Vol. 2. Boston: Norwood Press, 1907.

———. *Useful Birds and Their Protection: Containing Brief Descriptions of the More
Common and Useful Species of Massachusetts.* 2nd ed. Boston: published under
the direction of the Massachusetts State Board of Agriculture, 1908.

Fowler, Robert Booth. *Carrie Catt: Feminist Politician.* Boston: Northeastern
University Press, 1986.

Fox, Stephen. *John Muir and His Legacy: The American Conservation Movement.*
Boston: Little, Brown, 1981.

Fraser, Kennedy. *Ornament and Silence: Essays on Women's Lives from Edith
Wharton to Germaine Greer.* New York: Vintage Press, 1996.

Fridson, Martin S. *It Was a Very Good Year: Extraordinary Moments in Stock Market
History.* New York: John Wiley & Sons, 1998.

Gilligan, Carol. *In a Different Voice: Psychological Theory and Women's Development.*
Cambridge, Mass.: Harvard University Press, 1982.

Graham, Frank, Jr. *The Audubon Ark: A History of the National Audubon Society.*
New York: Alfred A. Knopf, 1990.

Grossman, Mary Louise, and John Hamlet. *Birds of Prey of the World.* New York:
Clarkson N. Potter, 1964.

Gurko, Miriam. *The Ladies of Seneca Falls: The Birth of the Woman's Rights
Movement.* New York: Macmillan, 1974.

Harwood, Michael. *The View from Hawk Mountain.* New York: Charles Scribner's
Sons, 1973.

Hearn, Lafcadio. *Japan: An Interpretation.* New York: Macmillan, 1904.

Hornaday, William Temple. *Our Vanishing Wildlife: Its Extermination and
Preservation.* New York: Charles Scribner's Sons, 1913.

Hult, Ruby El. *Untamed Olympics: The Story of a Peninsula.* Portland, Ore.:
Bindfords & Mort, 1954.

Ise, John. *Our National Parks Policy: A Critical History.* Baltimore: Johns Hopkins
University Press, 1961.

Jaques, Florence P. *Birds across the Sky*. 2nd ed. New York: Harper & Bros., 1942.

Johnson, Edgar. *Charles Dickens: His Tragedy and Triumph*. New York: Simon & Schuster, 1952.

Kaplan, Fred. *Dickens*. Baltimore: Johns Hopkins University Press, 1988.

Kaufman, Polly Welts. *National Parks and the Woman's Voice: A History*. Albuquerque: University of New Mexico Press, 1996.

Kirtland, Lucien Swift. *Finding the Worth While in the Orient*. New York: Robert McBride, 1926.

Klein, Carole. *Gramercy Park: An American Bloomsbury*. Boston: Houghton Mifflin, 1987.

Kosack, Joe. *The Pennsylvania Game Commission, 1895–1995: 100 Years of Wildlife Conservation*. Harrisburg: Pennsylvania Game Commission, 1995.

Kraditor, Aileen S. *The Ideas of the Woman Suffrage Movement, 1890–1920*. New York: Columbia University Press, 1965.

Krutch, Joseph Wood, and Paul S. Ericksson. *A Treasury of Birdlore*. Garden City, N.Y.: Doubleday, 1962.

Lamb, W. Kaye. *Empress to the Orient*. Vancouver, B.C: Vancouver Maritime Museum Society, 1991.

Lear, Linda. *Rachel Carson: The Life of the Author of Silent Spring*. New York: Henry Holt, 1997.

LeFevre, Edwin. *Reminiscences of a Stock Operator*. 1925. New York: John Wiley, 1994.

Leopold, Aldo. *Sand County Almanac*. New York: Ballantine Books, 1980.

Lichtenberger, J. P. *Family in America: A Social Interpretation*. New York: Arno Press and the New York Times, 1972.

Lien, Carsten. *Olympic Battleground: The Power Politics of Timber Preservation*. San Francisco: Sierra Club Books, 1991.

Line, Les, ed., *The National Audubon Society: Speaking for Nature; A Century of Conservation*. New York: Beaux Arts Editions, Hugh Lauter Levin, 1999.

Lytle, Mark Hamilton. *The Gentle Subversive: Rachel Carson, Silent Spring, and the Rise of the Environmental Movement*. New York: Oxford University Press, 2007.

MacColl, Gail, and Carol McD. Wallace. *To Marry an English Lord; or, How Anglomania Really Got Started*. New York: Workman, 1989.

MacKenzie, Norman and Jeanne. *Dickens: A Life*. New York: Oxford University Press, 1979.

Manthorpe, Victoria, ed. *Travels in the Land of the Gods: 1893–1907; The Japan Diaries of Richard Gordon Smith*. New York: Prentice Hall, 1986.

McMullen, Roy. *Victorian Outsider: A Biography of J. A. M. Whistler*. New York: E. P. Dutton, 1973.

Merchant, Carolyn. "Women of the Progressive Conservation Movement, 1900–
1916." *Environmental Review* 8, no. 1 (Spring 1984): 57–85.

Miller, Millie, and Cyndi Nelson. *Talons: North American Birds of Prey.* Boulder,
Colo.: Johnson Books, 1989.

Morgan, Murray. *The Last Wilderness.* Seattle: University of Washington Press, 1976.

Morris, Jan. *Hong Kong: An Epilogue to an Empire.* London: Penguin Books, 1988.

Muir, John. *The Yosemite.* With notes and an introduction by Frederic R. Gunsky.
New York: Doubleday, 1962.

Nasaw, David. *Andrew Carnegie.* New York: Penguin Press, 2006.

New, Christopher. *Shanghai.* New York: Bantam Books, 1985.

Norquay, Glenda. *Voices and Votes: A Literary Anthology of the Women's Suffrage
Campaign.* Manchester: Manchester University Press, 1995.

O'Neill, William L. *Divorce in the Progressive Era.* New Haven, Conn.: Yale
University Press, 1967.

Orr, Oliver H., Jr. *Saving America's Birds: T. Gilbert Pearson and the Founding of the
Audubon Movement.* Gainesville: University Press of Florida, 1992.

Orsi, Richard, Alfred Runte, and Marlene Smith-Barzini. *Yosemite and Sequoia:
A Century of California National Parks.* Berkeley: University of California Press
1993.

Pennell, E. R. and J. *The Life of James McNeill Whistler.* 2 vols. Philadelphia:
J. B. Lippincott, 1909.

Peterson, Roger Tory, and Rudy Hoglund, eds., *Roger Tory Peterson: The Art and
Photography of the World's Foremost Birder.* New York: Rizzoli, 1994.

Pinchot, Gifford. *Breaking New Ground.* New York: Harcourt, Brace, 1947.

Poole, Earl L. *The Bird Life of Berks County.* Narberth, Pa.: Livingston, 1930.

———. *Pennsylvania Birds: An Annotated List.* Narberth, Pa.: published for the
Delaware Valley Ornithological Club by Livingston Publishing, 1964.

Preston, Diana. *Lusitania: An Epic Tragedy.* New York: Walker, 2002.

Rajala, Richard A. *Clearcutting the Pacific Rain Forest: Production, Science, and
Regulation.* Vancouver: University of British Columbia Press, 1998.

Reed, Henry Hope, and Sophia Duckworth. *Central Park: A History and a Guide.*
New York: Clarkson N. Potter., 1967.

Rhondda, Margaret Haig Thomas Mackworth, Viscountess. *Notes on the Way.*
Freeport, N.Y.: Books for Libraries Press, 1937.

Runte, Alfred. *National Parks: The American Experience.* Lincoln: University of
Nebraska Press, 1979.

Russell, Carl Parcher. *One Hundred Years in Yosemite.* Yosemite National Park, Calif.:
Yosemite Association, 1992.

Schrepfer, Susan R. *Nature's Altars: Mountains, Gender, and American
Environmentalism.* Lawrence: University Press of Kansas, 2005.

Service, John S., ed. *Golden Inches: The China Memoir of Grace Service*. Berkeley: University of California Press, 1989.

Siegel, Jeremy J. *Stocks for the Long Run*. New York: McGraw-Hill, 1998.

Smith, Harold L. *The British Women's Suffrage Campaign, 1866–1928*. Harlow, England: Pearson Education, 1998.

Spence, Jonathan D. *The Search for Modern China*. New York: W. W. Norton, 1990.

Stevens, Doris. *Jailed for Freedom*. New York: Boni & Liveright, 1920.

Stone, Witmer. *The Birds of Eastern Pennsylvania and New Jersey: With Introductory Chapters and Geographical Distribution and Migration*. Philadelphia: Delaware Valley Ornithological Club, 1894.

Strachey, Lytton. *Eminent Victorians*. San Diego: Harcourt Brace, Harvest Book, 1969.

Strachey, Ray. *The Cause: A Short History of the Women's Movement in Great Britain*. Reprint, London: Virago, 1979.

Strong, Douglas. *From Pioneers to Preservationists: A Brief History of Sequoia and Kings Canyon National Park*. Three Rivers, Calif.: Sequoia Natural History Association, 1996.

Strouse, Jean. *Morgan: American Financier*. New York: Random House, 1999.

Teale, Edwin Way. *Autumn across America*. New York: Dodd, Meade, 1956.

————. *The Lost Woods*. New York: Dodd, Mead, 1945.

Terborgh, John. *Where Have All the Birds Gone? Essays on the Biology and Conservation of Birds That Migrate to the American Tropics*. Princeton, N.J.: Princeton University Press, 1989.

Terres, John K. *The Audubon Encyclopedia of North American Birds*. New York: Alfred A. Knopf, 1980.

Trefethen, James B. *Crusade for Wildlife: Highlights in Conservation Progress*. Harrisburg, Pa.: Stackpole, 1961.

Turgenev, Ivan. *Torrents of Spring*. Translated by Constance Garnett. Westport, Conn.: Limited Editions Club, 1976.

Vanderbilt, Arthur T., II. *Fortune's Children: The Fall of the House of Vanderbilt*. New York: William Morrow, 1989.

Vernier, Chester G. *American Family Laws*. Vol. 2, *A Comparative Study of the Family Law of the Forty-eight American States, Alaska, the District of Columbia, and Hawaii*. Palo Alto, Calif.: Stanford University Press, 1932.

Viney, Clive, Karen Phillipps, and Chiu Ying Lam. *Birds of Hong Kong and South China*. Hong Kong: Hong Kong Govt. Printer, 1996.

Von Harton, Marjorie, and Melissa Marston Macleod. *Man of Wolverhampton: The Life and Times of Sir Charles Marston*. Dalingworth, England: Coombe Springs Press, n.d.

Voorsanger, Catherine Hoover, and John K. Howat, eds. *Art and the Empire City: New York, 1825–1861*. New Haven, Conn.: Yale University Press, 2000.

Walker, Samuel. *In Defense of American Liberties: A History of the* ACLU. New York: Oxford University Press, 1990.

Wall, Joseph Frazier. *Andrew Carnegie*. Pittsburg: University of Pittsburgh Press, 1988.

Watkins, T. H. *Righteous Pilgrim: The Life and Times of Harold L. Ickes, 1874–1952*. New York: Henry Holt, 1990.

Weale, B. L. Putnam, ed., *Indiscreet Letters from Peking*. New York: Dodd, Mead, 1909.

Wells, Carveth. *Six Years in the Malay Jungle*. Garden City, N.Y.: Doubleday, 1925.

Wharton, Edith. *A Backward Glance*. New York: Charles Scribner's Sons, 1933.

Wheeler, Marjorie Spruill, ed., *One Woman, One Vote*. Troutdale, Ore.: New Sage Press, 1995.

Wilcove, David S. *The Condor's Shadow: The Loss and Recovery of Wildlife in America*. New York: W. H. Freeman, 1999.

Wilkins, Thurman. *John Muir: Apostle of Nature*. Norman: University of Oklahoma Press, 1995.

Williams, Edward Thomas. *China Yesterday and Today*. New York: Thomas Y. Crowell, 1935.

Williams, Richard L. *The Loggers*. The Old West. Alexandria, Va.: Time-Life Books, 1976.

Wingerden, Sophia A. *The Women's Suffrage Movement in Britain, 1866–1928*. New York: St. Martin's Press, 1999.

Winks, Robin. *Laurance S. Rockefeller: Catalyst for Conservation*. Washington, D.C.: Island Press, 1997.

Winn, Marie. *Red Tails in Love: A Wildlife Drama in Central Park*. New York: Pantheon, 1998.

Woodham-Smith, Cecil. *Queen Victoria: From Her Birth to the Death of the Prince Consort*. New York: Dell, 1974.

Woolf, Virginia. *Roger Fry: A Biography*. London: Vintage Division of Random House, 1940.

Worster, David. *A Passion for Nature: The Life of John Muir*. New York: Oxford University Press, 2008.

Zaslowsky, Dyan, and T. H. Watkins. *These American Lands*. Washington, D.C.: Island Press, 1994.

Index